TIME KILLS ALL THINGS
and other pleasant reflections

a handful of essays by
ETHAN RENOE

Hire Ethan to speak at your camp/conference/church/school/birthday party
at ethanrenoe.com

FOR DAAVE, my boy, my [swear word], my oldest friend.

Thanks for helping me think better thoughts
and care for people more deeply,
and for listening to every obscure thought I've ever had.
And just putting up with me in general.
Here's to many more bonfires to talk about girls and life.

We drove to where no people are,
escaped the urban sprawl.
We ran like dogs beyond the hill
to where no phone can call.

These things that men just love to build
will all soon be decayed.
So Dave and I went to the hills,
a place we should have stayed.

(and no, that's not a typo.)

CONTENTS

HOW TO LIVE
staying alive & doing it well

HOW TO RELATE
connecting with God, others & yourself

HOW TO FEEL
thriving in the land of death

HOW TO BELIEVE
reflections on God, faith, church and other trivial things

HOW TO THINK
you would think thinking would be easier

HOW TO QUIT
porn, drugs, sex and doughnuts

HOW THE WORLD WORKS
systems, structures, epistemology, and other fancy words

"Certainty is overrated."
            -my college roommate

"You're overrated."
            -my other college roommate

FOREWORD

This book should come with a warning label.

"You must be this high to ride this ride."

Stay away from theme park rides like *Insanity* in Nevada where you will be spun around over the edge of a Las Vegas skyscraper. Don't go near *Kingda Ka* in New Jersey where the ride will take you 450 feet in the air and exceed 120 miles per hour. And don't read Ethan's powerful, self-assured lines; they are not for the faint of heart.

If you are afraid of other's opinions – I am not – you are not tall enough to ride this read. If you only read those with whom you agree – I read everyone's point of view – you are not big enough to take on other's big ideas. If you do not think twenty-somethings have something to say – I believe everyone should be heard – then you should run, screaming, away from this book.

If you do not like to think about lascivious kisses, sex, masturbation, or pornography, choose the kiddie train for a gentle ride around the theme park. In fact, just plan on skipping pages 104-194 (and a bunch of others) if you can't handle discussions of S – E – X. Ethan's self-disclosures will cause wincing, tut-tutting, head-smacking, raised eyebrows, and other expressions of disbelief. Many there are, however, who will resonate with the struggle Ethan is so open about. Ethan is correct: Gnostic tendencies toward treating others as "pieces and parts" views people as bodies instead of people. And such fantasies chip away at our character.

If you do not want to read Ethan's opinions about theology, politics, economics, philosophy, or sociology, go get on the bumper cars. Ethan's twenty-something views are a smattering of ideas many in his age group will admire. You may not agree with some of his assorted thoughts about tough issues. I know I didn't. But what is important is that Ethan thinks about these things. He cares to offer a word of encouragement or argument as needed. Agreement is not necessary. [If you think it is, you should stop reading this book right here.] What is necessary is the conversation. By his own admission, Ethan is "wadding up thoughts" to throw at you. Read others who correct or give an alternative view. But don't discount the e.

xiii

If you think this book needs revision, go get on the merry-go-round. I have been teaching students how to write over four decades. Yes, some of e's writing needs reconsideration. The generation of 'e' thinks, reads, watches, and writes in a form unknown and unappreciated by other generations (including my own). So you may be frustrated by the *how* of Ethan's writing but don't miss the *what* of Ethan's writing. The vision is thoroughly, consistently, undeniably, and obviously about Jesus. The merry-go-round will keep you going in circles. Ethan wants you to join him in the Christocentric weight room.

If you think there is too much of Ethan telling you he's been in the weight room (I lost count of the numerous references myself) then maybe you should stay out of the theme park altogether. Stay on your intellectual couch to watch re-runs of *Andy Griffith* and eat ice cream. Yes, Ethan talks about himself – a lot. But the thousands of people who have read e's writings do so for just such a personal connection. Older folks may shake their heads but Ethan speaks to generation "Z" who wants to shake its booty. Scary theme park rides incite fear for a reason. You can't handle the ride? Get off.

The *Maverick* rollercoaster ride in Sandusky, Ohio will literally turn you upside down. But that is exactly the Christian message. In Acts 17:6 unbelieving residents of Thessalonica take Christians before the authorities, saying, "Those who have turned the world upside down, have come here also." The Roman culture had seen this "Christian thing" before and didn't want any part of it. You see, the Christian message is diametrically opposed to the views of any unbelieving culture; the strength of Ethan's words. The scariest ride in Ethan's prose – my favorite pages of the book – is perhaps his most humble; his discussion of Rembrandt's *Prodigal Son*. I won't tell you about it, go read it on pages 267-272.

One more warning label: Ethan *Mark* Renoe (yes, he was named after me) is my nephew.

And I love him.

Dr. Mark Eckel, ThM PhD
President, The Comenius Institute, Indianapolis
Professor of Theology, Media, Writing & Culture

INTRODUCTION

On my 18th birthday, I had just moved to Cape Cod and was living in a house with two other guys. One was a professional web designer, so on that summer morning I awoke on the couch (my bed at the time) to him shoving his laptop into my face.

"Happy birthday, dude," he exclaimed. "Look what I made you."

He had invested $13 into the domain **ethanrenoe.com**, and thus was born my website. It underwent countless transformations since June 19, 2009, but it has served me well over the years. I messed around with it, took a web design class of my own and performed countless Frankenstein-esque experiments on it, and eventually registered the domain on WordPress to optimize it for blogging.

In December 2015, a viral video shook my life and my blog exploded. This shot me to Los Angeles where I met with dozens of publicists, agents, and other media professionals, all of whom encouraged me to scour out my niche and produce "content" regularly. (I later realized I hate the term "content" because it seems like gray, meaningless matter produced for the sake of producing something, rather than pouring out meaningful pieces which connect with people and are true to me. Semantics, am I right?)

As a result, 2016 was the year I began putting out blog posts weekly and essentially filled up this book. This collection includes some posts as old as 2012, but is mostly comprised of post-internet-virality pieces, as that's when the bulk of my writing has been produced.

I have included over 170 of these posts (I lost count) in this book, although my website currently says I have 274 posts online. I cut pieces out of this book based on a number of factors. Many were based entirely on current events at the time, such as the death of Hugh Hefner or the riots in Charlottesville, and I thought that, while they were important events and thoughts, I wanted the book to be more universally understandable outside of a certain season in time.

The rest of the posts, let's just be honest, were not that good. All writers evolve as they age and continue to hone their craft, taking form like the hull of a canoe, and many of my earlier pieces have not aged well. Some have, and they have been edited and included, but after 274 blog posts, there are bound to be some duds.

So, this collection is a gathering of my best, revised, and expanded blog posts. None of them look the same as they do online because they have been combed through and edited. Any links which were included in the original posts have been footnoted, and many other footnotes have been thrown in wherever helpful.

I have repeatedly asked myself why I'd publish this book in the first place, since almost all the content is available for free online. The answer is simple and multifaceted. Essentially, I wanted to be able to hold these 200k+ words in my hand and refer back to them. It's a lot of work to publish weekly posts and put thoughts into them and receive feedback, et al. So it's really a personal project, much like my last book *Now Let Me Find A Stopping Place,* which was a collection of poetry I wrote over 10 years.

Secondly, I know many people, including myself, who would rather read words on paper than a screen. I'm sure many of you are like this as well. This book is for you. You don't need to sit at your laptop or phone and scroll through hundreds of blog posts since you have this aesthetic rendering of them which smells like paper and doesn't fry your eyeballs.

The sections. Divvying these posts up into neat categories was maybe the hardest part of the entire process. After all, they were written as blog posts, not chapters in a book. Because of this, they were not created to fit into tidy categories of a book, as they are presented here. I landed on the six sections as the best way to divide them, though frankly, the lines between the sections blur *often.* To help you understand these divisions, here is a quick description of what type of piece is in each section:

How to Live: These, for lack of a better term, would fall into the 'self-help' or life advice section. They are things you can do in your life in order to try to live a better life. Many are 'Christian' in nature, and some are simply ubiquitously useful observations.

How to Relate: This section is on intimacy and relationships, including the relationship one has with him or herself. It also includes thoughts on sex, dating, virginity and a few anecdotes from my own dating history.

How to Feel: These are my favorite types of posts, but they are ridiculously hard to define. So hard that many are just the date on which they were composed. They're more feelings than thoughts; they're about life and feeling alive. They're about death, God and the beautiful unity by which all things in the universe interact. You'll see.

How to Believe: Unlike the 'Live' section which includes tangible ways to live as a Christian, these are higher-end theological pieces. This is not to say the two don't interact, but where that section is more applicable/tangible, these are more ideal/abstract.

How to Think: Things I write about often have to do with how we think about issues, concepts and ideas happening in the world around us. If the world is a giant ongoing conversation, we need to know what the heck we are talking about. This section attempts to help with that.

How to Quit: Not only about porn—but mostly about porn—this section deals with addictions and how to fight them. Part advice, part reflection.

How the World Works: If you're familiar with my Systems posts, this section is comprised of them and other posts on the layout of the world, visible and invisible. It wrestles with big-scale interactions of history, politics, religion, race, and identity.

Feel free to jump around. Find a section that best fits your mood. Leave it on your toilet for some good bathroom reading. Leave it on your coffee table because it's pretty and thick and makes you look sophisticated. Buy another copy and leave them in both places.

To be honest, you can really read it anywhere.

Regardless of your location, thanks for picking up this ragtag collection of ramblings! I hope you find it enjoyable and helpful.

e

HOW TO LIVE

staying alive & doing it well

THE RUTS OF ROUTINE
the small adjustments and mundane habits determine where we arrive.

January 1st is coming, and for a gym rat like me, that only means one thing: A packed-out weight room for the next two weeks. Now, for an extrovert like me, this is a great thing! I love seeing new people in the gym, making good on their New Year's Resolutions, at least, for two weeks. Because after the first half of the month, the gym attendance begins to quiet back down and return to the ritual exercisers.

Of course there are a few exceptions. My favorite thing in the gym is seeing someone begin to make the gym a priority which they commit to and stick with. I love seeing them 3, 6, 12 months later when they are seeing the results of their labor and the gym has become a familiar home rather than a daunting torture chamber.

Now the question must be asked: What is the difference between those New Year Resolvers who fade away after the first two weeks and those who stick with it for the long haul? Why do some work long enough to see results while others give up quickly?

I think the answer is found in the way we think about resolutions. There is a lot of emotion and excitement around the beginning of a new year, and with it, a lot of brash promises are made. We do this all the time, don't we? Personally, I have had over 35 jobs, worked with 3 missions organizations, and moved countless times across all 6 inhabited continents, and every transition comes with a promise of some sort or another:

This time, I will read my Bible every day.

This time, I will tell more people about Jesus.

This time, I will quit that old sin.

This time…

Whenever we enter into something *new,* whether it's a job, home, or relationship, there is a lot of buzz and hype. We are confident that finally, things will change and our lives will be different because of the heightened emotion. Yet, as evidenced by the annual January gym attendance, hype wears off and we return to our established routines.

Two years ago, my father shared with me a piece of wisdom passed down to him by the late Denver Seminary president Vernon Grounds:

"The ruts of routine become the grooves of grace."

It's not the popular worship conferences or the emotional messages which will ultimately turn our hearts and desires to the Lord. It is the small, seemingly insignificant habits instilled in our day-to-day routines which make shifts in the long run.

Let's be honest: Many days, opening up our Bibles is *not* exciting and we would rather flip on Netflix or open a magazine. Spending time in silence and prayer is *not* the glamorous activity we expect to stir our hearts toward the Lord. But it is these small things which—if we are willing to commit to them daily—will bring about long-term change in our souls.

I think people expect their results in the gym to match their level of excitement around the new year. But when those gains don't come after three full weeks of sweat and soreness, they lose heart.

We do the same thing in our spiritual lives, don't we?

We resolve to read the entire Bible 17 times this year, but after a few weeks in Genesis, we still have the same temper, anger, wounds, or addictions we had last year. Because change doesn't happen over night. Or even over weeks. Or over months.

Real change comes from small, consistent habits installed into our lives which we are able to commit to for years…or decades.

One of my professors in college told us that when he first began reading the Bible, he would read three verses a day.

That's it.

Just three.

Yet he found that he was able to digest them and think about them throughout the day, and slowly came to know the Bible better. Of course, his study of scripture grew over time, but it was that small habit which initiated the shift.

Of course, reading the Bible in a year is a wonderful goal, but if you lose steam after two weeks and give up, what was the point? This year, try to pinpoint a *realistic* habit you can incorporate into your routine and actually stick with. Even if it seems insignificant, consistency is more important than lightning results.

Think of it like changing the direction of a giant ship: Even a one-degree change of direction will drastically alter where you end up.

Another way to think about it is the way you think about meals: Do you remember every single meal you've ever eaten? Of course not! Yet, without every single one nurturing your body, you wouldn't be here today. The same is true when it comes to nurturing your soul. You may not remember every single verse you read, or every prayer you pray, yet it is still wildly important to continue to feed your spirit.

At the end of our lives, when we look back across the paths we have traveled, may we be able to see how the small adjustments and mundane habits determined the destination where we arrived.

UNCLENCH YOUR FISTS
the body responds well to metaphor.

In 2012 I broke down crying in a Starbucks on Cape Cod. I was sitting before my Bible open to Philippians 3 and listening to heavy metal. The refrain of the song was, "Everything is hollow..." I realized that in order to walk fully in the Christian life, I needed to acknowledge that anything short of knowing Christ is empty and I needed to let it go. But I didn't want to.

I didn't want to admit that Christ could satisfy me more than a wife,
or that He was better than traveling the world
or having a great job and wild adventure stories.

4

One evening on the opposite coast, I was at a church in Los Angeles and the pastor was talking about how throughout the Bible, especially the Psalms, we see the worship leader giving instructions on what to do with your body while worshipping.

Raise your hands,

    bow down,

        fall on your knees,

            etc.

We probably read these things and assume he is just being symbolic. *Yeah, I'm on my knees in worship!* we think as we read those passages from the comfort of our recliner.

The body responds well to metaphor.

Do you think it's possible God may have *actually* wanted you to bow down to Him? Or to raise your hands? The one that stuck with me the most, however, was the unclenching of our fists. The pastor in this LA church told us to picture something we are having a hard time letting go of and offering to God. As we do this, he explained, we should start out with our fists closed and slowly open them as we release these things to God.

I looked at the beautiful fashion designer sitting next to me who I was dating at the time, and with great gravity initiated a conversation with God. I was torn about opening up my hands to Him and letting her go.

Think of it like this: Opening up your hands to God doesn't mean He is necessarily going to take this thing away from you; it just means that you're okay with whatever happens.

Want to know something scarier?

Marrying someone doesn't cement them into your palms either. I once spoke with an older man whose wife had cancer. He was about to lose her to the vicious disease and he remembers falling to the floor and walking through the same exercise. He opened his palms before them Lord, forcing himself to be content no matter what happened with his beloved wife.

"God, I love Sweet Sue and I don't want you to take her from me. But whatever happens, my hands are open and I trust you more than my own desires…"

It's hard to do. Try it. Maybe it's a job or a house or a car or a friend. I don't know what season you're in, but picture the thing your heart can't seem to release and clench your fists. Don't open them until you feel like you are legitimately opening it to the Lord; relinquishing it to His care.

The older man's wife survived cancer and recovered fully. God kept her in the husband's hands a little while longer. The fashion designer called things off with me.

Do you have an eternal perspective?

With an eternal perspective, we are able to recognize phrases like "till death do us part" for what they are: truisms that no matter how great or long your marriage is, you will depart from one another. What this means is that marriage is not the finish line, nor is it a promise of satisfaction. If one spouse dies before the other, does that mean the survivor is now doomed to a satisfaction-less remainder of their life?

It's a trap most of us fall into. With an eternal perspective, we can welcome the wisdom of Ecclesiastes 3:11 which tells us that God has put eternity into the hearts of all humans. If that's true, it means nothing can fill an eternal void which is not itself eternal.

God shakes everything and only the unshakeable remains.

Sadly, even the best spouses are shakeable—in this life anyway. It goes without saying that houses, fashion, cars, and jobs are easily shakeable.

What are you focused on?

In the words of Silent Planet, trade your certainty for awe.

How secure are you? Are you solidifying that savings account or are you content with the mystery of the future? How tightly are your fists clenched around the certainty of your own life?

I think the Christian life seeks to find a balance of being wise and making good decisions, but also clinging to trust in an invisible God because of our blindness to the future. You can have a swollen 401k, but what good is that if you're crippled in a car wreck?

The wisdom of Alcoholics Anonymous reminds us that everyone's future is opaque.

Unclench your fists.

Open your palms before the Lord in regards to your future, your spouse, your desires and dreams, and whatever it is that your heart craves. Let go of that grudge you've been holding. Let go of your situational anger.

Do you believe God is better than _____? Can you trust Him enough to open your hands to Him? No matter how tightly your fingers are wrapped around your idol of choice, He can still get it away from you. The only thing that will change is how you respond.

Will you be bitter or better?

The same mentor whose wife had cancer did lose one of his children to suicide. Because of his radical trust in God, even in such a dark situation, he could worship in the midst of his pain. His suffering was unable to shake his faith as he held his family in open hands.

Walking through incredible suffering and loss with God can make you stronger, but only if you let it. Only if you are able to open your fingers and trust Him with what He takes and what He leaves.

You know something else about open hands? You can put things into them. You can't give someone a gift if their fists are perpetually clenched. This isn't meant to whisper sweet notions of a prosperity gospel, but just a reminder that God knows what we need more than we do. He knows what to take away but also what to give.

This entire post, in case you couldn't tell, has been me wrestling with many things I need to release from my iron grip. I'm learning how to open up, finger by finger, a life which is open to the things God has for me, both enjoyable and painful.

HOW TO IMPRESS OTHER PEOPLE

there's really just one way that rises above the rest.

Yesterday I was in my gym and started talking to one of the trainers. I love the guy, he's a big sack of sweetness, but he's as insecure as they come (aren't we all?). While chatting with him, I quickly realized that every sentence to emerge from his mouth was an effort to impress the others listening.

He talked about a road trip he embarked on last year to various cities in the US, followed by future plans he has for overseas travel. There was some talk about exercise, where he was sure to fill us in on the best tips and tricks, despite the fact (perhaps because of the fact) that all of us listening were more fit than him.

The older I get and the more people I meet, the more I am able to *see through* a good amount of things. What I mean by that is, most people in the world are trying to impress you. And if you're observant and think things through, you become harder and harder to impress using the typical methods.

This next paragraph will come off as very haughty, I'm aware, but stick with me for a sec…

I can lift a lot of weight, and I'm aware that I'm not bad looking—I even won a bodybuilding competition. I wear relatively fashionable clothes (all from thrift stores of course), write books, play guitar, and can talk to girls *and* breathe at the same time. I have been on every inhabited continent, hiked ancient ruins, and I was world famous for a week or two, and during that time, met a fair amount of other famous people.

In other words, I'm the ultimate *one-upper* at a party.

But that's not a good thing, and when we look at the facts, it's really easy to deflate. Let's take a second and look at some of those things up close, not about me necessarily, but in general.

For instance, my friend in the gym bragged about his travels in the past

8

year. For many years I was quick to brag about my own. But realistically, travel isn't that impressive. When you think about it, anyone who can save up some money, buy a plane ticket, and leave for a week can travel. It takes no effort, no know-how, and no special skill. Sure, you become more adept and smooth at it and you, yourself get to experience amazing things in these diverse places, but is it really impressive when someone tells me they've traveled? Not really. For whatever reason though, it tends to make one seem *cooler.*

Same thing with lifting heavy weights and looking good. Anyone who looks like a Hollister billboard is simply someone who has spent more time at the gym than they'd like to admit. It's not hard so much as it is an addiction or insecurity. It's not necessarily something to brag about as much as it is a revelation of what your hobby is. People with model trains don't end up with washboard abs, but it's just as much a refreshing hobby as going to the gym is for gym rats.

So to be frank, no, I'm not really impressed by guys (or girls) who can put up heavy weight or have hulkish arms. It just means they've chosen to spend their time in the gym, which any of us could have chosen to do.

Stylish people may intimidate us, but deep down, they're simply people who pay attention to trends and choose to invest their money in clothes and accessories so they can show the world how observant they are. These people may also enjoy different films and music than you too.

My personal favorite is people who love to impress others by name dropping. I met Fabio at a sushi bar one time, which is funny to me personally, because everyone called me Fabio when I had long hair. I could try to weave my Fabio-meeting experience into every conversation just to impress people, but what am I really revealing?

I'm telling the world that I am not sufficient in and of myself, but I am only significant because I am attached to this or that famous person. I am not significant of my own merits, but I am significant because Fabio is significant and I met him once at sushi. You tracking with me? People who name drop constantly feel like they have to impress people, but can only do it by attaching themselves to people more significant than they are.

The list of methods we use to impress people could go on forever.

Think about yourself. What is your favorite method of impressing? Do you try to be the funniest in the group? Are you the tallest, the smartest, or the richest? Rather than exposing all these methods, I'll get to my point. And that is this: What AM I impressed by? How do you really impress other people?

In a word: *humility.*

It's the ability to feel like you don't need to impress anyone.

It's relinquishing the pressure to 'one-up' whoever you're talking to.

I'm impressed by people who ask me questions and who are genuinely more interested in others than they are in themselves.

If we're honest, most of our social anxiety or need to perform is due to insecurity or a feeling of being intimidated by others. We may be intimidated when someone is more hip than we are, or knows more, or makes more cash. But all of these things are simply things they've chosen to pursue in ways different than us. It doesn't mean someone wealthier than me is better than me, just different. Being intimidated by others simply means we are comparing ourselves to them and through some means of calculation, they come out on top.

Roosevelt once said that comparison is the thief of joy.

Humility does not mean that you simply think of yourself as this horrid being who is a terrible human and can't do anything right. Tim Keller has pointed out that there is just as much pride in someone like that as someone who thinks they're on top all the time.[1] The problem is that in both scenarios, you're constantly thinking of yourself and comparing yourself to others. Humility is the ability to let go of this comparison and embrace others.

You'll feel free.

---

[1] Check out his sermon called "The Man The King Delights To Honor"

Lewis put it succinctly: "Humility is not thinking less of yourself, it's thinking of yourself less."[2]

I can guarantee that whoever you're talking to will like you more when you show genuine interest in them rather than trying to impress them.

The folks who really impress me let their knowledge, accomplishments, and skills come to light naturally over time, rather than forcing them into conversation; they're the people who ask me how I'm doing and remember what was going on in my life last time we talked.

People who care.

Because frankly, being humble and caring about others is a heckuva lot harder than all the other "impressive" things I listed above (and it's the reason I'm not that impressive...I'm really bad at being humble...).

May we be Philippians 2 people, who "in humility, consider others better than ourselves, not looking to our own interests, but the interests of others." May we be people who are truly impressive and ask questions, rather than quasi-impressive and steal spotlights. And may we think of ourselves less rather than thinking less of ourselves.

IT'S CALLED SELF-CONTROL
life is 10% what happens to you and 90% how you respond.

"Things won't go your way."

This is one of those rare phrases which applies to literally every human on the face of the planet. And for many of us, this is good reason to worry.
To stress out.
To become anxious.

For many of us, myself included, situations arise in our lives which are out of our control and these breed a myriad of responses. Some of us respond to the unmanageability of our lives in healthy ways, while others respond in

---

[2] C.S. Lewis, *Mere Christianity*

unhealthy ways.

Galatians 5 lists a description of the Fruit of the Spirit, one of which is Self-Control. After years of having this list memorized and held in a rote category in my brain, something about it finally clicked. God instructs us to have *self*-control.

Not world-control.

Not others-control.

Not friend-control.

Not situation-control.

Not boss-control.

Self-control.

Because the painfully obvious fact is, we cannot control those other things. We cannot control diseases or jobs or world events, or family drama. But there is one area which we do have control over: Our own responses to all of these things.

My dad always tells me that life is 10% what happens to you and 90% how you respond.

To me, this maxim always seemed rather passive; if I want things to go as I want, I better get out and make them happen. In reality, there is often (always?) a massive disconnect between what I want to happen, or how I want things to go…and the actual outcome.

This longing to control the world, others, or anything else which is inherently out of our control results in a lot of angst and fear. There are a lot of *what-ifs* which can plague our minds if we let them, rather than concerning ourselves with our own personal reactions to people and events.

I recently began reading the acclaimed book by Townsend and Cloud, *Boundaries,* which has helped straighten out which things are within and outside of our responsibility. For instance, the fact that your boss parties, sleeps around, and wastes money is completely out of your control and out of your realm of responsibility. But what *IS* in your control is how you respond, how you love him, and whether or not you run your lips gossiping about him behind his back.

Think about it like the yard of a house. You are responsible for the lawn, flowers, and weeds inside the bounds of your fence, and your neighbor is responsible for those in hers. It is not your duty to try to mow her lawn for her or plant flowers in her soil. Nor is it acceptable for her weeds to spill over into your yard. You are responsible only for what is in your own yard, and this is truly the only thing you can really control anyway.

Essentially, the only thing you can really control in this world is what goes on within the boundaries of your own person. You can control your thoughts, the things you fill your mind with, the things you eat and what you do with your body. These things are *within* your boundaries and your control.

With this in mind, it therefore becomes *wrong* to try to control things which are outside of your boundaries, i.e. the actions or responses of others. Not only is it wrong, but it is the root of much of our angst, worry and stress. That's why the Bible describes self-control as virtuous. It's much easier said than done, but you *can* control your response to the world and your own actions.

One of the creeds in the first step of Alcoholics Anonymous states, "We admitted we were powerless over our addiction – that our lives had become unmanageable." When we see our lives as unmanageable and out of our control, we panic. Then we often deal with it through addictions like drinking, drugs, eating disorders, pornography, or anything else that makes us feel like we have some sort of control.

AA helps people understand that the future is opaque for everyone: It is unknown and mysterious. We cannot plan for it per se, but we can plan to control our own reactions to whatever happens. And this helps ease the angst of the unknown.

Leonardo da Vinci said "One can have no smaller or greater mastery than mastery of oneself,"[3] yet this is all we really *do* have control over.

You can choose to respond to your children with anger or grace, but you cannot control their actions.

You can respond to your unjust boss with love or malice and gossip, but you cannot control her management style.

Want to let go of anxiety, stress and fear? Stop trying to control the world and start trying to control yourself. It's not easy, but coming to understand the virtue of self-control as more than simply *not reaching for that last slice of pizza* has helped me understand my own limitations and remove some of the stress of life.

May we be people who know our own boundaries. May we come to have control over that for which we are responsible, and let go of the things which are out of our control. May we abide by the Spirit, who enables us to open up our palms which often hold too tightly the actions of others and the events of the world.

THE SCARIEST PRAYER YOU CAN PRAY

there is no humility in constantly ragging on how terrible you are.

Seven years ago I sat in Maroochydore, Australia with my YWAM staff mentor. Once a week we trekked to the Starbucks near the beach, sat on the patio, and watched the waves and people roll by. Isaac taught me a lot, and one thing I specifically remember him saying was about humility.

"You want to know a scary prayer to pray?" he asked one day while we sipped our matcha lattes.

I nodded.

"Ask the Lord to humble you," he continued. "That's a scary prayer because God will answer it and you will be humbled."

---

[3] From *The Notebooks of Leonardo da Vinci*

To be honest, I don't think I ever got around to praying that prayer. If you think about it, it's a pretty scary thing to pray. An invitation to God to reach down and put you in your place is downright terrifying. We have several misconceptions about humility and what exactly it is.

Humility is the opposite of pride. Pride also is an oft-misunderstood concept, as people think they are being humble whenever they speak ill of themselves or how much they hate themselves, when in reality, they are just taking on another form of pride.

C.S. Lewis defines pride as "ruthless, sleepless, unsmiling concentration on the self." If we can define pride this way, then both the cocky male model and the self-depricating high schooler are equally guilty of being prideful.

There is no humility in constantly bringing up how terrible you are.

Tim Keller talks about pride as a *calculation*. When we calculate ourselves against others, sometimes we come out on top, and sometimes we come out below them, but either way, we are being prideful. The pride is in the calculation. No matter who you compare yourself to, you're participating in pride. The devil doesn't care how you place as long as you keep up the comparison.

So, I never really got around to praying for humility. I was too chicken. In many ways, I didn't have to ask for it, because God will always send us opportunities to humble ourselves. We will always have the option to choose humility or arrogance in those situations.

For instance, take a look at my first year at Moody Bible Institute. I showed up thinking I was hot baloney. I thought I knew more about the Bible than all of my peers (and professors), and that I knew all about city life, despite never having set foot in Chicago before.

I had the opportunity to humble myself, learn from my classes and classmates, and create lasting friendships. Instead, no one wanted to be around me because I reeked so strongly of arrogance and I didn't learn as much as I could have because I went in thinking I knew everything.

Over my three years at the school, I learned something: God is not about humility as much as He is about humiliation.

They stem from the same word, but we don't often think of ourselves desiring humiliation. In fact, I think it's intrinsic to humanity to *flee* humiliation at all costs. We buy fancy cars, gym memberships and cool clothes to mask our humiliation.

When I think of humiliation, I think of total exposure. I think of total public shame. I think of the end of *Braveheart* when Wallace is publicly gutted and torn apart. And I think of Jesus.

I think of the mutilated body of the God-man dangling from a tree, utterly naked and humiliated.

Christianity is an open invitation to come and be humiliated.

To come and be exposed before our Creator. Like ripping the scab from the surface of the wound, so must we be rent open in order to be healed.

Many of us claim that we want to be like Christ, but we don't want to be humiliated. Yet, I think that if we are to truly embrace Christ-likeness, we should be open to humiliation. This is why a prayer for humility is so terrifying, not because we are afraid of being humble, but because we are afraid of being humiliated—as He was.

I think this is why the stories of Christian martyrs hit me so hard: These people were (are) willing to be humiliated to the point of death, all for Christ! Had they been too prideful or had they thought too highly of themselves, they would not have gone through with suffering for being Christians. But because they were humble, they allowed themselves to be tortured, killed…and humiliated.

Is Christ someone you are willing to be humiliated for? Or is He simply a coupon to give you a better/longer life? We may think of ourselves as humble people, but to what lengths would you sink because of your faith?

Over the course of my time at Moody, I would not say I was humiliated, but I came close. I had many beautiful and wise people speak into my life. And as they did so, they began to peel back this flimsy exterior skin I had built to protect the soft, authentic person underneath. There was an exposure of sorts as people began to see the "real" Ethan more than the cooler, stronger, mysterious version of myself I had spent so many years

16

constructing.

By no means would I consider myself a humble person. But I am more humble than the day I first set foot in MBI's courtyard, so focused on showing off that no one could get near me.

And as we seek to grow in humility, may we not flee humiliation for the sake of Christ. May we be people who are open to humiliation for the purpose of "knowing Christ in His sufferings, so that we may know Him in His resurrection."[4]

There is no resurrection unless there is death.

And there is no glory until there is humiliation.

May we be people bold enough to ask God to humiliate us that we may know Him better. That we may be healed.

SHAMELESS ATTEMPTS AT PRAYER
it's better to stay silent than risk messing it up.

Seven months ago, I did something I do not recommend to anyone.

I moved to a country where they don't speak English and I don't speak their language. Like, at all. Guatemala is a thoroughly Spanish country, and all my life, I took French in school. I think part of me assumed it would be like Europe, where everyone speaks English, even if they don't. Lo and behold, a third-world country is not the same as majestic Europe, where education grows on trees.

So I've tried to get by. I've been learning slowly and surely, although I bet the locals would beg to differ. I came here knowing roughly four words, and now I know about twelve, but I somehow scrape by.

When I first arrived, I lived with a host family and made several mishaps early on. I once came home from the gym, sweating and hot, and found the

---

[4] Philippians 3:10-11

mom in the kitchen. She turned to welcome me home and I announced, "Estoy caliente!"

She burst out laughing.

I soon learned that caliente does not actually mean 'hot,' but it's a colloquial expression for 'horny.'

Another night as we sat around the dinner table, I attempted to ask if there was more soup. Instead, I simply told the host mother that she is soup.

I have countless smaller stories of people laughing at my stabs at Spanish, but I've become accustomed to it. Early on, someone gave me a piece of advice I've taken to heart. They said that the people who will really improve their language are the ones who shamelessly try to speak it. The more you can let go of the fear of messing up, the better it will be. Sure, you'll mess up, but it's better than staying silent, or worse: Trying to get them to understand English.

I had initially stayed silent out of fear, but after being told that, I began just 'going for it.' I would shoot off all the Spanish I knew, trying to get the four words I knew to mean everything. It didn't become much better, but I think the Guatemalans appreciated the effort. At the very least, they get to laugh at another gringo.

I was thinking about this idea of 'shamelessly going for it' and realized that it applies in more than just foreign languages. It applies readily to prayer.

I cannot tell you how many times, both as a youth pastor and a teacher, I've asked teens to pray and they instantly fall silent, shy and sheepish. I imagine their mentality is similar to mine upon arriving in Guaté: It's better to stay silent than risk messing it up.

The problem with this mindset is, God would rather have us pray than not pray. He'd rather we take a blind stab at talking to Him than remain silent and not try at all. I think God is far more concerned with talking to His people than He is that they 'get all the holy words right,' as if that were a real thing.

In fact, Jesus taught the opposite many times: He condemned those who took pride in their righteous and eloquent prayers, and welcomed the lowly, humble and honest prayer.

I mean, do babies hesitate to speak before they've learned the language of their parents? Or do they just go for it without the social inhibitors of fear and pride? If you've ever been around a baby for more than five minutes, you know that they begin speaking years before they are fluent in any sort of language.

So why are we so afraid of speaking to God, whom Scripture tells us is a good Father?

The truth is, there is no special language you have to learn in order to pray well. My dad says that God cares more about the quantity of prayer and less about its quality. He cares less how you pray, and more just that you pray.

So, be like me who takes blind (foolish) stabs at the Spanish language: Go before God and pray. Be honest. Be thorough. Don't try to impress Him, as if He doesn't know you better than you know yourself.

POUR OUT YOUR GUTS
what I'm realizing now is that God is not a system.

"I want someone to worship me," said Allen. "I want her to be so in love with me, the way Tricia was, that she almost worships me...Right below God," he quickly padded his language. "She should worship God and then me right below Him."

Deep down, I realized the truth in Allen's words. He does not *want* to be second seat to an invisible entity who has not yet managed to satiate his soul's hunger to be appreciated, yet he doesn't want to cross the boundary of Christian-safe language. Better butter up the Big Guy and not say what you really mean.

That's the catch.

Say what you mean and step on some divine toes, or lie for the sake of Christian politeness.

Lose-Lose.

"I want to be on stage and hear thousands of people cheering my name," another friend told me some years ago. "But as they're giving me glory, I'll be giving God glory."

I looked at him with that emoji face that has eyes but no mouth.

There were no words to describe my confusion. Of course I understood my friend's sentiments. Who doesn't want the screaming applause and acclaim from thousands of cheering fans? But more than that, his thinly veiled attempt to mask his his true desires was nonsensical and contrived. Why even add that bit at the end? Why not just say what you really desire?

I've spent years of my life punching my way out of so-called Christian bubbles (which, by the way, are sewn together by pious American mannerisms, cultural guilt, and some marketing geniuses who carved out their own little niche in everything from music to movies to clothes), and have spent little time entering into people's lives. From the shallows of small talk and into the mire of who they are and the pain in which they daily wade.

I've spent too little time investing myself into others, opening up my ribs so my guts spill out.

And this is why the Psalms are so great: The word in the Bible which we read as "heart" in Hebrew really means "guts." It's the deepest parts of who you are. It's the thing that rises when you fall off a bridge, or in love. You may tell God what's on your mind. You may even share with Him some emotions you are weathering. But you haven't poured out your guts.

Even Jesus seemed unafraid of being judged for His words before God.

Jesus wasn't scared of pouring His guts out to God.

In likely the most intense moment of His life, Jesus is in the Garden of Gethsemane, wailing before His Father, sweating blood and begging for God to spare His life.

Take this cup from me...[5]

He cried.

Jesus literally told God that He didn't want to do what God told Him to do.

There's a professor at my college who always says, "Saints! You shouldn't swear. But if you're going to swear, swear when you pray. I cuss all the time before the Lord!"

If any of you are like me, there is a cognitive block somewhere in your soul that tells you, "these words are okay, but these over here...are not." There's something that tells me that too much honesty is sinful.

I am trying to undo this.

I feel that this barrier of politically polite language has actually built a wall between the Lord and I rather than enhanced our relationship. It's like I've been trying to paint a sunset without any red paint. You'll get the general idea, but the force of the fiery clouds will lose their vigor.

Language is important because it is the means through which we perceive, interpret, and communicate reality, communicate life. So in a sense, limiting your language before God limits the extent to which you can live with Him.

Earlier today I was trying to explain what Systematic Theology is to a friend, and as the words exited my mouth, they felt so small and limp. I was explaining that it's about creating a system in which the aspects of our faith —salvation, Christology, end times, heaven, et cetera—all work together to form a unified, functioning machine. It's about creating a simple, well-oiled system that makes sense to us and is easily digestible.

What I'm realizing now is that God is not a system.

He does not come gift wrapped in a cute little box with blue and red ribbons.

The moment you've got Him pegged as a pillar of fire, He reappears

---

[5] Matthew 26:42, Mark 14:36, Luke 22:42, John 18:11. When something appears in all four gospels, it's worth examining pretty closely.

21

somewhere else as a whisper. You start thinking He is a lamb and suddenly He rips out some organs as a hungry lion.

"Safe?" C.S. Lewis once wrote about the Lord. "Who said anything about safe? 'Course he isn't safe. But He's good."[6]

I fear that my conception of God has become far too small.

Let us pour out our guts before Him.

Let us demolish the walls in which we have placed Him.

HOW TO FEEL THE PRESENCE OF GOD
I feel odd claiming to have an answer to this question.

Someone once asked me, how do you describe the presence of God? He wasn't referring to the sort of omnipresent sense of God, but of the manifest type referred to by Brother Lawrence and other mystics throughout Christian history.

How does one define the intangible, unsensable notion of this presence of the Creator? Oddly enough, I had an answer for him and I still stand by it.

"Have you ever been in a room by yourself, reading or something?" I asked him. "At a very deep, unconscious level, you know you're alone."

He nodded, listening.

"Then suppose, someone comes in. It's your roommate. You both say 'hi' and then you go back to reading. He settles in on his bunkbed, also now reading out of your eyesight. You're reading your book and he's reading his book across the room, out of your vision.

"Here's the interesting part: There is now an undeniable sense of his presence in your mind. You are not looking at him, smelling him, hearing him, or in any tangible way conscious of his existence in the same room as you, yet you are fundamentally aware that he is there with you. You won't

---

6 C.S. Lewis, *The Lion, the Witch and the Wardrobe*

accidentally forget he's there because there is a deeper-than-your-five-senses-awareness of your roommate's presence in your room."

My friend, who was far less ethereal and more concrete in his thinking, politely nodded and then shrugged as if I was talking about my imaginary pet lizard. Nonetheless, as a Christian, this is still how I think about the presence of God.

Most of us, for most of our lives, will not have sensual experiences with God. By that, I mean any kind of experience in which we sense Him with any of our five senses. I know plenty of people who claim to have audibly heard His voice, or seen some sign from Him with their eyes. I myself have a basketful of similar memories, though it's easy to look back on them in my moments of doubt and dismiss them as emotional trips.

I even have a friend who told me that she was once praying and suddenly she knew she was "smelling heaven." She described it as the best scent she had ever inhaled and had no other way to describe it.

Stories like these will largely always be the exception to the daily rule of drudging on beneath a silent God. He is quiet. He is a Gentleman, meaning He doesn't spill Himself into our lives uninvited.

But what if we thought about Him as a presence we were previously unaware of. Not one you can sense, but that same idea of knowing someone is in the room with you? It's like in those million and one films where someone walks into a room and suddenly the light turns on: Someone has been sitting in the dark waiting for them and they had no idea (Spoiler alert: It's always either their enemy, boss, or parent).

If this has ever happened to you (usually it's a friend just trying to scare us, not James Bond emptying your pistol of ammo), you know what a shock to your system it is to think you're alone and discover you're wrong. It's disorienting for a few seconds to realize that someone is actually there with you.

I can't help but think that most of us are the person entering the room, unaware of this incredible presence there with us. Except in our case, the light rarely turns on and we go about our business.

But imagine two things:

1 // Imagine if God were to turn on the light and you spin around, amazed that you are actually not alone. I don't mean this as a "you better not sin because God will always see you touching yourself" type of way. But more in the sense of Emmanuel, God With Us. You are never alone because someone is always with you, cheering for you and on your team.

2 // Imagine if you were intentional about making yourself more aware of God's quiet presence, even when the light is off. Like the silent roommate in the room with you, you can continually draw your mind back to the profound knowledge that God is present with you. I am trying to get better at this, and 'practice the presence of God' more often. It's hard because of the number of visible, non-spiritual things there are to focus on, but if it were easy, everyone would do it. Or in this case, if it were sensed, everyone would believe it.

So wherever you're reading this right now, maybe just sit back and realize. Look up from the screen and acknowledge the quiet, invisible presence of Someone in the room with you. Or on the train with you. Or in the cafe or car with you. Like I said, it takes practice to focus on the mystical presence of God, but I'm trying to get better at it.

Wouldn't it be amazing to carry an awareness of Him while you were working? While you were doing the dishes, or stuck in a red light? What if you could even be aware of His invisible presence with you during conversations? While parenting or playing sports?

Let's do this together. Let's be people who carry this awareness of our God with us everywhere, and even make this awareness contagious.

IS IT OKAY IF I DON'T 'FEEL' GOD?

theology takes her time building up to an emotional crescendo.

Yesterday at the gym I started talking with a college student.

"I'm pretty sure you spoke at my school's chapel a few years ago, right?" he asked. I said yes, and we fell into some theological dialogue. After a minute or two, I could tell that his pressing question was rising to the surface. "So, I guess the thing I keep coming back to is, everyone else seems to feel God, whether they're feeling His presence, or they just have some emotion which I've never had."

He impressed me by quoting Pascal's Wager, which states that logically, the believer is safer than the atheist, and that was one of the driving forces in his faith. He reminded me of the Bereans in Acts, who were constantly searching the Scriptures to test the things the apostles were teaching them about Jesus.

"I feel ancient saying this," I told him, "but you honestly remind me of myself when I was your age." I told him I was with a mission organization where it seemed that EVERYONE was FEELING God constantly, yet I never seemed to have the same experience.

I even knew one guy who told me he would listen to sad music or watch a sad movie before every worship service he went to 'in order to soften my heart.' It seemed an awful lot like a ploy to make him cry and supposedly have a more 'authentic' experience with God...despite the fact that what he was crying about wasn't necessarily God-related...

The problem for me when I was with this organization was that I never felt any emotion about those things. I never teared up when I thought about the gospel, nor could I recount any specific episodes of 'feeling the presence of God.' I feared that something was wrong with me, and I wasn't really a Christian since I wasn't having these monumental experiences.

I didn't cry for over four years.

Then one day at church, I did. And a month or two after that, I did again.

And I wouldn't say I'm quite at the Jude-Law-in-*The-Holiday*-level yet, but I have found that my emotion toward God expands the more I learn about Him. I can't help but think that we have replaced deep knowledge of God and His Word with emotion and awe-inspiring performances at our (larger) churches. Theology often isn't sexy.

I don't want to make this comment as a rule, but couldn't we draw parallels between "emotional-pull churches" and one night stands? We want the emotional high without putting in the time to build up to a real and meaningful relationship; we want a shortcut to ecstasy. The man in the bar who wants sex with a stranger wants the feelings of intimacy without the patience and work.

Theology also takes her time to build up to an emotional crescendo.

At least, that's been my experience. I could have tried to squeeze the tears out all those years ago, and I did try, but they would have been false tears. What I have found is that emotion has followed truth. The more I learn, the more I feel.

Even this morning, the pastor preached a sermon on the importance of good theology. He said, "Years ago, I only knew *that* much about God and therefore, I could only worship *that* much of Him. But over years of study, my knowledge of Him has grown to *this* much and I can now worship *this* much more of Him!" Just as in a dating relationship, the more you learn about the other person, the more you are able to fully love and experience them as they are. You wouldn't want to remain ignorant and superficial in a marriage, but why would you in your relationship with Christ?

So what I told the kid at the gym was just that: Let your heart follow your head. You're in a good place, and the emotion will come when the time is right. Don't force it and don't think you're broken if you don't feel the way everyone else does. In fact, I would argue that there is danger in being led spiritually by your emotions.

Of course, a good balance is necessary, but I see most Americans swinging toward emotion and experience more than knowledge and truth. The whole notion of having a magnificent emotional rollercoaster of a worship service is very new to the Christian faith, emerging in the past couple hundred years. Does that mean that for the first 1,700 years of her existence, the Church was doing it wrong? Or maybe it's we who are a little off-track.

Do you not feel God? You're not alone. Many heroes of the faith felt very distant from God most of their lives, including the author of most of the Psalms, King David. He wrote, "My God, my God, why have you forsaken me?" Words which would be repeated by Jesus as He withered on the cross.

The best advice I can give is to keep learning about God. Keep reading the Word and filling your mind with Him. The act of these disciplines will eventually reorient your desires toward Him, and even though they are not glamorous or even fun, your emotions will follow.

"The ruts of routine become the grooves of grace."

The things you fill your head with will eventually trickle down into your heart; your emotions will be affected by what you put in your mind. There's no way they can't be! So don't try to rush it. I would argue that wisdom doesn't attempt to conjure up a false emotional experience, but simply remains faithful and lets the emotion come when the time is right.

I have reached a place now where I use words like 'kerygma' and 'ontology' and get a little misty-eyed. I sit in theology classes and feel stones rise up in my throat because I'm engaging with the material at a much deeper place than I could have seven years ago.

Most of you are the opposite. I recognize that I'm an outlier here. Different views of our beautiful God will choke you up and tug on your heart, but one thing is true across the board: You won't reach these deep places with Him if you're not filling your mind with His words and orienting your life toward Him.

It will come in time.

So may we be people who pursue God, not an emotional high. May we be people who see God working in all areas of our lives, especially many of the mundane and unglamorous nooks. May we be comforted by knowing that He is not simply an emotion to be conjured up at will, but He is a person; a Father who wants to walk the journey of our lives with us. And that means that there will be a lot of long stretches of road without emotion or hype, just many, many trudging footsteps.

IS YOUR CHRISTIANITY SUPERSTITIOUS?
it was a sort of demonic passover...

I was in Southern India several years ago and noticed an odd thing about most of the small children there: They all had little red strings tied around their bellies. These toddlers who were just learning to walk and run around were most often stark naked, save these shoelace-sized red bands tied around their middles.

I asked our host what they were for, and he replied matter-of-factly, "They are to keep the evil spirits away."

Like many Asian countries, these Indians (even in Christian villages) observed ritual superstitions in order to ward off evil or bring good luck. In Thailand, for instance, every restaurant or business we entered had small shrines in the entryway with ornate 'birdhouses' with fresh food and drinks set before them. These, we found out, were to appease the evil spirits at the doorway and prevent them from entering the building.

It was a sort of demonic Passover—stale noodles instead of lamb blood.

In the Western world, we may scoff at such petty superstitions, dismissing them as sophomoric or ignorant. *Of course the world doesn't work that way!* We say from our lofty towers of science and reason. As Christians in the West, however, we must remember two things: 1) That our culture—including our faith—is heavily postmodern and influenced by the Enlightenment in ways many third-world countries are not; and 2) that we each have our own sets of superstitions which may not be as apparent as a red string or food shrine.

We live in a culture defined by rationalism and empirical evidence. If something cannot be seen, touched, or logically explained, we tend to discard it and disregard it. One of my seminary professors said that we live in one of the few cultures in the history of mankind that has explained and reasoned ourselves out of believing in God and the spiritual world. If we have grown up in this culture, it is incredibly hard for us to believe that there are invisible forces or spirits at work.

This is the tension presented to Western Christians: We believe in this invisible force (God), but are raised by a culture which has done away with everything related to the spiritual realm.

Enter, the American version of superstitious Christianity.

We may not consider ourselves superstitious, but humanity is fearful to the core, and what is superstition but an attempt to harness our fears into submission? Catholic taxi drivers may hang their rosaries from the rearview mirror, or maybe you have a cross tattoo on your arm. We think that the amount of worship songs or sermons we listen to in a given week will sway the favor of the Almighty because of our obedience. More generally, we may keep a ledger in the very back of our minds of our good deeds and weigh them against our bad, just to make sure we're keeping up our end of the salvific bargain.

These things tend to go unspoken by most Christians, but the pattern certainly holds true; we tend to feel better about ourselves the more we do good and avoid doing bad.

This line of thinking is certainly not new to Judeo-Christian history. In 2 Chronicles 17, David tries to win God's favor by building Him a temple, but God never asked for the temple to be built. Fast forward several hundred years, and the Israelites have begun worshiping the temple more than the God for whom it was built. In Mark 13 when Jesus and His disciples are walking through Jerusalem, the disciples start to admire the stones which make up the temple, but Jesus simply states that they will all be destroyed. God never cared about things made by human hands, He cares about humans and making His home in and among them.

The Pharisees also seemed to fall into a 'superstitious trap.' Jesus rebuked them because they assumed their good works and observance of the law would save them. Isn't that all superstition is? Doing certain actions in order to garner some sort of reward or good luck (or simply avoid bad luck)?

Christianity, however, is anything but superstitious. From beginning to end, the work of redemption is done by God and God alone. With the first promise to Abraham (I will make you into a great nation...)[7] through the death and resurrection of Jesus Christ, the job has been done by Him, leaving nothing for us to do. This is why Jesus' powerful last words on the cross must be remembered: "It is finished."

Finished.

Meaning, there is no more work for us to do to hold up our end of the deal. Meaning, even if we tried, we cannot somehow add to our salvation.

If we really think about it, it's offensive for us to try to earn God's favor by doing good works. It's a subtle way of saying *What you did on the cross wasn't good enough, Jesus...let me help you out...*

So may we be Christians who flee from superstition in its many forms. May we be free to enjoy God rather than attempt to impress Him with religious superstitious actions or win His 'favor.' May we recognize our own use of talismans and return them to their proper place of decorations rather than magical relics or good luck charms.

ANXIETY & THE MYTH OF CHRISTIAN PEACE

we want our lives to be a model of peace and the absence of worry...

This holiday season, more than any before, has been stressing me out.

It's not so much the buying presents or parties or fears about the new year, or anything I can actually put my finger on. In fact, I think it has less to do with the holiday season itself as much as it does with the season of life I am in (three jobs, interviewing for a fourth, publishing a book, navigating singleness, sorting out my eschatology, etc, etc...).

I have never been a high-stress person. I have always had more of a chill, laid back personality, but for whatever reason, this past year has seen a

---

[7] Genesis 12:2

decline in that and an elevation in my blood pressure. I think too much. And becoming momentarily-almost-famous over a year ago certainly did not help to relax me. Quite the opposite in fact.

So for whatever reason, I have experienced anxiety for the first time in my life.

I used to always critique people in my mind who complained about anxiety because I was so ultra-chill and didn't understand the concept. I guess I still don't, as anxiety is somewhat undefinable, and I can't really put a finger on the source of this unrest in my bones. But whatever it is, I don't like it, and I can see the negative effects of it in my life.

The worst part is plugging this experience of anxiety into my beliefs about Christ, the Holy Spirit, and the tender love of the Father.

I mean, the Holy Spirit is referred to as "The Comforter,"[8] and Christ, "The Prince of Peace,"[9] so naturally, as a Christian, I shouldn't have to wrestle with foes like stress and anxiety, right?

I think the American conception of "Christian Peace" is a myth.

And here is what I mean by that.

I think we expect that simply because we wear the label of "Christian" our lives should be a model of peace and the absence of worry or fear. We expect our coworkers to approach us and say things like *Wow, you seem so at peace with the world…Why? What do you have that I don't??*

But realistically, how many times has that happened to you? To me? Far less than I'd like…if ever.

I say that *Christian Peace* is a myth—to Americans anyway—because we talk about it despite rarely having experienced it. To the outsider, most Christians I know are just as stressed out and anxious as the rest of the world. We may use our mouths to talk about The Prince of Peace, but not give much experiential evidence of knowing Him.

---

[8] John 14:16

[9] Isaiah 9:6

We have not experienced the peace we so adamantly proclaim.

We allow things to stress us out and fill our minds with worry just like everyone else; as if the Creator of the cosmos weren't watching over us. We neglect the small voice who whispers peace and life to us in favor of trying to grapple the reins from His hands and work things out on our own. Maybe we look peaceful on the outside but feel very differently. Despite how much we talk about peace, we are rarely shining examples of it.

I once had a friend who nightly drank away her fear of death. She was a Christian but had no trace of peace because of the anxiety which held her mind in a constant state of angst and unrest. I imagine you and I are no different, we just use different escape vehicles. For instance, I recently realized I could never drive in silence. My hands and thoughts were jittery until I had a podcast pumping through the speakers in order to distract my mind from the lack of peace within.

Silence became more of a nice thought, like a friend who lives on the other side of the globe, than a routine experience.

The worst part of this, as Francis Chan points out, is that *worrying is a sin*.[10]

In America, it is one of the most overlooked sins, right up there with gluttony and greed. Jesus specifically tells us not to worry.[11] Therefore, by worrying, we are directly disobeying Him.

I know how that comes off—like we are being punished for something that's out of our control...or for feeling like things are out of our control and clinging to that thought. But there must be a different way for us to look at it.

What if, instead of feeling dread about anxiety, we saw Jesus' words as an invitation *out of* worry? What if we believed Him when He said that He sees the birds and the flowers of the field, and we don't have to worry about ourselves? Why don't these words comfort us more than they do?

---

[10] He writes about this in his great book *Crazy Love*

[11] Matthew 6:25ff

There are some practical steps we can take away from anxiety, but they all begin with acknowledging that we are not in control of our lives, and that God is. Does an infant worry about what they're going to eat tomorrow when they are in the loving hands of their father or mother? We need to position ourselves like that infant, fully dependent and wanting for nothing.

This doesn't mean that our life's circumstances will always be ideal—in fact quite the opposite—but when we take on the mentality of a child of God, we can relinquish our tight hold of control and trust that God is moving. We may not have control of what happens in our lives, but we can control how we respond. Will you respond with worry, anxiety, and stress, or will you allow yourself to relax, knowing that the Prince of Peace and the Spirit of Comfort are at work, bringing all things together for our good?[12]

God never promised easy lives for His followers, but He did promise to be with us in the midst of the storm. So if the Prince of Peace is *with us,* who are we to be stressed out?

I want Christians to be a people who truly embrace the peace of Christ, no longer allowing it to exist only in theory, or a 'nice idea.' I want the peace of Christ to so radically invade our lives that the notion of Christian Anxiety vanishes and is replaced by total reliance on The Comforter.

So…

breathe.

We who confess Christ as our source and our sustainer are no longer allowed stress or anxiety. We breathe Him in with every breath and exhale our fears and worries. The more we allow ourselves to be consoled by Him, the more we can let go of our 'opaque futures,' to borrow Alcoholics Anonymous' terminology.

May we be a people who carry the peace of Christ with us. May we experience it in times of quietness and stillness, not only talking about it externally with our mouths, but demonstrating it through our interior life.

---

[12] Romans 8:28

SEVEN MONTHS OF SUFFERING

I fear that you have not comprehended how angry I have been...

May

This morning I stood in my classroom after my second class and had the same conversation with myself I always do.

Well, I'm still sick.

Well, I still can't taste a thing.

Well, my sinuses feel like they're going to explode every time I move and my throat is painfully swollen like I swallowed a melon.

I haven't caught up on sleep since the womb and on top of that, the world is a cold, scary place. In the words of Woody Allen, "Not only does God not exist, but try getting a plumber on the weekend."

I'm certainly not an atheist, but I'm barely a Christian as most days my faith is hanging on by a thread. Thank goodness it's not up to me, but most days it feels like I've wriggled my way out of the almighty grip of God and am wandering alone. I've been sick since Thanksgiving and 9 doctors haven't been able to tell me what's wrong.

I went viral again.

This time it was for being shirtless in the rain, so nothing really ever changes. There is nothing new under the sun: I have found my purpose in life. If there is one thing I am good at, it's being shirtless in the rain.

What a freaking one-trick pony.

June

"Not only does God not exist, but try finding a plumber on the weekend."

When I was younger and first heard this quote from Woody, I didn't understand it. Now that I'm older, have seen most of the world (it's mostly all the same: everyone wishing they were somewhere else), and have been sick since Thanksgiving (it's June now), it makes a lot more sense. I've realized that Allen's sentiment encapsulates life under the sun. He shrunk the book of Ecclesiastes down into one sentence and translated it to the 20th century.

If you think about it, a scarier way to put it, from a Christian perspective, would be thus:

> God exists, but try getting a plumber on the weekend.
> God exists, but what really matters is you can't get your crap flushed by Sunday...
> God exists, but He's not really pressing...
> God exists, but look at all the other stuff you need to focus on first...

My pastor said, "Most of the time when someone is having a crisis of faith, it just means God is smashing the little box in which they used to hold Him. He wants to show them He is so much bigger than they previously thought and He can't fit in that little box anymore."

It's easy to sit in that service when life is going well for you and say, "Heck yah, that's awesome! I agree! Amen!"

It's another to find yourself in the center of a 'crisis of faith' from a first-person perspective. It's another thing to feel like you're in a vast ocean where you can't touch the bottom or find anything to grab a hold of. Existentially, is there any way to feel like you're not out to sea with nothing solid to cling to? These are the questions I've asked after countless days of being sick with no hope of recovery on the horizon. Eleven doctors don't know what's wrong with me and my knuckles have put enough holes in the walls of my room to ventilate a comfortable summer breezeway.

In the midst of this anger, confusion, sickness, and of course, sin, where have I even seen God moving?

I haven't, but I think I'm learning something still.

We have become accustomed to talking about God using messages or experiences to bring us closer to Him. Go for a walk in the woods and call it church. Travel the world and find yourself 'out there.' Maybe if He's really good, He can use hard times to grow us and make us into better images of

His Son. A pleasant reformed pastor would point out that God was able to take the mutilated pulp of a body on Golgotha and turn it into something good, so I suppose he can take my enduring illness and wring some goodness out of it.

Some day.

Maybe.

August

I haven't sat down for two months because of traveling engagements and I'm tired.

It's likely that Abraham, the father of the Jews, upon whom rests the bulk of our faith, was a Sumerian who never became a total monotheist. YHWH would have been one of his household gods, yet in the progression of God's unfolding history, Abraham the philander was still able to be used.

This is a weird way of saying this: We don't know what Abraham believed about the afterlife. We also don't know what Moses or David necessarily believed about life after death because compared to their writings about this life, eschatological writings pale in comparison. When I first began looking more deeply into this, it scared me.

"Well, how can we trust anything the Bible says if the first half of it has no conception of the afterlife??"

After months of chewing on this, it turned out to be a more comforting revelation than scary one. Why? Because I discovered that God cares a LOT about this life. He cares what we do in this life and He cares about what is done to us. The psalms cry out for deliverance, and as a good non-denominational boy, I grew up reading those spiritually, as in,

God, deliver me from my sin and from hell and satan...

In reality, David and his ilk were crying out to be delivered from literal armies surrounding them. He was crying out to be delivered from illnesses and famine and other threats to a small tribal nation. In other words,

God is very, very, very concerned with what happens on this side of death.

This morning I stood in church trying to focus on God and other Christian stuff but the pain in my neck prevented me from going very far. This must be why God cares about human lives this side of death: How can someone care about the kingdom of God if they're in indefinite pain? How can someone worship when they haven't eaten in a week?

Better Christians than me are able to bypass their pain or illness and praise in the midst of it, but that's a level of mastery I have yet to attain. Anger and worry consume me night and day the longer my pain does not relent. Don't be fooled by my confident writing and my smiling Instagram pics.

It is a gnostic faith which pushes Christianity to the backburner until death, when we can actually reap the benefits of our faith. No, if the bulk of the Bible is about things happening in this world, that means we need to care about it too. It means we need to care about widows, immigrants, refugees, and orphans. It also means that God cares about my throat issues and that ultimately, I will not have suffered in vain.

It means there is a God who cares that you can't find a plumber on the weekend.

I have to keep reminding myself of this. Constantly.

FAME MESSED ME UP MORE THAN PORN EVER DID
there's a word for what I experienced: trauma.

In 2016, I was doing research for my book *The New Lonely*[13] by going to various high schools, churches and conferences to conduct surveys. One of the questions in the survey was "How important to you is fame?" Responses varied, but I'll never forget the answer from one tenth grader who wrote in, "Fame is everything to me. It's my number 2 goal." (Sadly, he did not mention what his number one goal was, so let's assume it's getting a really good perm.)

---

[13] It's really a terrific book. Definitely recommend. 10 out of 10.

We have a culture of children whose heroes are the Logan Pauls and Selena Gomez's of the world, and I have figured something out about this new fame operation system. It begins with a confession: I like Logan Paul.

A few months ago I went to see what all the hype was about with this YouTuber, and I honestly got hooked after the first video. He was hilarious, charismatic and entertaining. One thing I realized about his video style, though, is that you don't feel like you're one of millions of viewers tuning in to watch an über famous vlogger vlog. In the past, 'famous people' were those in the motion pictures. The ones you had to pay five dollars to see in the theater, and there was an obvious difference between their lives and mine.

You watch Clint Eastwood shoot the outlaws and Leo swoon over Rose on the Titanic, and no part of you thinks, This is attainable for me. I can do that too.

The difference with today's Hollywood is that you watch a good YouTuber do their thing and you feel like you're a pal. You're in the circle. You're riding dirt bikes around their mansion with them, or racing Lamborghinis on the PCH.

I think it's this inclusive nature that makes fame seem so much closer than it ever was before. They don't seem like famous people. And to some extent, that's true. That's actually the story of the Paul brothers who were midwestern nobodies from Ohio until their Vine accounts blew up, which led to YouTube superstardom.

Watch one of their videos and you'll soon forget that you don't have millions of dollars to throw on the world's largest pumpkin, or a customized Fortnite gaming room in your crib. The fact that this lifestyle is just a viral video or two away means that many of us have taken the bait. It means we're recording everything we do and tweeting every thought in our brains thinking that something will eventually catch, and we'll be on our way to LA next week.

Problem is, every alluring promise of fame turns out to be hollow. Their checks will always bounce.

Three years ago I was named the sexiest man on earth by CBS. Then I was asked for dating advice by both GQ and Cosmo magazines, and MTV called me 'stupid hot.' I was hit on by Luis Vuitton's shoe designer (he even offered to fly me out to Paris for a private weekend) and the followers flooded by the thousands.

I thought I had finally crested that glorious plateau of fame from which there is no descent, and for a delicious month, I had.

But then the calls stopped coming. The TV interviews slowed down and my follower number actually began shrinking. Three years later, I've probably lost more followers than most people will ever have. It seems like a pointless number, but can you imagine what that does to your psyche? To think that thousands of people don't want to hear what you have to say or see what you're doing with your life?

The thing is, most people (fortunately) won't know what it's like to come down from that because they've never gone up. Many people long for fame and influence without realizing the repercussions of their desires. They don't know what it's like to be hated by thousands of angry internet-people (once it became public that I was a Christian, thousands of strangers suddenly started sending me hate messages and writing terrible articles about me) or feel like you always need to please them all without offending any of them.

There's a word for what I experienced, though some of you may protest: trauma.

It's weird to think of myself as the victim of a trauma, because my life has honestly been pretty pain-free. Without delving too much into the philosophy of comparing sufferings, I think that's an adequate term for what someone experiences as an has-been internet celebrity.

When a counselor first told me that I had experienced 'trauma' in the experience of my viral video, I protested because I felt guilty. I had not been assaulted or abused. But looking back on it three years later, I'm realizing that 'trauma' just may be a fitting word. After all, how many celebrities end up killing themselves? We could name a few who took their own lives just this year.

Despite the staggering tragedy-like elements of the lives of many famous people, it remains something many of us seek as a high[est] priority. We probably feed ourselves lies like,

Naw, that wouldn't happen to me, I could handle fame.

I'd be happy with just a thousand more followers…then a thousand more…

My brain wouldn't be messed up by millions of fans; it would feel great!

The thing I've told everyone who asks me about the experience of being famous—and I never ever swear—is pretty simple:

Fame f's with your head.

Other side effects which you may not have thought about are things like:

Commitment issues: Since you know everyone is throwing themselves at you, no one is ever good enough. Found someone who likes you? Well there are probably better-looking ones out there among your horde of thousands of followers. Ever wonder why the celebrity divorce rate is so high?

An ever-growing feeling of inferiority: Your last Instagram post didn't get as many as the one before it? Uh-ohhhh…someone is slipping quietly into obscurity. There are 100 people who will take your place tomorrow.

Comparison and envy: You may have gotten 5 million views yesterday, but Jimmy just dropped a new video and it already has 7. Now we hate Jim but we also wish we were him. Returning to the attention of the public becomes an obsession.

Shame: In addition to mean articles and hateful comments about you, you become even more of your own worst critic. You beg yourself questions such as, Why would anyone follow me anyway? I'm worthless. I don't have as many followers as Catelyn and she's skinnier and has better hair and I'm not talented like her and…

Your fame becomes your identity: Three years later, it's hard to not try to associate myself as 'the shirtless jogger.' That's the reason people started to care about me, so that must be all I am. That must be the only thing to give me value.

Pride: In psychology, it's called the Spotlight Phenomenon. You think everyone is talking/thinking about you every second of every day. Forget intimacy when you have ego.

Fake friends: Everyone suddenly wants to be associated with the 'famous' person, or asks you to share their video of them doing slam poetry.

In light of the title of this piece, it's true. Fame messed me up pretty badly, and I wasn't even *famous* famous. I was just viral for a few days. And ironically, all the messing with my head worsened my struggle against porn rather than help it get better.

Don't long for fame. Don't long for your head to be f'ed with. Recognize that you're already loved and accepted by the only One who really matters; the only One who will never click Unfollow. The One who died just so He could be with you for all of eternity.

May we be people who remember that. May we be Christians who astound the world with our peace and identity whether we have 8 followers or 8 million. It's harder than it sounds, but be content with where you are. With who you have. Life will be better.

SETTLING DOWN WITHOUT SETTLING
it's almost like we weren't created to be uprooted.

This is for the wild ones.

This is for the people who never dreamed that sitting still was an option for them.

This is to myself, c.a. the majority of my life, as an exhortation.

I used to think settling down was the opposite of a fulfilling life. Adventure awaited me in the distant corners of the world, and I intended to fill those corners with tales of my travels. For many years of my life, the world shrunk down to a more digestible size and I trotted about her surface like Peleg over Pangea.

I loved it.

And still do.

I love the feeling of mystery when I step through the sliding glass doors of a foreign airport into the unfamiliar air. I love getting into a taxi and telling the driver to deliver me to an address I've never been to. I love standing atop high places and surveying fresh landscapes.

Not only is that way of life incredibly fun and exciting, but it looks really, really good online. The digital Ethan is at least twice as cool as the real one because all my travel photos are gathered and displayed in one collection which can be reviewed in a matter of minutes.

But living a life in pursuit of adventure is not sustainable.

Not only is it ultimately unfulfilling, but it bears little to no fruit. When our goal is to bounce from here to there every other week, we lose the ability to put deep roots down anywhere, or in anyone. And we lose the opportunity to be known deeply by others and therefore be poured into by them.

This described me pretty well for about half a decade. I was with various ministries around the world, thinking I was performing spectacular feats for the Lord, but in retrospect, my efforts were mostly in vain.

I used to think God had called me to a life on the road, ministering to people as I go. But since I've become a youth pastor, I've realized that real ministry never really happened in the fleeting glances I would cast at people while I drove through their city. I'd bounce from place to place, praying for people for a week here, and teaching them for a week there, but to what end? Any gardener will tell you that if you want to produce any kind of crop, you can't be throwing some seed and peacing out. It takes time and work over a long time to create fruit.

So now as a youth pastor, I'm committed to taking care of these kids. It may sound more boring than my trip across Brazil, but it is SO much more rewarding. Not only do I get to minister to them several times a week, but I actually get to stick around and see the fruits of that labor! I may go so far as to say that when I was wandering the world with various organizations, I did almost no *real, meaningful* ministry.

So last night, I came up with a question…

If that way of life is both unsustainable *and* unfruitful, would God really call anyone to it? Or do we concoct those phrases in order to justify our privileged jaunts around the globe? Many people in the missions organizations I worked with, including me, had this mindset of bouncing around and calling it ministry. And they had nothing but the best intentions, except for maybe a hint of millennial wanderlust.

Compare that to missionaries who move to a new country or city and commit to spending the rest of their lives there. How much more fruit will they see?

There is a story about Hudson Taylor, the great missionary to the people of China, and his devotion to the people he loved. He had relocated to China, but after many years there, his teeth began to rot and he had to go back to America to get some of them pulled. While he was on the dentist's chair, he told the dentist to simply pull all of them so he wouldn't have to leave his beloved Chinese congregation again.

Yes, he traveled to a different nation to proclaim the gospel of Christ, but his motives did not include envy-inducing Instagram pictures and cool stories. He wanted to take the name of Christ to the ends of the earth so they would be saved. And when he arrived there, he stayed.

Think about the way many of us view romantic relationships. I've been single since the introduction of the steam locomotive, and there is a part of me that loves the idea of being able to date anyone I want: This exotic beauty from the Maldives, or that Croatian goddess. The ability to date whomever I wish offers a certain type of freedom, but is this freedom truly what humans were made for?

There is a difference between settling and settling down.

Settling down involves making the choice to say, 'I choose this woman and I will give myself to her and enjoy her.' *Settling* implies that I am missing out on something better by choosing her.

I'm realizing that *settling down* is a good thing, and it does not necessarily mean I'm *settling*.

This is also true of ministry and choosing where to live. Choosing to commit to a certain place, a certain church and group of people can seem like a loss of freedom, but how much more rich is it! We gain the opportunity to be known and loved by others; we get to minister to others and see the long-term fruits of our labors; and we get to experience deep rootedness.

Everyone sacrifices some freedoms in exchange for other—often greater—benefits.

I recently got curious and did a Bible search of the word 'wander.' What I found was somewhat shocking. Not *once* is the word used positively. In fact, God often cursed groups of people by causing them to wander. Conversely, He blessed people by giving them land to *settle* and put down roots.

Our culture is one that praises the individual who is a wanderer, a traveler finding *her own path*.

But it seems as if God designed us to be rooted and nurtured by a stable and sustainable community. And that is the environment in which we can be most fruitful as well. If you think about it, travel is often a selfish endeavor. The one who benefits most is the one on the trip. No one has ever said to me, "That adventure you went on last month benefitted me so much!" More often, my journeys are simply envy-inducing and look better after they're digitally formatted.

The same is true romantically. Sure, I could go have emotion-fueled flings with a dozen women around the world, but it's far healthier to commit myself to one woman who will love me and spur me to grow, as I do the same for her.

Is it really *settling* if what I gain is greater than what I lose?

So I'm working on it. Learning how to be rooted takes time, as does growing actual trees and producing literal fruit. A big slice of me still longs to depart and breathe in that foreign air—and I probably still will fairly often—but I'm also learning how to settle down and develop healthy routines and rhythms here in Colorado for as long as I'm here. I'm training myself to appreciate this place more than I'm longing to take off and be elsewhere.

Wanderlust is an escape. It's something our culture romanticizes, but which is ultimately unhealthy. To be frank, it's immaturity.

May we be people who learn how to be rooted. People who are able to commit to others, to churches, to our spouses, and to locales, for the flourishing of ourselves and others.

BEING CONTENT WITH BEING

there is this place in each of us from which we need to operate...

I turned 26 two weeks ago in New Jersey.

Every birthday that passes, I try to remember what Henri Nouwen wrote about birthdays:

> Birthdays need to be celebrated. I think it is more important to celebrate a birthday than a successful exam, a promotion, or a victory. Because to celebrate a birthday means to say to someone: 'thank you for being you.' Celebrating a birthday is exalting life and being glad for it. On a birthday we do not say: 'thanks for what you did, or said, or accomplished.' No, we say: 'Thank you for being born and being among us.[14]

There was a vast disparity between my birthday this year and last. This year, I was with family and felt genuinely celebrated. I felt like they valued my existence. Last year I celebrated alone after being blown off by some friends who opted to go to a bar because a basketball game was on.

It is a valuable thing to feel celebrated for existing.

The title of this post may seem to some of you like an unfinished sentence.

---

[14] Henri J. M. Nouwen, *Life of the Beloved: Spiritual Living in a Secular World*

Perhaps there should be a blank space after the words: "Being Content with Being _____." Maybe you tried to fill in that gap with something to which you ascribe value.

I want to be content with being single.

I'm content with my job & my bank account.

Being content with being busy/at rest.

But no, there is not more to the title. I think something we can learn from birthdays is that there really is value in slowing down from time to time and being content to simply *be*. This is something I struggle with often, and it is a root of anxiety for many of us.

We feel like we must prove ourselves or earn our contentment. As Christians, many of us reach a mindset in which we allow ourselves to rest one day a week, but the rest of the time we are busy working for our merit, as if we are utterly useless if we are not busy.

But how many times does God command His people to be still? Dozens!

One of my favorite quotes about the Christian life is from a mystical writer named Muyskens: "The spiritual life is not about addition, it is about subtraction."[15] In other words, many of us try to add things to our lives in order to feel more 'full.' Yet in the spiritual life, the opposite is almost always true: The more we take away, the more we realize those things were just distracting us from what is truly important.

I spoke to my youth group recently about this idea of identity and compared it to what we are taught by our culture. If we are not careful, these notions will slip into our way of thinking too. For instance, the key line in *Batman Begins* is repeated a few times throughout the film: "It's not who you are, but what you do that defines you."

Of course, this is Bruce Wayne's motto to prove that he is able to do more than simply be a spoiled trust fund kid. But what happens when we

---

[15] J. David Muyskens, *Forty Days to a Closer Walk with God: the Practice of Centering Prayer*

inadvertently apply it to ourselves? We begin to think that unless we are constantly proving ourselves or 'doing good,' then we are a nobody.

This is completely antagonistic to what God tells us about who we are. He tells us that before we *do* anything, or prove anything to Him, we are accepted and loved. We are grafted into the family of Jesus not because of what we do, but simply because He loves us as we are.

So have you taken time to just *be* lately?

We are certainly called to work hard, serve others, and do good. But all of our actions need to come from a place of being content at our core with who we are. If you are a Christian, your first and most important identity is a beloved son or daughter of God. All else that you do or think comes from this deep place of realizing you are loved simply because you exist.

I'm walking my youth group through Genesis 1 right now, and last night we talked about God calling everything *good*. The trees and oceans didn't need to prove themselves to God before He called them good; He simply made them, saw how they were, and called them good simply because He had made them and deemed their existence *good*.

He does the same when He looks at us. Before you go to church or crack open your Bible, He looks at you and says, 'Hey, you're pretty good if I don't say so myself! I did a good job on this one!'

Haven't you noticed that the most comfortable, magnetic, and happy people are those who are most content with themselves? They're not trying to brag about their latest accomplishment or slave away at their job to be considered worthy. These are the kinds of people who love life. They enjoy what they do because their brain is not fogged up by fretting about whether or not they have earned anything.

I'm working on being that person. I want to be someone who has truly become content with being, with existing, rather than someone who constantly has to impress others or God.

Some of you may be asking the question then: What kind of steps do I take in order to become *that* kind of person? I think the answer is simple.

Take time to just *be*.

Make time throughout your weeks to not make anything, prove anything, impress anyone, or even try to learn or grow. Take time to just be and in that time, you will slowly become more and more content with just *being*. Whether it's sitting or walking or standing, just *be*.

May we be people who find our identity, first and foremost, in the belovedness of a Good Father who we don't have to impress. May we learn to still our minds and celebrate our own existence before trying to impress others or earn merit from the Lord.

May we become content with being.

TRAUMA + HONESTY = HEALING
addiction is the mask worn by trauma and honesty heals both...

Someone recently called me out.

I don't remember what they said because it was a small blip last week which sort of lingered in my mind, but they were talking about my writing, my internet presence, and my real self. The real Ethan Renoe.

"You have written really honestly in the past, but lately your writing has become more sweeping and theoretical than honest and open, like the way you used to write." Something like that.

Then yesterday I was checking in with my friend Brad, whom I talk to on the phone a couple times a week. He's one of the few people I consistently check in with on a deep level. I mean, really deep. I think many people (especially guys) flee from questions as cutting and deep as "How are you feeling today?" It seems like a simple query, but how often do you answer that question honestly? And then from there, how often to you take the time to analyze what brought you to feeling that way?

Years ago, Pascal said that the hardest thing for any human to do is sit alone in a quiet room for ten minutes.

Today I read an incredibly interesting article by Tucker Max which I intended to just skim and take a few pointers from, but ended up spending half an hour digging deeply into the whole thing. I was surprised because the premise of the article is Max sharing his experience with MDMA, colloquially known as Molly, in a clinical therapeutic way.

What he ended up talking about for most of the article, however, was his healing from a lifetime buildup of trauma and pain, and the gateway to opening this healing was the drug. I don't have firm opinions yet on treatments like these (supposedly they will be legalized in the next five years) but I think what Max brings up in the article is very worth examining as Christians.

I think many of us recoil from the idea of trauma and any sort of therapy which rings of New-Agey vibrations (even if it's not chemical in nature) simply because the human side of us is scared of *the Other*. We feel like we can only embrace Christ and to open ourselves up to any sort of 'therapy' to heal from our 'trauma' is to abandon our Savior.

I think that in this way, many of us become trapped within our own language and this is detrimental to Christian growth. What if you simply replaced the word 'trauma' with 'sin'? While the word itself has become more broad and ubiquitous in recent years, it is undeniably married to the Christian idea of sin. Trauma, put simply, is any sort of wound or pain and it can come from a myriad of sources. Perhaps you have trauma from neglect and not receiving what you needed. Maybe your trauma comes rather from a place of *commission*, meaning someone did something to you they should not have.

Whatever the root, all of us have trauma and the question is, will you address it or run from it? Will you be honest with yourself or keep wearing a mask? It's easy for us to conceptualize the idea of wearing a mask in public, but what I mean here is wearing one in front of yourself.

Yesterday on the phone with Brad, he began gently calling me out for making excuses for my behavior. If you're familiar with what I've written in the past, you probably know that lust, pornography and masturbation have been the behemoths I've wrestled throughout my life. Add to those the occasional angry or depressive outburst and you basically have my complete laundry list of vices.

The difference is, historically I've written about these things from a predominantly triumphant angle, making it sound as if I've conquered this foe of lust and my issues are now buried in the past. In reality, they are still very present demons I'm wrestling.

"I wonder if I'll ever be fixed."[16]

Brad and I began talking about how difficult it is to be honest with yourself and how most of us make so many excuses that we begin to believe them ourselves.

It is so ridiculously easy to become glaringly blind to reality.

As they say in Alcoholics Anonymous, the future is opaque. You are not guaranteed a better tomorrow so begin taking hold of your life today. When applied to addiction (Porn, alcohol, weed, social media, Netflix), it means don't keep telling yourself that there will be a magical time in the future when this issue will be resolved. Either you deal with it or you don't and in only one of those circumstances are you being honest with yourself.

Being honest with God is essentially the same as being honest with yourself. When you're alone in your room, are you able to pray with raw honesty to God, or do you clean up your prayers as if He doesn't already know? Most likely, this reflects the fact that you're not being honest with yourself *or* God. People who can approach the foot of the cross and just dump out their guts are those who are able to honestly examine themselves and take whatever they find to Christ.

How else do you expect to find healing?

Max described his first session with MDMA as "taking a giant [crap] which left him feeling hollow afterward." On the one hand, he just had a ton of poison (his trauma) leave his body, but at the same time, his body had become accustomed to having that poop inside of him.

We hold onto our own crap/pain/trauma/sin/addiction because sometimes

---

[16] Rival Choir, "House Fire"

that's more comfortable than addressing it and flushing it from our systems.

I met with a pastor a few years ago and when the subject of my addiction came up, he told me that I'm just eating feces and have somehow trained my mind to crave that taste rather than the satisfying palate of true intimacy and love. Why do we do this? Because more often than not, the fear of leaving our addiction outweighs the benefits of recovery.

Another friend once said that your addiction is your easy chair. It's comfy and you've broken it in just the way you want. Then you're surprised when it's *uncomfortable* trying to stand up from it and leave the easy chair of your addiction in the past.

Who ever said recovery would feel good?

I know I've sort of vacillated between talking about addiction and trauma, but I think the two go hand in hand. Trauma feeds us lies such as "you'll never be good enough...no one will ever love you," and we swallow them whole, leading to numerous addictions to numb that pain.

Addiction is the mask worn by trauma and honesty is the penetrating light which tears both apart and exposes them for what they are. This means being vulnerable with others (not *everyone*, but using discernment in our revelation). It means learning how to sit alone in silence for ten minutes without reaching for the phone or book or remote.

It means letting yourself be loved by the Creator of the universe with no mask or fancy, lyrical footwork in our prayers. If we can't be honest with Him, how can we even begin to be honest with others who are more easily deceived?

You are wounded. I am wounded. But as Henri Nouwen puts it, we can learn to become 'wounded healers' of one another. How can we do this if we don't first acknowledge our own woundedness?

May we learn how to come honestly to Jesus of Nazareth and be healed by Him. May we learn how to be refreshingly honest with ourselves so we can go on and offer the gift of ourselves to others.

SHAME 101

The other day I was exercising in the park and ended up diving headfirst into a deep conversation with a guy I met there. He's a student at Denver University, basically in the same tailspin I was several years ago, trying to figure out which way is north, how to look cool, et al.

We began talking about confidence and shame, and as I began referencing shame, I quickly realized he had no clue what I was talking about. Shame is not a topic normally breached in our day-to-day conversations. Everyone has some sense of what the term means, but often our understanding of it, and perhaps our experience of it, are skewed because of a lack of clarity on the subject.

So here is, to the best of my understanding, an introduction to shame.

Shame is not simply feeling guilty
One of the easiest ways to understand shame is by comparing it to guilt. When you steal a candy bar, you feel guilty. When you slip up and look at porn, you feel guilty.

Guilt is the feeling that you have *done* something bad.

Shame on the other hand, is the deep-seated feeling that you *are* bad.

Shame is the voice in each of us that whispers to us that we do not deserve love; that we are not worthy of grace or of friends or relationships, or anything good at all. While guilt can serve a useful purpose of calling to light things which we have done wrong, shame is unredemptive and destructive in nature.

Through guilt the Holy Spirit can come and convict us of a wrong action and get us back on track, but if we listen to the voice of shame, all we hear is that we are beyond the bounds of forgiveness and God and other people don't even want us. There is nothing within us even worth seeking out and reconciling.

The introduction of shame

When I explained this to my new friend in the park, I bent down and drew a circle in the dirt with my finger.

I explained that this circle represents the soft core inside each one of us. When we are born, there is this soft, authentic, vulnerable core within us which is who we most truly are. It's what David referred to in Psalm 139 when he writes, "You created my inmost being; you knit me together in my mother's womb...My frame was not hidden from you when I was made in the secret place. When I was woven together in the depths of the earth, your eyes saw my unformed body."

It's at this deep and central place that God knows us. It's who He intended for each of us to be. It's who Adam and Eve were before the introduction of sin, when they could be naked and not even realize it.

But at one point, we are wounded. It's inevitable. I draw another circle around the first.

This wounding can come from anywhere: Neglect or abuse by a family member, rejection from other kids, isolation, or any number of sources. Each of us is wounded and this wound informs us that we are not *good*. The subliminal message of this wound, whatever its source, is that we are not inherently worthy of love.

So in response to this wound—I draw a third outer circle—we create alternate identities to hide behind. We become the class clown or the successful business man. We hide behind our physical appearance or travel a lot so people will think we're cool.

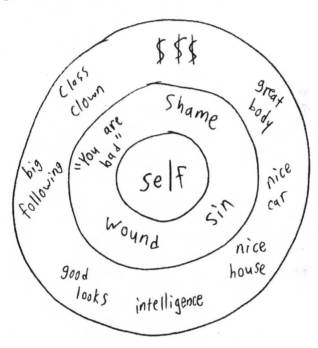

Shame, the second circle, has covered our true self and revealed (or instilled) a weakness within us that we feel we must compensate for. So we adopt new identities to try to 'win' love for ourselves or earn it or be good enough.

Just as in Genesis 3, shame always makes us hide.

After Adam and Eve ate the fruit, sin and shame were introduced to the world and the very first thing they did was run and hide. Shame causes us to try to hide our true selves because it convinces us we are not good enough as we are. It says, "You need to *impress* them or they'll never like you."

Shame and addiction

My pastor in Chicago once said that 'addiction is the one thing which unites all of humanity.' Each of us wrestles with one addiction or another, and the root of every one of these is shame.

Shame is what traps addicts in cycles of acting out, unable to break free from whatever vice binds them. It's a spiral impossibly hard to break out of.

He takes his first swig of alcohol at a young age and is instantly hooked on the taste, or the escape, or the confidence it provides. So he returns to it later. And then again. And again. And soon he finds that he can't stop.

And the voice of shame is swift to swoop in and whisper, "You're nothing but a drunk now. No one will ever love you because you can't stop drinking." Yet the only escape from this voice of shame is to hit the bottle again and flee.

Porn addicts return to the digital images because in a deep place they find themselves *unworthy* of a real man or woman. But of course, after each episode of acting out, she feels worse than before. Even less worthy. No real man will ever love her, so she returns once again to the digital actors to feel relief. But feels worse afterward...

The cycle is cruel and relentless.

The same goes for shopping addicts, food addicts, exercise addicts, eating disorders, and nearly every other form of addiction we can imagine. We have a deep knowledge that we do not measure up and seek out something to compensate for it or escape from it.

The unveiling of shame

Lately I've been realizing just how deep the roots of shame run in my own soul. I began dating a beautiful woman several months ago, and even though it didn't work out in the end, that brief relationship helped shed light on a lot of areas where shame was influencing me in areas I hadn't even realized.

The thoughts began the first night I met her: Upon seeing her walk into the room, my first thought was *Wow, she is beautiful. I'd never even have a shot with a girl like that.*

As time moved on, receiving attention and even attraction from her worked wonders on rebuilding my soul as a man. I realized that for so long, I had been operating under the assumption that I wasn't really worthy of a relationship with a real, breathing, Christian woman who was attractive and successful.

Where had these thoughts come from? They were the voice of shame conjuring up lies and convincing me to believe them with absolutely no grounding in reality.

If you're anything like me, there are these things you believe about yourself which, if teased out, are utterly ludicrous.

If I drove a nicer car, I'd have a girlfriend now.

If I were as funny as _____ I would have more friends.

If I had my dream job I wouldn't feel so insecure.

We often turn to externals like these to try to fix the deep shame dwelling within our souls. But putting more decorations on our exteriors won't help heal the wounds at the soft, vulnerable core of who we are.

Shame is very, very deep. The more you examine many of the things you believe about yourself, the more you'll find many of your core beliefs have been tainted by shame.

I want to begin examining some of the ways we begin healing from shame and all of its insidious effects. For now, remember that the Lord loves you at the deepest part of who you are; the innermost circle. The little *you* that was wounded all those years ago. He doesn't love you because you're funny, rich, attractive, or intelligent. He loves you just because of who you are.

This is the beginning of the unraveling of shame.

WHEN WORKING OUT IS HARMFUL

the most confident people are not always the strongest...

My first year of college, I remember lying on the couch Skyping someone on my laptop. I don't even remember who I was talking to, but I remember putting my arm behind my head, noticing how shrimpy it looked, and quickly putting it back down.

That was not the only time I had feelings of inadequacy regarding my body, but that was about the time I started seriously hitting the gym. *I couldn't go on being a little shrimp and still call myself a man!*

My friend Paul C. Maxwell wrote an amazing article called 'The Epidemic of Male Body Hatred,' in which he explored the phenomenon in depth.

> "'If I could look like that guy who played Thor, I would be happy.'
>
> It's a common belief among men of our age. Put more honestly, "If I can't appear confident, sexy, intimidating, competent, and super-human, I'm worthless."
>
> We compare ourselves to others in the gym. We come away from movies wanting to exercise for eight hours. We would rather jump in front of a truck than take our shirts off at the pool. We feel pathetic and small. We look at ourselves in almost every mirror we pass. When alone, we flex — not because we like what we see, but because we don't. We have spent hundreds of dollars on pre-workout, weight loss, and weight gain supplements. We research the best way to bulk, shred, diet, and binge."

Maxwell points out that there is a wide difference between being healthy and being shredded. Even as Christians we often excuse this excessive gym addiction as our way of "staying in shape" and "pushing myself." For many of us, myself included, these endless hours at the gym come more from a place of insecurity and self-loathing than a genuine desire for health.

Because in the back of our minds, we know that there are plenty of exceptionally healthy people who don't look like the cover models of Men's

Fitness. And conversely, not all those cover models may be healthy people, despite how chiseled their physiques are.

I have a friend who used to be a ballerina in New York City. She told me that when she began, her director handed her a box of diet pills and a pack of cigarettes and said "get started."

Because health was not the goal, looking good was.

And this is the attitude I often embrace when I walk through the emerald gates of my Swole Sanctuary. *I may not be able to woo her with my charm, my humor, my integrity or my character, but at least I can attract her with my body.*

Many of us perceive our body and our looks as the one aspect of ourselves which is easiest to address and control. We'd rather spend three hours on the dumbbells instead of spending time in silence, addressing these roots of insecurity and our lack of confidence. We see ourselves as unworthy of love as long as our bodies are 'undesirable.'

In *Fight Club,* the narrator looks at a Calvin Klein ad and scoffs, "Is that what a man is supposed to look like?"

You can always tell who is confident about which body parts at the gym by what they hide and what they show off. Dudes who love their arms don tank tops and those who don't wear t-shirts. Sweat pants are for the chicken-legged, but yoga pants are for people who want to draw the attention to their southern hemisphere.

Of course, being confident in certain parts of your body is not confidence at all. Ask yourself, if you were to be in a car accident and all your muscles evaporated in a month, would you still want people to look at your arms? Your legs? Your butt? Is your confidence rooted in your physical attributes, or is it rooted more deeply in who you are as a person?

We all hide behind something, be it humor, intelligence, or artistic skill, and for us gym rats, it happens to be our bodies. It's easy to hide behind this one especially because you can cover it up with the 'health' excuse, but as I said above, this is beyond the realm of staying healthy. So how do we diagnose this epidemic of male body hatred? How do we establish the symptoms and work toward a cure?

The *incarnation* is the theological term for God, the creator of all that exists, becoming human. The Creator entering what He created. The Eternal Spirit putting on flesh.

Our bodies are *good* no matter what shape they are in, not because of the amount of effort we pour into them, but because God Himself donned one. Whether chubby or bone-thin, your body is good.

The very fact that Jesus *incarnated* a body and walked around in it for 33 years shows that bodies in themselves are not bad or evil or shameful. On top of that, the prophet Isaiah actually tells us that physically, Jesus was not that attractive. We have done ourselves a disservice by portraying Jesus on the cross with a six-pack and toned arms.

The Greeks portrayed their gods with bulging deltoids and rippling quadriceps, but the Bible tells quite a different story about its God. *He had no beauty or majesty to attract us to him, nothing in his appearance that we should desire him.*[17]

The world looks for a strong and powerful king, but Jesus showed us one who was ugly, weak, and defeated. Not only was he physically unattractive, but he sunk to the lowest depths of shame when He was crucified naked and displayed for the public to look upon. He was physically unattractive, but he knew who He was and therefore didn't need to compensate by puffing up his chest or wearing purple robes.

The issue isn't that we have bodies and want them to look good; the problem comes when we try to root our confidence and self-esteem in that alone. We often ignore the health of our soul and spirit and try to compensate with hours in the gym.

Last night I was cleaning out my childhood room and found an old shoebox full of letters. As I read through pages and pages of rich affection, I remembered what it felt like to be loved unconditionally. I remembered being in high school and not feeling like I had to look a certain way to impress someone in order to be loved. And it felt good.

I've realized that people who are most confident are not the strongest, but

---

[17] Isaiah 53:2

those who are okay with their weakness.

I think the cure to overcoming our body hatred and insecurity is to remember that we are loved as we are: buff, chubby, or skinny. Health is good, as is working toward fitness goals, but not if we come to them to find love and acceptance.

In contrast to the world's message of finding approval through looks, spend time in silence and meditate on the fact that Jesus promised to be with us regardless of how we look. Dwell on the fact that we are loved despite weakness and always skipping cardio day. The Apostle Paul even urges us to *boast* in our weakness.[18] How contrary to the world's message of strength is *that?*

You are loved as you are. May we be people who experience the liberating feeling of unconditional love. May this come to define us more than the curve of our obliques as we learn how to relax and stop striving, but accept ourselves as we are, accept love from others, and accept the ongoing love of the Father who prefers weakness to strength.

I WAS TOLD I HAVE CANCER
my body was imploding within me and I didn't feel a thing.

"It looks a lot like cancer to me," my doctor told me over the phone.

It didn't hit me at first. It felt like when you first get a tickle in the back of your throat signaling a coming cold. I felt like the lumps in my lungs were just a problem which would come and go. But my doctor had used the C-word.

Cancer.

I was sitting in a Starbucks when my doctor called. Since people were sitting all around me, I tried to keep my voice down after he used the C-word. I

---

[18] 2 Corinthians 12:9

was almost embarrassed to say it out loud, as if saying it aloud would confirm my diagnosis.

"Are you sure that's…what it is?" I asked

"No," he replied, "but by looking at the CT scan, that's what it looks like. I'm not gonna lie to you, it's probably cancer."

A few minutes later I had hung up and was walking out to my car, dazed. I called my mom and told her the news. I got a text from my dad saying how much he loves me. My mind was churning out a million thoughts a minute.

I'm super healthy and young! I thought, followed by, *But cancer can happen to anyone, young or old. Think about all those kids with shaved heads. Or the film The* Fault In Our Stars. *They were in high school.*

One line from that film kept echoing through my head. The boy is talking about his PET scan and how his body "lit up like a Christmas tree," and I wondered if that's how my scan would be. I felt fine, but I guess most people do in the early stages of cancer.

The more my anxiety spun my head, the more I wondered if this was nearly the end of Ethan Renoe; if the scan would light up like a Christmas tree and the doctor would give me a grim prognosis in a hushed voice.

Suddenly every film about—or even containing—cancer ran through my mind. *50/50, Annihilation,* and a thousand tragic photo diaries of someone withering away and ending with an empty bed plagued my mind like hornets. It's one thing to watch those films as a spectator, but an entirely different thing to participate in them. I felt helpless, as if my body was also withering away and I couldn't stop it.

Over the next 48 hours I began to think about time wasted in the gym, performing a facade of health and fitness while my body was destroying itself inside. I regretted every fast food meal I'd ever eaten, or every drive I'd ever taken with my phone between my legs. Whatever it was that caused this, I regretted it. But not knowing was the worst part.

No. The worst part was thinking about what happened after.

Another line which rotated through my frenetic mind was from Brand New's song, "Jesus":

> "Well Jesus Christ, I'm not scared to die,
> I'm a little bit scared of what comes after
> Do I get the gold chariot?
> Do I float through the ceiling?
> Do I divide and fall apart?"

That's exactly what I wondered. What happens the moment my body stops? Does my consciousness continue? Does it go black until the resurrection? I imagined the quietest place I'd ever been, the backside of the great sand dunes, and tried my hardest to imagine a deeper peace which would be gifted me in that moment.

Or what if it hurt? What if I didn't rest in peace?

Suddenly every theological debate I'd ever had seemed trivial in light of reality. It seemed that when I talked about life and death before, I wasn't really talking about life and death at all, I was speaking about theories. The past decade of my life has been filled with doing Christian ministry and suddenly it was all being put to the test. How *real* was Jesus? How real was God? It was no longer a theory, but it became the center of my reality.

I thought about my grandma's email address: assurance46. When I was younger, I asked why that was her name and she said it's because she was saved in 1946. That's the year she received assurance of her salvation. That's the year she was given possibly the greatest gift a human can receive:

Assurance.
Some sort of anchor for your existence to latch onto.
Solidity in a sea of unbearable lightness.

Nothing is more terrifying than the void before us all: death. The Great Mystery. To those without this assurance, yes, it is a mystery. It is something to be terrified of. But in the hours I thought I had cancer, I hit my Bible more than I had in a long time, and more desperately. The passages reassured me. They were like aloe vera on my searing angst.

I can't describe it better than to say there IS something supernatural about the Word of God. They are not mere words on paper; it is the very breath of God. It's not nice thoughts to be spouted off as colloquial maxims; it is a very real rock on the ocean floor, anchoring us in the storms of our lives. And our deaths.

Two days after that phone call, I went in for my PET scan. I was shivering, both from fasting and nerves. The nurse inserted my IV and the contrast ran through my body, making me feel like I had pooped my pants. I lay in the center of the tube for 15 minutes, all the time wondering what it was seeing. Was I lighting up like a Christmas tree, or was it just an innocuous lump in my lungs?

I thought about cell mutation and the division of my own body. I thought it strange that my body could be imploding within me and I didn't even feel it.

When I came out of the tube I couldn't wait for the doctor, so I asked the technician what she thought. "You've done a lot of these, so how do I look?"

She told me she wasn't supposed to do this, but she showed me the scans. "It doesn't look too bad to me," she said. "Nothing is jumping out at me."

I hadn't lit up like a Christmas tree.
A million-pound burden fell from my entire body.
I was free.
I had more years to fill with life.

Later that afternoon I got a call from my doctor, who confirmed the technician's findings. It wasn't that bad, it was just something to "keep an eye on." I was overjoyed. Life was more real than it had ever been before. So was death.

Even though my doctor should *not* have prematurely used the C-word with me, I'm glad he did. I'm glad I had a wake up call to remind me of the reality of my imminent death. It may not have found me this time around, but it will. And when it does, will I be ready? Will I have filled every one of my days with meaning and sweet communion with Christ, or will I have wasted them all?

If you're reading this, death has not yet found you either. But it will. And I hope that when it does, you are ready. I hope you are anchored to the same rock that I am: Jesus Christ from Nazareth. A humble carpenter who was pinned to a tree outside the city, where people burned their trash.

But remember, the story doesn't end there. If you want to learn about death, listen to someone who went there and came back. That's Someone you can trust. He's someone you can trust with your life AND your death. He's Someone who can not only explain the Great Mystery, but Who has experienced and destroyed it.

John 11, the resurrection of Lazarus, shows us that Jesus has authority even over death itself, and if we bind ourselves to Him, we no longer have anything to fear.

> Jesus said to her, "I am the resurrection and the life. The one who believes in me will live, even though they die; and whoever lives by believing in me will never die. Do you believe this?"

POSSESS YOUR BODY
are you in charge of your own ship?

On February 24, 1989, United Flight 811 departed Honolulu en route to New Zealand. The plane had just crested 22,000 feet when the cargo door of the jet blew open, tearing a huge hole in the side of the plane. Nine passengers were immediately sucked out and fell to their deaths. The two right engines were damaged by flying debris, leaving only the two left engines.

They were 100 miles from land.

The captain, David Cronin, had been flying for 38 years and employed every ounce of his experience to try to bring the plane to safety. He slowed the plane to just above stalling, gliding it slowly back to land. When he began his descent, he found that the fuel was 100,000 pounds above recommended landing weight. Not only that, but the flaps which help the plane to slow were also broken and he came in 35 miles faster than the maximum landing speed.

In spite of all of these catastrophes, the flight crew reported that it was one of the smoothest landings they can remember.

Captain Cronin did not just fly the plane and flip some switches. He wasn't merely clocking in to his job to rack up some hours and get a paycheck.

He possessed the plane.

Robb Bell, in his book *Drops Like Stars,* writes about a guitar he owns. He paid for it and can play it somewhat well. He can construct chords and align them in a way that makes a discernible melody. He can evoke sound from it.

But Bell has a friend who comes over sometimes, and when *he* picks up the guitar, he can wring sounds out of it that are not from this world. He can make the guitar sing.

Rob may own the guitar, but his friend *possesses* it.

Last night, I sat in a coffee shop and cracked open my Bible to 1 Thessalonians. As I scanned the pages, one verse in particular jumped out at me. I was in chapter 4, and verse 3 was rather straightforward. Something we've all heard before:

> It is God's will that you should be sanctified: that you should avoid sexual immorality;

But then I kept reading and for some reason, verse 4 gave me pause:

> that each of you should learn to control your own body in a way that is holy and honorable

Again, for anyone who has been reading the Bible for a few years, this verse may not be earth shattering. But for some reason, I looked into the Greek behind the verse and was fascinated by what Paul is writing here. In fact, I feel like the modern translations do us somewhat of a disservice in their translation of the passage. The King James Version brings us closer to the target:

that each of you should know how to possess his own vessel in sanctification and honor,

The phrasing is reminiscent of the captain of a ship who has been sailing the seas for most of his life and has sea salt permanently trapped beneath his fingernails, and the north wind tangled into his hair. Paul is urging us to take mastery over our own boats.

He is urging us to take possession of our bodies.

For several years of my life, I dreamed of sailing the world. I had dreams of meeting exotic women on foreign shores and wandering the seas as free as the rolling waves. I wanted to earn the golden hoop earring only worn by seamen who have made the treacherous pass south of Cape Horn. I longed for that breed of adventure. I still do.

As I read that passage in 1 Thessalonians last night, a new longing came over me. A fresh desire to take mastery of my own body the same way a captain of the sea does. I want to possess my body the way Captain David Cronin possessed United Flight 811. I want to have control over it the way Rob Bell's friend possesses his guitar.

To me, this involves a number of things. To continue Paul's metaphor, when the hard winds of lust or sexual desire wash over me, I am able to have mastery over my ship and sail it to calmer waters.

When the cargo hatch flies off—say, I get rear-ended or a friend betrays me with gossip—rather than getting angry and punching holes in the wall, I want to be able to maneuver my plane to smoother air.

I think part of the *how* here involves orienting our desires, so when the gusts of desire blow, they are slightly less powerful. When we desire holy things, our longings for sexual gratification and other addictions begin to fade.

Another part is simply preparedness. Just as Captain Cronin's 38 years of flying prepared him for disaster, Jesus was able to resist temptation by having scripture pre-loaded into His mind to dispense when He needed to, and thus combat the attacks of satan.

To some of you, this may seem like just another Purity-Movement-esque call to keep your V-card until you're married. To me, it seemed more like an artful call to mastery over my own 'vessel.'

Bruce Lee could break bricks just by touching them because he had such control over his body.

Are you in charge of your own ship?

Do you possess your own vessel, or are you blown hither and yon by every stray breeze of desire that comes over you?

The captain inside of me wants to be able to say 'Yes, I have mastered myself. I can pilot myself away from the storm and into the holier spaces.'

A SIDEWALK CONFESSION

Christianity is easy when it's only digital.

"Is that a Bible??"

I was almost to the door of this coffee shop in Denver where I was going to sit and write a blog post about something spiritual, poetic, and reflective. But now there was a woman stopped in the middle of the sidewalk a few feet in front of me, pointing at the weighty book in my hand.

I nodded and said "Yup!" hoping to resume walking and enter the sanctuary of the shop, where I could pop on my over-ear headphones and narrow in on my writing.

But this woman, no more than five foot three, stood and stared at me, her mouth slightly ajar. From the way she talked and stared, it became evident that her brain was dancing to a different rhythm than mine. Autism or Aspergers maybe?

My patience ran short, but I tried not to snap off a rude comment.

"I love the Bible!" she said after a few seconds.

I smiled with a politician's grin to mask my shrinking patience and asked her what her favorite book is.

She fiddled with something in her back pocket. Then her front coat pocket. Then said "John. I'm doing a Bible study of John right now."

"That's great," I said, "What do you like about it?"

"I like how it shows that He knows what we're going through. And that He is love."

It took me a second to realize that the antecedent to those pronouns was Jesus.

And then my heart was melted. Conviction slammed into me as I realized that the very Person I was in such a hurry to write about would have stopped and talked to this lady for hours, giving her full attention. Yet here I was, trying to rush past her in order to write about Him and look good online.

The headlines would read:

> *Ethan Renoe, Ultra-Spiritual Blogger, Spares 47 Seconds for Sweet Handicapped Woman on the Sidewalk as He Rushes into Coffee Shop to Write About Jesus*

> *Youth Pastor Urges Students to Be More Like Jesus, Doesn't Want to Spend Time with Fellow Disabled Believer on the Street*

"Whatever you did for the least of these," said Jesus, "you did for me."[19] In other words, if I could only give this lady a few seconds of my time, I would probably give Jesus the same amount.

Jesus did not come as a YouTube star or Teenage Sweetheart. People didn't follow Him around because of His political pull or cultural savvy. I doubt He would have sported those tight black jeans with the knees torn out and paid an extravagant amount on a haircut.

I think He would appear more like this woman on the sidewalk; the one I could barely give a minute of my time. The plain, sweet, unpretentious lady

---

[19] Matthew 25:40

68

who was more interested in making a new friend than in how she appeared. And I think that if Jesus had been in my place today, He would have sat her down to a cup of coffee and heard her story, regardless of how awkward and choppy the dialogue was.

I was convicted today realizing that to be like Jesus is to make time for the un-fun and un-glamorous people. The mouth-breathers and acne-infested. Ministry is about loving real people more than it's about theories, words, or hermeneutical gymnastics.

Because Christianity is easy when it's only digital. It's easy to caption a picture with a Bible verse or have your bio be some hymn lyrics.

But when it puts on skin and takes up your time on the sidewalk, how will you respond? Will you be too busy to stop and talk for a sec, or will you take time to show the love of this Christ whom we confess? In my own heart, I've realized that it's far easier for me to be drawn to the affluent and beautiful people—the ones who give me street credit or a step up the societal ladder.

"What's your name?" I asked her with renewed softness.

"Sabrina," she said as she fumbled her hand out of her coat pocket to shake mine.

"Great to meet you," I said, wishing I had felt that way from the beginning.

This morning as I ate my cereal, I read a few pages from N.D. Wilson's book *Notes From the Tilt-A-Whirl*, and it happened to be the passage where he recounts meeting a handicapped woman in a wheelchair on the sidewalk. The woman asked him what his name was, then asked him to be her friend. Then he has a similar epiphany about generous love. (What are the odds??)

I wish I made friends the way these people do. They don't care who you are, nor do they think too lowly or too highly of themselves. They just want to make friends.

They are the epitome of Henri Nouwen's longing to be 'free from the weight of having to judge others.'[20]

Free to love others instead of judge them; free to love themselves instead of heaping baggage and shame upon their backs.

I think this is a step toward what Jesus described when He talks about having the mindset of a child. Children don't strategize friendships to make steps up the social ladder, nor do they select more aesthetic people so they look better on Instagram. They just want to love people without tether or chain. It sounds way more fun than whatever mindset I've been stuck in.

Praise God for unexpected wakeup calls.

May we be people who love like Jesus did—the unattractive, the sick, the lowly, the least—even if it means burning a few minutes on the sidewalk to talk to a sudden friend. May our love be childlike, and may our patience expand. And may we make friends just for the fun of it.

ON LOVING 'SINNERS'

or, why the simplest things are often hardest to grasp.

You know how there are those really simple things which often take years to click with you? For example, the jingle for Kay Jewelers—"Every kiss begins with Kay"—took me over a decade to realize that it was referring to the letter K in 'kiss.' (Do you respect me just a little less now? I don't blame you.) I thought they were just saying every kiss involves our jewelry.

Anyway, I have recently been going through a similar season of epiphany which has to do with returning to the subject of a million sermons and Bible verses: Love. There are so many basic truths and maxims and passages we hear repeated so much they lose all their meaning. I have been returning to their origins and in a way, rediscovering their meanings. These verses include, but are not limited to:

---

[20] Henri J. M. Nouwen, *The Way of the Heart: the Spirituality of the Desert Fathers and Mothers*

"Remove the log from your own eye before removing the speck from your brother's."[21]

"There is no fear in love."[22]

"The world will know you are my disciples by your love."[23]

Something clicked which, honestly, should have clicked years ago but didn't. That is, we need to be people who love others before we judge, condemn, and correct them. I'm going to try to word this right: Other people's sins do not affect your life at all. You do not gain heaven points by pointing out other people's sin and trying to make them better.

Barring, of course, violence or abuse which *does* affect you or others, trying to mold and form other people out of a religious motivation is most likely not love. When we try to change people, we are usually not loving them, but trying to form them in *our own* image.

The most common argument for this—which I have employed in the past —is that correcting their sin *is* loving them. Granted, that may be the case 5% of the time, and only with close, Christian friends, but is this how we tend to live our lives?

For example, I have some friends here in Guatemala who are a married gay couple. I had dinner with them a few nights ago and it was so much fun! They are intelligent, vibrant and attractive people. They are not Christians, but they are aware of both my faith and my different views of homosexuality. But they also know I put my relationship with them over my beliefs.

Sure, I could lecture them on 'the evils of their twisted ways' every time we hang out, but how long do you think that relationship would last? Is their marriage harming me in any way? Am I losing heaven points by not calling them out?

---

[21] Matthew 7:5

[22] 1 John 4:18

[23] John 13:34

I would much rather live like Jesus who welcomed the sinner and the outcast to His table. I would rather my friends encounter Him before they ever hear a word about their 'sinful lifestyle.' Frankly, they've already been told that by a thousand other Christians in the name of love. To summarize:

—I *gain* nothing by pointing out people's sin to them, especially those who don't even believe in God.

—I *lose* nothing by befriending them, loving them, eating with them, seeing them as beloved of God and made in His image.

I'm using the homosexual population as an example for two reasons: 1) They are one of the most stigmatized and alienated populations in the world, especially in the Christian community. Their suicide rates are staggering, and we have the option to contribute to that, or to help heal it. 2) This issue is a very present and ongoing debate in our culture, especially in Christian circles. I want us to remember to humanize our brothers and sisters in the LGBTQ community rather than use them as a pawn in an argument, regardless of which side of the aisle you're on.

I can't help but think that God is happier when we reach out and love the other (in this case, the homosexual) than when we preach at them and drive them away. I wonder which is a more heinous sin: To be gay, or to drive someone away from Jesus' church because they are gay.

Maybe it's not just homosexuality. Maybe you see someone smoking a cigarette and fear that by loving them, you are encouraging smoking. Or alcohol. Or weed. Or dancing. Or reading Rob Bell. Whatever it is, don't let it become a wall between you and this human.

Yesterday I sat in a Chick-Fil-A and listened to these two old ladies gossip about their friends for an hour. Personally, I'd rather welcome a kind gay person into my church than a gossiping straight person. They are included in the same list of sinners, are they not?[24]

I think I've spent much of my life in fear: fear that if I was *too* loving to those outside of Christian circles, I would somehow be in error and sinning.

[24] Referring to 1 Corinthians 6:9-10, which lists homosexuality among sins such as slandering and greed.

I feared that by accepting them and loving them, I would also be approving of their sins and therefore, God would be angry with me.

This is the definition of having fear mixed into our love, which is directly opposed to John's words, "there is no fear in love."

Isn't that stupid? Do you ever think like this in the back of your mind, or am I alone here? I think we need to ask ourselves some questions to root out the basis of this thinking. Do I trust that God knows what He's doing in them, and my sole mission is to love them, regardless of the sins they're doing? Do we trust the Holy Spirit enough to do His job of convicting people of their sin, or do we feel like we need to do it for Him?

(I worded it like that intentionally to sound sophomoric and naive. I mean, you accept your close friends despite their own sins and struggles; chances are, their sins just look more like your own. We are more likely to sin in the direction we already lean. If you're a Democrat, you're probably not going to suddenly become a white supremacist. If you're a Republican, you're likely not going to spontaneously start celebrating abortion…Make sense?)

I think there is a balance here, of course. The Bible says Jesus is full of grace AND truth.[25] We need to strike a balance, just like in everything, but I've realized that much of my life has been lived with 90% truth and 10% grace.

I'm beginning to understand what an old school pastor meant when he preached, "If I'm going to err in one direction, I would rather err toward love and grace." I just can't read the Bible and come away with this mentality of alienation, judgment, and any sort of lifestyle that would further push people away from Christ.

So may we be people of grace AND truth. May we be people who focus on drawing people toward Jesus, rather than pushing them away (in the name of 'love'). May we look more like the repentant prostitutes than the pious Pharisees, recognizing our own sinfulness long before calling out others'.

---

[25] John 1:14

DEAR CHRISTIANS, WAKE UP

"I think a lot of Christians will wake up and say 'oh sh!t, I missed it!'"

In the words of Kendrick Lamar, I got a bone to pick…I'm mad.

I've had a rising frustration in my chest the past few months, and it can be represented by this pattern: My most popular blog post of all time is entitled "Why I'm No Longer Waiting Till Marriage," and it's about wisdom in dating and singleness, though the title implies something sexual. Almost every other popular post of mine is on dating, porn or sex. I know that if I want clicks, all I have to do is throw in a suggestive title and Christians will gobble it up.

But then I write about systemic racism, poverty, human trafficking, and a Christian response to injustice: 12 reads max.

I'm obviously not mad at people's readership of my blog. I'm mad at how it functions as a synecdoche of American Christianity overall. We are so focused on things which immediately affect us to the point that we refuse to even read about issues being faced by others in the world; in our own city even.

Of course, that was me before I got 'woke.'

I remember being in Australia and one of my teammates was researching where different chocolate companies sourced their cocoa, and I thought *Who cares? Just eat your candy!*

The more I learn however, the harder it is to turn a blind eye to the monstrous amount of injustice in the world. For instance, there are more human slaves in the world right now than at any time in history, millions of whom are sex trafficking victims who are being raped 15-20 times a day.

But this coffee shop's wifi is too slow so let's move to a different one; I'll just have to buy another latte…

First world problems are the foothills which prevent our eyes from seeing the massive mountains of injustice in other parts of the world.

Writing as a white male, I've also become increasingly aware of the level in the world's economy I was accidentally born into. Am I a 'racist' because I've benefitted from a system that favors me over other demographics, despite the fact that I've never cognitively had hatred toward others based on their skin color? I've felt pressure to feel guilty the more I learn about history and the creation of the current system in which I live, but I have found that it's better to turn that feeling into action. I can't help but wonder if 'racism' is becoming aware of these issues and then remaining complacent.

I recently came across an incredibly disturbing work of art while researching for a paper which stirred me so much I set it as my phone background for the past few months. It's an African piece of art which

slams the suffering of Christ into the experience of the black slave.[26] I can't shake it.

The thing my blog readership has reflected to me is that people are far more interested in themselves, and how their Christianity affects them, than they are in bigger-picture issues like justice and poverty. Thousands of refugees have been evacuated from their home country in the past year, but hey, at least you finally got the right angle for that Insta-selfie. Where are the kingdom-minded Christians? Where are those whose reading of Scripture prompt them to action rather than just a few colorful highlights and maybe a sophisticated Bible study discussion?

The other day I was in a coffee shop and overheard the conversation between two thirty-something married mothers. The more I listened, the more angry I got. I don't know them or their lives at all, but what I heard made me angry. They were evidently Christians, but it seemed that church was all about them, and God's grace was merely to enable them to live more comfortable lives. They talked about their families and their kids and a dash of local gossip, and anger stirred in me. I've wrestled with that anger for a while, asking myself if it's justified or not, and here is what I've come to: Paul calls us to judge those who are inside the church, not outside. So, would I berate those two women for their seemingly consumeristic Christianity? No, of course not! But, am I regularly having conversations with my own close Christian friends about how we live, how we spend our money, how we work and how we use our time? Yes.

I wish I could do more to open the eyes of fellow American Christians to the suffering of so many people in the world. It's so easy to hear a statistic like how millions of people in the world survive on a few spoonfuls of rice every day, then close the article and go on with our days.

Today I sat down with a fellow Denver Seminary student and we talked about this. "There will be so many Christians," he said, "who will wake up and say 'Oh shit! I completely missed it! I was so focused on my job, my marriage and family, and myself that I missed Christ's call to the rest of the world!'"

---

[26] When I first saw this picture I tried for an hour to find the source of it or the artist and came up with nothing. It wasn't even credited in the book.

"I hate, I despise your religious festivals;
    your assemblies are a stench to me.
Even though you bring me burnt offerings and grain offerings,
    I will not accept them.
Though you bring choice fellowship offerings,
    I will have no regard for them.
Away with the noise of your songs!
    I will not listen to the music of your harps.
But let justice roll on like a river,
    righteousness like a never-failing stream!"[27]

God, through the hard words of the prophet Amos rebukes His people for fattening themselves with the very things He blessed them with. To help translate some of what he says:

I hate the fact that you go to church and sing.
I don't care that you drop a few bucks in the offering plate,
I don't care that you have your 'quiet time' daily.
The rock concert-style songs you sing are hideous to me
because you've taken good things I've given you
and stored them up for yourself.
Why not open up your wallets,
your homes,
your time,
and let equality and justice flow?
I literally can't hear your worship songs
because I see how you live your life.

Is your faith primarily about you?

Are you intentionally keeping yourself uninformed because to become educated on certain issues would demand action? I have lived that way for years.

---

[27] Amos 5:21-24

In a recent conversation with a passionate friend of mine, she said something which lingered in my brain: If the Christian can still worship unperturbed (or un-outraged) at the site of violence and injustice, I say, "take your god back."

I believe it was Francis Chan who lamented seeing so many Christians who were fiery with zeal in their younger years, but got older, married, settled down, and the sole aim of their life shifted from 'kingdom things' to 'American Dream things' like family, mortgage, and Netflix.

What is the goal of your life? Where are your eyes set?

I know that if you've read this far, I've done a good job of beating you up, but here are two pieces of hope to balance it out:

Not all believers are called to all fields. It is literally impossible for one person to single-handedly make big differences in the arenas of race, trafficking, refugees, war, poverty, and every other issue faced by the world today. I've been meditating on this line from Merton lately:

> To allow oneself to be carried away by a multitude of conflicting concerns, to surrender to too many demands, to commit oneself to too many projects, to want to help everyone in everything, is to succumb to violence. The frenzy of our activism neutralizes our work for peace. It destroys our own inner capacity for peace. It destroys the fruitfulness of our own work, because it kills the root of inner wisdom which makes work fruitful.[28]

In other words, find your calling. Learn. Become aware. Find what makes you angry and set out to fix it.

The gospel is not about doing, but about being. We are not saved because we donate x-amount to charities each year, or pull more people out of slavery than Django Unchained. We are saved through our intimate union with Christ, and that alone. However, the question must be asked: If you have experienced this grace, is it merely enabling you to be more comfortable and eloquent in your coffee shop conversations, or is it a spark which catalyzes social action? If 'works' are the smoke which are a sign of

---

[28] Thomas Merton, *Conjectures of a Guilty Bystander*

the fire beneath, do you have the smoke? Is your faith real, or are you merely imagining a smokeless fire?

My seminary professor yesterday told us not to give up striving for a utopia here on earth. It's easy to become discouraged by a lack of progress in the world, but that doesn't mean that we give up and layaway all our hope for the eschaton.

Work to bring the kingdom to earth.

Here.
Now.

Participate in the economy of heaven in this life.

Pray, *Maranatha! Come quickly Lord Jesus and reorient our lives toward justice and mercy.*

THE LEPROSY OF LONGING
"you literally prefer to eat crap than a filling meal. your senses are fried."

Beethoven lay on the keys of his piano going deaf, shaking a fist violently toward the heavens. No longer could he hear the heavenly compositions of his youth.

There must be no god.

Grant Aschatz is less famous, but not less talented. After years as an award-winning chef in Chicago, Grant found a white lump on his tongue. It turned out to be cancer and he had to have much of his tongue and throat removed. The Michelin-starred chef couldn't taste.

There must be no god.

I've had a sinus infection for weeks now and after two rounds of antibiotics, it doesn't seem to be moving on. I can't taste. I'm in one of my favorite Guatemalan cafes sipping my mocha, but for all I know it may as well be hot water. I taste nothing either, and the anger wells up in me. I'm contemplating smashing my half-drained mug of coffee against the wall.

Is there a soothing balm for this sort of anger?

There is situational anger which you can affect, but then there is anger because you don't seem to fit right in this reality. It's something you can't escape and no matter how many holes you've punched in the walls, no matter how much money you have, you can't change your reality.

You can leave friends, jobs, houses, countries, and even spouses to change your situations, but there is still a God sitting sovereign on the edge of our experience calling the shots. As Beethoven's eardrums weakened and deflated entirely, no amount of anger or tears would have restored his lost sense.

I often feel this sort of anger. It's existential and big.

In the gospels, we often see Jesus interacting with the lepers—folks with leprosy— and I don't think it's an accident that this disease is singled out. For one, the reason they live in colonies is because the ailment is highly contagious. In 2010, I went to a leper colony in India and saw firsthand the effects of the condition.

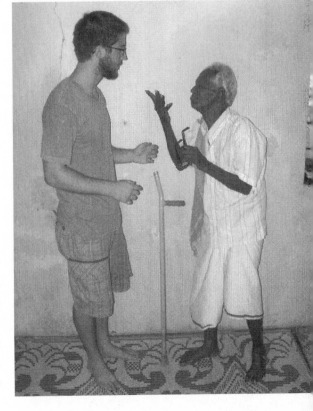

The thing about leprosy is, it doesn't necessarily destroy your body. What it does is ruin your nerves so you could be leaning on a hot surface or a sharp edge and not even know it until you've already burnt a finger off. The people in this

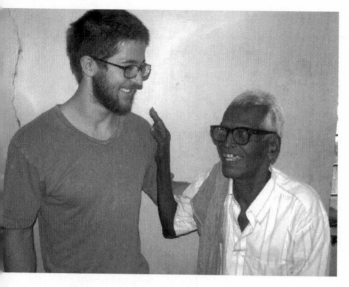

colony had nubs for digits, missing eyes and noses, and a myriad of other physical defects. Leprosy had damaged their bodies by decimating their sense of touch, leading them into a world of odd physical confusion and ultimately destroying their own bodies without them even realizing it.

And I don't think it's an accident these people are highlighted often in the story of Jesus. My present sinus infection serves as a reminder of how nice it is to have all 5 senses functioning properly and how often I take that for granted.

But I think there's another type of desensitization: That of our souls and spirits.

Years ago, I met with a pastor and the topic of my struggle with pornography came up. He raised his hand up like he was holding a glob of manure.

"The problem, Ethan, is that you've acquired a taste for crap," he explained. "You literally prefer to eat shit than a filling meal and you don't even know it. You've fried your senses."

He was totally right. When we try to numb the pain of existence; to soothe the existential ache which sleeps in our bones with artificial comforts, we shouldn't be surprised when things don't improve. I think much of the problem with our current situation is a refusal to accept reality as it is, so we escape into a digital realm of Netflix, YouTube, porn, or substance abuse.

We're lepro-fying ourselves.

We're applying the soothing balm of desensitization because it's easier than living with pain, discomfort or disappointment. Kierkegaard pointed out that just beneath the surface of each of us simmers a well of blocked and unmet desires. John Eldredge describes our angry outbursts in the line at the bank, or on the freeway not at the person before us, but at the existential anger at the fact that we continually go hungry. Our desires repeatedly go unmet.

We speak the language of desires as if they didn't directly affect every iota of our lives.

Isn't it easier to shove those desires under the carpet and settle for a temporary fix? We're fine to eat crap as long as we won't be hungry again for a few hours.

Often, that's far less painful than accepting the fact that there's a void between us and *eudaimonia*—satisfaction. I'm sitting here just wishing so badly I could taste my coffee and take pleasure in its warm froth.

I've spent most of my life wishing I could sense God in some way, big or small. I just want to hear a whisper or sense something supernatural and be reminded of the transcendent. But I haven't. I've raged on, desire unmet, senses left thirsty. When Beethoven couldn't hear, he shook his fist and spat at the sky. When Aschatz and I couldn't taste, we break our saucers against the wall and clench our palms. But this spiritual leprosy is even worse. Rather than explode in anger, we simply replace the desire.

God hasn't showed up to satiate my soul's palate, so I'll acquire a taste for casual sex or drunkenness. God doesn't exist, so I'll numb my desiring bits and fry them senseless with porn and Netflix.

It's been over-quoted a million times, but just in case you haven't read it before, here's what C.S. Lewis brilliantly wrote about our desires in *The Weight of Glory*:

> It would seem that Our Lord finds our desires not too strong, but too weak. We are half-hearted creatures, fooling about with drink and sex and ambition when infinite joy is offered us, like an ignorant child who wants to go on making mud pies in a slum

because he cannot imagine what is meant by the offer of a holiday at the sea. We are far too easily pleased.

It seems like a hopeless position, waiting indefinitely for a whispering God to show up and alleviate our suffering. It's almost as if we forget that God Himself suffered, and continues to. I mean, do you think Jesus was giggling as they tickled Him on the cross? Or was He asking His Father why He had turned His almighty back on Him and left Him to hang like pulp on a stick?

If anyone in the universe knows about suffering, it is our God.

I don't know why Jesus seemed to have a big soft spot in His heart for the lepers, but if there is one group of people I can continually identify with, it's them. They probably longed for a lifetime just to feel warmth or to know the touch of another human. I often find within myself longings which may well not be satisfied in this lifetime, and I'm left with the same option the lepers were handed: Go to Christ, or spit on Him. Shake my fist in senseless anger, or reach out just to graze the dirty edge of His skirt.

May we be healed. May we move toward Christ, even when our senses seem to differ. May we blindly grope about for Him, ultimately realizing it is He who has found us all along.

WHERE IS OUR BALM? REFLECTIONS ON ANGER

I slammed my fist on my desk, hard. then again, a few more times.

When I was in college, I founded a tradition where once a month, I'd jump in Lake Michigan. Every month. The worst one was December, 2013 because it was 27 degrees and the thin sheets of ice carved blood from our shins as we waded in. We were too cold, however, to even feel the gashes until later when we warmed up. We saw the blood pouring forth but felt nothing.

For three years, I jumped in Lake Michigan without fail. The lake didn't care.

At the time, it seemed like some massive commitment bound me to the body of water, and what did it offer me in return? Nothing.

The same was true of the summer I was a surf instructor on the East Coast: I was in the ocean every day of summer, but did the ocean care?

These are not legitimate reasons to be angry—nature's indifference is something you've probably grasped by now. But I think it symbolizes something much deeper that exists in many, if not all of us. I mean, I want the world to care that I'm here. When I depart, I want it to have mattered that I was. Truth is, I'm just the cotton candy salesman at the Catholic street parade of life, trying to make a quick buck off the glorious procession.

I think the root of much of our anger is the feeling that we won't matter. Sure, you may leave a mark on a generation or two, but what about in a thousand years? What about in a million?

I don't want to take this piece too cosmic, but I do think there is something to be said for feeling like you don't fit correctly within this reality (or is that just me?). To some degree, we all feel like aliens in a human world, or a giant trapped in a small cage. Maybe you see God as some cruel prison guard dangling the keys just inches beyond your fingertips, and if you could just reach them, you'd feel...*alright.*

Do you ever feel stuck in this reality and you can't escape? On a smaller scale, do you feel like your energy and talents would be better spent somewhere else, doing something else? I think this nearly everywhere I go, thinking that just around the corner of this next international jaunt will be the spring of eternal satisfaction.

The secular world is no stranger to the power of anger and resentment. Fictitious billionaire Bobby Axelrod summed it up, "Hate is nature's most perfect energy source; it's endlessly renewable."

Eldredge wrote that most anger comes from desires which go unmet. Whether we acknowledge them or fry them, we have deep longings which probably go hungry, if not completely unrecognized most of the time. We often fall into the trap of numbing our desires with porn, Netflix, alcohol or a myriad other distractions which don't satisfy our deep longings, but simply take away their intensity for a few moments. Like the December ice slicing into our shins, we don't feel the damage we're doing to ourselves. It takes different forms in each of us but it's summed up in Ecclesiastes 3:11:

"God has placed eternity on the hearts of men."

How do you feel about knowing that your desires are not only big, but infinite? It makes me itchy, like I'm wearing a shrink-wrapped wool sweater.

Last week after an especially stressful string of classes, the students had left and I slammed my fist onto my desk. Then again. And a few more times.

Why?

If you were to ask me in that moment, I may not have had an answer for you. I'd probably vent some cop-out answer, like how stressful the students were that day, but the truth is, that's just the pebble atop the thousand-ton burden; the straw through which we press the ocean.

What is this burden? What causes these angry flare-ups at times which may even mystify ourselves? If you're like me, there's often a well of lava simmering just beneath your surface, waiting to erupt.

Poe screamed alongside the prophet Jeremiah,[29] 'is there no balm in Gilead?' Why can't we be healed? Gilead was a place in Biblical times famous for its healing spices and ointments. The prophet asks God why even there, even at the Mayo Clinic of the Ancient Near East, no healing could be found to nourish the hearts of his people. Is there no way to soothe this burning anger which flares out of control on a moment's notice?

Last month I asked God where He was and I have yet to hear back.

Recently, a friend showed me this 18-minute documentary about a 97-year-old philosopher contemplating his imminent death. He's not a Christian, so for all of his poking and reasoning about the amorphous substance, or event, to which he drew near, he ended up nowhere. He was like a blindfolded child taking swings at a distant piñata which the gods kept cruelly yanking above his reach.

"So I just go on existing and waiting," he laments toward the end. "Waiting until I have to say goodbye."

---

[29] Edgar Allan Poe's poem *The Raven* cites Jeremiah 8:22

In his gutwrenching and hopeless pontification, he had decided that 'the best' was indeed behind him. With his wife died much of the joy of his life, and all he had left was to die. So he spent his final years wobbling around his empty house, reading with a magnifying glass, and painting.

Too often, Christians adopt this mindset and assume *this life* is all there is. When this life does not align with our ideas of our dream life, disappointment sets in. Depression and anger creep in.

Perhaps worst of all, hopelessness creeps in.

Have you ever wondered why the idea of hope seems to be so emphasized in the Bible? Hope affects everything. Hope affects how we live now, and the more we realize this—the more we can live into the reality of hope—the easier this life becomes to digest. How?

Tim Keller explained it this way: Imagine you take two men and give them identical jobs. It is toilsome, drudging work, not the ideal choice for anyone. You tell one man that when the year ends, he will receive $25,000, barely above the poverty line. You tell the other man that after his year of labor, he will be given $25 million.

Do you think that *during* their year of work, they will have different mentalities and mindsets? Of course they will! One will be complaining constantly about his work and how hard and ridiculous it is. The other will be doing the same work, but rejoicing: "Is this *all* I have to do?? This is nothing!"

During the year, they are in identical situations. The difference between them is hope.

The heart of Christian belief is that we are the latter man, eagerly anticipating the coming glory when our years of toil are over. This means we do the same work as the rest of the world, but we do it with joy. We suffer along with the rest of the world, but we suffer with joy.

Do you have hope?

Or are your (my) angry outbursts reflections of a hopeless heart? I catch myself constantly wondering why my life isn't *better*. Why the world never seems to align with my vision of how it should be. Unlike the 97-year-old philosopher, we do not merely exist, awaiting our nearing oblivion. We work hard and we hope hard.

We take our cues from a Man who *has* tasted death and lived to tell about it. We trust in the One who killed death. Because of Him, we are *not* trapped in our situation. We are not limited to the offerings of this dying world.

Jesus heals reality.
Jesus heals reality *now.*

As Plato would say, we exist in the realm of the *becoming,* while Christ calls to us from the plane of *being.*[30] Much of my anger comes from expecting perfection from a land of brokenness. Our universe is in flux, but I find myself striving for that one *moment* and *place* and *community* where things will be *good.* I think there is much more joy to be found in accepting that I won't obtain them until the eschaton. If the Apostle Paul could rejoice while being tortured in prison, surely we can rejoice in our cubicles.

May we be people who look forward to the future, knowing our best is yet to come. May we be people who gladly accept our present situation, whatever it is. And may we take the difficult swings to clear away the anger in our souls, digging to the root that we may be healed.

May we rediscover hope.

---

[30] In Plato's *Timaeus,* he outlines the comparison between the world of forms and the tangible, physical universe. The forms are the things that *are.* Unchanging, they dictate a solid aspect of the universe. Beauty, for instance, may be a form which is unchanging yet we can only catch glimpses of it through this world which is *becoming.* A rose may reflect a portion of the form of beauty, though the rose itself is not the entirety of beauty. The rose is becoming, while the form of beauty *is.* Plato lived roughly 300 years before Jesus, though, and his brilliant analysis of the universe has led some to call him a 'pre-Christ Christian.' In Jesus, Plato would see the marriage of the *becoming* and the *being.*

WE MUST CELEBRATE!
God is serious about parties.

I exited the season of Lent somewhat downtrodden and guilt-ridden. I had tried to give up sugar and failed miserably. Not only was I beating myself up and feeling bad every time I slipped a few spoonfuls of ice cream into my mouth, but I had a friend who would (half-seriously) remind me of how much I was failing (She was right, of course, but I still felt bad).

I told my dad halfway through Lent, "I can't wait for Lent to end so I can stop feeling guilty every time I eat something sweet."

He said, "You sound like a good Catholic."

The reality, is, the more I think about it, Christianity often comes off more like *that*. Like an institution made of restrictive rules and seasons in which we strip away the enjoyable bits of life and favor minimalism and solemnity. And for the past couple centuries, I think the Church has tended to lean that way, in favor of 'steering clear' of indulgence and licentiousness.

However, when we look back to the Israelites and even crack open some of the (gasp) Books of Law in the Old Testament, we see numerous laws about celebrations, feasts, and years of Jubilee which the people were commanded to observe. They weren't optional. That's why God dedicated significant portions of His Word to detailing just how massive and grand these parties needed to be.

God is serious about parties.

He is serious about His times of Lent and solitude as well, but I think that many of us see Him as a more repressive God, bent on eliminating fun and delight from our lives at all costs.

Turns out, He's not.

I mean, look at how Jesus lived His life! He even attacked the Pharisees for seeing Him as no more than a Greek party boy! (get it?) He said, "The Son of Man came eating and drinking, and you say, 'Look at this glutton and drunkard, a friend of tax collectors and sinners!'"[31]

In other words, we would probably be more likely to mistake Jesus for a frat boy than a serious and mopey ascetic.

So with a little bit of establishment that Jesus loves fun, feasting, and festivities, the next question is *Why?* Why is it so important for Christians to celebrate? What are we celebrating?

The Israelites believed that when they had their monstrous feasts which would last for days on end, they were foreshadowing the feast which is to come—the eternal party; the heavenly celebration. God knows that human beings are very tangible and tactile, needing physical images and symbols to help us understand and remember things. This is why we get married—in part to understand the commitment of Christ to us. This is why we *physically* eat the bread and wine, to remind us that the Spirit of God is also now inside of us, nurturing and sustaining us.

The feasts and celebrations are the same way: We must celebrate to remind us to look forward. We must celebrate as a reminder of the good things God has already given us, and of the good things which are coming our way. I love how Matt Chandler once described worship being everywhere. He said that sometimes he has better worship times eating a hearty burrito than he does singing songs in church.

I wonder if part of the problem is that we put strict limitations on what worship can be, and have often relegated things that are enjoyable as 'outside the bounds of worship.' In other words, if it is enjoyable, it can't be honoring to God.

While there certainly are indulgent extremes, I think that this impression of God is incredibly toxic. To think that He is *against* human pleasure and enjoyment is simply ludicrous. He did not create this beautiful world with all of its delicious food only to have us suffer through life by abstaining from it all.

---

[31] Matthew 11; Luke 7

Intentional celebration is a necessary part of the ebb and flow of life. Our liturgy subsists of seasons of fasting and seasons of abundance. To neglect either one is to miss some element of what God has mandated as part of human flourishing.

My roommate and I are throwing a behemoth of a party this Friday (And no, I didn't write this post just to plug my party...mostly) and we are beyond excited. Christians and Non-Christians alike will be in our backyard enjoying a bonfire, hot dogs, s'mores, and a myriad of other party essentials. It's going to be awesome and exhausting.

It's going to be both a foreshadowing of the coming feast, and a conscious celebration of everything good God has given us in the present.

We must celebrate!

We must celebrate as a means of worshiping a God who made marmots, beef jerky, and Niagara Falls. We must enjoy these things, not out of drudgery or obligation, but because, as John Piper points out, the natural overflow of enjoyment is praise.[32] When we enjoy something greatly, we naturally sing its praises and tell others about it. By celebrating a 'God from Whom all blessings flow,'[33] and enjoying His gifts, we honor and praise Him.

We must celebrate!

Because Christianity is not only about suffering and pain, but about a coming party which will never get shut down or grow stale.

We must celebrate as a means of looking backward, forward, and at what we have now.

As a people filled with hope, partying is mandatory.
We must celebrate!
"Rejoice always."[34]

---

[32] John Piper, *Desiring God*

[33] *Doxology*

[34] 1 Thessalonians 5:16

F%#&!

the last time I did it was in 5th grade...

The other night when I was wrapping up a workout, I started talking to the girl at the front desk. At some point, she said something like, "...what the hell—I mean heck..."

I laughed and asked her if she was trying to stop swearing.

She said yes, so I pried a little further.

"*Why* are you trying to stop cussing?"

She said something about it being wrong, about certain words being unprofessional, but ultimately realized she didn't really know why certain words were so *wrong*.

Unless you're a student at a Christian college or an English major, you probably have not given much thought to the language you use beyond *These words are good and these are bad*. Chances are, you fall into one of three categories. There are those of us who are strict with the words that fall from our mouths; those who know there are words they shouldn't use but let slip on occasion; and those who don't give a second thought to releasing a string of expletives.

But perhaps there is a fourth category, which hopefully more of us (Christians especially) begin to wander into: That of the thoughtful language user. Someone who gives thought to the words they use, and why they choose to use them in the way they do. This is not a comprehensive post, but just a few thoughts I have to offer for now.

The Heart of the Issue

I have not sworn/cussed/used an expletive since 5th grade. (And it was kind of a funny story when I did.)

However, I have come to realize that this feat is incredibly meaningless. I've subtly dropped this fact to others before and they are always amazed at my restraint. But there are more insidious elements of this subject below the surface.

The most evident is that it is a sort of shortcut to pseudo-righteousness. I look way better than you, because *I* haven't sworn. There are few ways to look more like a Pharisee than to keep track of your swear count.

The next is also somewhat obvious: You can go your whole life without cussing and still find a myriad ways to hurt others, cut them down, and dehumanize them. This has been me countless times in my life. Sure, I won't say the f-word, but I'll still ruin someone's week with a degrading comment or a sarcastic insult.

Alternately, you could spill expletives like a tipped-over thermos and be one of the kindest, most gracious people on earth.

So who is right?

I think some better questions to ask are, what is language, how should it best be used, and what does God think about the words we select?

(Spoiler alert: I'm not going to give you a black or white answer. I'm going to give a few differing arguments and end with my own philosophy of swearing.)

Of course, God cares much more about the heart behind our words than the actual sounds coming from our lips. Any sort of language that does violence to another person is wrong from the start. So then why does it matter if we use expletives as a means to loving other people?

Abuse of Language

A commonly cited argument *for* swearing comes from Tony Campolo, who once said in a sermon:

> I have three things I'd like to say today. First, while you were sleeping last night, 30,000 kids died of starvation or diseases related to malnutrition. Second, most of you don't give a shit. What's worse is that you're more upset with the fact that I said 'shit' than the fact that 30,000 kids died last night.

Initially, you feel convicted. As you are meant to. The point he is making is valid, but when deconstructed, the means by which he got there is by shock value more than by a well-constructed argument. The reason this paragraph works so well is because he introduced language to a context in which it is foreign and expects people to overreact.

Philosophers would call this an 'abuse of language.' He took a word which is commonly used outside the context of a church sermon and inserted it in such a way that people's mental environment would be jarred so that he could make his point. Because if people heard that language used *anywhere* else outside a church building, they wouldn't have flinched. In fact, there is a good chance that most of them use that same word any given day of the week.

So when people point to examples similar to this in order to defend the use of expletives, they are not realizing that they are being manipulated into reacting exactly how the speaker wants. Which begs the question, is cussing still justifiable?

Revealing Inauthenticity

As a youth pastor, I get to hang out with high schoolers several days a week, and I love it. It's a complex position to hold, as people tend to think pastors are some sort of holy men, with whom they must act more righteous than they really are. In other words, when a student lets an expletive slip during youth group, they immediately look at me with this nervous, sheepish look, expecting a disapproving look from me.

But it never comes.

Some of the other leaders will reprimand them for the language they use, but I never do, and there are several reasons for this.

The first is, I am more saddened that they try to transform themselves into *better* kids when they're at church than the fact that they swear. I would rather they bring their whole, authentic self to church than some phony, calculated version of themselves that only uses 'clean' language. The fact that there is still a dichotomy in their minds between 'holy' and 'unholy' places shows that the church has not served to teach them well about the nature of our God.

I always think of Jacob in the Bible, who encountered God in a random place in the wilderness. Prior to this time, people only interacted with the gods in temples, or 'holy places.' But at the end of his encounter, Jacob mutters "Surely God was in this place all along and I had no idea."[35]

Many of us still live in the mindset of only meeting God in churches. And this is tragic, because it likely means that we are cleaning ourselves up before going before God. We have trained our minds to think, *God is over there in the church building, but not here in my public high school.* The subject of sanctioning out swearing is simply indicative of a larger issue: People don't see God in every aspect of their lives.

I would rather have my students bring their whole, uncensored selves to youth group and not have to fear judgment from their leaders. From there, I can only trust that God will begin to work in them from the inside out, rather than in a way where they try to transform their external behavior even if they aren't really sure why.

Swearing is the least of my concerns for these students. If it helps them communicate in a more authentic way with me, I'm never going to reprimand them for it.

The English Vulgate

In 382 AD, the Latin Vulgate Bible was published by Jerome. Prior to this time, there was only the Latin Bible, which was written in language which could only be accessed by the highly educated. The Vulgate was written for the common people; the masses.

When most people think of the term 'vulgar,' they think the definition has something to do with being dirty, crude, or offensive. But originally, the word simply meant 'for the common (read: uneducated) people.'

In other words, using *vulgar* language simply makes you seem uneducated or ignorant. And for this reason, I try to employ a richer vocabulary. I think God has given us language as a gift, and we can choose to either refine it and use it well, for the edification of others, or we can squander it and continue to speak foolishly and uncreatively.

Conclusion

As I wrote above, the goal is not to earn *Heaven Points* by simply not cussing.

---

[35] Genesis 28:16

And we all could find plenty of ways to verbally destroy one another without dropping a single expletive. The goal, above all, is to use our words to encourage and love one another, and to worship and glorify God. For some of us, this will require the occasional strong language, while others of us have weaker consciences.

Wherever we land on the spectrum, may we be people who use all of our words to love one another and to love God. May we be creative in our exploration of language and our construction of thought.

ADULTING IS (NOT) HARD.
growing up has its difficulties, but more than that, it has its promises...

It's New Year's Eve today.

Today we sit on the edge of another 12 months of possibilities, disappointments, and discoveries. In essence, it's the same as any other day but we tend to assign more weight to it than it's due, and this is why gyms will fill up the first two weeks of January, then return to the normal hum of fitness regulars. We expect tomorrow to be greater than it is.

Which is (kind of) why I wanted to write about a trend, or phrase, I've been seeing lately. All across the worldwide web, I see people regularly complaining.

"Adulting is hard," they say.

We—upper to middle class Americans—have every opportunity known to man. And those of us who have passed from high school to college and have now graduated have literally all the freedom in the world to go wherever we want, make investments, start organizations, start families, work hard, save money, move, read for fun, and *literally* anything else we could imagine.

And what do we do with this freedom?

Complain.

We invented the word "adulting" just so we could complain about how difficult it is. And don't get me wrong: With this new form of freedom and responsibility, there are new problems and difficulties which arise. We are suddenly thrust out of the comfort of a structured life and into a totally foreign realm of malleable time, resources and opportunity. But I find it odd that people prior to our generation never complained about this as much as they simply rolled up their sleeves and got to work.

I mean, in certain African tribes, boys go out into the wilderness and kill lions in their mid-teens as their rite of passage into manhood. Then they begin their grown-up life. And here I am, ten years older, tempted to complain about how difficult my life is.

The fact is, as a middle-class American, I will not go hungry. I have tried dozens of things since graduating high school, and many of them failed. And I have certainly been a whiner at numerous points. Yet there was not one day I worried about going hungry or not having clean water to drink.

Rather than embrace our opportunities, make daring attempts, or even just work hard, we stress, flip our phones on, and whine about how hard it is to 'adult.'

The irony here is that those who are truly in need and who are really struggling with life are those who are not complaining about 'adulting.' The single mom working three jobs to provide for her kids, or the family in India who splits one sack of rice for their weekly meals are the ones who deserve our sympathy and help more than the recent college grad who can't decide what color Jetta to buy, or which plumber to call.

I don't mean to build arguments on hypothetical situations, or guilt you into sympathy. But I do want to call something out in today's American Christianity.

When it comes to ranking our sins, we are good at averting our eyes from certain categories and focusing on others. One of the more overlooked areas of sin is complaint. Let us not forget that in Numbers 21, God allowed snakes to kill several *thousand* Israelites simply because they were complaining.

They weren't worshiping other gods or sleeping around; they were complaining.

Yet today, we feel a liberty to complain without consequence. I think this comes from a notion of entitlement Americans are raised with, and when things don't go our way, or we feel a bit of discomfort and stress, we have a *right* to complain about it.

Why is complaining such a big deal? Why would God let thousands of His people die simply for complaining? I think the short answer is because complaint is the opposite of gratitude. The height of anything a human can ever give to God is gratitude. We literally have nothing else to offer Him. Gratitude is the root of worship. It all begins with giving thanks for what God has given to us, from the big things to the small.

When we complain, we are giving God the middle finger. We are telling Him that what He has given us is *not* good enough for us; that He is not good enough for us.

So it seems odd that people my age would complain about becoming adults. We now have the opportunity to build something with our own hands. We have the materials and the resources to really make differences in our communities, but rather than embrace this new season, many of us simply complain about its difficulties.

'Adulting' has its difficulties, but I think more than that, it has its promises. It is pregnant with opportunity and excitement. Don't let the hardships of this new season lead you to depression and complaint. Instead, embrace it. Help the needy. Try something new and fail at it. Then fail a few more times. 99% of you won't go hungry so stop worrying about it. Create new things and start something that matters.

This year, I intend to work more than I complain, to create more than I stress. I hope you'll join me. We don't need to dispose of the word 'adulting;' we need to see it as a positive thing rather than a negative. We need to embrace this new season we are entering.

Sincerely,

Someone who is kind of tired of complaining

GETTING A FULL-TIME JOB WAS THE BEST THING TO HAPPEN TO MY CREATIVITY

I thought it would grind against my 'artistic, creative gears.'

I'm about to say something I never thought I'd say. It's something which ground against what I thought were my 'artistic, creative gears.'

For years my dad would tell me that "if you want something done, ask someone who is busy." The implication being, if you ask someone with a lot of free time to do something, it most likely won't end up getting done.

Irrational, right?

I never believed him until moving to Guatemala and starting a full-time job.

I wake up at 6:15, eat breakfast and leave by 6:40 to catch the bus. As soon as I get to school, it's lesson prep until classes begin a half hour later, at which point the day whizzes by faster than Jim Carrey pumping his arms in *Dumb and Dumber*.

By the time classes end at 2:30, I have a pile of grading to tackle for an hour, mixed with some prep for classes the following day. My goal, which I am still working on accomplishing, is to do no school work outside of school hours. 1.5 weeks in, I have yet to master the fine art of speed-lesson-prepping, but I feel like I'm getting there.

The bus drops us off around 4:30pm, meaning I have three and a half hours before my host family has dinner. One and a half are spent walking to the gym, working out, coming home and showering. I try to hit the hay around 10, so the time after dinner is spent winding down and getting ready for bed, or writing as I am now. And this doesn't consider any sort of social activities I have throughout the day

The point is, now that I have a full-time job, every free hour (or minute) counts.

For the past handful of years, I consistently thought that if I only had a bit more free time, I could really get creative and be like those other guys: The Casey Neistats, Gary Vees, and Austin Kleons.[36] The thing those guys are constantly telling their followers, though, is that if you want to do something, you just

make

it

happen.

For me in this season, that means wrapping my creative outlets around the skeleton of my teaching routine.

Many of you creative types reading this may think that the term 'routine' means someone is sharpening an axe against the stone of your soul. What I have found (and what countless others have affirmed) is that the opposite is true. Being forced to cram my creativity into an hour or two in the afternoon or evening has actually made me *more* motivated to get on top of it. I can't explain the exact psychological rationale behind it yet, but staying busy—in a healthy way—has made me more excited to do everything better.

Life has somehow transformed from an amorphous mush which was unable to sustain any sort of foundation to an exciting puzzle, where I find places I can fit everything and still make it work. I don't know how I never realized it before, but when I was working a handful of part-time jobs, most of which were rather flexible with the hours, I always expected to accomplish more than I actually ever did.

When I had all the time in the world, I could take an hour to cut my own hair and shave and shower. Now, once a week, those things are forced into the 20 minutes between gym and dinner. With all the time in the world, I

---

[36] 2019 update: Some of their advice is to work so hard you are burnt out and have no joy in life—and then keep working. They may be motivating, but this must be taken with a grain of salt, especially for Christians who believe rest is an essential part of work. See Mark 2:27.

didn't have to get my sermons planned ahead of time, because there was always tomorrow to get it done as well.

With a full day of freedom, I would anticipate being productive for most of it and checking errands off my list. Instead, I'd sleep in, leisurely eat breakfast while soaking in some Netflix, and take forever just to get around to doing anything. In fact, this typically meant that an entire free day was spent with maybe an hour of productivity. Which is *less* than I output now while working a full-time job!

Again, I'm still working on the mechanics, or psychology running beneath it all, but I have never felt so accomplished in my life. I go to bed having worked out; written, photographed, or shot video; and taught a full day of classes, influencing young minds toward the Kingdom. Every day.

Ideas may burst into my head in the morning or afternoon, but the best I can do is jot them down and stew on them for a few hours. Historically, when I got inspired I whipped out my laptop and wrote up the post. I have learned that patience may also be a key to the creative process: Rather than shuffling a piece right out to the public, I've begun starting something and letting it simmer overnight, or over the course of the day.

And none of this is to brag. Rather, I feel like I'm a bit disappointed in the Ethan of the past for having so much time on his hands and filling so little of it!

And maybe you can glean something from this as well: Fill up your time.

I'm learning that there is actually a wide chasm between having a full schedule and being an unhealthy workaholic. God doesn't want us to solely define our lives by our vocational output, but He doesn't want us to be slobs either. Remember that work existed in the world before sin did.[37] There are plenty of Christian books on rest and Sabbath, but you can just

---

[37] It's true! Work was not a result of Adam and Eve's sin, but their labor became *painful* as a result. See Genesis 2:15, and then look at what God says in the next chapter when He is rolling out their curses. Work was never supposed to be a bad, painful thing, and we have hope that in heaven it will return to being enjoyable.

as easily err in the opposite direction. Don't let your theology of rest become a ticket to Lazyville.

So, may we be people with high output and full days. May we remember that our days are numbered, and we are only given so many from which to wring the sweet nectar of productivity. May we labor for the glory of God and expend out effort to make earth look more like the kingdom.

May we be people who do work.

SAY THE SAME THING 100 TIMES
another breakthrough in how to think about creativity and productivity.

A friend recently introduced me to a guy named Gary Vaynerchuk, or GaryVee as he's better known. He is constantly filming or recording himself, or outputting SOME sort of thought online. Every day. Multiple times a day even. To me, that sounds exhausting. And it's not the act of filming and speaking which is necessarily tiring for me, but the thought of having to have fresh and original ideas to produce every single day.

However, the more I listen to what Gary is saying day-to-day, I noticed something. He is not necessarily coming up with a new idea every time he flips on the camera, but he is often reiterating the same thing over and over. The thought of GaryVee can be summed up in two words:

"WORK HARD."

I noticed that he doesn't really stray very far from this simple idea. He pushes people to work hard. Gary himself is the child of immigrants who built himself from nearly nothing to a thriving entrepreneur who shares stages with the likes of Tony Robbins and Dwayne "The Rock" Johnson. He relentlessly spouts pithy lines such as, "If you have ever spent five dollars on a Starbucks cup of coffee, you cannot complain about your life situation."

His main idea is simple, but he somehow always comes up with new ways to communicate it. And I (and evidently millions of others) continually tune back into his videos because he is inspiring. His redundancy reveals the passion he has for hard work and pushing people to be their absolute best (fair warning: he cusses excessively).

I realized that I often create in an opposite manner. I write a single blog post on, say, God's interaction with our emotions, and think to myself, Welp. I've covered that. What else can I come up with?

The ironic part is, I often get messages from readers saying how grateful they are for a certain post or video because it helped them see x, y, and z in a new way. The only problem is, the things they picked up were not exactly what I was trying to say (and sometimes, they're way off).

All this means is that it's time to take a chapter out of Gary's book: Talking about the same things repeatedly, but communicating them differently. Maybe with only slight differences. The reason being, some things may click a certain way with some people, while other ways of saying the same thing click with others.

For instance, I am passionate about speaking against pornography, and I often feel like I'm beating a tired rhythm on the same old drum, but others don't seem to think so. In fact, an influential person in LA once told me so. He said that you actually need to narrow your scope of things to talk about. Become 'the Christian porn guy,' or the 'motorcycling yoga girl.'

There's already a GaryVee online telling people to work hard. And there's a Matt Komo teaching people how to shoot beautiful film. And there's a FunForLouis hippie galavanting around the world with dreadlocks. But what exactly is your passion? What is the one thing you feel like you could talk about 100 different ways without running out of things to say?

I'm asking myself this. The problem with being an extrovert is we have a tendency to be a mile wide and three inches deep with our interests. Someone may dedicate their life to playing guitar, while I prefer to reach a certain level of competency before moving on to my next big interest.

But really, all of this is to say that I'll be continuing to write and shoot videos and podcasts, and if you hear a topic which sounds familiar, this is why. As a creator, I think the most important thing is to keep creating, even if it's reformatting an old idea.

What do you think though?

What's your big idea?

HOW TO RELATE

connecting with God, others, and yourself

HOW TO BE ATTRACTED TO SOMEONE
it's just confusing and perhaps a little awkward.

There's something I think a lot of Christians struggle with talking about. And it's not because it's necessarily shameful like pornography or revolting like racism. It's just confusing and perhaps a little awkward.

And that is, attraction.

In my quest to find that one person that will satiate my endless romantic antics and abate my lonely groanings, I hear a lot of advice. I've been single far more than I've been in any relationship, so the maxims and pop-dictums on how to find "the one" have flooded my ears for years.

The most common topic deals with a certain dichotomy that supposedly exists in all of us, especially Christians.

Look at her soul, not her body....

Ethan, How can you be so shallow as to like her personality and not be attracted to her INSIDES??

Her character is what REALLY matters.

Essentially, many Americans are functioning Gnostics.

The Gnostics were an ancient group of heretics that believed in a firm division between the physical body and the immaterial soul. Their theology allowed them to believe that God only cares about the soul, therefore, you can do whatever you want with your body. This thinking had taken hold of the Corinthians, and Paul addresses this issue in 1 Corinthians 6:

Food for the stomach and the stomach for food, and God will destroy them both." The body, however, is not meant for sexual immorality but for the Lord, and the Lord for the body. By his power God raised the Lord from the dead, and he will raise us also. Do you not know that your bodies are members of Christ himself?

The Corinthians had this saying about the stomach and food, which implied the same was true of sexual arousal. *When you're hungry you eat; when you're turned on, you hook up...*

Paul points out that no, the body is *NOT* meant for pure pleasure and disposal, but it is meant to honor God. Human bodies *ARE* in fact important, because Jesus Himself, the very Son of God, entered into one. Therefore, what we do with our bodies matters.

As a single Christian man, I have been critiqued by many of my friends for often just looking at 'a girl's outside,' rather than some unseen quality that we often refer to as one's heart, soul, personality, etc.

And yes, if you were to marry someone simply because they're a fox, you would be a fool. There is definitely the trap of putting *too much* emphasis on the physical body, but that's for a different time.

But it's equally foolish to only look at someone's invisible qualities as if their body did not exist!

Our bodies are our God-given vessels through which we experience, act, and take part in our life. They are meant to be healthy, serve others and honor God. And they reveal a lot about our internal lives as well.

For instance, who wants to eat food from a skinny chef? Would you get a tattoo from someone with bare skin or be trained in a gym by someone whose shirt cannot contain their belly? Sometimes you'll see a man who is *too* fit, which often speaks to some kind of masked insecurity. Our bodies matter and they say things about us.

I think that to divide an individual up into little parts is, in essence, to do violence to them as a whole human being. We are not effervescent spirits floating in some abstract realm, having conversations and thinking together. We have tangible bodies that can hug, spit, slap, poop, pinch and break. We feel pain when our skin is sliced, and we indulge in the tenderness of a lover's kiss.

Yes, we humans have bodies, souls, and spirits; we are multiple but we are also one. We are not divided entities, but are united into a single person. I believe the membrane that divides the three is far thinner than some of us have been supposing, and from this has come some breezes of Gnostic theology. We are scared to embrace our physical bodies. We are scared to be attracted to another human.

If and when I ever end up falling in love with a woman, it will be because she has a splendid heart and a love for other people.

BUT,

it will also be because my eyes and my hands find her attractive and are drawn to her. Her body will draw my own to it, and hopefully she will feel the same. We will not be divided persons, but will be holistic humans, loving each other emotionally *and* physically. No one loves another person solely using their unseen attributes.

That's just ridiculous.

I want to be attracted to an entire person. Organs and all.

I do not think good looks are just 'the cherry on top.' They're certainly not everything, but I think as Christians, we have undervalued physical attraction.

You have permission to be physically attracted to someone.

DEEP ROMANCE
when #RelationshipGoals don't cut it anymore

In writing this post, I admit up front that I am a contributing culprit in this endeavor. As a wedding photographer, I have shot the perfect picture countless times from *just* the right angle so as to make the bride and grooms' nuptials look flawless. I can take *those* pictures they will share on social media in order to evoke emotion (or envy?) in their friends and followers.

There is so much that goes into the *aesthetics* of a wedding that sometimes the actual purpose of the day can get overlooked. I've seen it happen and can tell a difference between the fiancées who just want the wedding to look good, and those who could care less about the aesthetics as long as they get to unite themselves to their best friend.

There is a difference between something appearing to be romantic versus what I'm calling *Deep Romance.*

As an example, let's look to theology in relation to the sacraments. Depending on your denominational background, there are a million ways to view them, but I like the illustration of a road sign. Imagine a yellow sign with black squiggly bacon on it, indicating a curvy road ahead. The sign points to the *reality* of the curvy road without actually *participating* in the curviness of the road. The sign is neither wavy nor a road.

The sign represents a physical reality.

In the same way, the communion cup and bread point to the very real body and blood of Christ to which we have united ourselves. They themselves are not what saves us and unites us to Him, though they do play an important role.

They are elements of the relationship, not the relationship itself.

I once dated a girl in New York who, soon after our first date, told me that she *absolutely* needed a diamond ring before she got married.

"Not a little dinky one either…It needs to have some *real* diamonds in it!" she would say.

I had never planned on purchasing a real diamond in my lifetime because of the ethical questions behind their origins. Not only that, but the entire concept of gifting a diamond ring to your beloved emerged in the early 1900's as an advertising campaign from De Beers, spiking sales of diamond engagement rings.[1] In other words, the entire notion behind them has nothing to do with real love, romance or affection in a marriage, but a massive advertising push not even a century ago.

---

[1] Analytics. *Great Depression and Drivers of Diamond Market.* 2009, www.rough-polished.com/en/analytics/30783.html.

Yet in our Western culture, it is nearly unheard of—though it is slowly becoming more common—to have an engagement without a diamond ring. As if the covenant could not *possibly* be complete without the carbon allotrope atop her knuckle.

Though I've never planned on purchasing a diamond for my beloved, I do plan on finding something deeply personal and symbolic to represent our love. My cousin's husband proposed to her with a ring bearing her birthstone which happened to also be her favorite color. I know another couple whose husband crafted the ring himself from materials he sourced all on his own. Aren't those so much better??

Yet this girl in NYC was unrelenting in her persistence for a costly diamond ring. She had conflated the artifact with what it represented—true love, deep romance.

To her, the symbol of the love was more important than the love itself.

And that's exactly what this post is: An encouragement to sort through and prioritize what is *real* in a relationship (things like commitment, trust, honesty, and intimacy), versus what is just extracurricular (Mushy Insta-selfies, diamond rings, wedding hashtags and monstrous cakes) because we often conflate the two.

Now, none of this is meant to suggest that those bonus things are bad. They are important and valuable, just like road signs are necessary to alert us to the reality of the road conditions. They are ways of communicating love to one another, and creating mementos or symbols to remind our family of the love we have for them. And they're so much fun! But often we lose sight of the line dividing what is sustaining versus what is just pleasant, but ultimately hollow if there is no substance beneath it.

Deep down, we all know that what our souls crave are honest intimacy, deep affection and nurture, and loyal commitment. But so often we settle for hoping for a diamond ring or a flashy wedding because frankly, those things are easier to attain. They are easier to point to and identify in concrete terms.

I have no facts to back this up, but I wonder if part of the reason for a continued rise in divorce in my generation is because we long so desperately for *Superficial Romance* that when someone comes along who seems adequate enough to supply us with fluffy feelings and expensive gifts, we leap for them. How many women have been wooed by a giant diamond ring without fully knowing the integrity of her suitor? Or maybe he was just 'nice' to her for a few months. How many men have been so eager to place a beautiful woman by their side that they wed the first one who said yes?

There is a lot of deceptive fluff in the world.

Yet when I look at people like my grandparents who are approaching 80 (they met when they were 14), it's not the diamond ring, gifts, or romantic social exposure that has held them together all these years. It's something much deeper. It's combination of honesty, intimacy, hard work, longsuffering, trust, and a myriad of other factors which, frankly, are not as immediately alluring, nor are they immediately evident. Who wants anything to do with *longsuffering?* I've summed them up into the phrase:

Deep Romance.

Because that's what I want. I think that's what we all want: To be deeply known and still loved. To be embarrassingly vulnerable, yet accepted. To be committed to. And none of these are things that cameras can capture or money can buy, so for that reason, many people in our world overlook them in favor of easier, more superficial things like #relationshipgoals.

Deep Romance takes time. It takes painful honesty and a lot of trial and error. It takes patience.

And then it takes more patience.

Growing in this is difficult and takes a lot of experimenting and wisdom. Hang out with older couples who can help reorient your #goals toward things that are deep and lasting rather than flashy and fleeting. Look into the Word to see what God's intent for marriage truly is: Which elements are integral and which ones are expendable or invented by modern marketing gurus?

I hope that we, especially those of us who are Christians, will continue to see romantic gestures and symbols as *good* things, which they are. There is nothing that makes you feel alive like a first kiss or a letter in the mail.

But I hope that we keep them in their proper places: As symbols pointing to a romance much deeper than what others can see. I hope we remember it's not the ring holding a husband and wife together, but the love, trust, and intimacy they share.

It's the Deep Romance.

A WORD ON TATTOOS & INTIMACY
let's all get tattoos...

So a few days ago my family and I got new tattoos.

I essentially got a backward "D" which mirrors the opposite shoulder and is symbolic of Christ making all things new.

Tonight I was in the gym and caught myself looking in the mirror and, for lack of a better phrase, *checking out* my new tattoos and how they looked on my skin: Fresh, puffy, shiny and new.

Before I got my first tattoo (the word "hero" in typewriter font on the back of my right shoulder) I imagined how it would make me more intimidating. I would be on a run and people would see me and think *Wow...that guy has a tattoo!* Or maybe the women would flock to me because I looked like I was in a rock band.

Whatever the motivation, I know the desire to get a first tattoo was urgent and eager. And the first few weeks, or maybe even the first months I had it, I felt tougher. I felt like I could get into a fight and win. Or like I could dive into a mosh pit and actually belong there.

Now I look at that ancient ink sunk beneath my skin and it's not jarring or fresh. I am not surprised to see those letters resting just beneath my first layer of skin; they have become a part of me.

(I am going somewhere with this, stay with me.)

Tonight in the gym, (yes, most of my writing inspiration hits at the gym. No idea why.) I started talking to a guy who also had a brand new shoulder piece and we chatted about it. His was significantly larger than mine, and most of his arms were equally covered in rich colors. I wondered if he had a similar feeling of empowerment in the moments he caught quick glances in the mirror of his family crest newly portrayed on his arm.

Heck, if I got pumped up seeing a tiny little "D" on my shoulder, he must feel *really* good about that giant piece on his shoulder. And he should! It's a beautiful and unique art form.

But my mind continued wandering.

I wondered about someone I met recently who had a prominent tattoo on his forehead above his right eye. I wondered if he still *saw* his forehead tattoo, or if it had become a part of his flesh the same way you have a little freckle on that one spot on your forearm, the same way I don't really *see* my old tattoos anymore.

I imagine it was a big deal for him for a while, but eventually it just became a part of his body—like his elbow; I imagined his friends barely saw it anymore when they looked at him either.

I bet his friends, like any of our friends, look at his eyes when he talks instead of distractedly staring at the ink above his brow. They're used to it.

And I think that's what any of us want: Someone who can see past the ink and look at our eyes. Someone who sees through the things we employ to make ourselves more cool or intimidating and sees us as a friend. Someone who doesn't necessarily see us the way *we want* to portray ourselves, but sees us the way we *are*.

Isn't it comforting when you can let down your armor of 'hipness' or 'toughness' and just be seen authentically? Aren't those the best kinds of relationships, where you can feel like a vulnerable little kid in front of this person, yet feel completely loved as you are?

It's refreshing.

I think this is why Jesus tells us to be like the little children when we come to Him. He doesn't want us trying to impress Him with our facial tattoos, swollen biceps or bohemian clothes; he wants us to come to Him vulnerable and raw.

Because if He isn't saving *that* person—that person who is most truly you as you are—then who is He saving?

Someone cooler?

Someone tougher?

Someone stronger or prettier?

Forget that.

The antithesis to shame is vulnerability. If you want to feel *completely* loved, you must expose *every* part of you. Otherwise, how can someone love you? Kind of makes sense when you think about it.

So I'm trying not to hide.

I'm trying not to hide behind the fresh ink on my shoulders or the number of pounds on my bench press. I'm trying not to hide behind how intelligent I can appear or how hard I can make you laugh.

Because I, like all of you, am looking for someone who can see through my tattoos; someone who can look me in the eye.

Whatever your forehead-tattoo-of-choice is, I want to leave you with this charge: Put it down. It doesn't *actually* make you tougher, even if it feels empowering. It doesn't *actually* make you prettier, even if it feels exfoliating. It doesn't *actually* make you cooler, even if it feels ridiculously hip in the moment.

Fads pass, but intimacy grows. If you let it.

So let it.

May we be people who lets others see who we are beneath all the ink. May we be people who let others look us in the eye, and may we be people who can look others in theirs.

Vulnerability is hard.

Intimacy is hard.

But let's try it anyway.

THIS IS WHY YOU'RE STILL SINGLE.

make excuses or moves.

"There are just no good options in my life right now..."

"I'm just waiting for the right one to come along..."

"When God's timing is right, He will bring the right one to me..."

I begin by admitting that I've had each of these thoughts, and billions of others, at various times in my life. The past 9 years have basically been an extended experiment in singleness, though not for lack of trying. I'm a relatively bold and forward person when it comes to dating, though it hasn't always been this way, nor have I refined the 'techniques' (for lack of a better word) for finding my spouse. But I'm getting there! And simply by looking at some of the attitudes and actions of many people I know, I see patterns which reveal why many of us are still single, despite a desire to be married or in a relationship.

So, without further ado, here are a few thoughts and observations on why you (or that lonesome friend of yours) may still be single.

"There's just no good guys or girls around/They've all been taken/I don't meet anyone new!"

While this may be true for 3% of the population who live in small towns, the majority of us, if we're honest, don't have this excuse to fall on. Without realizing it, we have a pattern or routine in our lives which generally dictates exactly who we will encounter throughout our days and weeks.

You work somewhere and depending on where that is and what you do, you probably know everyone where you work. You see familiar faces at the gym and the grocery store. Your church, depending on several factors, seems to always come up dry as well.

You travel through roughly the same routine every week without changing anything...and expect something to change! For a dashing new man to walk through the door of your church, or a ravishing young woman to get hired at your job. Not that these things never happen, because of course they do, but why not take things into your own hands? Why not make small adjustments to your routine?

Go to a different coffee shop or a new grocery store. Sign up for a class where people who have the same interests as you will gather. Check out a new church (honestly...just to scope out the prospects. Been there, done that...) or go to a party you'd normally say 'no' to.

Unless you are actually in a tiny town where all the inhabitants know each other, there's a good chance there are plenty of fish in your sea, you've just missed them by falling into your routine. So mix it up! Do things you normally wouldn't. If you spend all your Friday nights playing board games at Vicky's apartment, how do you possibly expect to meet new people there?

Of course, if all these options fail, call upon technology to save you from your singleness. The stigma seems to be fading regarding dating apps and websites. Don't count them out just because of the awkwardness, or the embarrassment of having to tell people you met online.

How to meet new people

I admit that I'm a freak of nature. An 'extroverted-extrovert' who not only enjoys being around people all the time, but even meeting new people! So, this step is relatively easy for me, but I recognize that's not the case for many of you.

So, you've signed up for a class or shown up at a party where you don't really know anyone. Now what? As someone who actually walks up to people and starts a conversation, I can say that there are clear signs that someone actually wants to chat and be open to meeting new people.

Step 1? Eye contact.

Even if you're not the type to walk up and meet people, you can accidentally give off the wrong message simply by avoiding eye contact and looking away. This tells people that you don't want to talk, you're not interested in opening up to new people. Would you want to go over and chat with someone who looks away immediately, or someone who makes eye contact and *maybe* even smiles a little bit?

As a guy, I can tell you that a girl maintaining eye contact and giving a little smile sends a pretty clear invitation! You don't have to wear the pants *per se*, just show that you're open. Many people close themselves off without realizing it and then wonder why no one ever approaches them and asks for their number.

Think about some of your married friends: Even when they were single, were they closed off and awkward, or were they outgoing, friendly and open? I've realized that there are reasons certain people get married sooner than others, and almost all of them have personalities which are not only open to connecting with others, but show it really well.

And if you're the guy? I've said it before and I'll say it again: Man up. Gather your courage and think of something to say. Breaking the ice is the hardest part and it's usually downhill sledding from there. Remember, it's shame which is the root of all these insecurities and fears of rejection, which leads me to the next point,

Sometimes the factors are internal

I cannot fully state how much of an impact shame makes on our day-to-day lives, and the places our lives take us. Shame makes us run and hide and take cover behind anything but our true selves.

Perhaps the reason you're still single is that you have these voices of shame and insecurity feeding you lies about yourself. Maybe you've never pursued a woman, or seen yourself as worthy of being pursued by a good man, so you settle for either an abusive partner, a toxic partner, or simply your own vices like porn and alcohol.

Until you adjust your view of yourself, you'll always think you're only good enough for digital women on PornHub, never enough for a real human.

But when you start from the place of acknowledging that you're already accepted in the deepest place and operate from *there*, things change. The masks you once donned to hide behind in public fade away and you can be yourself before others. And *that* is an attractive quality! People can always tell when someone isn't being their most true self, and this can simultaneously repel quality guys and girls and attract the less-healthy sorts —people who are looking to satiate their own thirsts and hungers in unhealthy ways.

Often, becoming more "attractive" has less to do with losing weight or donning more makeup, and more to do with being a person whom people want to be around; the type of person who *attracts* people by being positive, encouraging, and confident.

Conclusion?

I myself am chiefly guilty of making more excuses than moves. I've called out to God about 'bringing the right one along,' all the while neglecting to put in the effort to make that happen. They aren't always big changes, but often the smallest changes of direction or habit make the biggest difference in results.

From the inconclusive list I made above, perhaps the hardest change will be the invisible ones. Shedding shame and putting on authentic confidence (not to be confused with cockiness) in order to attract the right types of people is easy to type but hard to employ. When you begin to see yourself as someone who is worthy of a relationship; someone who someone else could actually be attracted *to* and excited *about*, I'd wager you start to see things change on the outside as well.

If you were a hungry person, you could complain for years about your empty stomach, or you could take up your plow, work your field, and make food happen.

Don't blame your status on your circumstances, change them.

GUYS: HOW TO DATE A WOMAN

<u>whether you have six-pack abs or a beer gut, you can do these things...</u>

I have been on a fair amount of dates in my lifetime.

I'm not perfect, but there are a lot of things I hear from both female friends and the women I date on which we men could improve. This post is not to say 'all women are perfect and men need to step it up,' because that's certainly not the case. But this post is directed toward men in the hopes of encouraging them to become the man that their girl will want to date.

You don't need a six-figure income or bulging biceps to woo a girl and show her you mean business. So here are some simple observations that all of us can employ to become better daters. If that's a word.

Be Confident
Easier said than done, right? Easy to say for millionaires, models and ivy league grads, right?

Wrong.

I cannot tell you how many girls have lamented that the guy they like simply won't ask them out or respond to their hints. Many women don't want to don the proverbial pants and ask the guy out, but there are plenty of hints they may drop, such as texting, calling, being physically close to you, touching your arm, etc.

To this, the guy will respond, 'but how do I knowwwwwww that that's what she means?'

There is literally one way to find out. Ask her out! If you like her, take the risk! Many guys I have talked to have the same response: "But I'm not sure if she'll say yes…"

Well, that's exactly the risk you take. And in this case, you have so little to lose. Worst—and I mean *the worst*—case scenario is that she says no, she would just rather be friends. And if she is mean about it, then you probably didn't want to pursue her in the first place.

We have come to fear rejection so much it's a little absurd. Girls are definitely scary but not *that* scary.

Don't be timid.

There are times where you may not be attracted to a certain girl for one reason or another and don't want to ask her out. In this case, assuming you see each other a fair amount, communicate that to her, so she's not left wondering when you'll ask her out. Yes, it will be awkward but just do it.

CALL IT A DATE!

Recently I have been seeing a ravishing woman who has recounted her own tales of past dates (or were they dates…?), and she is not alone.

It has become common for guys to ask women to
hang out,
chill,
get some dinner,
stargaze,
go to this event or that,
do some homework at a coffee shop,
et cetera.,
and all of these leave the woman wondering: *Did I just go on a date, or does he just want to be friends?*

If you like a girl, let her know by using the simple 4-letter term when you request her company. If not, try to make that clear as well (Though whoever asked my current crush to go 'stargazing' wore a pretty thin veil).

The struggle I've had in the past, being a guy in this situation, is not yet knowing whether I actually do want to pursue this girl, so I'm colloquially dipping my toe in the waters. And that's a valid place to be. There is no easy answer, as every individual situation is unique. There is quite a bit of gray area here. Just try to be as clear as possible with what it is you two are doing.

Tips for a good date
Ok, so you've asked her on a date, she said yes, and now you have to figure out what to do. So here are a few simple do's and don'ts to keep in mind on the big night:

Do: Go into the night with an open mind. You're getting to know her, so do just that, and nothing more.
Don't: Have wild expectations that you'll get married next week, that you'll fall in love, that she'll sleep with you because you paid (That's another whole conversation), or that you'll know everything about each other by the end of the night.

Do: Have a plan. Make reservations. Call ahead. Set a time. Know where you're going.
Don't: Go in blind. It's not caring or thoughtful to just ask her where she wants to go, or what she wants to do. You're the one who asked her out, so you should be the one with the plan! Women like a man with a plan.

Do: Pick her up at her house.
Don't: Tell her where to meet you.

Do: Open the door for her (restaurant *and* car).
Don't: Be weird about it.

Do: Listen and ask questions. And listen more.
Don't: Talk about yourself the whole time or try to impress her. Just be real. Confidence comes in being who you really are and owning it, not inflating yourself to someone you think she'll like.

Do: Pay.

Do: Breathe.

Conclusion

I know this post seems very black and white. I can already hear the resounding chorus of AMENs from all the single female readers (Don't get too excited, you're next...maybe. If I find the courage). But I know that there are a million different situations and these things are constantly in flux.

But there are a lot of things I see as patterns happening in our culture, and not all of them are healthy. Centrally, I hate to see men miss out on great women because no one has ever encouraged them, taught them the right way to do things, or told them to be bold and courageous. I was fortunate enough to be raised by a father who loves my mother well, and taught me to do the same, but I realize that's not everyone's story.

I guess the overarching themes boil down to these:

Communicate your intentions well.

Be thoughtful and considerate in all of your actions. Your job is *not* to impress her, but to care for her and get to know each other authentically. Good men don't lead by overpowering or impressing, but by serving.

Plan, make decisions, and be confident. You can do it.

Let's be men who treat the women in our lives gently and courteously. May we be courageous and tender at the appropriate times. And may we give the women we date a story they can't wait to tell their friends about (or at least, may they respect us despite the outcome).

A LETTER TO AN ATHEIST I KISSED

that's what good kisses do—they put a little bit of fear inside of you.

You were, for all intents and purposes, an amorphous mist I tried to cling to as if you could resuscitate my arid heart. We kissed in your sweltering apartment in New York.

"Come over," you said, "But they don't turn on the A/C until later this month, so it's a thousand degrees in my apartment."

You came down to the lobby to let me in. I had driven over instead of biking, despite the warmth of the night, and you assured me it was okay to park there, across the street.

You were short and beautiful. Your Mediterranean features were high and olive-colored, framed by dark hair which tonight was messy. When you pulled it up into a tight ponytail, you looked like a freaking Persian princess who had become matriculated into the business world of the Eastern seaboard.

Only in hindsight do I realize that you were not very fun, but you did have a solemn strong allure. For instance, that evening we got caught in the massive downpour, I skipped down the sidewalk rejoicing while you sought shelter beneath the nearest skyscraper that would lend its ledge.

We didn't create this city, we just got caught in the rain and begged for its charity. And it was all too happy to oblige.

New York was the bustling metropolis where an atheist and a Christian could meet in a Chipotle and initiate a summer fling. You don't know this, but our story actually began with a bet. My friend and I had just crumpled our foil wrappers and put our silver trays atop the trash cans when you walked in wearing a black cut-off classic rock tank top.

"Wow," I muttered to my friend. "She's gorgeous."

He was always quick. He whipped out his wallet and pulled out a bill. "I'll give you five bucks if you get her number."

"Nahh," I said and we walked out to our bikes. But I couldn't stop looking back in the window at you. You got your taco salad and sat down in a corner booth.

"Really, five bucks?" I said to my friend.

"Yah!"

I walked back into the restaurant and approached you. You wore a confused expression as I walked over, as if I was wearing a gorilla costume and juggling and didn't belong in a Chipotle, talking to you. You weren't cold to me, just confused.

"Hi." I spat out a staccato greeting. "You're really attractive. And I just wanted to come over and talk to you before I regretted not doing it."

You smiled like it happened all the time. "In a Chipotle??"

"Well…" I mean, what do you say to that? "Would you want to get coffee some time?"

"Sure." I handed you my phone to enter your information.

You and I texted that night, and after earning one another's last names, we were able to commence the mandatory social media background checks.

"You're a Christian?" you asked me in a message.

"Yah!" I replied, hopeful.

"Well I'm an atheist. Is that a problem?"

I thought for several minutes about how to respond. I'll go on a date with any open-minded atheist, but won't marry one. But you were also hotter than a Guatemalan tamale, so I didn't want to slam the door shut. "For being friends, of course not…for marriage, probably," I ended up replying.

But we still got that coffee. We chatted for a while, then walked down the street to my favorite thrift store. You didn't smile often, but your chilly demeanor was offset by your severe eyes and toned calves which slid just above your lacy sandals as you walked.

& & &

The night I came to your apartment, you cautioned me repeatedly that you were gross and had been poolside on a rooftop all day without a chance to clean up. I assured you I preferred the natural look of your skin.

The sharp ledges of your lips drew me in, with their gentle curves and pointy corners. The way your cheeks softly folded over them into a dimple spelunkers wouldn't dare to disturb. I began to wonder, sitting in the chair adjacent to the couch where you sat, why you would allow me into your space. Into your apartment. Into your home. And why there were no better suitors found to fill your sheets this evening.

You told me you stopped believing in God because He just kind of stopped mattering. You simply realized that He didn't exist anymore, the way one realizes they only got 11 chicken nuggets in their box for 12.

For you, God was nothing more than numbers that didn't add up.

I told you about how Jesus is, like, everything, and there is nothing beyond Him.

Zoom out far enough and you always get to Him.

But I was zoomed in. I was focused on the sharp slivers of your eyelids as they rested above dark irises as you examined me back. I was talking about God but you were studying me.

"I need to go home so I can shower," I announced. "Got an early morning tomorrow."

"I have a shower," you lowered your eyes, deadly serious. "And you know what's here that your shower doesn't have?"

"You have a steam shower??"

"No...me."

My stomach twisted into a complex knot of premature guilt and intense desire. I imagined your small, tan body pressed to mine while we stood in the tub. To accept would be to break a barrier from which there is no retreat.

"What if we were just friends?" I asked. Deep inside my head I plotted out how I would befriend you, continue these lengthy talks on religion and God until you finally caved and asked Jesus to come live inside of you, and I could properly woo you, wed you, and follow you behind that shower curtain. But that was at least…seven months away.

"I could never be friends with you," you stated bluntly. "I would just want to make out with you all the time."

I thought for a moment, but I'm not sure about what.

I moved from the chair toward you, into an awkward crouch-slash-bend over the edge of the couch.

And I kissed you.

Your lips were the exact right elixir of soft and firm. They were possibly better than expected. Not only were they phenomenal to the touch, but they left the most delicious tang on my own lips. Not a manufactured fruity taste, but a very human flavor. The kind you would imagine if you were to try to conjure what an exotic woman tastes like.

I knew in the back of my mind that kissing atheists was wrong.

"Wasn't expecting that," you said, authentically surprised.

I can't remember what exactly was said in the following minutes, but I ended up seated directly in front of you on the ottoman. We faced each other and spoke closely. Our knees touched. My hands held your elbows and I noted how soft the skin on your arms was.

We kissed more.

You told me I was bad, but you would help me get better.

"Just do less," you said in a low voice. "Let me…"

You kissed me again. And to this day it was the greatest kiss I've ever had.

And when I'm honest and alone, I miss the nearness of your skin. I miss the red warmth of your sunburnt shoulders and the naturally succulent tang of your lips.

And you know what? I'm afraid. That's what good kisses do; they put a little bit of fear inside of me.

Fear that, when this one doesn't work out—which it won't, our religious differences have made sure of that—I'll never have another kiss like that. Perhaps the next girl's lips will be too smushy, or her flavor won't be like yours. Fear that, when I do meet the right one, her body will be all wrong and maybe she won't put her hair up into that sleek black ponytail like you.

I've had dreams since then that I stayed longer, that I spent the night and woke up holding you. But I didn't. After the third or fourth round of kissing, I stood up and departed. We both knew it was over. We both knew it never had been.

I remember turning to talk to you in the doorway, said something about moving a mattress you wanted to get rid of, and was off. We both knew I'd never be back for that mattress. No kiss goodbye. It was over the moment we rose from the couches. We both knew it, and to this day I still wonder if it ever did exist.

Ontologically, I can't help but wonder if we are different, you and I. Is it more than a line on a form that segregates our religious differences, or is it more? Apples and oranges, or is it more like the difference between apples and a 10 million tonne glacier floating lonely in the Arctic?

I kissed you, but what was it? What is created when two bodies touch? What was that substanceless thing we held between us like a child passing water from one hand to the other as he sits in a pool? The problem with trying to hold water is it runs quickly and before you know it, you're sinking your hands beneath the surface again to scoop up more.

You left me thirsty.

Because that's the thing about substance. It is satiating. It doesn't leave you wanting like a burrito made of celery.

You were beautiful but you left me wanting.

Ours was a relationship made entirely of negative calories.

Ours was a kiss that reverberates through a thousand punk rock songs but will be forgotten in the High Country to come.

When everything is shaken and only the unshakable remains, that night in your apartment will be lost in the dusty annals of trivial—but pleasurable—mistakes. And I am eager to consume something substantive once more.

SOME SCATTERED THOUGHTS ON DATING
we all gather these expectations of what our 'soul mate' will be like...

As a single Christian man in his mid-20's, I give a lot of thought to the subject of dating (in case you couldn't tell). The past several months, a few things have risen to the forefront of my mind which I thought were worth throwing into a post on here. It'll be a good time.

In the summer of 2013, I made a friend I'll call Lanie. Lanie and I became immediate friends, mainly thanks to her incredibly outgoing nature, big smile and bigger laugh. There was nothing Lanie wouldn't do. We went cliff jumping once, and I recommended she go off the low 10-foot jump first to get used to it. She neglected my advice, bypassed the 20-foot jump as well, and climbed all the way up to the 40 foot ledge.

Her zest for life was unmatched. There was no one she couldn't befriend and everyone loved Lanie.

Fast forward a year and one of my best friends at college is named Mindy. Mindy is infinitely creative and I am drawn to her hard-working nature and constant innovation. She seemed to dream of a new idea every time she slept because they flowed from her without ceasing.

And it wasn't hard to see where much of Mindy's inspiration came from: She loved all sorts of music most others hadn't yet discovered, was fascinated with documentaries (and really any sort of art you could think of), and had a boundless curiosity about everything and everyone she encountered. In lieu of dissecting every female friendship I've ever had, I'm going to refer back to these for the purpose of illustration.

Fast forward to the present. As I continue my search for the one woman who will *surely* satiate my desires and put to rest all my searching, I'm beginning to notice a pattern happening inside my skull. I have subconsciously developed a sort of ideal woman drawn from all those I've known in the past.

I expect her to have the *joie de vivre* and extroversion of Lanie with the creativity and productivity of Mindy. And the _____ of Sarah and the _____ of Lauren, and the list goes on. I wonder if we travel through life gathering these expectations of what our 'soul mate' will be like, taking just the scraps of others' personalities and crafting them into some ideal romantic messiah who will deliver us from our woes.

But that's not a human…that's Frankenstein's monster.

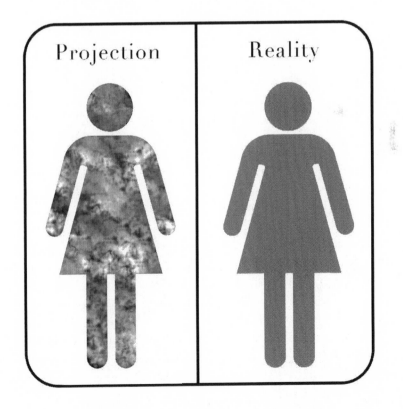

For the first time in the history of EthanRenoe.com, I have made visual aids. However, since this book is only black and white, the left person has a tie-dye rainbow of colors except blue and the right one is solid blue. Imagine that Lanie's qualities are yellow, and Mindy's are green, and the other colors are all the others I *expect* in my ideal spouse. They are collected scraps and pieces of others I've known throughout my life.

To be frank, there are physical characteristics mixed in as well. Perhaps Aladdin was my favorite movie growing up (it wasn't), so I've always been drawn to Arabian women, and that is represented by orange. The list goes on and on.

Yet in reality, if I do meet a girl crazy enough to settle down with me, she will not be like Mindy, Lanie, or Princess Jasmine. She will be herself. She will be a totally unique hue I could not have imagined on my own, even with the help of all these other wonderful women. She will not have the exact same interests or appearance as past flames, nor will she fit into the slim box I've created for her.

Now, why would I spend 578 words making tie-dye bathroom people? Because we all have expectations. Each of us has painted in our minds this vision of who best suits us, and we pull from a myriad of factors. Maybe we subconsciously look for our most beloved character from a romantic comedy, or perhaps we look at the relationships of friends and envy what they have. I don't even want to get into what Freud would tell us.

Each of these influences inflates the bubble of what we hope for romantically, and when it bursts and reality sets in, we are often disappointed. I can't count how many times I've called my friend Elliot after a first date, disheartened by how it went, and he is quick to call me out for having incorrect expectations.

The reality of our situation, as single people, is that we won't find what we are looking for. We won't find the exact combination of colors we have conjured in our heads. I like the line in *500 Days of Summer*, when one of the characters spends a minute describing his ideal woman. The interviewer then asks him if he'd rather have this imagined person or his wife. He thinks for a moment, then says,

"No, that list would be nice. But I'd stick with Beth. Because she's real."

Reality is better than projection. It's better than imagination. Your dream man won't hold you in the night as you weep, or if you're cold; a real one will. A real one with bad breath and farts and a porn problem.

Your bodacious dream girl won't listen to your tiring day and rub your feet, but a real one will. And she won't look exactly like you've pictured and she may have an annoying habit or two.

So is the solution to lose all hope of a romantic future and settle for a Boring Betty or a Bland Bill? Now way! I'm romantic as heck.

I think the solution is to have *realistic* expectations. Enter into each first date with a blank canvas in mind and allow him to paint his own color. It's important to note that the entire canvas won't be filled in all at once. Coming to know someone in a deep and meaningful way takes a lot of time.

I think the biggest cause of blind infatuation is meeting someone, knowing just a dearth of information about them, and filling in the rest with only good things. (Uh-oh…here comes another diagram!)

How much I think I know about someone after a first date

How much I actually know about someone after a first date

It's easy, especially when you've been single since the invention of light like me, to want to fill in all the parts we don't know about someone with what we want them to be. Then, in our minds, the end of our single lives is just *that* much closer.

(We all know that once your single life ends, your *real* life begins.)

As hard as it is, try to be like rappers Rae Sremmurd who declare, "I ain't got no type."

My roommate in college once told me, "I try not to have a 'type' of woman. In a lot of ways, that eliminates the freedom for them to exist as an individual and be themselves. If I have a 'type,' I'm essentially creating a box I want them to fit into, rather than giving them the space to authentically be *other* from me. I'm just looking for another version of myself."

Obviously we all have traits and characteristics, even appearances we are looking for. And I don't think that's a bad thing, but work out what is set in stone and what is flexible. Figure out which things are the immovable rim of the trampoline, and which things are the springs with which you can be flexible. Without both components, a trampoline wouldn't work.

Identifying false desires in whomever we are seeking can help with disappointment and keep us more grounded in reality.

Happy hunting!

SHOULD CHRISTIANS GET MARRIED YOUNG?
or, learn how to open up your fists.

I don't know how I made it out single.

Shortly after my first year of college, I went to Australia for a school with YWAM. Some of you may be familiar with the missions giant whose acronym *officially* stands for "Youth With A Mission," while those of us who have survived it know it stands for something completely different:

Young Women After Men

Yes, We Arrange Marriages

And the list goes on…

After YWAM I headed to Chicago to attend Moody Bridal Institute—I mean *Bible* Institute. My first roommate got married between Freshman and Sophomore year at the wizened old age of 19. I know a dozen similar stories yet for whatever reason, I've remained single through all my 28 years. (Though I'm beginning grad school at Denver Seminary, so perhaps the third time is the charm?)

There's a reason nearly every Christian institution has jokes about how young her members wed: They're accurate! What's more, everyone knows why, whether it's stated subtly or explicitly.

SEX!

As one of the pockets of people who still wait for marriage in a hyper-sexualized culture, it doesn't take much to figure out why Christians tend to get hitched so young. Most of us agree that sex outside of marriage is wrong, yet we still have sensual urges within us, so the easiest solution is to follow the apostle Paul's admission that 'if we cannot control ourselves and are burning with passion, we should get married.'

This verse in 1 Corinthians 7, however, comes after a long plea with the Corinthians to remain single! Growing up in Christian circles, I heard a dozen feats of hermeneutical gymnastics explaining away why this doesn't *really* apply to us, and God really wants you to get married and He was just kidding before, etc…

But what if Paul was telling the truth? What if it really is better for us to remain single instead of diving headfirst into marriage?

Before most of us can digest this statement, we need to take a cold, honest look at the culture which raised us. For as long as I can remember, I was inundated with "Happily ever after" messages. I was brainwashed (no, that's not an overstatement) by plots which taught me that once I met the right girl, my life would finally be complete.

Would she sit next to me on an airplane? Or even more romantically...a train? Or maybe I'd bump into her in a coffee shop near my house, or perhaps, in a fun plot twist, she would be an elementary school flame who resurfaced after *getting hot* in college.

For years, our brains tease out these possibilities until the idea of marriage and sex are idolized far above anything else in our lives. What's worse is the American Christian culture has taken this bait and teaches us the same "Happily ever after" ideals. I mean, there are entire bookstore shelves dedicated to "Christian Romance," a phrase the world would be much less gross without. Let's not even get into the sub-genres, such as "Amish Romance."[2]

The point is, our desires, those things we see as ultimate and necessary as the source of satisfaction, are malleable. We *can* change the way we see things and reorder our priority list, though it's hard to undo decades of messages teaching us that *Yes, even as Christians, our main priority in life is to find our soul mate, get hitched, and make some love.*

As Christians, our primary calling in life is not to gratify our sexual desires first and foremost. It is to glorify God, enjoy Him forever, and bring others into this sphere of blessedness. For this reason, I've come to see many of the young marriages of Christians as more of a detriment to the work of the church than a blessing.

What I mean by that is, if we really believe that Jesus, not sex, is the source of our satisfaction, it should affect the way we live our lives. It means perhaps we would spend years of our lives giving to the world in sacrificial and beneficial ways before settling down with our sweetheart to raise children (The sacrament of marriage and the discipleship ministry of raising children is another article entirely...) rather than diving into marriage just because we can't keep it in our pants longer than two decades. I think too many of us have hopped aboard the "I'm Burning With Passion" train rather than authentically giving ourselves to the Lord and the work He has for us as singles.

---

[2] Yes, that's a real thing. No, I have not read any AR, but I am terribly curious.

I've seen so much fruit in this as a single 28-year-old, as I look back on the countless trips around the globe I've made and the lives I've impacted thanks to my singleness. I don't say that to brag at all, since most of that time was spent complaining to God about my singleness. I say that to tell you that you too can survive well into your twenties—even your thirties or whole life—as a single Christian. Not only that, but you can thrive! You can dedicate your life (or years of it) to serving others in ways you never could if you were married!

Rob Bell once explained that some of the most sexual people he knew were chaste Christians.[3] His definition of sexuality here is beautiful in that it relates to one's relational capacity rather than physical gratification. They were not sexual because they wore tight clothes and did yoga; they were sexual because they were available and free to give themselves to others in meaningful ways. They were free to serve and love others rather than having all of their time and energy absorbed by a spouse and family.

And my friends who married young? They fall into three categories. Some have begun families which continue to glorify God and actively advance God's kingdom on earth. Many have simply settled down and are simply enjoying life together; they don't really contribute to the world in meaningful ways outside of attending church and occasionally mentioning God in their Facebook posts. And tragically, some are already divorced. They dove in far too early, before giving themselves time to even get to know themselves, much less another human being, and ended up as a divorced Christian in their early twenties.

We have become blinded by a culture that teaches that the best source of satisfaction is sex, so it makes sense that many of us would marry young for a taste of that ecstasy. But when it turns sour, we are just as swift to abandon ship.

This is not meant to simply turn you away from getting married; it's an invitation to see your life as bigger than simply a hedonistic pursuit of sex. Give yourself to others before settling down and becoming limited by your spouse. Spend time seeking the Lord and His plans for this crucial season

---

[3] From *Sex God,* by Rob Bell

of your life; how can you best spend it in a way that reflects godly priorities?

We have decades ahead of us to settle down and be married. Spend your younger, more energetic years doing things you can't do as a married man or woman! Go get lost in South America or start a business. Despite what our culture has programmed us to believe,

there

is

no

hurry.

WHY I'M NO LONGER WAITING TILL MARRIAGE
I'm just tired of being patient...

I remember being in 6th grade and watching some cheesy family movie where the princess fell in love with some peasant shlub and they lived happily ever after. I remember the film stirring up longings within me for that same kind of whimsical romance. I wanted a beautiful and innocent mademoiselle to fall helplessly into my arms after I had heroically come to her rescue, whatever form that took.

Over the years, Hollywood continued to program my desires. I remember movies (tacky as they were) like *Fever Pitch, A Good Year,* and literally hundreds more which taught me that all my problems would be solved once I met the right girl, fell head over heels in love, hit a rough patch where we didn't talk for a minute, then came rushing back together to live indefinitely in a state of heavenly bliss.

Yes, once that happened I would be good.

So I eagerly waited. I knew in the depths of my being that one glorious day, God would orchestrate a *meet cute*, and I only wondered when and where.

Would she walk in the door of a coffee shop with an adorable lost expression on her face, or would she happen to sit next to me on the airplane? The options were endless.

But the troubles this presented me were manifold.

For starters, the romance film industry programmed me to believe there is *one* perfect woman out there for me, and all I have to do is meet her. According to the criterion plot line, we will have everything in common and enjoy the same hobbies. (Of course, there are the cute discrepancies which cause cute little arguments, but those can be overlooked.)

But there are no perfect women. And I am as far from a perfect man as you can get before you start getting into the "Murderous Dictator & Collegiate Rapist" categories.

I also failed to account for insecurities arising, both in myself and in others. I overlooked more base factors such as farts, B.O., and faint moustache hairs. I didn't think about how the timing is usually bad, and she'll be going home for the summer. I didn't think about arguments and disagreements, and how my anger can boil over.

All that is to say, my ideas of marriage, and life in general, were programmed into me by the media. The media did not simply *influence* my thinking about these things; it literally programmed me.

I'm going to repeat that once more just to be clear: The things we allow into our minds rearrange our desires, and even create new ones that were not there before.

I've been reading a book lately called *You Are What You Love* by James K.A. Smith, and it is reshaping the way I think. It is mind-boggling. Smith explores our desires, and what shapes them, and I have been able to identify certain desires in my life that have been programmed into me, with an idyllic image of marriage being at the top of the list.

Marriage became something I looked forward to, to the degree that I couldn't be happy until there was a woman in my life.

And apparently, I was not the only one to buy into this. Look at the number of people on Tinder, eHarmony and the like. The dating industry rakes in over $1.4 *billion* a year. A lot of us seem to feel lonely, and think a relationship (even a one-night relationship) will fill in the gaps.

There is no place in the Bible that points to marriage as the source of our fulfillment, yet we Christians are terribly guilty of elevating marriage to a toxic source of satisfaction.

A friend once told me, "If you're not happy as a single person, you won't be happy as a married person." Marriage was not invented as a means of solving all your personal issues. If anything, it will likely bring to light *more* issues that lie dormant beneath the surface.

Marriage is a reflection of the gospel; of God's relationship to His people. It is a covenant. It is living in a perpetual state of forgiveness. It is not a happily-ever-after utopia where all your problems are vanquished.

Recently, however, I decided that I don't want to wait until marriage...(long pause)...to be happy.

I can enjoy the friends I have right now rather than wish I had someone *more* than a friend. I can buy a house by myself. I can pursue hobbies like painting, dancing or snake charming on my own. (Insert cheesy inspirational line about how doing the things you love will lead you to 'The One' you're supposed to be with. Then stop and think about how even that sentiment reflects how deeply you have been programmed to see marriage as the ultimate destination.)

I'm attempting to undo years of programming and enjoy the present moment, single as I am. I go on runs and stop to talk to people. I bike really fast and simply enjoy the adrenaline rush, rather than trying to impress anyone. I take time away from social media so as to not stalk countless women to determine if they are The One.

More so, I am working on enjoying God, and my times of quietness with Him. My prayers are no longer a begging-session of me complaining about my celibacy (I've reduced that to about 50% of my prayers now), But I can zoom out and focus on others. What does the world need? Who does God's heart hurt for?

Since deciding not to wait until marriage, life is more enjoyable. It's almost like experiencing freedom from a big weight that always loomed overhead. The pressure is off. And *if* it happens, it will happen in God's time, so I can relax.

I hope the rest of you single people experience this same degree of freedom.

Don't look to romance to fill the voids within you.

Don't wait till marriage.

(I bet you thought this was about sex, didn't you? Sickos.)

WHY I AM WAITING TILL MARRIAGE
ok, this time it's for real.

After that misleading title, I thought I should make a post about sex and discuss why I *am*, in fact, waiting until marriage to have sex for the first time. This will be a very surface-level survey, because this is a conversation that is definitely deep and ongoing. Brace yourself for a fistful of euphemisms because I got tired of using the word *sex*.

A few months ago, TMZ broadcasted to the world that "Ethan the Shirtless Runner is the new Tim Tebow...HE'S A VIRGIN!" and people went wild. Some accused me of being a prude. Many assumed I was gay. But for some reason, I remained silent on my reasons for waiting until marriage to *park the car in the garage*.

I think the best way to go about this is in two sections: One with my 'Christian' reasons for abstinence, and another more broad section that anyone can apply, Christian or not.

The Broader Reasons

I'm not even going to waste my time expounding on STDs and unplanned pregnancies, as MTV and public schools have talked about those to no end, and they seem to do little to deter anyone from waiting until marriage (that, and they can usually be prevented with a quality contraceptive).

Instead, I think there are a lot more unseen complications that arise when two people *put the bread in the toaster* prior to marriage. For one, having sex with someone creates a chemical bond to them in your brain. The more sex, the stronger the connection.

So, for people going out every weekend and *holstering their pistols*, they are creating these deep chemical brain-bonds with dozens or hundreds of people. You can imagine what this does to a person. It essentially confuses your brain into a dysphoric state of being deeply committed to many people.

Not only will they have a much harder time committing to just one person in the future, but it may even become harder to maintain other relationships in their lives. Because the chemical used to bond together two lovers is the same one used to bond a mother to her child during breastfeeding, people who have had a lot of sexual partners may even have a harder time bonding with their own children.

Let's not just talk about chemicals; look at how hard it is emotionally to move on from a good (or even bad) relationship! In my life, I can clearly see how much more complicated things were with the girls I kissed versus those I didn't. The ones I smooched seem like a much deeper connection was formed. I can't even imagine trying to get over someone with whom I had shared even deeper physical connection!

I've seen friends of mine who had been sexual and then broke up, and how they were so much more devastated than other friends who had chosen not to have sex. My friends who couldn't wait to *plug it in* suffered so much more unnecessary heartache.

One of the arguments I hear the most is that "we REALLY love each other!" The cold hard truth is simply that there is no foundation in that. It is a foundation built on emotion and impulse rather than legal, financial, spiritual, and contractual bonds. There is just no guarantee, no matter how poetically you slice it. At any given moment, she could cut things off, or he could run away with a prettier girl and there is nothing anyone can do to stop them.

When I give myself entirely to someone else, I want the grounds upon which I do so to be one of firm trust and deep-rooted love, not just because we really really really like each other.

The 'Christian' Reasons

Growing up in the church, it was easy for me to simply point to a number of Bible verses and say, 'See! God says not to do *it!*" However, after walking through several years of Bible school and countless conversations with people exponentially smarter than me, I have come to realize that such a simplistic argument doesn't always hold up.

As with anything, I think the best approach to take is to 'zoom out' to get as much of the bigger picture as we can. So in this case, this means examining the purpose of marriage, our bodies, and sex. Granted, I have about 200 words left so this will be a very superficial survey.

Bodies

The first thing to note is that our bodies are *good*. I think that often we inherit this gnostic idea that our bodies are somehow dirty or gross or bad. This mindset perpetuates cycles of shame, which lead us into deeper spirals of sinful activity. If our bodies were inherently bad, then how could Jesus have entered into a human body and through it, worked out the whole of our salvation?? Bodies are good and useful, and from them, good can come.

However, because we live in a sinful and fallen world, we can also do harm and evil with our bodies. We can beat and kill. We can selfishly take things. We can 'unite ourselves to a prostitute' (Paul's phrase for sexual immorality in 1 Corinthians 6).

So when it comes to *boogy-woogy*, we have to ask ourselves, are we using our bodies to give to others and glorify God, or are we using them for selfish means of satisfaction and temporary pleasure? Jesus used His body for the ultimate good when He took it to a cross and let it be tortured and killed in order to save the whole of creation. Are you using yours to the best of your ability, or are you using it to take from others and feel some fleeting good feelings?

Sex

In 1 Corinthians 6, Paul describes a husband and wife becoming one flesh with each other. This is not to be taken lightly, as the next thing Paul says is that the Church becomes *one spirit* with Jesus. When a husband and wife *do the horizontal tango,* they are physically demonstrating something far bigger than the two of them. They are acting out a microcosm of what Jesus does spiritually with His Church.

Confused yet?

Another way to think of it is through the sacraments. When you take the bread and wine into your digestive system, you are *physically* acting out a *spiritual* reality. We have spiritually taken Christ into ourselves, and eating and drinking the communion elements physically demonstrates that.

Looking at sex in this light, we can see why the Bible is so adamant about maintaining purity outside of marriage. To sleep around reflects a Christianity in which Jesus is *not* faithful to His bride, the Church. We have taken Jesus into ourselves, so let us live in a way that reflects this spiritual reality.

Marriage

Lastly, marriage is the context in which sex happens. It is the covenant on which all of these actions rest. *Covenant* is a biblical term for a contract or promise. When you enter into a covenant with someone, there is no breaking it. The Bible speaks of blood covenants, which were so serious that, if broken, blood would be spilled. Not only that, but they were sealed with blood, usually of animals.

When a marriage is initiated between two people, there is a sort of safety created between them. They are free to be themselves. Free to give themselves wholly to the other without having to fear being left or abandoned or taken advantage of.

I think the Bible has a much higher view of marriage than most people in our culture, and as Christians, we should be working to restore this. We should be examples of marriages that are strong and built on sincere love and steadfast trust (Something Christians have not been great at the past several decades).

Conclusion

So if you've got *Getin' Jiggy With It on repeat*, it may be time to think about retiring the charade and making the choice to wait. For the sake of a life lived wisely, as well as a life that reflects well the spiritual realities we embody, join me in placing sex within the boundaries of marriage.

And if you're not a virgin, don't think it's too late for this to apply to you! The God who makes all things new has grace sufficient for all of us. He is eagerly chasing after you, virgin or prostitute. It's never too late to start.

VIRGINITY DOESN'T MAKE YOU A GOOD CHRISTIAN
your sexual status may not be QUITE as important as you think.

Several years ago, I was walking around Boston with an old friend and one of her friends whom I had just met. I can't remember exactly how the topic came up, but her friend ended up saying something along the lines of, "Yah, we're both Christians…we both still have our virginity."

It was such a small comment, but it clearly reflects something many of us raised in Christian homes subconsciously believe:

That being a Christian=Being a virgin

and

Being a virgin=Being a Christian.

There are a number of problems with this mindset, that the sole factor in you being a Christian is your ability to control your private parts, and I want to look at a couple of them here. But before we get started, I'll dispel any notion that Ethan is *actually* against purity now. Nope. Still a virgin and will be till my wedding day.

Problem #1: What about non-virgins?

I imagine anyone overhearing our conversation who was not a virgin would have immediately been turned away from Christianity. The notion that virginity is core to the Christian faith erases any chance for those who have slept around in the past to be saved. It's as if their previous relations have disqualified them from the one relationship which is enduringly life-giving and soul-nourishing.

The Jesus I've come to know is one who reaches out to those who are *especially* filthy; to those who feel the *most* unworthy. Nowhere in the Bible does it say that our sexual transgressions are what make us unworthy in the eyes of God.

In fact, it would appear that the things which disgust God the most are things like pride and religiosity, the pointing of fingers at 'sinners' without first examining one's own heart. Jesus seemed to chill with the prostitutes more than with the religious leaders of the day. Maybe the prostitutes had a unique view of God's grace in a way the religious leaders never did with all their rules and laws and judgment...

Problem #2: Sexuality isn't the only category of holiness

A couple months ago, I was in a thrift store thinking deeply (We've all been there) when a simple yet profound line came to me:

> He is no better a Christian who can control his penis but not his angry thoughts, his gossiping tongue or his worrying heart.

If you grew up in the church, your mentality may persuade you to believe that you are fulfilling your Christian duties by keeping it in your pants until marriage and maybe even reading your Bible every now and then. Some pockets of American Christianity have put so much emphasis on sexual ethics that the rest of Christianity has been mitigated to the back burner. Things like work, money, missions, friendship, food, and justice have taken second seat to the mammoth topic of Christian sexual ethics.

We would much rather debate "How far is too far with my boyfriend?" than discuss how the Church can work toward ending human trafficking, or how we can make our inner-city neighborhoods safer.

Have you worked on growing in holiness in *all* areas of your life?

Keeping yourself sexually pure is a noble and admirable feat, which all Christians should strive for (inside *and* outside of marriage...one needs to remain sexually pure even after the wedding day and remain faithful to their betrothed). But have we focused on this one topic to the neglect of other categories of holiness?

Do we still lust for more money and nicer possessions? Are we generous with the money we do have, or do we spend it solely on ourselves, improving the quality of our own lives?

Do we have a handle on our emotions, especially in areas like anger and envy? Are we patient with our coworkers and loving to everyone we meet?

Or are we merely concerned with how far we can get with our girl before God starts to frown?

What a small religion.

God cares about our sexuality and what we do with our bodies, yes, but He cares about so much more than that! If sexuality is the only area in which you pursue holiness, perhaps take a look at Scripture and see what God spends the most time talking about (Hint: It's not sex...).

Problem #3: It removes the need for grace
Virginity, by definition, is something someone chooses to keep. Therefore, by your own willpower, you could hold onto it until your wedding day, and share that very special gift with your spouse.

But when we conflate this (very good!) choice with our faith, then the Gospel suddenly becomes more about our own willpower than it is about the *gift* of grace. We don't get a special trophy in heaven because we kept our hands to ourselves until the honeymoon. We don't earn our salvation, period.

If the focus of our faith is on our own restraint and self-control, then it entirely removes the need for a Savior to come and lift us up out of our sin and death; we could just get there on our own. Praise God it's not up to us or our decisions to get ourselves into the kingdom!

Problem #4: It places sex on such a ridiculously high level

This is similar to #2, but with a few slight differences.

We live in a culture in which everything is highly sexualized. TV ads, Facebook ads, magazine covers, and yada-yada-yada. To ignore the topic of sexuality in the American Church would be a huge misstep, but we also must not let our culture's fascination with the topic define our own views of it.

My friend's friend in Boston seemed to think that because she was sexually pure, that counted as evidence of her faith. However, this does not reflect the teaching of the Bible, but a specific subculture of American society which waits for marriage. If we as Christians let our faith be dictated by our sexual views, we are not thinking biblically, but rather floating along with the cultural tides of American trends. Our priorities are being dictated by popular culture rather than by the Bible.

In other words, our faith should dictate our sexual beliefs, not the other way around.

Conclusion

Jesus did not come so that all may be virgins again.

He did not come to save only the sexually pure, nor does He turn His back on the 'unclean.' If anything, He moves *toward* those who feel the most ashamed and draws them into the sphere of His love so they can feel clean and new again.

American Christians have somehow married virginity to our faith in such a way that we have come to frown on those who screw up and cast out anyone with different beliefs than ours in the arena of sexual ethics. Yet, nowhere in Scripture do we see Christ doing this. In fact, just the opposite. He rescues a woman who was caught in adultery from her punishment and tells her to be free from her sin.

And *that* is a religion I want to be a part of. I wan to chill with a God who doesn't mark me down for my sexual misdemeanors, but who sees past them to a wounded soul and a struggling spirit, inviting them to come and cast my cares upon Him.

My virginity cannot carry the weight of all my sin; Jesus can.

May we be people who look to Him, rather than our own sexual restraint, to cure us of our sin, shame, and fear.

SEX IS NOT SEXY
is your view of sex unrealistic?

It was my second year at Bible college when I first had this mini-revelation.

Like most young red-blooded Americans (especially of the virgin persuasion), I had this notion that marriage and sex would assuage all feelings of emptiness and quell all my upset desires. I looked forward to finding and marrying that one person who, once found, would satisfy me once and for all. For years I have worked to awaken from this misguided belief and cultivated more realistic expectations.

I specifically remember where I was this one night in college, though, when the seeds of this realization first took root. I had grabbed a couch from the sidewalk in Chicago and used it as my bed for an entire school year. At the time, I was reading Sarah F. Winner's book Real Sex, which argues for a holistic and healthy view of sex and chastity, so the topic was heavy on my mind. I was grappling with this question of whether or not to continue pursuing a girl who was in my life at the time, and there on that tattered couch-bed, it hit me.

Sex will not satisfy me once and for all.

This ethereal entity which seemed like a haven of ecstasy and satisfaction would leave me no more permanently satisfied than a good meal fills up my stomach once and for all. No matter how good the food is, you'll be hungry again.

Give it enough time and the well runs dry.

This thing which, since middle school, had seemed like the finish line to the human race would not satisfy me once and for all. I still remember the scene playing out in my imagination. I imagined myself married to a woman, regardless of how beautiful and (ahem) sexy, once the act was over, I would be in the same place I was in reality: Just trying to fall asleep, get a good night's sleep, and go on with life.

The act of sex would not permanently fill the elusive voids within my soul. After the act, physically speaking of course, I'd be content for a while but life would continue madly on, and the urge would return again. I realized it is not a permanent fix-all for whatever ails the insides of me.

You could say I realized that sex is not sexy.

I mean, what sort of terms come to mind when we think of the word sexy? Isn't it some sort of glamorous, polished, and unrealistic ideal which is constantly sought after but never actually grasped?

Sexy is arousing.

Sexy smells nice and doesn't have morning breath or hangnails.

Sexy is airbrushed and may or may not have had some plastic work done.

But then I stir from this fantasy long enough to look around and tame my wild expectations. I look at those elderly couples who have weathered 50+ years together and are anything but sexy. Yet there is something which keeps them together all those years. There is something deeper and more attractive which draws him to her and vice versa for all those decades. In their essence, 'sexiness' and pornography depend on novelty. There are always new people and new bodies and new, flashy ways to turn someone on. Intimacy, however, is the opposite. It depends on getting to know the same person over a long time.

I remember something an older mentor told me a few years ago which has stuck with me, which I turned into a poem. Here is a clip from it:

he said,
sure sex is great
and a good body is exciting at first,
but eventually,
it's just good to be naked,
it's nice to be naked with the same old person.

Of course, this nudity runs far deeper than a physical lack of clothes. It's a raw, performance-less sort of nakedness. Unlike Adam and Eve who realized they were naked and ran and hid, this sort of intimacy reveals itself to another in a beautiful and unabashed way.

Real sex is not a one-and-done sort of event, but an ongoing, dare I say, mundane practice between a husband and wife, like keeping the dishes clean. If we single people go into marriage expecting a cinematic (read: pornographic) experience every time we come to the marital bed with our beloved, we will be sorely disappointed. This is why thousands of married men and women still struggle with pornography after the wedding night. Because sex is not a cure-all for all of our desires and fantasies. No one person can satisfy all of our deep longings, as they have been programmed by media and magazine covers.

No, real sex is not sexy. It is intimate and longsuffering. It is selfless and other-focused in nature. It is not the object of marriage, but a reflection of the intimacy which should already exist between the two spouses.

Think of it like communion: At the table, we take into ourselves the bread and wine; the body and the blood of Jesus Christ. It is a physical representation of a spiritual reality. It is a shadow which points to something beyond itself. The bread and wine are not special in and of themselves, but they are important because of what they point to.

Sex, similarly, is the *physical* coming together of two people who have already united themselves to the other socially, financially, emotionally, and spiritually.

It's a visible symbol of an invisible reality.

Nowhere are we promised that the sex itself will satisfy us. In fact, if we expect sex alone to fulfill us without the fullness of the relationship being present, it will be hollow and lifeless and we will walk away empty. But when sex follows all the other areas of an intimate relationship, consummated in marriage (the covenant is the consummation), it is life giving and fruitful (literally).

And when we think of it that way, we must remember: Sex is not sexy.

It is real and it is ongoing. It happens amidst the vacuuming and the errands. It is not always made-up and gorgeous, and occasionally gets sick and vomits. The question is, are we going to commit to this person who will have very un-sexy days (increasingly so as the years roll on), or are we going to keep holding out for some sexy fantasy which will never materialize?

This year, I want to attempt to un-program my mind from what our culture has taught us is "sexy" and reclaim a more holistic and realistic ideal of sex. I want to return it to its proper place in my mind, undoing years of being formed in the image of our pornified culture, and embracing a view which is sustainable, healthy, and quite frankly, un-sexy.

So are you with me? Are you ready to help reform our culture in favor of real sex rather than the plastic version we are bombarded with daily? It won't be easy (or pretty) and will take a lot of rewiring our brains to think according to reality rather than Insta-glamour. Let's be people with eyes who can see truly and not be deceived by what media tells us is 'sexy.'

6 COMMON MISCONCEPTIONS ABOUT MY VIRGINITY
some questions I got tired of answering.

"So have you lost your virginity yet?"

This is possibly the most common question I get from people with different beliefs and practices from mine. They never ask about my writing, my travels, my heart or my other friends.

Just my sex life.

Which is still non-existent.

After years of being asked why I'm still a virgin (*"You religious or sumthin?"*), and having to sum up volumes of logic and theology into about two sentences, I decided it's about time to write about why I'm waiting for marriage. I want to address some misconceptions folks seem to have about those of us who remain chaste until their wedding day.

We have zero sexual desires. None whatsoever.
No!

No!!!!

No one could be **more** excited for their wedding day than me! I'm hoping for a 16-second ceremony so we can sprint up the aisle, spit out some vows, and sprint back down the aisle and speed to our hotel room!

There will be no photographers; no family pictures. If you want to remember this day, blink your eyes people! Mental snapshots are the only non-blurry ones you'll get of us!

We who have chosen to wait until marriage do not magically have *less* sexual desires than the rest of y'all. They are there and they are just waiting to be unleashed.

It's just because we're "religious."
For me, this is a big factor in my decision to wait until marriage. I want to honor God with my body and with my use of His gift of sex.

However, a lot of it also comes down to logic and a love for my future spouse.

I have an atheist friend who told me once about how powerful sex is. She explained how amazingly spiritual and bonding it is to unite yourself to this other person; it's really magical. In the next text, she told me that she has probably slept with over 150 people.

To me, this just seems like a logical oxymoron. How could something so beautiful and powerful be shared with such a gigantic number of people?

If sex really is as powerful as she said it is, I want to save that for the one person in my life who deserves it: The person I will have committed myself to and don't have to worry about them taking off in the morning. Someone I can trust wholly and completely, and fully give my whole self to without fear or insecurity.

I'm sure many people have similar reasons beyond simply "I'm religious," so try asking them about it!

Virginity is simply a matter of *that one line* you can't cross.
The other day, a girl asked me about my virginity and followed up with questions like "But what about oral? Or touching?" as if abstinence were about a singular point you don't want to walk past rather than a holistic pursuit of purity.

A friend at college once explained his views on virginity as more of a sliding scale than a matter of steering clear of penetration. He said, "He who has kissed a girl is less of a virgin than he who has not. She who has had oral sex is less of a virgin than she who has not, and so on."

It's not simply a matter of not having intercourse, and then you're suddenly not a virgin; the goal is to live a pure life holistically so you have as much of yourself to share with your spouse and carry less baggage altogether into your marriage.

Now, I'm not saying kissing is terrible and everyone should wait until their wedding day just to give a little peck on the lips. The "line" will be different for everyone. We all have different convictions.

We look down on those who have not waited.
Of course I can only speak for myself here, but a lot of people get embarrassed or ashamed in front of me because I have chosen to wait. I wish this was not so! As a Christian, I must recognize that all of us are on level ground before God. I may not have had sex with a girl, but I have millions of other sinful areas in my life, so who am I to judge?

My pursuit in maintaining my virginity does not have the end goal of shaming people who have not; it's simply because I have found that this is the wisest way to prepare for a future marriage and honor the Lord with my body.

I have no moral high ground to stand on when it comes to pointing fingers. After all, Jesus Himself said that anyone who looks upon a woman lustfully has committed adultery with her in his heart.[4] God knows that by this definition, I've slept with a LOT more than 150 people...

We would never date a non-virgin.
This is a question I have fielded countless times.

But what if she's not a virgin? Dealbreaker?

No, of course not.

Again, if God is able to forgive my myriad sins I've committed throughout my life, I would be a terrible person with no understanding of the gospel if I were to hold a woman's past mistakes against her. I would be someone unable to show grace because I probably haven't experienced it myself.

Virginity, or lack thereof, does not define a human being.

If you've lost your virginity, you're damned to be impure forever.
I have talked to many people who despair because they have already lost their virginity. I see a lot of people who think that they are damaged goods because they have screwed up and can't take their virginity into their marriage.

I think the concept of *being a virgin until marriage* is a modern day concept. The Bible speaks very little about *waiting until marriage,* and our culture has put more emphasis on this than the Bible itself has. (Though it certainly calls for purity and fleeing sexual immorality!)

What the Bible speaks a lot about is renewal and restoration. Broken things being fixed and shattered things being made whole. If you have had sex in the past, don't let that fact, and the shame that may accompany it, determine your future. You can choose right now to live a chaste life. Some

---

[4] Matthew 5:27-28

people refer to this as being a 'spiritual virgin,' as God has already forgotten the things you've done in the past.

It's never too late to begin walking in the light and living a pure life! May we all be people who, from this day forward, long to live in the light and use our bodies wisely and for the building up of others, rather than out of a selfish pursuit of pleasure. May we learn to walk with others in understanding and love rather than judgment and pretense.

AN APOLOGY TO THE GIRL I KISSED ON THE FLOOR OF MY OLD HOUSE
she climbed down beside me, tangling the two of us in blankets...

I once wrote that "The past holds nothing for me but dreams from which I've already woken." I love that line, but there is something I've overlooked. Perhaps the past holds one real thing: lessons. Wisdom. It holds an equal amount of regret and pain, but to completely neglect it would be foolishness.

For instance,

I owe a hefty apology to the girl I kissed on the hardwood floors of my old home. It was the center of winter and she came over for a film double feature: Horror followed by comedy. For the horror, ironically, she lay on the couch while I lay on the floor. I'd rather lie on the floor than anywhere else when I watch a film, and it wasn't until we started the second movie that she joined me.

Our home had very weak heating since it was 113 years old. It took our house a good hour to warm itself into a snug cocoon of comfort on the chilliest nights, and she was shivering.

"If you're cold," I told her, "you could join me down here on the floor."

She smiled.

She always smiled.

And she climbed down beside me, tangling the two of us in a web of half a dozen blankets.

The pressure of her head on my bicep is a weight which seems so alien to me now. It seems like a sweet scent you smelt once in a dream, but woke up knowing it was too good to be real. Nostalgia weighs heavily on me now as I wish, like I have for a handful of other moments, to return to that instant and hold her again.

Beside me, she curled her body into my side.

"That's a good shot," I uttered while the film played. It was a wide, panning shot.

"I like watching movies with you," she said with her right arm draped over my torso and her mouth close to my head. "I never would have noticed something like that."

You want to make a man feel like a man? That's how.

Build him up. Tell him he's good at what he does. Tell him he makes you see things differently. That's how.

I don't remember what else was said that night. I don't remember our first kiss, or how it started. I vaguely remember the credits of the second film rolling in the background until the DVD clicked back to the main menu.

I remember telling her I was sick, and I wouldn't want to get her sick, but she said she wanted to risk it anyway.

I remember liking her a lot; her tan skin and clear complexion added to the effect and the atmosphere of that night. I remember her quick wit and easy laugh. In fact, that was what had first drawn me to her—her sharp sense of humor. Not a krill of my sarcasm was permitted to swim past her without an equally funny response. She seemed to *get* it.

And she smiled while we kissed, I remember that.

Not many people smile when they kiss someone for the fist time. To most, it is a serious responsibility. It is something you need to be careful about, or else you'll screw it up. You can't look like you're enjoying it or you'll spoil the sexiness of it.

But she didn't care. She liked what she was doing and she wordlessly let me know.

It was a couple hours after midnight when we rose from the floor so she could drive home. I didn't want the night to end. I didn't want her to go. I was a youth pastor at the time, and even if there was no dirty play involved, I couldn't have my kids finding out that I let girls spend the night at my crib. That, and I didn't need the added temptation to begin with.

I hugged her goodbye and walked her to the frosty door. Not only did she leave the warm cocoon of our old house, she broke some invisible but very real barrier which exists for moments like that. It's there for nearly every first kiss, and gets broken the instant one of the partners turns away or checks their phone. It's there in my family's home on Christmas mornings while we open presents beside the tree, but it bursts like the thin membrane of a bubble as soon as one member gets up and goes to do something else. Just as a bubble cannot go on existing after something passes through its wall, the atmosphere is shattered when one person leaves the moment.

It was well below freezing outside, so she let her car warm up before pulling away from the curb and driving home on the icy streets.

We were never able to recover the magic of that first night together, and the fault is mine. The next time I saw her, it wasn't the same. We fell to deeper conversation and my boundary-ridden brain wouldn't permit me to have grace where it should have abounded.

If she doesn't believe exactly as I do, I would think, *then there is no hope of a relationship.*

I like to think I've softened since then. I like to think I've expanded my boundaries to allow a few rays of grace to leak in. Grace is a weird thing. It's a two-way street. It can't go out of you if it's not allowed in, yet once it does get in—*really* in—you can't seem to contain it.

The biggest dispensers of grace are those people who know that they have been forgiven deeply. You don't have to be a murderer or thief to drink deeply from the chalice of grace and forgiveness. Maybe you're just a run-of-the-mill heartbreaker like me. Or some form of addict or narcissist.

Also like me.

I learned from the fragile fabric of that night that I have the power to heal or destroy. I have the ability to break someone's year or ruin them for a few months. I have the ability to cast a dark spot on the timeline of someone's life, and I'm learning from that. I'm learning how to be a source of light more than darkness, but of course that light doesn't come *from* me, but merely *through* me.

Have you learned this yet? Have you learned what grace is?

I'm 27 now and I'm still learning. Nights like tonight when I reflect on the past help me to glean something real from them: An awareness of my selfishness. My depravity. They help me to experientially formulate the type of man I want to be in the future.

So may we all learn from the past. Though it's vaporous and passes through our fingers like sand through a screen, may we remember what we have learned and grow wiser as a result. May we fill our baskets to the brim with memories we've learned from, digging into them often that we may grow in wisdom.

AFTER THE BREAKUP

being dumped hurts. here's some wisdom I've gleaned over the years.

We didn't even go into the coffee shop because our silent walk there had erased every appetite for a beverage either one could have had. She hadn't spoken to me for a full week, so I knew the prognosis was not going to be good. I knew that after today—after this conversation—our relationship wouldn't be the same as before.

We sat in the cold metal chairs beneath an overcast sky as—I haven't the slightest idea as to what she actually said—she told me that there was no more hope for a romance between us. We could be friends, but…

It was as if all the dominoes inside of me that had been lining up over the past two years had been flicked and were beginning their spiral tumble. They weren't all down yet; but the pieces had begun their descent.

It's almost the same as going into physical shock: Your brain somehow prevents the pain from setting in right away, despite what you already cognitively know. Though there seemed to be a physical weight on me after the succinct conversation, I somehow made it back to campus and we parted ways in the courtyard.

I took the elevator up to my dorm room, still stunned. Still wishing that her week of silence had *really* meant something else, as thin a hope as that may have been.

Now, this is the part that has always stuck with me: I entered my room and couldn't do anything. I fell onto my bed in a half-sit/half-lie amidst the mess of pillows and blankets and didn't move. I didn't text or call anyone. Didn't open my laptop. Didn't read. Didn't cry. Just sat/lay there for over an hour unable to think of what I should possibly *do*.

Breakups are hard.

It's easy to observe someone else's relational collapse and perhaps feel a pang of sympathy followed by moving on with your day (perhaps that's just apathetic-old-me), but from within, as I can attest, they are crushing. They are suffocating and shocking. I can't even imagine the deep wells which are demolished within people who undergo a divorce or an affair.

Nevertheless, in a season of rupture, words of wisdom, advice and encouragement are needed. So, here are some of the best I've accrued over the years.

The World's Second-Best Spouse

A number of days after my motionless hour, I met with a deeply southern professor at the school. He's the one we all sought for our romantic advice, and there's a reason. He was simply bursting with experience and wisdom. I told him my situation, and in his thick yet snappy southern drawl, he replied,

"Nahw Ethan! Cecilia may be thee second best wahfe for you. But when it comes to something as serious as marriage, we don't want number two, do we? We want number one! So if the door is closing with Cecilia, that just means that, at best, she was thee *second* best wahfe for you!"

Open your hand, even after the wedding
While his sentiments were accurate, the execution was still painful. I really liked Cecilia a lot and for all intents and purposes, she seemed like my #1 option! I knew her pretty well after two years.

What my professor said next was something I'll never forget as long as I'm alive, especially if I'm ever married. He pulled a pencil out of his shirt pocket and held it in an open palm.

"Nahw Ethan, this is Cecilia," he meant the pencil. "And what you want to do right now (he closed his fingers) is hold her tight and refuse to let her go…But what you need is to learn how to keep your palm open before the Lord. And if He wants…"

He used his other hand to lift the pencil off his palm.

"He will either keep her there, or He will remove her from your hand. He will do what He wants either way, but it's easier for *you* if you're already holding her in an open hand."

What he said next is the part that blew me away.

"I married my wife Sweet Sue decades ago, and when I married her, I thought that, *Yes! She was mine forever!*

"But Ethan, just fahve years ago, Sweet Sue got cancer. In that season, God told me that even though she was my wahfe, I had to continue to hold her in an open hand because he may take her out of it."

I was floored.

The last thing I wanted was to think about getting married and *then* having God take her out of my hand. Fortunately, his wahfe had recovered and is still alive and well today. God allowed him to keep her for a few more years. But what that taught me is that marriage is *not* the finish line. There is no time in this life that we get to close our fists on what we want (or what we have) and hold onto them for eternity.

On letting go

In the case of Cecilia, she used language which lacked black and whites and was very gray. She left me hopeful that the time wasn't "now," but maybe "later." What that means is that I spent the next three months refusing to actually move on from her and violently held onto hope that "later" would come.

If you find yourself in a situation where the person hasn't closed the door completely, but has essentially hinted that there may be hope in the future, you need to shoot them straight. Just yesterday I was on the phone with a friend in Cape Cod who had just been dumped by a very serious girlfriend. When she made the cut, however, it was not clean.

"I'm sad, but I'm still hopeful," he told me on the phone. "She didn't say it's over for good, but she just needs some space."

For his sake, I hope she's telling the truth. Also for his sake, I hope that whatever her decision is, she tells him sooner than later. My advice to him was this:

"Don't wait forever for her. Set an ultimatum. She won't know any more in December that she will in June as long as you two are separated and not talking. Force her to do the respectful thing and be straight with you sooner rather than later. It's not fair of her to expect you to just wait indefinitely while she sorts through things. Eventually, she'll realize that she likes you or she doesn't, and when she does, she needs to be up front. For your sake."

I've been on the receiving end of that conversation more often than I'd like to admit. People will use all sorts of softeners to reduce the impact, but often these do more harm than good. I think it's only human to be infatuated with someone and cling to a hope that they'll change their mind. This may be the first step in the grieving process (denial?) but we can't stay here forever.

If the person dumping you is using ambiguous language, set an ultimatum. Let them know that you'll give them space to sort through things, but you won't wait forever. Force them to be the bigger person.

Conversely, if you're the dumper rather than the dumpee, be straight. Don't dance around the issue and don't avoid the difficult and honest conversations. It stings in the present, but is healthier in the long run.

Don't rebound right away.
Don't rebound right away.

Conclusion
Yes. Breaking up sucks for everyone involved. It's a sort of pain which is deep and lasting and can lead to all sorts of insecurities and festering wounds if not properly treated and cared for.

No. Break ups are not the end of the world. In the words of this shark,

You will move on and there will be other people on the land.

Hope that helps!

HOW TO GET OVER ANYONE
try this one step; it works every time!

Wait a long,

long,

long,

long,

long,

long time.

Works every time!

HOW DATING A GUATEMALAN TAUGHT ME PATIENCE

or, how to learn a foreign language in a month.

I spent my first several months in Guatemala mostly isolated and alone, going to work, gym, home. One day, after the rhythm of the season had been well established, a five-foot-nothing Guatemalan woman threw a wrench into everything.

I was wrapping up a back workout on the ancient, rusty cable machine and she walked past me. I had seen her in the gym for several months, but always assumed she was 'taken' because of the confidence in her shoulders and the dark depths of her Latin eyes. She passed by and I took my shot.

"Hola!" I said smoothly, like Lego bricks on the carpet. "Como se llama?"

She told me her name was Claudia, and I told her I'm called Ethan. I asked if she knew English and she said, in Spanish, "no."

Now, there's one more thing you need to know about my escapade in Guatemala: I moved there without knowing a lick of Spanish. I worked at an American school, so I spoke English throughout my workday, but outside of the school, I was pretty lost. By this point however, I at least knew how to ask someone's name and introduce myself.

And that was it.

We fumbled through the next stage of conversation and had to pull over a friend who knew both languages. He helped translate for us and somehow I still wound up with her phone number.

First it was coffee. Nearly all of our conversation was done through our translation apps rather than actually verbally speaking. To be honest, I don't know why either one of us followed through after that first date because it was basically an hour of texting the person via the SpanishDictionary app while sitting across from each other. It was painful.

Then it was dinner, then spontaneous hangouts, then afternoon movies, and over the course of our time together we figured out how to communicate. We were together most days and our talking began to look

162

more like actual conversation as her English improved as did my Spanish. We slowly continued to learn, and only occasionally had to use our apps when we couldn't pinpoint a word.

If you ever want to learn another language instantaneously, date someone who speaks that language. Nothing motivates you toward fluency like romance and the ability to communicate more clearly with the object of your affection.

Our first kiss was after watching the film *Pan's Labyrinth*. I had to practice in my head repeatedly: *puedo besarte? puedo besarte?* After that we were basically 'dating,' however you want to interpret that today.

One day I realized something about our relationship which was new to my dating experience. I enjoyed being with her. I liked showing her things and I liked our occasional kisses. It was relaxed and fun. It was the way dating should be.

I met her after school and greeted her with a kiss. Most days she tasted sweet like a summer day, but today she was smoky like a backyard barbecue.

We were going to a cafe near our gym and with my arm around her, I made a joke about her height. Then she called me *gordo* for missing the gym two days in a row and then I pretended to punch her in the head. She was laughing and I began to wonder why I had scarcely reached this point with the other women I've dated. Months later, I think I have an answer.

On our very first coffee date, I discovered something about Claudia which previously would have been a deal breaker: she told me she was Catolico, and I explained that I'm not Catholic, but I am a Christian. That was about the extent of our religious conversation on the first day. The boundary was essentially forced upon us due to the language barrier. I wanted to know more about her beliefs, as well as share more of mine with her, but the difficulty of communicating all that just made me forgo it. I accepted it and moved on.

Looking back at first dates with other women before Claudia, I realized what a disaster I've been. Sure, I'm a theology nerd but that doesn't mean I should call things off with a girl just because she's an Arminian. Or maybe she didn't share my views on predestination or the spiritual gifts. It's almost like I was looking for a little trigger to nitpick; a spiritual reason to call things off. You could say I dated with a fearful mindset more than one that actually wanted to find a best friend to eventually marry. I was scared if her beliefs varied too much from my own, and always had to call it off.

Dating Claudia taught me patience in a number of ways. Obviously, having entire conversations by typing them out and translating them is toilsome, but the biggest was learning how to pace a relationship. I've learned that it's a big mistake to try to cover the five points of Calvinism on the first (or sixteenth) date. Spending time with Clau forced us to just have fun; to enjoy each other's company and talk about things which were simple enough to communicate in Spanglish. It took mammoth effort to try to have a deep, intricate conversation about politics, religion, etc., so we just didn't until we knew better how to communicate with one another.

Just as a child learns to read with Dr. Seuss before he can read Schopenhauer, Claudia and I were forced to take our time learning all of the elementary things about one another before advancing to the more divisive issues. Moving forward, I intend to institute this method of not-diving-into-the-deep-end-on-day-one, but simply having fun getting to know the person before making a serious judgment call.

I came to enjoy Claudia's company in a unique way because I got to know her as a person—as a friend—before I projected a panoply of beliefs and political categories upon her. People are not just a collection of opinions, but they're humans. If you're dating, get to know the human before you discard them based on a differing opinion.

Date with grace, not fear.

I'm grateful for Claudia, the fun we had, and the lessons she taught me.

INTIMACY PART 1: DREAMS
or, what a sheep-monkey taught me about love.

A year ago, I sat down and blasted out a four page essay on intimacy in the middle of the night when I was struck with inspiration. I wrote it as a letter to my best friend, and much of what is in these 'intimacy' posts will be derived from that essay. I hope it speaks to you. I'm really excited about it.

The essay opened with (and was the result of) two dreams I had within about a week. Without spending too much space on them, I will summarize them thusly:

In the first dream, I was in an enormous mansion with a girl I knew from grade school. I assumed we were married, and we had just finished making love. The physical act was downplayed in this dream, and the focus was on what happened next. We simply lay in the bed in this huge mansion, whispering to each other. I distinctly remember thinking about how lying there was more enjoyable than the physical act of sex itself. Rather than a fleeting fleshly pleasure, we were sharing something at a deep and intimate level. I *knew* her and she *knew* me. I loved her and she loved me. I wasn't scared that she would get up to leave, nor was she. Granted, both she and I were acting within my subconscious, but the feeling was enough to leave an indelible mark on me upon my waking.

The second dream was more strange, but equally moving. I was in a submarine with a small monkey/sheep hybrid. He was my best friend and I was his. We also shared a relationship that was deeper than the average human friendship. He stayed with me wherever I went on the submarine, but as a companion, not an annoying chihuahua that won't stop following you around. The ship eventually opened its door like a garage, and we found ourselves not underwater, but in an idyllic park where the sun was setting over families playing in the lush green lawn. My monkey/sheep and I climbed a tree and watched the sun set behind the mountains. We spoke in words that we had made up, and always knew exactly what the other meant. As we watched the sun sink over the purple hills, I felt the same sense of camaraderie and intimacy I had had with the girl in the previous dream.

Once more, it was not sexual, but purely a sense of knowing and being known; loving and being loved.

Yes…This was the foundation of my thoughts on intimacy.

I don't know why it took me 22 years to realize this, but it did. I realized that all the physical consummation shown on television and in movies is nothing more than a fleeting glimpse of the potential of intimacy available to us as humans. I had been brainwashed by our society's depiction of 'normal' sexuality. I never realized what I had really been craving was not sex, but intimacy.

We long for it. We need it. We were made for constant, near, unconditional intimacy with both each other and the Lord. I believe both are necessary, and one is not at the expense of the other.

In the Garden of Eden in Genesis 2:18, God says, "it is not good for man to be alone." He had just finished saying everything else in creation is "good," and this is the ONLY thing in the UNIVERSE that is NOT good. Being alone. Now, take note of a very important fact: this was before sin entered the world, and Adam had perfect and unbroken relationship with the Lord. In other words, his relationship with God was not quite enough. We understand that He came down everyday "in the cool of the afternoon" to walk with Adam.

God descended to walk with us.

And even in Genesis 3 after the first sin was committed, God continued to come down to walk with man. It was Adam and Eve who felt ashamed and ran and hid from Him.

Shame drives us to hide. Whether behind lies or jokes or masks or makeup or false identities, we are a hidden people. Our culture has reinforced this hiddenness tenfold with the onslaught of social media and other media we intravenously pump into our heads.

A wise friend of mine made a brilliant observation tonight: We joke most about the things we are most ashamed of; the things we have perverted and tainted in our own lives. It's a way of hiding behind a guise of lightheartedness and laughter rather than facing our own history and mistakes, our sins and our pain.

And in our culture, nothing is more skewed than our views of sexuality. Look at an episode of nearly any TV show or movie. What is the repeated subject of joking and theme of progression? Sex. The characters relentlessly make light of the topic, while at the same time seek it out as the be-all end-all source of satisfaction. Our culture is ashamed of its sexual perversion.

I am really excited to share on this topic that is constantly moving and shaping me, drastically overlooked by our culture and our church, and is key to knowing our relational God. I will conclude with a meditation on a line from my favorite hymn. In *Rock of Ages*, the age-old line resounds:

> Foul, I to the Fountain fly
> Wash me, Savior, or I die
> Wash me, Savior, or I die,
> Wash me, Savior, or I die.

The writer is not singing of a painless bubble bath type of washing, but the painstaking scrubbing that induces aches and rashes. It takes some skin off with it. It's the washing that destroys infections the way alcohol poured on a gash bubbles and foams and sends waves of pain from our limb to our brain.

It's not an external washing necessary for our cleansing, but a washing of the deepest parts of who we are. Our guts and muscles. It goes deeper than flesh, even bone.

It's the sort of painful washing that the Lord—and only the Lord—can accomplish.

He is infinitely gentle and painstakingly thorough.

He is gracious and loving.

He is tough on stains.

INTIMACY PART 2: LONELINESS

"that's exactly what I would do if I were depressed too."

A woman went to her therapist and asked him to tell her what was wrong with her.

He said, "I think you're depressed."

She said, "I can't be depressed. I go to parties all the time and I'm always meeting up with people."

He said, "Well that's exactly what I would do if I were depressed too."

I have become fairly certain that loneliness is not simply the result of a lack of friends. Surrounding ourselves with other human bodies won't make that nagging ache inside our bones magically disappear. Nor will sex, drugs, porn, or a few cold ones. I want to point to one of my favorite passage in the Bible, Ecclesiastes 3:11, which reads, "He has set eternity on the hearts of men." We are filled with a longing that nothing in this world can satisfy; only Eternity Himself.

In 1 Kings 19, Elijah is on the run from an evil king who is trying to hunt him down and kill him. God tells Elijah to wait at the entrance of this cave, for He is about to pass by. This is what happened:

> Then a great and powerful wind tore the mountains apart and shattered the rocks before the Lord, but the Lord was not in the wind. After the wind there was an earthquake, but the Lord was not in the earthquake. After the earthquake came a fire, but the Lord was not in the fire. And after the fire came a gentle whisper [literally: 'a sound of silence']. When Elijah heard it, he pulled his cloak over his face and went out and stood at the mouth of the cave.[5]

Elijah waits for the Lord to pass by at the mouth of the cave, and what is he met with? A great wind, an earthquake and a fire, but the Lord is not in any of them. It's not until he is face to face with the silence of the hills that

---

[5] 1 Kings 19:11-13

Elijah is able to witness the Lord. The other things may have been ferocious and mighty, but all they ended up doing was distracting him.

In our world today, how easy is it to glue our attention to a church service, an electric worship set, or a charismatic conference? These are good things (just as God also showed up elsewhere in scripture as fire, wind, and quakes), but they are not to be the center of our focus. When we are face-to-face with the Almighty, in the intense silence of His presence, we have no response left but to hide our face like Elijah.

In my own life, I recall going to high school Snow Camp every winter. I remember looking forward to it because "I'll get closer to God...I'll make a *real* change this time!" I'd go, get ultra hyped-up for about a week after camp, and then be back where I was before.

But God also lives in the spaces between events.

He meets us in the silence of the morning and the cool of the afternoon.

The cure for loneliness has little to do with our external circumstances and almost everything to do with the weather going on inside of us. Michael Cusick describes it this way: "When you are empty, being alone with yourself is almost always a scary thing. But when you are full, it's almost always a joy—like being with a good friend."[6]

An old mentor of mine named Ethan once told me that knowing God was nearly identical to knowing yourself. How can you love God, and know that He loves you, if you barely know yourself?

Let me give you a tool which has helped me greatly the past few years in battling loneliness and its effects, like addictions and insecurities. It's an ancient practice called Centering Prayer, and the goal is silence. It may seem counterproductive to fight loneliness with solitude, but believe me, learning how to be alone is key to knowing yourself.

In Centering Prayer, you get completely alone, without phone, internet, music, books, or even the Bible. Next, say a little prayer inviting God to come and simply be with you. Sit comfortably and close your eyes. After

---

[6] Michael John Cusick, *Surfing for God*

that you just wait in utter silence. The goal is not to work your way up some spiritual ladder, or even to pray to God; it's simply to *be with* Him. Set an alarm for fifteen or twenty minutes and try to simply enjoy the silent presence of the Lord. Maybe He will speak to you and maybe He won't, but either way, I promise that if you make this a regular habit, you will notice differences in your life.

I have seen myself grow more patient and less anxious. There is a greater peace and clarity as I go about my day. These 20 minutes help to clear away much of the stress and distractions from the rest of my day.

As believers, the deepest part of who we are—our center—is the Holy Spirit. Paul tells us in 1 Corinthians 6:19 that our bodies are temples of the Holy Spirit. What's in the middle of a temple? God. By deafening ourselves with endless social media excursions, iPods, texting, TV, and movies, we have become distracted. We have wandered 'off-center.' That's why it is so hard, if not impossible, to sit alone in silence for 20 minutes. It's absolutely foreign to us.

(If any of you are afraid that all this talk about being centered sounds too "New-Agey," it's worth noting that New Agers stole this practice from Ancient Christians, not the other way around. The Bible repeatedly commands us to be still, or to meditate.)

Suppose you're a guy who wants to date a girl. Would you only get to know her by going to rock concerts and movies and loud bars, or would you spend time talking quietly, watching sunsets and shooting stars, and walking on the coast? The same is true of our relationship with God. We will never get to hear the still, small voice of God if we are always drowning Him out with the noise of the world.

Talking. Listening. Being. Together.

That's how relationship is formed, and how it grows and molds. Intimacy is not built during the rock concerts and dance parties, but in the silence that fills in the gaps between the noise. It's when we catch a fleeting glimpse of another human soul that deep connection is made.

There's so much more I want to say. Let me try to wrap up this bundle of ramblings by pointing to the most secure and self-aware Person I know: Jesus.

Peruse the gospels and you'll see how He is constantly escaping the noise of the crowds and the company of His friends in order to be alone in a quiet place with the Father. No one walking this planet knows him or herself better than Jesus, and the reason for this is evident.

He even gave us the instruction in Matthew 6:6, "But when you pray, go into your room, close the door and pray to your Father, who is unseen. Then your Father, who sees what is done in secret, will reward you." It's no mystery as to why our generation struggles with intimacy so much. The private things have bled out into the open. We don't know ourselves.

Cure your loneliness by getting alone.

Get to know the Lord and yourself on deeper levels.

INTIMACY PART 3: GOD IS NOT A HIPSTER
nothing is serious. nothing is deep.

In his amazing posts[7] on the Superflat culture of 21st century Japan, Mark Sayers describes the existential crises many young Japanese people experience upon arrival in the Australian outback. Since the atomic bomb was dropped on their homeland, they have retreated to the opposite extreme of anything with gravity. They have breathed artificial life into a bubbly and cute culture where the adolescents are blinded by the flashing lights and noisy colors.

Nothing is serious. Nothing is deep.

Sayers writes about many of them graduating from college, vacationing to some foreign land like Australia, renting a car, and driving to the center of the continent where there is nothing but vast expanses of red ground and

---

[7] Visit marksayersthinks.com, or read *The Road Trip That Changed The World*

blue sky. "Deprived of stimulation, outside of their superflat world, they would have a spiritual and existential breakdown," writes Sayers. "The superflat distraction was detoxed out of their system and the big questions of life, God, human existence and death were now at the forefront of their mind." They find God in the middle of the desert.

The trouble for us, though she wears a different colored dress, is we live in the same kind of culture. Think about how we go about meeting people, especially those of the opposite sex. The conversation is built upon a foundation of sarcasm and small jokes.

'Flirting.'

We wash away our troubles, stresses, and fears by immersing ourselves in the oily waters of sitcoms and YouTube clips.

The notion of a hipster is someone who has built their core values on irony and satire. They wear a corny wolf t-shirt not because they think the shirt is cool, but exactly because it is not. They don ugly sweaters and nasty shorts to poke fun at them—the style is a fashion of irony. It's a way of hiding in public, saying that you can't make fun of them because they are already making fun of everything. Life to them is a joke that you're not *in* on.

Have you wondered why the concept of a hipster has taken such a dominant position in our culture over the past decade?

On April 20, 1999, two teenage gunmen marched through Columbine High School killing over a dozen people, mostly fellow classmates. This would result in countless copycat shootings over the following decades. September two years later, terrorists steered planes into the World Trade Center towers. Eighteen years removed, we can't seem to bring any sort of weighty issue to the public mind. And if we do, it is quickly satirized by talk show hosts and late night comedians. Death is taboo, and what happens after is irrelevant. For Americans, it has become easier to escape into the world of comedy and irony than to honestly look at our spattered history and present reality.

I have recently realized that many of my relationships are built on nothing more than inside jokes and our shared ability to quote *Nacho Libre* or *Monty Python*. Internet memes and social games. It's no wonder, then, that I have been battling loneliness while simultaneously wearing the smiling face of someone else.

We humans were not made to function alone. We were designed for intimacy with God and one another. As Dietrich Bonhoeffer put it,

> Let him who cannot be alone beware of community...Let him who is not in community beware of being alone...Each by itself has profound perils and pitfalls. One who wants fellowship without solitude plunges into the void of words and feelings, and the one who seeks solitude without fellowship perishes in the abyss of vanity, self-infatuation and despair.[8]

However, true community is not gathering together to stream *Portlandia* marathons or hop on the Youtube flow for hours on end. These are not bad things, but to initiate true fellowship, we need to shut off the electronics, the distractions, and dive deep. People of my generation in particular struggle with this because we so desperately avoid looking in the mirror and being vulnerable. Not physical reflective surfaces (we love those *too* much), but the spiritual mirror that allows us to know ourselves and be known by others. Conversations where we are allowed to ask hard questions and required to answer them. Simple questions like,

What has the Lord been teaching you lately?

What do you want? Really want?

Why do you keep returning to your porn/drug/alcohol/one night stand addiction?

What are the times in your life when you felt hurt the most, and, can Jesus meet you there?

What does God think of you?

I have realized that these conversations do not start themselves. We need to take initiative to begin them; to begin healing ourselves and one another. Each of us is wounded from something (read: many things), and many of

---

[8] Dietrich Bonhoeffer, *Life Together*

these are wounds from intimacy. From people who were supposed to love us, but left instead. Parents who hit us rather than holding us. From middle school kids who closed their circle of friends while we orbited in the atmosphere of rejection. Of 'almost cool enough.' I've been there and you have too.

It's easier to float in the ethereal and substance-less realm of comedy and satire. It is both a shield to our vulnerability and an escape from reality. It's even easier than letting the Lord love and heal you.

Look at Jesus, the most genuine and substantial human to ever live. Examine His interactions with people, even strangers, and you will not find small talk or sarcastic jokes. Rather, you will find that He dives straight to the deepest parts of who we are and gets to work healing old wounds.

In John 4, Jesus meets a Samaritan woman at Jacob's well in the middle of the day. She would have gone at that time because no one else would be around and she wouldn't have to face anyone. She was a person drenched in shame. In her initial interaction with Jesus, she even seems a little snappy.

But Jesus, rather than avoiding the issues at hand, goes straight for her heart. He tells her that there is water that is better than this liquid, water so good she will never thirst again. He tells her to go get her husband and return.

But she doesn't have a husband.

Jesus knew this, and pointed out that she has had five husbands, and she is currently living with someone new. He did not dance around the point, but rather pointed directly to her weakness. He saw that she had been trying to quench her spiritual thirst with man after man, but none could satisfy the resounding thirst in her soul.

He then discourses on the coming time when all people will worship together, and invites this hurt, broken, thirsty woman to join in the feast. Jesus was impatient in the best way possible. He did not wait to build relationship before he began loving them. He started upon contact, going straight to the deep wounds, thirsts, pains and longings.

I want to be a person who is not scared of vulnerability or hesitant to engage the spiritual lives of others. I want to build relationships on a foundation of depth and trust rather than sarcastic pokes and hollow attempts to impress. I want to be someone who doesn't hide behind a veneer of satire and a shield of cultural irrelevance. I want my identity to be firmly rooted in my relationship with the Lord.

And my guess is, you do too.

Let us initiate this deeper conversation.

INTIMACY PART 4: WRESTLING WITH A QUIET GOD
when the little god you believed in loses a fight.

I stood by the Literail tracks waiting for my train into downtown Denver, wondering if I still believed in God. I remember the sound of the Pentecostal preacher's voice crackling through my earbuds as my train pulled up and I boarded. He was giving a message on why it's important to 'win souls', as he put it. I wondered why any of it mattered.

I was a handful of months out of my first YWAM trip around the world. When sharing my story, I typically tell people that trip is the reason I'm a Christian today. Because of what I saw God do. But this winter day nearly a year afterward, I was wondering if there even was a God. And if there was, why would he care about us? About me?

I lived in this place for months, wrestling.

It wasn't until I left Colorado and went through two of the worst months of my life in Boston that something shifted. I was backpacking from Boston to New York City, and found myself in a tiny mountain town in Connecticut, in a stranger's guest bedroom. He and his girlfriend were gone for the night, so I was utterly alone in the quiet apartment, and then I met God.

It's not something I can explain or even fully understand.

That night I experienced the intersection of so many loose cords I had been tripping over for months. The Lord spoke to me with some language deeper than words. The only way I knew how to respond was to put in my earbuds and play the most 'spiritual' music I could find on my iPod. And that night, in the middle of nowhere, Connecticut, I worshipped for the first time.

I had always sung the words on the church screen and prayed the proper words when the time was right. But I don't think I had ever worshipped from my heart until that night.

You might say I had never *felt* God before.

I went on from there to Pennsylvania to NYC to Nigeria. After the night in Connecticut, it was as if a light switch had been turned on for the first time in my life. The remainder of the trip was perpetually riddled with Spirit-driven conversation and learning new things from the Lord. People cried when we prayed together. God moved.

Today I was bathing in Chicago when something hit me. More lines intersected.

It starts with Genesis 32 where, as I was, Jacob is wandering around looking for some unknown utopia. He is attacked by a nameless man and they wrestle all night long. The man saw that he was overpowered by Jacob, so he touched his hip so that it was wrenched. After some spotty dialogue, Jacob wrests a blessing from the man. The man changed Jacob's name to Israel, which means *he struggles with God.*

I often point to this text as an image of the Christian life. As we approach the Almighty God, there is struggle. There is difficulty in letting go of the things of this world, of the things our flesh desire. There is pain in transformation into the image of a Holy God. These are the things I had always seen in this passage, but tonight as I washed myself, I understood something I had been missing.

Now, my soteriology is anything but solidified, but I'd argue that most people in our generation long to wrestle with God; to feel His flesh against ours as we struggle against His strength, whether they admit it or not.

Tendon against tendon and muscle and bone. The reality is, most of us wrestle with ghosts while longing for a visible, tangible god. The secular age has raised a society of humans declaring themselves enemies of an absent god. As I stood on the train tracks outside Denver, I would have killed for God to come to me, that I may wrestle Him and try my strength against His.

But I, like most humans on the planet, was left with silence.

As he traveled on his path, Jacob was encountered by God in the most unlikely place. This is why I resonate with his story so much. He is the homeless wanderer, seeking God in the unknown and unscheduled wild. In all of his years of wandering, it is not he who stumbles upon God, but God who comes to him. The encounter so moved Jacob that he named that place Peniel, which means *face of God,* "because I saw God face to face," he says. When he least expected it, God came to Jacob and allowed him to struggle against Him; to test the merit of His sinews.

Our struggle is just finding a God to wrestle with.

In a culture where only the visible is consequential and the immediate is contemplated, it is very hard to connect with an invisible God. As I said in the previous Intimacy chapters, distraction is a central factor in our feeling distant from God. We have a trillion bits of media and advertisement vying for our attention, making it exponentially more difficult to reach out and touch God. So we choose instead to settle for the hollow and empty cavern of secular religiosity. It fulfills our dues to the god who needs *our* attention, and allows us to go on calling ourselves Christians.

However, what God wants from us could not look more opposite. In 1 Chronicles 17, God says He does not want a temple to be constructed because He prefers to move with and *be with His people.* In Matthew 22, Jesus states that the first and greatest commandment is to love the Lord your God with all your heart, soul, mind, and strength.

He wants relationship with His people.

He loves us deeply.

Intimately.

And sometimes, intimacy means you wrestle with the one you love. It may look like sitting in silence, beholding the beauty of the Lord, or it may look like yelling at a God who is more often silent than present. Whatever the emotion is, do not bar it from your relationship with the Lord. He is big enough to take it. He can handle your humanity, fraught with anger and fear.

I want to go on for another 18 pages about being loved by God, but I'll wrap up with a word from Rich Mullins that has helped me over the years:

> I'm always being asked by people, 'how do you feel closer to God?' And I always want to say, 'I don't know.' When I read the lives of most of the great saints, they didn't necessarily feel very close to God. When I read the Psalms, I get the feeling that David and the other psalmists felt quite far away from God for most of the time. Closeness to God is not about feelings; closeness to God is about obedience...I don't know how you feel close to God. And no one I know that seems to be close to God knows anything about those feelings either. I know if we obey, occasionally the feeling follows. Not always. I know if we disobey, we don't have a shot at it.[9]

Continue reaching for the invisible God.

Yell, if necessary.

INTIMACY PART 5: CRYING LIKE DAVID
how blessed is he who dashes your infants against the rocks.

Sorrow is better than laughter, because a sad face is good for the heart.
~Ecclesiastes 7:3

The thought began with all of our new best friend: Netflix. I can't pinpoint exactly when this began for me, but I'll start from the beginning. Hopefully many of you will resonate with this.

---

[9] This was from a live recording of a show in Texas, and fragments of this speech appear in the film *Ragamuffin*, a film about Mullins' life.

I remember being in middle school and having my first major crush. A girl liked me and I liked her and there was much rejoicing. My musical tastes, awful as they were in 2005, turned to the upbeat and joyful sounds of spunky guitars and hopeful lyrics. Then came heartbreak. For some unfathomable reason, it didn't work out between this cute thirteen-year-old and me. Sure, my musical tastes devolved into this poppy form of mourning, but what did I seek out? Some kind of comedy or romantic chick flick to make myself feel better. A happy book with a hopeful ending. Rather than experiencing the full pain of the rejection, I turned to something with a predictable and controllable happy ending.

Fast forward to today. If any of you are like me, you'd rather watch something with a happy ending than something that takes a realistically depressing slice of life and lays it out before its viewers. We are quick to call this form of entertainment an 'escape.'

It's easy.

When I feel lonely, do I want to watch something depressing to make me feel worse? No, I turn on *Friends* reruns or stream *Arrested Development,* in which the protagonists are always in some sort of comedic peril, always with their close friends or family, and always lighthearted. We viewers can make quick friends with these characters who always seem to be there for us, to cheer us up and make us chuckle.

There has to be a reason comedies rake in billions at the box office and sad dramas are reserved for the sparsely-attended art house theaters. (Granted, it is just as possible to escape into any series with a good plot and realistic characters. i.e. *Breaking Bad* or *House of Cards.* Just track with me for a minute.)

How different is this from the way the psalmists walked through suffering and loneliness!

By far, the Psalms of lament outnumber the other categories of psalms. They compose about a third of the psalter, which in itself should be a wake-up call to this laughing generation. In these psalms, I've found that the writers don't avoid the tough and ugly parts of what they are going through. Nor do they try to make their trials sound prettier than they are. In many of the psalms, the writer is angry at God or his enemies, and states what he wants to see happen to his opponents (i.e. Psalm 137, which ends by saying how blessed is the man who takes the infants of my enemies and dashes them against the rocks. Note that the author is not *doing* this, but being honest in saying what he wants to see happen. He is being honest with God. But the imprecatory psalms are for another day and a smarter author).

Take for instance Psalm 88, arguably the darkest psalm in the book, as there is no glimmer of hope, even at the end, but rather, an ending Simon and Garfunkel would be proud of. Note several things. First off, the psalmist is totally honest with God. He spouts phrases like, "my life draws near to the grave," "You have put me in the lowest pit," "Why, O Lord, do you reject me and hide Your face from me?" and finally, "the darkness is my closest friend." I think that if Christians learned to be honest with God the way the psalmists were, rather than dressing our prayers in a polite spiritual piety, we would experience a nearness to Him that is foreign to so many in our Christian culture today.

Also note that the author engages his troubles rather than brushing them under the rug. He says that he has cried out to God day and night; his eyes have grown dim with grief; he has called to the Lord and spread his hands to Him. The writer repeatedly talks about crying out to the Lord, in the morning and in the evening. It is clear that He faced his sorrow head on. In other words, he didn't jot down this honest little poem and then flip on *The Office* to relieve him of his burden and shoo the ugly suffering under the carpet, laughing to avoid the pain.

He faced it in the morning.

He faced it in the evening.

He faced it day after day and gave it to the Lord.

The last thing I noticed is that the psalmist does not lose sight of God in the midst of his trial. He opens up the psalm by calling God the "God who saves me," and offers up other statements to declare truths about who God is. We need to do this too. We need to remind ourselves and remind one another who God is and what He has done for us, even when we don't feel like He is with us.

Is your tendency like mine? Do you flee your pain and loneliness and scroll through any number of social media outlets, looking for the one laugh that will satisfy once and for all? Or perhaps you just soak in hours of Netflix comedies, feeing closeness to these digital people.

I think there's a reason there's no book of comedy in the Bible.

I think we need to learn to grieve and suffer better.

Next time a trouble comes upon you, or if you are in the midst of grief right now, put down the TV remote. Shut the laptop. Get alone from the noise and the distractions and pray. Journal. Read the Word (hey, try the Psalms!). But don't escape the Lord. Don't run from Him, but to Him. He cares about your woes. David was deemed The Man After God's Own Heart, and he somehow learned to walk through the hard times of life *with* the Lord, rather than by keeping his problems in the closet and out of sight.

Learn to emote well.

Be honest with the One who understands.

INTIMACY PART 6: DISPOSABLE TROPHIES
it may lead somewhere, it may not. either way, it feels good.

"I shouldn't have even come out here tonight," she cried, shivering in Chicago's winter. It was a cold Friday night in January a handful of years ago, and this woman (we'll call her Maggie) was embodying something we saw on a weekly basis.

I ran a street ministry when I lived in Chicago. We stood outside of clubs and bars simply to talk to people, pray with them, and tell them Jesus loves them.

As mascara ran down Maggie's cheeks, she explained that she knew she should not have come out tonight. She felt like it was a mistake and she was so glad she ran into my friend and I on that street corner. After we had finished talking to her, Maggie called a taxi and went home. She did not go home with a stranger that night.

She had been looking for something meaningful, she was just looking in the wrong place.

Years later, I was baffled as I listened to my friend's voice on the other end of the phone.

"Sex is such a spiritual and intensely intimate experience," he mused.

On that we agreed.

"...yah, that's why I've had sex with over 150 people," he concluded.

I didn't speak for a moment.

It seemed as if his view on sex was incredibly contradictory. How can something be so spiritual and intimate, where two people connect in the deepest possible physical way, and simultaneously be so disposable and expendable?

Sadly, my friend's view on sex is now the majority view in America. Sex is both meaningless and it is a god. It is the ultimate prize and it is effortlessly dispensable.

Since the introduction of contraception, the value of sex has plummeted. No longer does sex potentially mean long-term commitment. It's not just for sweeties who intend to get married. Now that there is no risk of getting pregnant, the weightiness of sex has been reduced, and it can solely be a pleasurable endeavor.

There are dozens of TV shows centered around people's pursuits of one-night stands, hookups, and other sexual exploits. No longer are they reserved for the after-dark specials either. They are prime times on the family channels. They have normalized our crooked views on sex.

Instead of mourning the fact that characters regularly wake up next to one another, completely forgetting the others' name, we have made it a situational comedy. It's *funny* when people perform the criterion *Walk of Shame*, or air their regrets about settling for a '4' because they were drunk.

Simultaneously, these hookups are the ultimate pursuit throughout the course of every episode. They have arrived at the golden doorstep of satisfaction if they have connived or stumbled their way into bed with a bombshell.

It boggles my mind how we arrived here as a culture.

Real life hookups are not that pretty. They are not that clean cut, and they're definitely not that comical. I've spent enough Fridays on the streets of Chicago at 2am to be familiar with the system.

There's the calculation of looks; a 7 stooping for a 5.

It's a premeditated recitation of the proper lines and soft touches.

It's not a relationship, it's a transaction.

In our pursuit of satisfaction, we have reduced the value of our own human bodies. We have all but demolished the value of other peoples' bodies by treating them as some sort of 'disposable trophy.'

It may lead somewhere, it may not. Either way, it feels good.

Jesus gave ultimate value to the human body when He entered into one. He shows us that ours are not disposable pieces of flesh meant to be thrown around from person to person.

He also calls to us, promising deep intimacy and ultimate satisfaction. When we stop trying to fill that void in our hearts by sleeping with strangers every weekend and focus on filling it with the One who invented intimacy, we will find peace.

This post is not to condemn people who have immersed themselves in this culture. Not at all. It is an invitation to a richer and more substantial view of sex. It is an invitation to be cleaned and made whole by Him who gives us life and life to the fullest.[10]

God invented sex as a means of incredible pleasure, connection, and intimacy with a loved one. My friend was right when he said sex is both spiritual and intimate, and that's exactly why I want to share it with *only* one person. I want to grow old with my wife, knowing her body as well as I know my own, and vice versa. There is an immense beauty to chastity that many people in our society are missing out on. You can't grow old with *all* the girls in the club.

Don't settle for being a disposable trophy on the mantle of a stranger's bed.

Join me in seeing through our hookup culture for the hollow lie it is. It's not satisfying and hurts far more often than it heals.

HOW WOULD YOU LIVE IF YOU KNEW YOU'D BE ACCEPTED UNCONDITIONALLY?

are you tired of living how you think other people think of you?

Two weeks ago I moved into a house with four other guys. At the time, I only knew one of them but as a consequence of the move, I inherited their web of friends as well. I did not realize how well connected the house is to their own little bustling community, so that has been one of the best surprises of this season.

In the past two weeks of getting to know my roommates and their friends, I have been overwhelmed by a sense of grace and acceptance. Everyone shares their food and possessions, they are quick to encourage and slow to criticize. And each person, as a result, receives the liberty to be unapologetically themselves.

For example, I was talking to one of my roommates a few days ago. He is a construction worker who comes home every day covered in dust, paint and

---

[10] 1 Corinthians 6:11; John 10:10

other construction debris. He has a big beard, loves hiking, climbing, and any other form of being in the mountains.

One of the first nights I was in the house, he and I were having a late-night kitchen talk and he began telling me about his night out dancing. It wasn't *that* unusual, I thought, for a guy like him to go out swing dancing.

But then he told me he goes out about four times a week to dance.

I stared at his face, trying to read if he was serious or pulling my leg.

Then he said, "Yah, no kidding. I would consider dancing one of my passions!" His face spread into a wide, sincere smile. Then he did a hop step and turned to descend to his basement bedroom.

The great thing is, everyone here is like that. They don't fit into one specific category, and I guess the more you think about it, no one does. The difference is, many of us are scared to live out our full *self*-ness in front of the world. I began to form this into words tonight as I soaked in the hot tub after a workout.

It came to me as a simple question which I've been gnawing on for about an hour now:

> *If you knew you'd be accepted unconditionally, how would you live? Would you act differently?*

I've been bouncing this question off myself and realizing that a fear of rejection has often fueled much of how I act with others, both friends and strangers. At a party, if a favorite song of mine came across the speakers, the little inner Ethan would be dying to break into a foolish jig, but the image-conscious defense mechanisms prevented it.

Because what if I was *too* goofy?

Because what if these people don't like people who dance goofy?

(After years of experimenting, the results prove that everyone likes people who dance goofy.)

I often feel like I'm a little man inside a big mechanical body and I'm always rushing around pulling the levers and oiling the pipes to make sure everything is running smoothly, rather than just inhabiting my own body comfortably and relaxing into my own personality. After all, wouldn't people rather hang out with a human being than a mechanical, but impressive, puppet?

I can only speak for myself, but I'm sure many of us construct these ideas of expectations *others* have for how *we* should act and behave around them. We should conform to the expectations *they* have laid out for us...which we made up in our own minds.

In reality, most of us are happy to be with our friends and family without expectations for how they should act. So why do we construct false ones for ourselves in the minds of others? See how backward that is?

Years ago, my friend Tony laid it out like this. He said, "There are essentially two types of people in the world. The first walks into a room of people and thinks, 'I haven't done anything to offend these people, so why wouldn't they like me?' The second type walks in and thinks, 'I haven't done anything to prove myself to these people, so why would they accept me?'"

If you're anything like me, the second person describes you but you wish you were the first. I'd love to walk into a room of unfamiliar faces and not feel pressure to impress them or woo them into liking me; I'd like to just be myself.

This bears repeating again: The only one with that pressure and those expectations in their minds for you is *you*. In other words, assuming you're out of Middle School, you can genuinely be yourself in the midst of others and not have to worry about being judged or rejected.

(I'm speaking generally here. If your natural tendency is to act out in a violent rage, or tickle strangers with emu feathers, perhaps work on those things first...)

So I bring myself back to this question for myself: How would I act differently in the absence of that fear? I don't know yet, but I intend to work toward it and find out.

I can tell you two things for sure though:

1. Most people will like you *more* the *less* you try to impress them. They are probably not scheming to make a fool out of you or holding expectations for you to meet. The truth is, most people like folks who are just themselves, no pretense or image polishing.

2. God accepted you before you were born and He is most pleased when you live as who He made you to be. He doesn't see someone rich, or funny, or intelligent, or whatever factors you use to disguise yourself. He just likes you as you are, so live that out. Be content in that. Adopt the mentality of a child who loves to be with their parents, not because they have impressed their parents first, but because they are loved first and act second. Remember that Jesus died for you before you even took your first breath.

A month before he died, Eugene Peterson was interviewed and asked what he thought about his life. He thought for a moment and part of his reply was, "I'm happy that I just got to be Eugene. I never felt pressure to be anyone else, I was just happy to be Eugene."

Wouldn't you love to reach the end of your life and be able to look back and say the same thing? Learning to undo years of social pressure takes time and effort, but I think it's worthwhile. I think it will be worth it in the end the more we can live as if we are already accepted and act secondarily.

So, how would *you* act if you knew you'd be accepted unconditionally?

Would your life change if you really believed that?

HOW TO FEEL

thriving in the land of death

A MAD HOPE
life is a collection of feeling woozy in various locations.

"I've come to realize my life is a collection of me feeling woozy in various locations," I told my roommate as we walked into our friend's coffee shop downtown, and it's true. You ever have days—or strings of days—from which it seems like you'll soon wake up and return to reality?

I think pornography has drowned much of my life in a whirlpool of illusion and fantasy. Walking away from it has been very much a return to contact with reality. No longer do I hover above my life like a spectral observer, but I have returned to the full and rich experience of life, and life to the fullest, as Jesus promised us.

Life to the fullest does not subsist of some austral experience of floating. We do not float on like the musings of Modest Mouse, nor do we depart and drift away from reality like some dust in the wind.

In the summer of 2016, my favorite book ever became *The Great Divorce* by C.S. Lewis. He writes about humans in hell who are clinging to things that don't matter in the end. They hold onto things which are nothing more than vacuous mist, and when the lights come on, they are simply closing empty fists. One of the sages in the book says,

> "Hell is a state of mind – ye never said a truer word. And every state of mind, left to itself, every shutting up of the creature within the dungeon of its own mind – is, in the end, Hell. But Heaven is not a state of mind. Heaven is reality itself. All that is fully real is Heavenly. For all that can be shaken will be shaken and only the unshakeable remains."[1]

No book has more thoroughly rocked me to my bones and left my skin holding on for dear life. No book has so vigorously flipped me upside down and changed the perspective from which I see life, death, and the eternal value of all things.

---

[1] C. S. Lewis, *The Great Divorce*

Do I cling to the real; the things that last, and the imperishable? Or am I merely running after shadows and fog?

I think about this as I sit in this coffee shop. I'm feeling woozier than normal today (a state in which I should probably not be publishing any sort of writing but here we are...) and my removal from reality is in full effect. It may be my roommate's haphazard driving, or the incredible amount of caffeine I've ingested today.

Sometimes, as a single man passing the midpoint of his twenties, this theoretical arrangement of heaven and hell doesn't help when all I really want is a girl with two hands for holding and at least one functioning ear to hear my rambling thoughts.

The tangibility of heaven doesn't bring much comfort to those nights where I'm so lonely there is a physical ache and I lie in bed starved for human touch. Sometimes our mad clinging to hope in the man of Jesus Christ doesn't *feel* very helpful. I think this is why so many people my age are leaving the church.

We are very, very impatient.

Sometimes as we stumble through our daily routines and forget to emerge from our shells of anxiety and fear, we miss the very *real* things passing us by in this temporal world.

This life only happens once so make sure your eyes are open.

It's hard to look for reality and permanence in a world where time exists. Today has pretty much happened, and as I sit on this half of it, do I look back on it with joy and satisfaction? A triumphant cry of *"tetelestai! It is finished!"*? Or do I look back on another wasted day which could have been better spent attaching myself to things and people which will last forever?

Possibly the biggest danger of a pornography addiction is the fact that it will attach you to things which will blow away. Do you want to be real? When the world is shaken and only the unshakable remains, do you want to be among the ranks of the remaining, or do you want to blow away along with the worthless things you've attached yourself to?

Priority lists matter.

The higher something is on your priority list, the more it orders the rest of your life. It preoccupies your mind and runs through your thoughts like a fawn through a wooded glen.

One of the best way to examine our own priorities is to observe how we spend our time. The other day I was in a different coffee shop and overheard a conversation between two ladies. I didn't hear the context, but what I did hear punched me in the n@rds. One of them said,

> "You're supposed to make a list of all of your values and how you think people should live. Then, over about a week, you keep track of what you do every day and see how those activities line up with your self-professed values."

This is exactly what Paul is talking about in Romans 3. Everyone is a hypocrite. Therefore, everyone is "a law unto themselves." I think holiness is less about following a certain set of rules and laws, and more about becoming less of a hypocrite (Maybe? Remember...I'm feeling pretty woozy today).

I have a lot of feelings inside me today; not so many thoughts. Sometimes it's hard to filter feelings through the thin sheet of language and present them to another, but I guess this is today's attempt. In summary:

Love God. Love others.

And pray that today's woozy feelings are reduced to a minimum.

MORE THAN IMMORTAL
yesterday I was skipping cracks on the sidewalk; tomorrow I'll be dust.

Today I watched a little boy walk down the sidewalk after timidly crossing the street. He wore snow boots which looked three sizes too big for him and his little winter coat (also too big) slid down his shoulders.

He wasn't in a hurry to get home (or wherever he was going), but seemed to stop and look at every crack in the sidewalk as he went, stepping on some and skipping over others. I drove by slowly, watching and wishing I was as not-in-a-rush as he was. I wished I could have not only been as carefree but as furiously curious as he.

Yesterday I was this boy on the path, reciting sidewalk superstition and imagining aliens in the sewers; tomorrow I will be dust.

Life is both very short and very long. A lot has happened in my 26.5 years on this planet, and simultaneously, not much has happened, as there are presently 7 billion human experiences of this planet happening right now. I've experienced the world temporally (within the confines of time, as opposed to atemporally: outside of time, as some posit God as being) and have been pretty grateful for it.

Today I was thinking about Jesus and the Bible and eternal life.

I was thinking about the film *A Ghost Story* in which the main character's ghostly life is never ending, though it is not enriched. He passes endlessly through time, though in his passage there is neither joy nor purpose, identity or community. It is lonely and indefinite.

I was thinking about how Jesus promises that those who love Him will not experience death nor will they be cut off from Him. Those who love Him will have eternal life, as promised in John 3:16.

But it's not merely *eternal* life.

It's not simply immortality Christ has promised us—it is far more than that.

If all Christ did was prolong the lives we are currently living, we would have little hope for anything being *better* in the next life. We don't merely get an extension of the lives we currently possess, but LIFE!

We don't have to wait until we die to experience what Christ has promised us. It means that we gain glimpses of freedom and purpose *now*. You've been living life through the fog of pornography/drugs/alcohol, and Christ's gospel for you is not *Just wait till you die, then you can be in heaven.*

No, life with Christ begins far sooner than that.

Like, right now.

You don't need to wait till death to see the fruition of Christ's promises coming true: His presence and peace is here and now.

I think the key here is understanding life. Jesus doesn't say that we will *survive* eternally, or that we will simply *exist* without end. We have *LIFE!*

Elsewhere, He promised that we will have "life, and life to the fullest." Even in my best moments of this life, I would be cautious to say that I had 'life and life to the fullest.' Sure, I have had great moments, but every one has ended.

Every moment of 'life to the fullest' has been bookended by pain, sorrow, rejection and disappointment. Every rollercoaster dips and rises. Every height of ecstasy eventually plummets.

But this is what Jesus is saying: That in our everlasting life with Him, it will not be a dry spell of immortality. Our lives after this one will be perpetual livelihood and joy, as unknown to any human this side of the kingdom, except it will not end. Our hope is not in a fleeting glimpse of satisfaction, nor is it in a boring extension of the lives we currently tumble through.

I remember being in college and going to swing dance nights at the University of Chicago in buildings that looked like they belonged in *Harry Potter.* I remember standing on the balcony breathing in the crisp winter air with my sweetheart, dreaming about what life would be like when I finally *arrived.*

On my more melancholy days, I wonder if those dreams are the closest I'll ever be to experiencing real life. On my hopeful days, I realize that the finish line isn't going to appear in this life, so that I may cross it. The finish line is at the tail end of this life like a rattle on a snake. It follows her from behind, haunting the path of the being, but rarely in her thoughts.

I think heaven is what I dreamed of standing on that ancient balcony while the big band swing played nearby in the warm indoors. I think heaven is what we catch glimpses of in the poems we read: Not the boring ones which lose our train of thought halfway through, but the ones which suck us in and uppercut us in the jaw. Or the stomach. It's the lively sort of life pointed to in Anis Mojgani's poem *Sock Hop,* or in the wakefulness Annie Dillard seems to capture in every word she's ever freaking written.

I've said it before, but time is the means by which we experience beauty. Without time, your favorite song is merely a note held for eternity. Without time, there is no decay in the fabric of the universe and there is no vineyard fermentation.

Without time we would never die, nor would we ever be fully alive.

So don't pray to be stuck. Do not fear your death, but see it as a starting line.

In summation, two mistakes we make about the life after this: That it will be a mere continuation of the tedious, painful experience through which you are passing now; or that it will not really be *everlasting.* It seems too good to be true, but I think this is what Christ has promised us.

Most of all, this life we are promised is centered around the person of Christ Himself, for He is the source of healing. He is the source of joy, of peace, and of hope. He is the reason we have this mad hope of something better and more solid than anything we could experience here.

Tomorrow you will be dust.

Today, Christ says, come to Me and taste life
and life to the fullest
and life everlasting.

DEAR FRIEND, VOLUME 1

I still love you passionately...

The other day I rediscovered the old shoebox in my childhood bedroom crammed full of ancient letters. These letters range from professions of love to friendly notes passed in the hallway. I spent hours upon hours reading through all of them and gathering the best passages from them because they were far too good to keep to myself. They are in no order and from dozens of different people from the past decade. There is no real purpose to these posts, save their aesthetic and poetic value, so without further ado, enjoy!

Every night when I close my eyes it is your face I see and every morning when I wake up, before I open my eyes, I see your face. (Was that a run-on? I don't care. I like you too much.) My arms ache to be wrapped up around you and my hands are lonely. My eyes long to see you and my mouth greatly desires to speak with you. My ears are going deaf because they only want to hear your voice.

I became as offensive as all the things that broke my heart or confused me. My only coping mechanism was vulgarity, and I don't mean dropping frequent F-bombs, I mean my worldview, my laughter, and my crass personality became vulgar. If you are *bad,* the bad things don't hurt.
Does that make sense?
I've had a bit of wine.

I still love you passionately. Why don't we leave for a trip to Paris tomorrow and not just Paris, but everywhere.

Wherever you go there you are, and I met a man who's broken like me and fun like me and my appetite for tragedy got the better of me again.

I like all the little names you call me, like this morning you called me Peachums. You always use them at the perfect times too. Today I was upset about something and you said something in response, but you threw Darling in there and I could feel my entire body relax.

I'm doing pretty good, it's not as bad I thought a rehab would be. Most of the people are in here for heroin, meth, benzos, and pain pills. I kinda feel like I'm in here for nothing, but I know that's not true.

You said in your letter that we've gotten to know each other and then grown together. It's like if you plant trees near each other, their roots grow together and sometimes the trunks become one and it is like one tree instead of two.

Today's the kind of day where I wish you could come pick me up and we could listen to sad music and you could laugh at me cry my heart out. This life sure is giving me a run for my money. Luckily, we serve a big God.

It's 2:19am EST. I'm beat. Thank you for helping me unwind. Even though you won't get this for days. Thank you for being there. I wish you were here so that I would have somebody to just BE with. Somebody to listen to the sounds of the earth with and to watch the beauty of each other and all that is around us. That not to say that I'm beautiful, but that I find our friendship beautiful.

We are already making it where others have failed. We have bashed the wall of outside beauty. We have stripped each other to nothing and have found that it is better than anything else.

The best thing about writing to you is that all you can see are my words. There's a quaint comfort in the anonymity of it all. All you can see are my thoughts, my emotions. I think I always say more than I should when I write, but it's how I truly feel I suppose.

I love you too much for this to end.

Man, I would be really bad at writing a true love letter. I wouldn't know what to say. "Um. I think you have a nice smile and you make me laugh so my heart is ever indebted to you." LAME.

I read this book over the summer and the main character was a girl and her older brother went away to school. She wrote him a letter and all that was on it was 'I love you and I miss you.' Sometimes that's all I want to write to you. I love you. I miss you. I love you. I miss you......

I feel like I can't win. My life is a vicious cycle of letdowns and failures and pain. I'm in the midst of the wilderness in its truest form and I'm so tired.

This is a dangerous cliff we are standing on and we are young and if we take a wrong step it could come crashing down and we will tumble into the darkness. Right now I don't care. I don't see the black abyss below us and I don't really care about the danger.

I could go on for hours about how wonderful of a person you are and how thankful I am to have you in my life, but I really have to poop.

DECEMBER 27, 2016

look, I made something that will be read when I'm gone...

I remember the late nights at Moody heading North a mile to the 24-hour Starbucks. The train ride would usually take as long as walking because the Brown Line ran so infrequently late at night unless you caught it at just the right time. I remember Lila Carvell and I making the trek more times than I can count, though it was probably fewer than my brain conceives, because the mind has a way of painting infinite layers over a few small events, making the quality compensate for the quantity.

The mile went fast or slow, depending on the night. Perhaps the distance itself was fluid. Perhaps it depended on the company I walked with. Lila made all time fly by. I remember many days with her, wasting time in coffee shops, supposedly doing schoolwork but talking endlessly instead. I don't know why a beautiful, creative, and curious mind like her put up with me, always talking about myself, where she was always, *always* interested in others.

It's hard to find anyone to match her level of energy, creativity, and most of all, her curiosity. I think the thing I miss about her the most was her curiosity. Hanging out with curious people makes the world burst into fitful life, endlessly entertaining and always unraveling new mysteries.

To those who have the world figured out, the world is bland, redundant, and tiresome, as if you're watching a film you've seen a dozen times and you're just waiting for it to be over. But to the curious, it's exciting. You're turning a page and you have no clue what the next one contains, what you'll learn from it or experience on its canvas.

Lila was curious about me. She wanted to read what I wrote—my stories and poems—and I was excited to share them with her. Just like tonight, as I write these things down in my favorite late-night coffee shop in Denver, I'm thirsty for someone to pick up this page and pore over these words with the same intense curiosity.

Tonight I just wanted to write something. Something that may or may not be read by anyone else, but the fact that I created it stands. So I'm pulling from the ever-present alphabet and arranging these letters for you, whoever and wherever you are.

Perhaps all creativity is a quest to not be forgotten when we're gone. To say, *Look, I made something that will be read when I'm gone. Look, I'm not really gone.*

Perhaps all creativity is a battle for immortality.

The thing I realized about my blog posts as of late is that they have become far too formulaic. I get an idea and lay it out in the same pattern and the same level of intensity—that of a baby canary.

But tonight, I'm creating a new formula. It's a free-form formula, like that category of math that uses letters instead of numbers. It's a formula that doesn't look like math because really it's not, and this post is more of me sitting here and slicing my stomach so my innards can pour out before you onto this page. Or screen.

There is another point I remember in Chicago.

There were times in my life when I would look at actresses like Emma Watson and wonder if it were possible for me to find someone as beautiful as her. But then one night, when I watched the movie *Noah* seated beside Lila, I saw Emma Watson on the screen and thought *meh*. Because I looked next to me and suddenly saw someone so much more interesting, so much more curious, so much more beautiful than any distant A-lister on a screen.

What can a 2-dimensional character offer me that's better than a 4-dimensional relationship with another human being? How much more tangible is the girl sitting next to me in seat H6? Look at the way I can ruin her night with one word, or make her feel like a billion bucks with a different one! Look at how I could reach out and touch her nose if I wanted.

I feel like in some ways, I have retreated back to that place of longing for distant two-dimensional actresses and models because there is a hunger and thirst for artificial beauty. Because I haven't been touched in a while.

Look at the way a man can touch a tree, a brick, or a computer and feel nothing. Look at how a woman touches her light switch, her carpet, and her tabletop, and feels no attachment.

But watch the two of them touch.

Watch her calf touch his under the table of a crowded restaurant and the entire night shifts. If it's the first touch of a relationship, it's a rush, like cracking open the lid of a chest discovered underground. If it's a familiar touch, there is comfort in it, like the smell of your house when you return for Christmas.

There is value in skin touching skin. Solomon wrote in Ecclesiastes that a man who lies alone will grow cold, but two who lie together remain warm.[2] Skin is unlike any other surface. It's dynamic and raw. It flinches and it slides over bones. It bends and it's warm. It smells both good and bad and in many ways, the feeling of it is what all of us are after. Touch from fathers who didn't hold us when we were younger or mothers who misused their skin against ours. I don't know what this is like, but I know something of the deprivation of touch. Of wandering the world like a passing thunderstorm; it's looked at and talked about, but never really touched.

Skin is a nice thing.

I'm sitting in this coffee shop watching a girl run her boot along her lover's leg. Even through shoes and jeans, it seems like human touch is enough to melt men made of even the strongest of materials.

I don't know why I sat down and wrote this today, nor did I know where it was going when I began. It feels like the night I sat on top of a skyscraper drinking other people's leftover wine and writing poetry with Lila. She inspired things in me I haven't felt in a while but hope to again. Sometimes I wonder if maturity is some kind of letting go of these passionate feelings and settling down into routine and mundanity.

I hope not.

---

[2] Ecclesiastes 4:11

I hope God was more creative than that when he crafted men and women in His own image. I imagine that the Creator is exactly that: Creative. And therefore I must conclude that, if we are made in His image, we are meant to have nights like these. Nights wondering about the world and where the next turning of the page will take us. Of what we will learn and who we will be when the page turns again.

There's no way to know; the only possibility is to fill up the page I'm on with the best possible combinations of words. So here it is: A post I've created for no other reason but to leave something here, like a footprint which lasts longer than I will, but ultimately, as language and syntax march on and are forgotten, will blow away with the eroding of the world.

It was fun while it lasted and I enjoyed this particular string of metaphors.

Hope you did too.

EXPERIMENTS IN GLORY

your body was in my arms but you were not.

Forget these temporary pleasures.

Forget the lover's kiss and the gentle pressure of her hand against my arm. Forget the parties, the clothes, and the electrical circuiting in the palms of our hands keeping us alive. Forget the blanket we lay on in that field that cloudy midnight. Culver City was electric. Take me back there and I would spend endless days just dwelling in that feeling.

That emotion.

It's the free fall where your organs elevate within your ribcage, erasing all other places and times, presenting you with only the very raw Here and Now.

I would trade all that for a taste of glory.

I'm after something more intense than a free fall and more intimate than a simple touch. After all, how much nearer can one draw to another than to simply reach out and touch them?

The tragedy of our fallen, time-bound flesh is that every touch ends. Each one exists only a fleeting matter of moments before the sun comes up, the lights come on, and the magic escapes. I think every close call I've ever had with glory ended before it could climax. The curtain falls and the actors retreat to the greenroom to rub the stage makeup from their faces.

I touched you in Escondido. I kissed you on the mouth. I pushed the hair from your neck and held you in the dark. But like each close encounter with the infinite, you grew tired and drifted away from me.

Your body was in my arms but you were not.

The mystics in their quiet rooms speak of a glory that visits them in their shiny silence. Sometimes I feel it in the rain. Foreign monks build temples from blood money then reach for glory through the emptying of their minds. Sometimes I've felt it on the road—those silent drives in the dark as the white stripes slip rhythmically beneath the car.

I've never been able to wrap my mind around a God big enough to make All This, so I made idols of women instead. At least I can wrap my arms around them. At least I can hold them for a little while (Though I always wish it were a little while longer).

All my life I've been looking for glory.

Hunting it, really.

I remember that rainy day on Cape Cod when I faced You in the forest. We were dressed like Adam and splashing through the mud. The Glory was so near, I thought the next raindrop to slap my skin might finally burst the bubble once and for all.

My Chicago boys and I ran to Lake Michigan because the sky was pouring warm rain. We dove in and listened to the world; silent, save the impact of the drops on the water's surface. Those gentle waves lapped at our chests in the windless afternoon. I was convinced the glory was waiting for us in the mist just a little further out on the water.

But once again, the clouds departed and the rain stopped. The puddles evaporated and we toweled off.

We were so close.

I missed glory when I sat on the bare back of an elephant while we paraded through a Thai jungle. And I missed it again when I played soccer with the Nigerian kids—But I was close! The way you can taste the meal your mother is cooking just by inhaling its scent.

I think that's the best this world can be—close.

I think we can only catch a hint of its flavor. Glory eludes us like that phantom in the attic—always calling out our name, then vanishing when we get too close.

The house lights come on, the actors bow then retreat to the greenroom to hang their costumes on the rack.

All this tells me is that glory is somewhere, but it's always somewhere else. Somewhere we can't touch in this life, but we can sniff it out. C.S. Lewis said that we can't attain it on this planet, so we were probably made for another one.[3] This world is not all there is.

It tells me I have a home I haven't seen yet, but my name is written on the door of my room.

I've come close to glory several times, but have yet to hold it without it wriggling from my fingers. I've come close, and will arrive there soon.

The Lord is glorious and I draw near to Him. I've chased Him through the trees and sat with Him in silence. I'm longing for glory so I'm binding myself to Him.

After all…He's the best chance I've got.

---

[3] C.S. Lewis, *The Weight of Glory and Other Addresses*

DANDELION KYLE
learning about God from a hippie

Kaylie and I hopped onto the Blue Line train and quickly sat down across from the door. Immediately I nudged Kaylie and nodded to the man beside her. He had a long red beard and multiple colored bandanas wrapped around his neck. He wore a renaissance-style vest beneath a brightly colored 80's wind breaker, and a straw hat rested gently on his head. He had bags with him like he was going somewhere.

He seemed to be going in and out of consciousness. Or a trance.

When he noticed us looking at him, he granted us a big grin and nodded back at us. We began talking, and he told us he was in a psychedelic folk band called Bowl of Dust, and that he was heading to Kansas City. He told us his name was Dandelion, but he sometimes goes by Kyle.

Throughout our conversation, whenever a lull in conversation arose, Kyle would return to his meditative trance. A large smile would consume his face, his left hand would be elevated openly as if gently asking for nickels, and his eyes would close.

I thought about what a beautiful image this was to us believers. I don't know exactly what Dandelion was doing, but he inspired me to worship more. He seemed to be aware of the constant presence of…something… and it was awesome. Whenever we spoke to him, he would graciously open his eyes, smile at us again, and continue the conversation. It was as if he were recharging, or re-finding his center whenever given the chance, and those brief moments filled him with more joy, peace and rest.

I asked myself why I am not more like Dandelion. How come I am not constantly seeking to be in God's presence? How much more joy and peace could we bring to our days, and to those around us, if we were ever aware of our Lord's perpetual presence!

I asked him if he ever goes to church. He said yes, but he doesn't totally agree with Christianity's theology. He subscribed to "a more feminine and caring aspect of the divine."

As we walked out of the train and toward the stairs, I exclaimed my desire to be like Dandelion Kyle. I told Kaylie that we should be constantly retreating to the awesome presence of God, and carrying it with us everywhere. How many times in scripture are we told to pray without ceasing? Or to meditate on the Law day and night? And yet so often, we are put to shame by the friendly feminine diviner. Whatever spirit he is carrying with him is obviously no match for Yahweh, our God, but are we constantly aware of His presence in our lives? I know I am not.

Spending time in His presence, whether we are in silence at home, or working, or on the train, or eating brunch, is crucial. It brings joy. It removes burdens and breaks chains. It is one of the most overlooked aspects of American Christianity.

My friend Andrew has recently been telling me about his hatred of the dichotomy between "sacred time" and "other time." He says that, as Christians, we should never use a phrase like, "Ok, I'm done eating. Let's go worship." Andrew gets heated as he exclaims that eating IS worship! And every single thing we do can be worship. But as Americans, we have often stripped down the term 'worship' to meaning 'those three songs we sing before the pastor gives his message.'

It is so much more. It is constant.

It is marveling at the greatness of God in every single aspect of our lives, down to the smallest quark. We should enjoy God while we enjoy a great burger, a great song, or a swim in the lake.

Let's be more like Dandelion, and constantly tune in to the presence of the Lord, every chance we get.

Let's live as if God really were omnipresent.

DREAM SMALLER.

<u>I gained some much-needed perspective from a third-world country.</u>

There was an economic parable I once heard about a businessman who ended up on a small tropical island. After several weeks on the island, he began talking to one of the locals.

"Hey, I see that every day, you wake up early, go fishing, come back and cook it with your family," he said to the man. "Then you relax on the beach most of the afternoon, eat more food, and hang out with your community into the night."

The local listened intently as the businessman continued.

"You seem to know these waters well enough, and I think you could be doing more. You could hire a whole fleet of boats, bringing in exponentially more fish than you are now! Your profits would be huge! You could retire young!"

The local man paused and thought for a moment. He then asked the businessman, "So what would I do when I retired?" There was a pause for a moment and he continued. "I feel like when I retired, I would wake up, go fishing with my friends, and spend the rest of the day on the beach with my community...Just like I do now"

This parable provides a tangible insight into something I've been thinking through lately, and have discussed with some friends. As a westerner living in Guatemala—a developing country—I have gained some much-needed perspective.

One thing I've noticed is the massive difference in goals and aspirations here. For instance, there are countless people here whose family runs a small shop or business of some sort. For the sake of illustration, we will say their parents make tortillas all day. These parents have children who, when they grow up, will likely inherit the tortilla-making business, as will their children and so on.

My initial reaction to these people's lives was pity. I felt bad that I was offered so many options in my life, while they seemed somewhat limited in their scope. I could go to school and be a lawyer or doctor! I could become a YouTube star and be followed by the masses, or maybe go back to seminary and found my own church! The possibilities are virtually endless.

But after being here a few months, my perspective has shifted. On the one hand, is it sad if someone wants to change their current situation, but does not have the resources to rise above their current position? Of course! However, what about people who don't even know these possibilities exist?

There is probably a fancy term for this, but I'm coining it as The Low-Ceiling Paradox. It looks like this: As a westerner, I have a higher 'ceiling' of potential than most people in the third world. I have health, education, disposable income, et al. The tortilla-maker's son has a much lower 'ceiling' as he doesn't have as much (if any) education, his health is generally poorer and his network and vocational potential is more limited.

Now, you would be more tempted to feel bad for him, right? If you're like me, you may think Aw, poor guy! We should push him into a higher-ceilinged world so he can be happy!

What I realized recently is that people with lower ceilings are more prone to be happy.

Unlike me, the tortilla maker has realized his dream. He gets to do the work he knows and doesn't long for all the crazy things advertising has programmed me to want. For instance, if I constantly stream the videos of YouTubers with millions of followers, I will never be happy until I have caught up to them (and even then, probably not). I will always envy best-selling authors until I am one. Et cetera. Insert your own internet-induced desires.

Perhaps America's cultural exports of raised blood pressure and an overwhelming sense of competition don't actually lead to happiness. Maybe productivity and notoriety are not keys to the door of satisfaction.

I've been trying to convince myself that this is true, or at least, that I could stand to take a few steps in that direction for the sake of balance and internal peace.

Since moving here and working a full-time job, I have seen productivity as a key to unlocking meaning and purpose. So if work hours and output are what give meaning to our lives, what does that say when our output is lower? What about when we get sick for a week and can't meet our normal quotient? Accordingly, it would mean that we become less valuable and have no purpose during that week.

That simply can't be true.

Whenever I get too caught up in work and productivity, it's easy to forget my own inherent value and purpose, grafted into me by the Creator of the universe. Yes, He made us to work and be productive in all we do, but that work was never designated to be the thing which gives us our worth.

Perhaps pulling in the reins on our crazy dreams or expectations can help us return to peace and clarity in our lives.

Maybe it's okay to take a day off.

I find myself trapped in a tension of wanting to constantly be productive, but also to be able to be still and meditate and be in the presence of God without having to work for it. It's important to remember that that time is not wasted. Minutes spent in stillness and solitude are not squandered minutes.

Maybe those of us living in wanton excess can learn a thing or two from those born with less. Maybe we can learn that happiness is less about material or opportunistic benefits and more about gratitude and presence.

Maybe it's okay to just sit still for a minute, looking at the day. And maybe God will meet us there as well, once we stop trying to impress Him and simply enjoy His world.

DON'T PLAN YOUR LIFE
something I wish I'd read before my 20's.

This morning I woke up with my toe in a dog's mouth.

He's a mastiff the size of a horse with a head bigger than a basketball which constantly spews drool from an endless reservoir of slime. After chopping my toes off I realized that, in no way was this what I had planned to be doing with my life at the ripe old age of 28, but here I was, dogsitting for a family from church while they're out of town.

That's an odd way to say that I'm really glad my life has gone the way it has and I cannot bring myself to understand 'planners.' I've never been the type to set goals or to attempt to gaze into my own deep future, deliberating where I'll be in 5, 10, or 60 years. It's easier to look back on where I've been and marvel at the weird and wild doors which have opened without my trying. When I was fresh out of high school, did I think that I'd be speaking at a camp in Scotland or teaching history to Middle schoolers in Guatemala? Of course not, yet I was doing both of those things this year.

I don't want to rant against people whose natural tendency is to make plans and stick to them; those people become great dentists, lawyers and pilots, which the world needs. However, I've often felt ostracized—whether overtly or covertly—for not having a 'plan.'

There are the Leslie Knope types who can see down their paths all the way to the grave and know exactly where they're going and how they're going to get there. It's easy to look at them and feel inferior in some way, like they're a better class of person and have a better life. Just because their 401k may be a bit more swollen than yours.

Or because they know what a 401k is.

We often feel pressure from our parents, teachers, counselors, or our competitive peers to map out our future to a tee and stick to it. Some of us, however, have dimmer torches which only let us see a few footsteps up the path.

And maybe that's not such a bad thing.

For example, as a non-planning person, look at my life and where my non-planning has brought me. It took me 6 years to get a bachelor's degree but that's because I kept putting school on pause to hop to other countries and work with different organizations. I hit all 6 inhabited continents before I was 21 and (I like to think) understood the world more richly because of it. I am writing my fifth book—one of the others was a #1 best-seller. I was homeless several times, both intentionally and accidentally, and even co-founded an organization in Nigeria during one of those periods.

I have worked somewhere in the ballpark of 40 jobs, not because I can't keep them, but because I kept moving, or wanting to try something new. Because of that, I can talk to a barista about pouring perfect latte rosettas; a rock climber about which belay device to use, or a pastor about some theological issues he's walking through.

Now returning to complete my Master's Degree, I'll enter my 30's just as 'equipped' as my peers who took the traditional route, but with vastly different experiences. I don't want to say one is better or worse—I'll let you decide—but I could not be happier, now on this side of my 20's and looking back on them.

I don't write all this to brag, but to say that if even a meandering schlub like me can get stuff done, you can too. I never set out to do any of those things, yet they happened nonetheless. The world spins madly onward and the future comes at you whether you've planned for it or not, so like countless other pieces of energetic writing out there, I want to encourage you to make the most of it; *carpe diem,* seize the day.

Are you like me? Do you swell with angst every time someone asks you what your five year plan is, as if it would actually happen anyway? I write this in the hopes of quelling your fears about the future. Maybe you're just starting your 20's as I near the end of mine, and you have no idea what awaits you beyond graduation. Maybe you don't even know what to study.

Here are a few things I would think through as you approach that precipice.

'Not planning' is not the same as 'not working.'

None of this is meant to encourage you to sit around in hopes wild things happen to you while you're Netflixing from your couch. They won't. Life happens when you're out and about and meeting people and saying yes to things. One of my most common prayers has not necessarily been foresight or complete knowledge of the future, but simply for God to open the right doors and close the wrong ones.

There have been numerous times I thought I had a great job lead, or a cool opportunity, just to have the door slam shut in front of me. I often responded with anger, but as time went on, I've realized that this is just one of the ways God communicates with us: He leads us in the right directions and away from the wrong ones. It probably means that if that job in NYC *had* worked out, my life would have exploded, so it was for my own good that it didn't!

Many of the best things that have happened to me dropped right into my lap, like my job in Guatemala, and my job as a paddleboard instructor on Cape Cod. (Don't say yes to everything though—I was also offered a hefty wad of cash by Playgirl to do a photoshoot, but turned them down for obvious reasons.)

Pray and pray a lot.

Pray for wisdom and discernment.

James 1:5 tells us that when we ask for wisdom, God does not find fault but gives it generously. I think the reason for this is because wisdom is the one thing He could give to everyone who wants it and the world would get better as a result.

Experiment with things, for two reasons:

The only way to know if you'll like accounting is to go and do it for a while. How will you know if underwater welding is your thing? Become an apprentice and do it for a year. Maybe you like the romantic idea of being a barista, but after being yelled at by angry customers for a month, you find it's not quite the right fit. Better to find that out about something before studying it for 4+ years.

The other reason is to see if you're good at it. Maybe you really like photography, but after a bit of exposure (get it?) you find that you just don't have the eye to do it professionally. This takes humility; you'll need people who can tell you that it's not a good fit for you, and hopefully these same people will also tell you what they think you are good at.

For example, I have worked construction jobs in 3 cities, and all 3 of my bosses basically told me it's not my thing, some more kindly than others. On the other hand, I have been speaking and writing for a while and not only do I love to do it, but I get told that I'm pretty good!

I think our 20's are for this very purpose: To experiment and discover. I don't think it's helpful to pressure others (or ourselves) to have all 80 of our years mapped out by graduation day. I do think it's helpful to encourage bravery,
risk,
hard work,
hard prayer,
and humility

and everything will work itself out, even without a plan.

"CARPE DIEM"
you won't be around much longer...60 years max till you're worm food.

Last night I watched *The Dead Poet's Society*, and two immortal lines stood out to me:

"We're all just worm food, lads."

and,

"Medicine, law, business, engineering, these are noble pursuits and necessary to sustain life…But poetry, beauty, romance, love, these are what we stay alive *for*."

It's one of those films that really just pumps you up. It makes you long for life. It makes you long to not merely BE alive, but to FEEL alive. The thing about emotional rides like these is, they often lead to immense excitement and passion, but it's undirected. What does it MEAN to be alive? How exactly do you write a prescription for all of mankind for One Daily Dose of Passionate Life?

The *Joie de vivre?*

The *Carpe diem?*

Everyone has their own answers, don't they? Some suggest that if you just 'get out and see the world, your life will be complete. Don't just stay in the same place! Get out and find yourself!' Others find their answers to a fulfilled life in sex, success, fame, and crazy experiences. Some think that the harder you laugh, the more fulfilling your life is.

Some think that the more religious they are, the more fulfilling their life will be.

I've thought a lot about this and I have a few thoughts. A few years ago I put out a book on loneliness called *The New Lonely*. The thesis is this: 50 years ago, people were lonely because they were cut off from other people. Widows, orphans and prisoners were truly alone. Today, nearly all of us complain of being lonely constantly, despite the fact that we are more connected than ever before. This leads me to believe that the problem isn't the number of connections we have; it's the depth of those relationships which has suffered.

We may have more connections but they're shallow. Hence the title, the NEW Lonely.

I think about this as it applies to being truly alive and wonder, is this true in other areas as well? Are we experiencing a shallow toe-dip of life rather than diving on in, full submersion? Are we settling for the photogenic Instagram capture of us on the mountaintop instead of just taking time to BE there? Richly? To really experience and dwell in that moment?

It's weird and it takes time, but I think that as Millennials, we are missing our lives in favor of the shallow substitutes. This is true of our relationships and it's true of our lives! We are not only sacrificing deep, authentic intimacy on the altar of digital acclaim and attention, we are missing the passion of being alive where and when we are in the moment!

You see, I'm a Christian, and I believe in a God who feels things. I believe in a God who is also fully alive because He made us to be like Him!

I believe when we get stoked about something, He is stoked right alongside us! And that when we weep, he weeps with us as well.

You may have heard the colloquialism, 'Jesus comes and lives inside of you,' and I think there's some truth there. But do you ever really take time to think about what that means? That He—the God of the universe, Creator of all—lives life through and in and with you?

Acts 17:28 says that 'in Him, we live and move and have our being...'

God never called anyone to a bland, passionless life! He doesn't call you to spend your days swiping on your phone, scrolling through your various feeds!

I think deep within our soul is this longing to be roaringly awake, to dive headfirst into the pool, but we're content to sit on the side dipping our big toe in repeatedly and wondering why we still feel dry.

C.S. Lewis said, "We are half-hearted creatures, fooling about with drink and sex and ambition when infinite joy is offered us, like an ignorant child who wants to go on making mud pies in a slum because he cannot imagine what is meant by the offer of a holiday at the sea. We are far too easily pleased."[4]

We live life through and in the God of the universe! Doesn't that get you stoked? Doesn't that make you want to dive deeply into the ocean of experience out there? Even in your "boring" day-to-day routine, life is happening. And it's crazy. And it's always changing and different.

---

[4] C. S. Lewis, *The Weight of Glory and Other Addresses*

N.D. Wilson says, "This is not a sober world."[5]

Are you aware of this, or is it slipping away from you already? You won't be around much longer....another 50 or 60 years MAX before you're worm food.

How's it gonna be spent? Asleep or awake? Bored or alive?

I think the biggest mistake I could make in this post is to get you all pumped up to go out and 'live your best life now' and then the inspiration will wear off after a few minutes and reality sets back in. Inspiration without perspiration is useless. So what is the point here?

I think it's about recognizing not only what makes us most alive, but who. I believe that life is found in Christ, and He even says that He came that we may have life, and life to the fullest. So I guess this is just a reminder that Jesus isn't boring, nor does He want you to be bored.

If Christianity were boring, why would anyone want to draw others into that?? You only invite people into something when you're stoked about it!

So come on in! Come fully alive, in Him. Because outside of Him is where there is boredom, monotony, and more accurately, pain, anger, war, darkness and hatred. There's not really much middle ground here.

I HAVE NO IDEA WHAT I'M DOING.
I was born omniscient.

My parents were a smidgen older than I am now when they thrust me into existence. I didn't have much say in the matter, but I showed up and immediately started acting like I did.

Despite the fact that I was born omniscient (it seems to have faded after my teenage years) I thought my parents were all-knowing, all-powerful and all-benevolent. I was right about one of those. But with that belief came the

---

[5] N.D. Wilson, *Notes from the Tilt-a-Whirl: Wide-Eyed Wonder in God's Spoken World*

assumption that by the time I reached the ripe old age of 29, I'd be as all-knowing, all-powerful, and all-benevolent as they were.

Unless something drastically changes in less than two years, I plan on being far from all three.

You see, the thing most of us tend to forget is, moments before we emerged into this humid, chilly world, it was spinning along just fine without us. History was being made without our say, much less our observation.

In two days, I will teach my first history class and I have a monstrous task ahead of me: Convince my middle school students that the universe was extant far before their arrival here. Heck, I was extant long before their arrival. I guess that's something you have to experience to understand: you see a new generation of self-proclaimed geniuses rise up and you realize you never were as smart as you thought you were.

It was chilling recently when I was talking with a high schooler who was born after 9/11. To me, that was one of the most earth-shattering events in my lived history. To them, it's simply "Pre-Me" history.

But now I'm off track. What I wanted to say is this: I have no idea what the h-e-c-k I'm doing.

Like I said, my parents were a bit older than me when I burst into the world, but they were a bit younger than me when they got married. I have this tendency to think that certain milestones denote 'arrival'. Arrival on some glorious, invisible plane upon which life becomes more clear and easy and…lively.

Marriage is one of these planes, despite the fact that every wedding I've attended in the past three years has been for couples younger than me (in other words, they've 'arrived' and I haven't).

My most recent book is called *Now Let Me Find A Stopping Place*,[6] and the implication is that I'm looking for a place to set roots down. While this is true, geography is not the only thing you can set roots into. There are

---

[6] Really, really terrific book.

businesses to haunt. You put roots down into cuisine, guilty pleasures and routine.

Then there are people.

There is *that one person.*

This year, three of my best friends got married and one entered a serious relationship.

I moved to Guatemala.

Two years ago, I wrote about living life in a gradient.[7] The more I live, the more I realize how accurate that post was. You expect 'light switch changes' to occur in your life, but more often, you're fading from one season to the next. It's a slow change, a gradual turning of the seasons.

June 21 may be the first official day of summer, but we all know that mother nature pays no heed. Her gears are turning the clock toward summer over the course of many weeks. Months later, those same gears will shift away from the heat and toward the face-stinging cold of a Chicago winter.

I found myself there on multiple occasions: Once for college, once on the news, and a few times since. My Chicago season never ended abruptly, it faded out (I was even there for a day this summer…yes, a day).

So, fellow millennials, what fuels this desire to *fade* rather than to *be*? Why does it feel like we're slowly ascending a mountain rather than stopping at a plateau? Seems like that would be a simpler way to live.

I'm in Guatemala now, but don't know how long I'll be here. Don't know if this is my 'Stopping Place.' But one thing I'm not doing anymore is looking back. I've nostalgically lived in the past for most of my life—although I may occasionally lapse into longing for the future—and that eternal longing never seemed to satisfy.

---

[7] It's the next chapter, "Gradient"

I don't know if I'll go back to Colorado. Or Cape Cod. Or California. Or Chicago. (Or apparently, any other place that starts with a C.) I think I'm figuring out how to have my eyes set both on the present moment as well as the nearish future.

The past holds nothing for me but dreams from which I've already woken.

My Spanish is non-existent but I'm loving the experience of living in this disorientation. Every time I feel a longing for home, I remind myself that this is exactly why I wanted so badly to leave America. I can only speak for myself, but I badly wanted to experience this disorientation for the sake of waking into life rather than pacing through a stagnant routine. It's same reason I go to church, if it's done right.

You can go to a service which has conformed to the exact 'pattern of the world' with the simple rock-concert-plus-TED-Talk formula and know exactly what's going to happen. You will not be disoriented for the sake of relying on a transcendent God; you'll be mildly entertained and then ask where people are going for FroYo afterward.

No, I prefer to be lost in a liturgy. It's the pattern the Church has carried for millennia, yet it never ceases to be alarmingly different from the rest of our weekly routine. I went to a liturgical service on Sunday and loved it. I didn't know what was coming next. The Scriptures sang with Adele-strength power as if they came from the mouth of God Himself (huh…).

If nothing else, travel casts the same spell on me. It loses and confuses. It spins me upside down and, in this episode, takes Ethan to a country where he can't communicate with anyone else except via pointing and waving money around.

To be frank, I go back and forth between whether or not I think travel is beneficial for the Christian. On the one hand, it's a first-world luxury which very few people get to enjoy. On the other hand, pilgrimage has been a spiritual discipline for eons, so who am I to argue?

All that is to say, who knows where I'll fade to next? Who knows what type of human I'll fade into, and if I'll find that one special person to fade with? I could waste time and lose sleep juggling these questions in my mind, but for now, I want to be here, now. Because I will spend a good amount of my life not being here, and likely looking back on it wishing I was here again.

I don't know what I'm doing yet, but I hope to give it my very best. I hope to play my part in the history of the world, so that when I'm long gone, my memory may last just a few days longer than the grass which grows on top of me (better yet, the waves which roll above me!).

Maybe when it comes my turn to spring a child into existence, I'll have a better sense of what I'm doing. Maybe not, and I'd be okay with that too.

May we be people who live here now. May we not fret about tomorrow, for tomorrow will fret about itself. May we be people who number each and every day, for the days are evil (I have met but a handful that weren't).

GRADIENT
try to pinpoint the spot where the pink fades to blue, but you can't.

May, 2009. Colorado. I walk across the stage at my high school and shake the principal's hand. I put my diploma in a drawer and now I have no idea which drawer it was.

March, 2010. I'm in Haiti after the earthquake. I see the miles of blue tarps stretched out over the recently homeless families as I pass by the pop-up village, but the thing that strikes me the most is the crunch of gravel beneath my sneakers. It sounds the same as a crunch of gravel in America. I'm still figuring out compassion.

Tonight at around 1:24 am, my friend asked why I was going to Starbucks to write. I've got a word in my head, I told him: *Gradient.*

October, 2010. I'm on a plane from Thailand to India writing some emotional poem in my spiral-bound about the Brazilian girl I met in Australia whom I'm in love with because I had a dream about her when I lived on Cape Cod.

My story is a dizzying one. Maybe one day I'll write it all down and fill in some of these gaps. But not tonight. Tonight I've got a word on my mind: *Gradient.*

You see, my parents' generation was one of blacks and whites. Of light switch moments, where all at once, everything was illuminated and your future was determined. There was no YouTubing instructions, there was either total mastery or, 'Honey hand me the phone book so I can call the guy.'

I think it's July, 2011. I'm on a ferry in Brazil as we made our way from Sao Paulo to Rio. I'm playing worship songs with some kids on the ship. Their parents would give us dinner and a warm bed that night, even though only one of us knew Portuguese.

The next day. I had my first drink ever: Vodka and lime at the Gecko Hostel, Paraty. The fat Australian guy named John told us Thailand is a party. Then I ran 5 miles barefoot up the coast, this time thinking about a Brazilian girl I met in Brazil.

Two days later in Rio. We're being held up at gunpoint and the guy is asking for all our valuables. *Well,* I thought, *If Thailand is a party, Brazil is a poem.*

My father knew he wanted to be a pastor before he graduated high school. An older man at his church one day told him that he saw in him the skills to be a great pastor. So he became one of the best freaking preachers I've ever heard. And I've heard a *lot* of preachers.

I graduated high school a long time ago and I still have no idea what singular calling beckons my name. Perhaps it's because no one spoke it into my life the way the old man did to my father. Perhaps it's because the options are endless these days. Perhaps technology is to blame for presenting so wide a platter of options. Perhaps it's okay to live in a gradient.

February, 2012. I'm on the phone with my mom from a hostel in Boston. I'm telling her I'll be going to Nigeria in April because a friend and I are starting an organization. She sounds calm and makes a joke about Nigeria being nervous about me coming.

August, 2012. I'm homeless again. I'm living on the beach and teaching paddleboard lessons. I don't know how hard the transition will be when I move to Chicago and begin my third college. This time, it's for real. This is no community college; this is the number one Bible school in America. And maybe by the time I finish, I'll know where I'm going and what I'm doing and who I am.

My transition into adulthood has not been a light switch. There was no moment of epiphany to suddenly illuminate the path I was to take. Some people are fortunate enough to have that. However, for me and most people my age, the abundance of information and opportunities have made the decision to 'iron out our future' nearly impossible. If not impossible, at least a more time-consuming one.

January, 2014. I'm at Starbucks with a favorite author of mine. He gave me a hundred bucks and explained how to have intimate relationships with others. Including myself. I'm learning that travel experiences make you look cool, but wherever you go, there you are and blah blah blah...

Whenever I see a sunset, I always try to pinpoint the place in the sky where the pink stops and the blue takes over. What I've come to find is that you can't. There is no single point. God was the inventor of the gradient. He was the first one to say, Okay, you fade into this color here. But make it wide. Make it vast. Make it so the lines blur and the beauty in this hue carries into the next. Make it so this color gives way to this one, but not too soon...

Not all at once.

August-December 2015. I'm driving to and from the house where I work nannying two little boys. I listen to a punk rock song about never growing up, dropping out, and sleeping on a twin size mattress your whole life.[8] I feel it so hard every time.

My transition into the world of suit jackets, briefcases, and grown-up conversations has been a slow one. It's been a gradient. It's been a slow fade. A slow clap. Perhaps soon the uproarious applause will

---

[8] The Front Bottoms, *Twin Size Mattress*

break out into full-blown adulthood, full-blown responsibility. You can't slow clap forever.

December, 2015. It's raining in Chicago, so I lace up my kicks and go for a run. I see some newscasters on the deserted beach and get curious.

One month later. I move to Los Angeles and learn how to see through the deceptive media machine. I learn that the demigods of television and the legendary descendants of Zeus known as pop stars are not that far off from the Wizard of Oz hidden in his little room. There's a big curtain called the Imagination and they're all huddled behind it hoping no one sees.

I'm in a Starbucks at 3am in Chicago and I'm still wearing a damp swimsuit from jumping in the lake earlier. This Starbucks in particular still reminds me of a girl who broke my heart in college. She and I would come here often and study into the thin hours of the morning.

When I was 18, I was positive I'd be married by the time I was 22.

My life so far has been a gradient. It's been a slow fade into adulthood.

And I think that's okay.

There's this pressure to feel guilty about being halfway through my twenties and not know where I'll be next year. Next month. Or who I'll be, what I'll be doing, et al. And this pressure is unnecessary. I think God is sometimes okay with slow fades.

I'm not writing this post as an excuse for laziness and slacking off, I'm not about those things. But I am for bravery. I am for courage and trying new things. And I'm for patience. Sometimes God doesn't turn on a light switch, but He'll at least give you a candle so you can see where your foot should fall.

Sometimes you bump into a few walls.

I'm okay with living in a gradient, in a transition period. Sometimes one season fades into the next and you can't quite see why or how, or even where you're going. Sometimes you end up in Paris with two people who work for you in this Nigerian organization. Sometimes you're driving across Utah in the middle of the night to see about a Brazilian girl you met online. But the fact that there's a gradient means change is coming. It means soon the moon will be up and everything will be peaceful. And after the night is a sunrise; a fading into day. A transition into the *next* season.

Many of us will have a slow fade into adulthood and that's alright.

Be at peace and enjoy the gradient.

WAITING IN A BUS TERMINAL IN BOSTON
some thoughts on God & traveling from a journal entry on the road.

It's just this itching of discomfort that calls me by name—names me. The lusty trains of wanderloss have beckoned me to the loss of all that I know in homes and online. Here, there are no codes or formulas. Rather, there is a presence of lives guided only by emotion and desire—driven only by this madness to dwell in the state of passionate searching.

Have you found this plateau?

The peak is named travel and the ascent is called departure [from home].

In this, the season of motion, few things that can be gathered, accumulated, or touched are longed for. These pinings are replaced, rather, with a collection of memories—with a desire to *be* touched, to be beaten out of sleep for trespassing; and to be with people. With someone to accompany you on this sojourn—to hear your thoughts and to share theirs as you sit on the [surprisingly clean] stone floor of the bus terminal.

When I rid myself of the internet, of security, and of all I own, save a handful of backpack essentials, I gain the freedom of the open road and the liveliness that accompanies a commercial-free life.

Every girl becomes just that much more beautiful; every man that much more accommodating. The color in the sky and the cool wince of my skin under the rain is magnified exponentially. Ripples of a passing river offer comfort while before they would have been overlooked. And where in all of these glimpses of thriving life does God fit?

Everywhere.

Every raindrop which touches skin is an envelope of His love, a reminder that He hasn't forgotten you. I may weary of manmade dramas and what the world tells me my life should look like, but I believe that to seek Him is to travel, to violently escape comfort and find a solace in omnipresent companionship. In this relationship, and in this relationship alone, I can share my thoughts with someone who never tires of hearing them; and I can seek His perfect wisdom any time a Bible can be found, or a prayer can be muttered. One of the beauties of His Word is that I can read it in Brasil and it is just as true and accessible as in Boston; in Nigeria as in North Carolina.

My advice to you, dear readers, is to get out and find this discomfort. Get out and discover the joy of full reliance on YHWH.

THREE MOMENTS IN GUATEMALA
the world is singing a song of static and the lyrics are 1's and 0's.

A while ago I poetically declared, 'you live in a foreign country long enough, meaning eventually comes from the alien voices which were initially mere babbling noises.' I conjured up that sentence out of seemingly nowhere, seeing as how up until this past Tuesday, it had been six years since I had left the country.

Tonight, however, was a poem in itself.

The power went out halfway through my push-up workout in my room. I sweated in blackness until I heard the sounds of dinner flow under my closed door and emerged to find the daughter of the woman who owns the house setting the table by candlelight. The world was silent against the flickering glow.

A couple weeks ago, I saw the film *Skyscraper*, starring Dwayne Johnson. It's not his character that stood out to me, but the antagonist; a Chinese billionaire who had finally accomplished his dream of constructing the tallest building in the world, and it's basically his child.

I pictured this fictional man in his own airplane, wrapping his ears in noise cancelling headphones and complaining if his soup arrives four degrees too hot. His character is the archetype of the modern man drowning away the world with electric noise; one escaping from the collective pain and angst of a culture with a history of mass death and suffering: poverty without explanation, oppression without God.

The world is singing a song composed of static and the lyrics are ones and zeros.

The daughter at the house where I'm staying is the image of a Central American youth: Olive tan and adorable. Tonight while our faces were illumined by the small candles, she spoke with rolling R's and the exaggerated gyration of her small hands. Her voice is a tight string, elevated and plucked in staccato.

There were moments when the conversation (none of which I understood) would cease and we would sit in the utter silence and near darkness, crunching our tortilla chips dipped in corn mash. Few moments are so unique that I am caught off guard by their simplicity, but that happened tonight. Tonight was the reason I asked the director of my school if I really need a cell phone while I'm here (he said yes), because the quiet of the night was life giving.

Six people around a table, almost all from different countries or states, sitting near candles in the dark, quietly crunching on tortilla chips.

Then the Spanish conversation would resume and I was lost once more. At least in the silence, I understood what was happening.

Or maybe I didn't;

maybe thinking I did is the biggest mistake I could make.

One of my favorite stories in the Bible is found in 1 Kings 19. God is about to speak to His prophet Elijah in a cave in the middle of nowhere, so Elijah is chilling. A fire, wind and earthquake come, but God is not to be found in the loud and monstrous demonstrations. Then silence falls upon the area and it is so violent Elijah covers his face and moves toward the cave's mouth.

God meets us in the silence. He meets us with the screens off and the power out. I don't know for sure, but I don't know if we find God in the noise cancelling headphones which filter reality to our comfort. I don't know if we find Him on the private jet or the world's tallest skyscraper (Do you see us more clearly now, God/when we ascend to metal heights?).

But I know we do meet Him in the silence. I know He's been found there before, and has spoken into the unpolluted stillness.

So may we seek Him where He may be found. May we not drown out the gentle call of the Spirit of God with things we think we need more. And may we soak in those rare candlelit moments in Guatemala around a table of strangers, crunching on tortilla chips.

& & &

The latte goes down incredibly smooth with a punchy bitter aftertaste. Coffee shops in Guatemala have done all they can to look and feel like American shops, and this one comes remarkably close.

You know how you see those black and white photos of a flurry of pigeons taking flight over colonial cobblestone streets? I just saw that a couple minutes ago near the giant concrete gazebo with the Roman pillars here in downtown Quetzaltenango. The thing is, however, these moments always look different in person than they do on the screen or in a print. I could have captured it with my camera in order to make you wish you were here. However, I would conveniently leave out the poverty, the decimated streets, and the polluted smell which often accompanies certain parts of the town. You may wish to be here, adventurous as me, but at least you have hot and clean water.

Without looking it up, I've been trying to determine if Guaté is a third- or second-world country. I'm pretty sure I've landed on second-and-a-half. Parts are so beautifully developed, especially where the ancient landmarks have been restored and refurbished. Other parts have been allowed to be polluted and crumble. Regardless, today for the first time, I'm going out with my camera to try to capture a lick of this beauty. It's a vibrant and active sort of beauty, embedded with millennia of rich history and colorful culture.

& & &

Today we paraded around a huge *cementario*. Many of the bodies were buried above ground in the walls or shelves of the yard, unable to afford their own plot of ground to occupy for the foreseeable centuries.

I found out that the family must pay rent for the space, or else the body will be exhumed and returned to them.

Death rent.

I used to think rent would stop following me around like a curse once I died. Chew on that one for a while.

PRETTY CITIES FADING

soon it will be my turn to suffer again.

My eyes seemed to faint with longing as I passed through *Parque Central* earlier today, beholding the beautifully rich and ancient buildings. The colonial columns with the Gothic curls atop brightly painted facades form architecture almost too magnificent for me to bear.

When I was in high school, my mom would take us to the dump, which had a little shop off to the side called the Swap Shop. You brought items you wanted to leave, and took others you wanted to take (One year, Mommy got all my birthday presents there and I've never let her live it down). Because it was Cape Cod, full of wealthy retirees, you could often make out with a decent haul.

It was in this tiny building by the dump I found an ancient book titled *The Paris I Love*. It was primarily black and white photos of Paris circa the 1940's. It's everything the world imagines Paris to be: Cobbled roads, beautiful architecture, cafes, a million pigeons in a flurry above the widow's bench.

After flipping through this book in the early 2000's, I thought utopia was attainable. Or at least, that it had existed for a brief flash in Paris in the 1940's. The cafe I'm in now is participating in that manmade utopia: These gorgeous buildings flock around the *kiosko*, which is a round concrete gazebo made of Roman columns crumbling in just the right places. Right now, a traditionally dressed Mayan woman is kissing a business man leaning against one of the poles.

From the center of the park, you could look around and see open-air balconies where lovers could easily be serenaded à la *Say Anything*. Olive-skinned Mayans parade around the perimeter, selling jewelry and chiclets in their bright and ornate dresses. The climate has been described as 'the land of eternal spring.' If there ever was utopia, Quetzaltenango would be pretty close.

But look a little closer.

I just paid 1Q (12 cents) for a pack of gum from a girl who should be in kindergarten. Instead of learning, she is peddling her family's goods because children rake in more money than adults.

Pollution lingers in the air thanks to a lack of emissions control (Side note: I'm now grateful America makes us go through those annoying emissions tests), and I'm realizing that beauty must be more than aesthetics.

As painfully pretty as this city is, appearances alone won't sustain a soul.

I'm presently reading through C.S. Lewis' book *Out of the Silent Planet* and the protagonist just had a compelling conversation with an alien poet. The alien told him that they mate only once for the sake of bearing young.

"Isn't the process of creating the offspring pleasurable," he asks the alien. (I'm paraphrasing here)

"Of course it is," replies the alien, "and because it only happens once, the beauty of the event grows in my memory like the progression of a great poem or song."

The protagonist is confused for a moment and the alien elaborates, "You can read a great line of verse over and over again, but without the context of the entire poem, it loses its power. Time, like a song, must move forward for the fullness of beauty to be witnessed."

I've been stuck on that line of thinking for a while now. Why do something pleasurable over and over again when you appreciate it more if it only happens once? It's a tension I'm facing. I mean, if you only ate once more for the rest of your life, you couldn't dwell very long on the sweet memory of its taste. You wouldn't live too long. You can't be hugged one more time and call it good for the rest of your life.

Time and life are complex. There are three views, check it out:

Eastern: Time is cyclical. Reincarnation. All things repeat. Think of a circle.

Western: Time is linear. Moves forward. Birth, life, death. Picture a straight line.

(Can you see how these views of time inform the way these various cultures have grown and morphed over millennia? This last view is the one I find the most accurate.)

Hebrew: Time is seasonal. Picture a slinky, slightly pulled apart. Winter fades into spring which moves into summer, which becomes fall which goes back to winter. Winter, 1940 is not winter, 2018, but it is still winter. There is repetition *and* progression. My grandfather was once young and spritely like me, but now is my moment.

Soon it will be my turn to fade into the soil.

I'm enjoying this idyllic afternoon, but soon enough, pain will return. Soon it will be my turn to suffer again.

I was just offered more chiclets, this time by a little boy, reminding me that I'm really longing for a city not built by human hands. Beautiful as these exotic towns are, they're not where I belong. I can only stay here so long; 70 more years if I really like it.

Now let me find a stopping place.

The more we see ourselves as aliens on this world, the less attached we will be to the fleeting goods it has to offer us.

I'm still trying to find a way to describe the beauty and power of these words from Hebrews 11, but I can't. So let me end by just saying that I hope all of us may be humans of whom this is also true:

> For he was looking forward to the city with foundations, whose architect and builder is God. . . All these people were still living by faith when they died. They did not receive the things promised; they only saw them and welcomed them from a distance, admitting that they were foreigners and strangers on earth. People who say such things show that they are looking for a country of their own. If they had been thinking of the country they had left, they would have had opportunity to return. Instead, they were longing for a better country—a heavenly one. Therefore God is not ashamed to be called their God, for he has prepared a city for them.

THE OPTIMIST'S SUICIDE
when you don't want to end your life, just a part of it...

I had arrived in Australia two days prior, but already felt like I wasn't fitting in. The harsh adjustment not only to a new community, but an entirely new country was tough. I don't remember who I was speaking with, I just remember angrily mumbling something about 'I'm not sure if I'll stay or if I'm gonna leave.'

Did I know where I'd go? Of course not. I just wanted to *show them*. As in, *That's what they get for not letting me fit in.*

It's always worth pointing out that most, if not all of these feelings have more to do with what happens inside of me and my own perceptions than with how other people actually treat me.

Years later, I was sitting in a Starbucks in Chicago. I had been at Moody Bible Institute a total of a week and a half and was sitting with the guy who lived two doors down from me. I told him I didn't know if I'd stick it out at Moody.

"Not even sure I'll finish out the semester," I told him in an attempt to act casually apathetic. He later told me that's why he couldn't ever connect with me on a deep level: He always felt like I was about to take off.

A few nights ago I was on the phone with a good friend of mine and we began talking about our childhoods. He was bullied in 5th and 6th grades, and this sense of not-fitting-in led him to dip his toes into thoughts of suicide. "I even held a pocketknife to my throat at one point," he confessed, "but ended up throwing it across the room."

Now a clinical psychologist and counselor, he pointed out an important note: Most people who contemplate suicide don't want to die; they just want out of their current situation. As a middle schooler, he saw no other path out of his reality of being a bullied outcast. As adults, though, this can look vastly different.

Last night I was on the phone with another close friend who confessed similar feelings haunting him throughout his life. Like me, he has traveled the world and bounced around. Like me, he struggles to find a comfortable niche within society and even within a church. Like me, he often opts to leave rather than stay.

But unlike me, he has suicidal tendencies rise up from time to time.

And that's when it clicked.

We who bounce about the globe under the veneer of 'finding ourselves' or 'world/self exploration' are simply self-destructive misfits too afraid to pull the trigger.

He gave breath to the phrase, I just named it: The Optimist's Suicide.

I have never had suicidal thoughts, so it was jarring to realize that much of my behavior throughout my life reeks of some sort of watered-down suicide.

> I want to leave my current situation because I feel like I don't fit in: Check.

> In some deep-seated, angsty way, I want to *show* the people who didn't accept me: Check.

> But at least I'm hopeful that OVER THERE, things will be better: Check.

When you want the simultaneous attention and seclusion of/from society but you don't want the downsides of suicide (read: death), you leave.

You move.

You take a job in a new country because not only does the grass look much lusher, but your extant problems don't exist there [yet].

"I've spent most of my life hiding behind a veneer of cynicism and critique when in reality I'm terrified every time I talk to another human being," my friend told me on the phone. I was stunned because my friend is not only brilliant and funny, but has always carried an air of confidence and self-awareness.

Turns out no one is as healthy as they appear.

The demons inside of me look different than the ones inside of you.

"I'm just a lonely intelligent dude who's suicidal. Hanging out in Turkey as a vagabond is the closest to oblivion I can get. The anonymity makes me invisible; people walk by as if I'm not there and I crave that. I'm sick of being an outcast, so it's better to not exist."

The optimist's suicide is to pack your bags and dip out. Leave without permanence. You don't want to end your life, just a chapter of your life.

"The last time I went on a date," he said, "I immediately told her it wouldn't work out. I had to end it before she inevitably did. I told her it was over even though I was painfully interested in her."

I'm sure many of you are familiar. Perhaps you have not committed this specific disappearing act, but you've been tempted to. Perhaps your roots are a bit more healthy and deep than ours, but for those of us with a penchant for rolling out, it's tempting to catch the wind as she blows.

But I feel like this watered-down form of suicide affects the majority of us. We fear the setting of deep roots and yearn instead for an aesthetically beautiful departure. Who among us hasn't felt the pangs of social anxiety in a room full of strangers? Who has never opted for Netflix when invited to a party?

Why are these minuscule forms of retreat so alluring to this generation? And why haven't we realized that drawn out to their logical extremes, we are all myopically suicidal? We're familiar with the phrase "social suicide," but don't many of us commit such acts on a weekly basis? Don't we always pull away?

Years ago, my friend Tony pointed out that one of the main things that separates God from man is that we have a tendency to move *away*, while He has a habit of moving *toward*. We were Jonah, charting ships away from Him, all the while that Hound of Heaven was hot on our scent.

We were the sheep wandering away; the coin getting lost; the son who wished his father was dead[9]—whatever metaphor you prefer—and God is always the one relentlessly pursuing us. He always has been and always will be the Unsatisfied Stalker until He's gotten what He craves—you and me.

While we're busy disguising our coward's suicide as some Instagram-friendly mystical sojourn, He's busy creating a home for us to belong; to fit in once and for all.

We're dressing our corpses and anointing them with oil and makeup while He's trying to rouse us from the dead.

---

[9] All stories found in Luke 15

I also don't think He's satisfied with mere life; I think He thirsts to be intimate with His people. He wants to know us and be known by us. Can a transient vagabond ever know or be known?

Sure, it varies from person to person, but we're all guilty of running. We're each guilty of fearing people more than Him; fear of losing our reputations more than fear of losing Him.

May we be people who choose to tear down the thin fabric insulating us from one another, truly connecting with those around us. May we recognize that we are already loved and accepted how we are and where we are, that this may give us peace, hope and life.

THE FAULT IN OUR STORIES
I think the issue is these two words: happy endings.

I've been thinking a lot lately about the stories we tell.

Or more accurately, the stories we hear. The films we watch and the books we read. And if I were to make a monstrous generalization about modern Hollywood's ideals, it would be summed up in two words: Happy endings.

I touched on this in the chapter on Waiting Till Marriage, but wanted to expound on this idea of a 'one-fight life'. Even the best romantic movies fall prey to this outline of a plot: Meet, flirt, fall in love, roll romantic montage, and here is where the drama sets in. A secret from earlier in the film is revealed, or maybe a trait that she wasn't supposed to see appears. A battle erupts, but peace is eventually restored and they make out.

Take, for instance, one of my favorite films of all time, *Beginners*. Realistic as it is, it is heavily laden with artistic takes and romantic whimsy. The film reaches a place where the protagonist unravels years of psychological threads; his noncommittal character breaks down and he leaves his beautiful French girlfriend. Without giving away too much, there is a happy ending. A reunion after their singular conflict. The jazzy piano croons on as the last shot gives way to the credits.

And after the credits roll, the audience is left with this vague good feeling because the conflict has been resolved and in our minds, the two romantic leads continue on in their blissful romantic utopia, never to fight again.

In our optimism, we have adopted this repetitive plot into the liturgy of our lives.

What I mean by *liturgy* is a repeated action or input into our lives that eventually develops certain rhythms within us. For instance, I used to work in the Chicago Juvenile Detention Center and would always ask the guys about their influences. They talked about characters like Lil' Wayne, who glorifies getting money above all. Right under money was getting girls and shooting their enemies.

Their 'liturgy' was one that glorified money above everything else, as well as exalting a lifestyle of violence and self-glorification because they repeatedly put those concepts into their minds via Wayne, Eminem or Chief Keef. A lifetime of this liturgy led them to prison, because it became the entirety of what they hoped for and worked toward. Their end goal fueled their actions. (Of course this is an oversimplification, but you get the concept of how liturgies affect our lives).

My uncle says we should never take in media with our brains turned off. Always be aware of what your movies and music are *saying*. Everyone is always saying *something*, so learn to recognize how your media is affecting your desires, your actions, and your thoughts. There is no neutral ground. It is either orienting you toward God and His grace, or it is pointing you toward yourself, money, sex, pleasure, et cetera. It is pointing you away from Him.

We often fail to recognize our own liturgies—repetitive actions or thoughts in our lives—because they are less explicit and cloaked in the innocent spirit of rom-coms and love songs. Even commercials promise that *this one simple product* will be a quick fix for whatever ailments your life has accrued.

We expect every situation in our lives to be resolved simplistically and offer a permanent solution to whatever ache or conflict we are engaged in because that is what our postmodern liturgy has promised us. Especially as

Christians, we often associate coming to faith in Jesus with the elimination of our sins, struggles and conflicts.

I wonder if this is why so many marriages end prematurely: We think that when the first winds of conflict stir, it means there is a problem with the person we have chosen. Or when your porn habit simply *will not* go away, even though you repeatedly pray to Jesus to take it away, you wonder if you're really saved.

Because there *should* be a quick fix and a happy ending, right?

Hardships, trials and conflicts will continue as long as sinful people continue to walk the earth. This is why so much of premarital counseling teaches the prenuptials *how* to fight, rather than how to avoid fighting.

Because in real life, there is more than one fight.

There are a lot more than one fight.

I once was in Florida and this beautiful couple that must have been hovering around 80 years old invited me to dinner. They were cuter than plums on the porch, and I expected to witness a couple that only said kind words to each other with the gentleness of a baby's rear end.

Instead, I was privy to an ongoing (hilarious) bicker battle between the loving couple. They were still very much in love with each other, and both knew it, but she yelled at him for getting the wrong flavor of ice cream, and he jabbed back that there was too much sauce on the salad. It went on most of the night in the cutest way possible, like two puppies wrestling.

I was trying hard not to laugh out loud.

They had learned how to fight well. They did not expect a one-fight marriage followed by a Pax Romana. Rather, they accepted that they would never agree on *everything* and engaged in a life together in which conflict was an acquired skill.

This doesn't just apply to relationships either. I feel like every episode of *Modern Family* offers some kind of pithy moral throughout the course of the plot, as if life change happens over the course of 21 minutes and endures the rest of our lives.

If my life is any indicator, this is clearly not the case.

Because sin is ongoing. My pride and selfishness are ongoing. My fallen human nature creeps up again and again and I find myself falling into the same pit,

climbing out,
and falling in again.

At the end of his life, well-battered and weathered, Brennan Manning sat in a chair in his Kansas home and told a camera crew, "Let yourself be loved by God, as you are and not as you should be, because none of us are as we should be..." After struggling with alcoholism for decades and only finding relief in the arms of a gracious God, Manning found only one cure for the repetitive liturgies sung to us in the smoothest voices from Hollywood and television: the love of God.

Repeatedly returning to God reminds us that there is not one solve-all solution for our brokenness and pain. Creating *new* rhythms that engage with His Word, His body, and His Spirit are what begin to reorient our lives toward what is true. Maybe this is what Paul meant in Romans 12 when he wrote, "Do not conform to the patterns of this world, but be transformed by the renewing of your mind."

Yes, you will continue to battle the urges to look at porn, or to lose your temper at your husband. These may be lifelong struggles that take years to eradicate, but implementing new rhythms and liturgies into our lives will help us change; they will help us see God in everything as His Spirit works and moves through the mundane and ordinary things in our lives.

May we be a people who integrate holy rhythms into our lives in order to orient our hearts toward God daily.

Not just once.

RECOVER YOUR IMAGINATION

part of me is still in that field, killing imaginary foes alongside Dave.

It's just a kids book, I thought. *I won't get anything out of it.*

Today my sixth grade class finished reading *Bridge to Terabithia*, so we started watching the film. Normally, I'm not a fan of children's films, and I guess the film itself warrants no outstanding attention, but while I was watching it, something clicked.

When we were in fifth or sixth grade, my best friend Dave and I were behind his house. I was on the cusp of being allowed to watch PG-13 films and I was dying to see the *Lord of the Rings* series. I had caught five minutes of the first one on a flatscreen at Sam's Club and it was irreversibly etched into my brain.

It happened to be the scene in the Mines of Moria when the Fellowship is battling some orcs and trolls. My attention was especially drawn to Legolas, who fired his arrows with laser precision while doing some sort of medieval parkour. He was not only the heartthrob of female viewers, but the idol of every tweenage boy.

Behind Dave's house was an open space with a creek running down the middle. In the winter months, the reeds hedging the creek lay flat and gray. To us, however, they became the setting of the most epic battles we'd ever fight. Looking back on those days which slowly sunk into colder and darker evenings, we would lose track of time swinging our branches around and slaying orcs. (We fought over who got to be Legolas every time.)

The crazy thing is, looking back on those days, I don't only remember the physical scenery, but also the exact things I was envisioning there with us as well. I remember the armies of orcs the two of us would singlehandedly (doublehandedly?) overcome. I remember how we would make our way through the hearts of mountains without ever leaving the field. I recall the trolls disguised as trees which we toppled with ease after a few minutes of hacking at them.

It's strange, but I remember my imaginings as well as I remember the reality.

Anyone who has seen *Pan's Labyrinth*, any *Narnia* flick, or read *Calvin &* *Hobbes* sleeps in one of two camps: You either think all the magical elements are meant to only exist in the child's imagination, or you think they actually happen and the stories predicate themselves around the reality of the whimsical world. I think people who fall into the latter category believe this for a deeper reason:

We so badly want it to be true.

It isn't because it makes for a better or worse plot; it's because we want to believe that our five senses aren't telling us the whole story. We want an adventure to live and giants to topple. We don't just want the bad guy to be a mean stepmother. We want the key given by the goblin to actually lead to another world. We want the stuffed tiger to actually be alive.

Like the horse says in *The Velveteen Rabbit*, "What is real?"

Is it that which exists in the imaginations of children, or is it limited to what is observable by everyone? In that case, are sunsets real, as blind people have no evidence of their existence? Are any of Beethoven's symphonies real, since they can't be sensed by the deaf?

I know I'm not exactly making a rational case, but a poetic one. Maybe I just want the orcs slain by Dave and I to count for something. And maybe that's exactly why imagination is so important in the development of human beings. If nothing else, it taught Dave and I about battle, valor and victory. Our fantasy-scapes allowed us to craft worlds in ways reality does not. I'd like to think that experimenting with imagination leads to bigger thinking later in life.

I've lived all over the world and few places have had the same type of magic as the cold gray field behind Dave's house. Not because of what was *actually* there, but because of how we saw it.

There's one more thing I'd like to recapture from those days. Despite the fact that dozens of houses backed to that field—and therefore could see us —we hacked away at the trees and the ice and the ground nonetheless. We didn't care who saw us slaughtering orcs by the dozens because we were in Middle Earth, not Littleton, Colorado.

I wish I still cared so little what other people think.

I wish my imagination still existed outside the boundaries of the opinions of others. Maybe recovering some of that free-spirited indifference will help our imaginations to once again expand to their proper size. I'm pretty sure that a big imagination and caring what others think of you are mutually exclusive. You can't have both. Dave and I certainly didn't care what people thought of us as we ran around with our sticks and wet sneakers.

A pastor in Chicago once gave a lecture[10] on 'The Christian Imagination,' and it is still one of those mind-shattering half hours. He defines imagination as the ability to see the invisible. For instance, you can even be imaginative about next month's vacation: You don't see it, yet it is a real thing. In this case, it *will* be a real thing; it *will* be visibly manifest.

As Christians, are we as imaginative as we could be? Are we good at being aware of the invisible and acting as if it is real? Just like a future vacation, we must always keep in mind the coming reality of things unseen[11] and live as if they are real.

When we lose our imaginations, we lose our witness to the world.

Part of me is still in that field, killing imaginary foes alongside Dave. I'm dying to see like that again. I'm trying to live like that again.

May we be folks who disregard what the world thinks of us as we seek to live with reckless imagination. May we train our minds to see abundant invisible things and communicate them to the world, to the glory of God.

---

[10] Fr. Aaron Damiani, Immanuel Anglican Church, *The Baptized Imagination in a Pornographic Age*. You can listen to it on Soundcloud.

[11] Hebrews 11

DEAR FRIEND, VOLUME 2

you can't count the waves, the sand, the stars, or the ways I love you.

Here's another batch of fragments from my ancient love letters. I have this shoebox full of them in my room and thought some of these lines from friends and lovers alike were too beautiful not to share. They are from a dozen people over the past decade, in no order whatsoever. Enjoy!

I don't know what to say. I 'something' you. You are my stronghold and I really just want to bury my face in your chest and cry because I know you would be exactly what I need.

Ahh! I love you. Is it strange to have this much passion for one thing? Not a thing—YOU!

Writing something for you was really difficult. I wrote and erased tons of letters for you. So I decided to only write about what I'm sure of, and I'm sure that I'm really happy that I had the chance to meet you.

You can't count the waves, the sand, the stars, or the ways I love you.

Basically, I wanted to tell you, Friend, that the only way I've ever coped with chaos is creating more chaos. I only feel good when I'm orchestrating disaster. I am bored and numb until I am anxious or sad and then I f*** something up on purpose to make myself laugh.

I always enjoy myself when you're around. Thank you for being weird. I'm weird. You're weird. We're all weird and I love it.

My cousin eats cereal (for Ethan)
He is downstairs.
I tell him,
I'm glad you're here.
He says he's glad also.

We wave
and I go to type this.

There isn't one night that passes when I don't wish that I had hugged you goodnight or I was staying up all night talking with you. There isn't a morning when I don't wish yours was the first face my eyes came across or your eyes were the first I could look into. I miss you and there is so much more in that phrase than appears on the paper in ink. I love you and when I say that it is only a surface of the ocean of feeling inside me. There isn't enough paper in the world that could hold it.

When I am home next we should have deep conversations.

Sorry if the paper is smudged, I just got in from the rain and my hair is dripping and not just a little. I don't mind. I really like being attacked by the weather.

You said your romantic fire is being doused by the liquid of distance. I think the liquid of distance can be flammable.

I am drowning and burning at the same time. I miss you and I need you. My hands ache to be touched by your hands; my fingers long to be entwined with yours. My nose misses your scent. My eyes tear up when they look around and can't find you. My head misses the comfort of your shoulder and my ears are stubbornly deaf to any sound because they want you to whisper a secret to them. This could be considered a form of torture.

I think my poetry isn't very good because I was writing and there was no music to it, I was just giving information.

Loneliness is hard to live with. I kinda think loneliness is a good friend a person has with them their whole life and getting to know it and having it reflect a person's self is important, good, hard life work. I hope I develop my vocabulary with myself and my friends. Sometimes relationships get stunted because they rely on outdated or immature vocabulary.

I don't think we should have just one 'song,' it should change as we change. There are specific lines from different songs, but not always the whole song. I'll think about it.

To me, my brother's wedding was blue, but the kind of sky blue that reflects beautiful things. Usually blue feels like a bruise. This blue was lace, delicate and strong, like an ocean or a dress.

I can tell when you are really angry or sad or bored or annoyed. Maybe we need to spend more time together and I'll memorize you. I'll pick through your head. I want to finish your sentences and I want to know everything.

I'm reminded that this is not all there is. That I don't have to stay here, get married, become a mom, hate my life. Thank you for your ambiguity.

I think I'm going to send this before I think better of it.

APRIL 3, 2018
random theological thoughts and a handful of pop song references.

I'm always tempted to laugh when someone tells me that they're a 'super strong Christian.'

"My faith is really strong," the kid in the gym locker room told me the other day.

Like…did Jesus die extra good for you? Did you do more to earn the overwhelming, never ending reckless love of God? Did you pay for your grace?

I'm always curious.

It's like those people who superstitiously believe that if *this* famous pastor laid hands on them and prayed for them, they'd be healed of that chronic disease. And that's how those deceptive pastors get rich.

Call yourself an Apostle.
Call yourself a New Prophet.
Call yourself a Strong Christian,

but you're just the same as the rest of us. I feel like the strength of your Christianity (that phrase...ugh) can be measured in a single question:

Have you ever sinned?

If not, then yes, you *are* a strong Christian and you are, indeed, the Messiah.

If you have, welcome to the club. There's a seat for you here at the table, scooted up by the sinless One Himself.

You can add as many scoops of ice cream as you want to a pile of roaches, but you'll never make it an appealing platter. However, all you need is one insect to utterly ruin a giant bowl of ice cream. It's easy to taint and contaminate; it's much harder to cleanse and redeem.

Are you a strong Christian? Does your dessert have a few less roaches on it? Or are you down here with the rest of us, kneeling on the level ground before the cross?

A month ago a girl broke my heart.

The fact that it hasn't healed shows that it was broken more deeply than I previously thought. Sometimes the ripping off of the bandaid hurts more than the actual wound. Sometimes you need to be wounded again to see where the deepest cuts hide.

Maybe this is why God sometimes allows our tissue to be severed. So He can not only heal the fresh, superficial laceration, but so that He can get to the root of the issue. That porn addiction or alcoholism. That reason you gotta stay high or always be in work mode.

I heard an old Jewish idiom once. A rabbi said to a young disciple, "My son, do you know why the Scriptures say to set the Word of God *on* your heart, and not *in* it?" The boy listened intently as the rabbi continued. "So that when your heart breaks, Scripture will run down into it and fill the cracks like water into a fractured dam."

I've said it once and I'll probably say it a billion more times before I go:

Me: "I struggle to fall in love with invisible things."

Paul: "Those who live according to the flesh desire the things of the flesh, but those who live according to the Spirit desire the things of th ___"12

Me: "Yah I know, Paul but howwww do you desire the things of the Spirit? How do you long for the Glorious Unseen? How do you pine for the Intangible? I've held a girl or two in my day, and (not to give too much undeserved credit to Hozier here), sometimes I feel more in those moments than I do in church!"

Paul: "What's a Hozier?"

It's easier to wrap your arms around a human and feel love flow between the two of you, requited. Or, if you're eternally single like me, to long for that moment. It's much harder to wrap your arms around our God, whom Scripture tells us is a Spirit, and feel much love flow in either direction.

We've got Stockholm Syndrome for the world.

She's taken captive our attention and our desires and is refusing to give them back. She doesn't play fair. She invents things like women's soft shoulders and lamb jerky risotto and expects us to stay focused on invisible (or tasteless) things.

But look, now I've gone and waxed Gnostic.

They preach, *All matter is bad and all spirit is good.* Not true of our God. He made a good world. A world that spins and pops and sizzles. A world that sometimes is too hot and sometimes is too cold and sometimes is just right. And risotto is very good, as are these funky bodies we inhabit. I think the mindset I'm looking for is that wonderful balance: That ability to worship the Creator of these good things *more* than the objects themselves.

Right?

---

12 Romans 8:5

Paul: "For everything created by God is good, and noth—"[13]

Me: "Stay out of this, Paul, I've got it from here."

(I'm making this up as I go along, can you tell? Thanks for letting me think out loud. [Who did it better, me or Ed Sheeran?])

Sometimes it's hard to imagine any goodness remaining in this flesh of mine.

Sometimes it's difficult to acknowledge beauty untwisted by lust.

I've only been at this whole *living* thing for about 27 years, but it hasn't gotten much easier to figure out. When I was 17, I thought I'd have the world figured out by now. Turns out, 10k years of human history takes a little bit longer to sift through and learn from, much less 2,000 years of Christian history alone.

But God is good.

And like that freaking wonderful song says, I long for that day when my faith will be sight.[14] I also long for the day when my faith will be touch, smell, hearing, and *taste!* For that reason, as I often do, I conclude with the earliest of Christian prayers: *Maranatha! Come swiftly, Lord Jesus! Make all things new.*[15]

So may we fall in love with invisible things.

May you join me down here, with the other weak, frail, and dirty Christians.

And may your heart break, that it may be filled more with the Water of Life.

---

[13] 1 Timothy 4:4

[14] *It Is Well With My Soul* by Horatio Spafford and Philip Bliss, obviously.

[15] See Revelation 22:20

RAIN: A THERAPEUTIC MEMOIR

when the floodgates of heaven open, pay attention.

The swell of clouds rode into Dennis, Massachusetts that afternoon like a demon tangled in a little girl's white dress. Today I realized that almost all of the best days of my life involve being caught outside in the rain. I think it's something about the atmosphere shift that illuminates the previously arid world we once inhabited.

Derek and I sprinted from his car to the outdoor patio of a seafood place in this tiny surf town. Earlier that day I had sprinted along the coast as the clouds gathered opposite the sand bank protecting the shore. There was a shark watch at the time, but I saw the heads of seals bobbing in and out of the water, so I knew it was safe to dive in at the end of my run.

Today I'm working on an exercise given me by my counselor which delves deep into my past and the highs and lows in the life of Ethan Renoe. It's simultaneously really hard and beautifully illuminating. Some of the memories are hard to revisit because they introduced a painful belief or a longsuffering wound. Others ache to call to mind because of how beautiful and pure the moments are and I want to return to them with everything inside of me.

But I can't. Time only moves in one direction and I'm caught in her cruel current.

The summer of 2012 was easily the highlight of my life. It was the summer I was homeless on Cape Cod and living on the beach working as a stand-up paddleboard instructor. I had no car and no home. Every day was as fresh and exciting as the sunrise spattered across the morning sky. I didn't even have a smartphone yet, so my mind was yet unadulterated by constant updates and anxious scrolling. I have very few pictures from this summer despite how beautiful the entire season was (The picture above is one of the few saved from my flip phone).

There was the day Elbita and I were showing her cousin around and once again the warm rain struck. We had driven quite a way to find a ridiculously long dock which you could jump off at several spots.

One of my favorite things in the entire world is jumping off of things into water. (Even when I happen to kick a barnacle)

It was the end of July, as it is now, and we were caught in the warm rain, springing from the falling droplets into the brackish Atlantic; the tide was barely high enough to dive into the bay and we carelessly threw ourselves in.

Later, after driving back toward the mainland, we stopped at a path I'd wandered many times growing up. Today was different though. The woods were silent save the rain hitting leaves and the mist rising around the trunks of the trees.

The three of us were dressed in swimsuits and took off through the mud and puddles, dashing barefoot through the wet woods and experiencing a very surreal moment.

Then there was the rainy day in Thailand we walked past the trees draped in orange priest robes to reach the giant white Buddha resting atop the mountain.

The same happened years later when a storm rolled into Chicago and some boys from my dorm and I ran to the lake to see the gray sky penetrating the gray waters. Rain has a way of making even the busiest cities fall silent beneath its droplets. We dove into Lake Michigan as it was being broken up by the falling water.

Even years after that, I returned to the same lake during a midnight thunderstorm with my best friend. We ran barefoot through the city's streets, even diving into the lake as it was being struck by lightning. (Not the best idea, but a heckuva rush)

The rain makes me feel alive.

There's something messy about it, but at the same time cleansing.

It's paradoxically peaceful yet active.

It's vibrant but gray.

Rain is a singular thing made up of billions of things.

I'm teaching through Genesis for a few weeks at my church, and Rain is an interesting character in the book. Chapter 2 tells us that prior to the flood, rain never fell on the ground, but rather, streams rose up from the ground.

This is awesome because it makes Noah seem even more crazy to the people around him, telling them that water will fall from the heavens and flood the earth. Because that had literally never happened before. Knowing that gives new shape to the amount of faith Noah had when God told him a flood was coming. It's one thing to hear that rain is coming that will flood the world; it's another entirely when rain has never fallen from the sky before!

And when the rain does come, the Hebrew says that "the floodgates of the heavens were opened." Put yourself in the shoes of a Hebrew several millennia ago: You have no idea what the sky is, what clouds are, or how far up anything is. You don't know what the sun or moon is, nor do you know that stars are the same as the sun, just further away.

Suddenly all these things vanish and water starts to fall. Like it does today.

To this day, the floodgates of the heavens still open and refresh us and bathe us. The water grows our crops and quenches our thirst. Little pieces of heaven still fall on us, renewing our world and reminding us that there is peace in the chaos and stillness in the commotion.

One droplet of rain won't flood the earth or change your life, but a collection of many millions will. And it is the chorus of raindrops that moves us and stills us. It is this gathered water that transports me back to that bay off Cape Cod or the Thai mountaintop.

When the floodgates of heaven open, pay attention.

Maybe it's just me, but crazy things happen when we find ourselves caught in the rain. There is an enormous amount of freedom in letting go of your kempt and dry conditions and letting yourself run free, letting yourself be washed and allowing your skin to drink in the water.

Perhaps your preferred method of communing with the Transcendent is something else. Maybe it's snow, books, motorcycles, or stargazing. Whatever it is, pay attention. The Lord is vast and imminent. He is both incredibly far and unutterably close. For me, the rain is something that brings the heavens down to earth and reminds me of the nearness of God.

What's yours?

APRIL 7, 2017

on creativity & passion

I realized today as I was making a left-hand turn from Coal Mine Ave. onto Wadsworth Blvd. that all language is some type of amorphous mush that we squish between our fingers and form into semi-recognizable sentences, paragraphs, and similar concentric circles, in order to communicate.

Chefs can smash grains together in a thousand different ways, yet I can only construct a peanut butter and jelly sandwich. They see something in the ingredients that the rest of us don't. They look at a wheel of parmesan and see a billion complex curves and chemical reactions leading to a thousand different plates of food.

I fill my belly with 29 cent ramen.

Some people look at a pile of words and arrange them into the most base of sentences, making spartan use of their opportunity to communicate. They use language the same way I use food: Easy, cheap and simple. And there's nothing wrong with that!

But lately, I have been inspired. I have realized that I am a chef in the kitchen of language, responsible to pick up this pile of words that the ancients left on the floor and arrange them into something powerful and delicious.

Maybe you're a designer who arranges pieces of color and shape into something relaxing to the eye. Or maybe you simply staple drywall to beams so people can live in warmth. Or you're the farmer creating new and innovative ways to insert flavor into simple crops.

I once thought God hated creativity.

That time was earlier this week.

To be honest, these struggles come and go as I see a thousand knock-offs, like the imitation Banksys which pop up around the world. Inspiration means originality and authenticity, and I have grown weary seeing millions of photographers/models on Instagram contributing a 'new' idea to the internet.

#LiveAuthentic is possibly the biggest oxymoron in human history.

Am I being too cynical, or am I starved for fresh inspiration?

When you stumble upon true and original creativity, something shifts. I recently started watching a show about the best chefs in the world, what inspires them, and what gave them their starts.[16] The way they work with their ingredients initially made me want to go out and start a farm/3-star restaurant, but then I thought better of it. When these people are inspired, they make new culinary plates which the world hasn't seen before.

But what about when *I'm* inspired?

I write. Sometimes I paint, make music, or photograph.

One chef's wife relayed a story about when she and her husband were in a theater watching a movie. Afterward, she asked him what he thought of the film and he said he didn't really remember it because he was imagining a new way to arrange pasta in his mind.

I can relate, except in my case, it's not food that distracts me from reality, but words. Look at how these two words sound when you mash them together. What happens when you throw an article or linking verb into the mix?

I can waste hours thinking about simple phrases.

That same chef also talked about what initially attracted him to his wife. He used a phrase similar to one I've employed in the past:

"We spoke the same language."

Ironically, he was Italian and she was American, but I knew exactly what he meant. It's not a language of understood syllables and vocabulary, but of aligned experiences and ideas. In many ways, this goes far deeper than

---

[16] *Chef's Table* is definitely worth a watch.

simply speaking English together; the language of creativity connects people at a deep, deep level.

I think this is why the artists seem to feel things at a much deeper level than many of us. At times, they seem more alive, and at others they seem to die at the onset of heartbreak.

One day as I was driving up 6th Ave. toward Denver, I had a question pop into my head: Who gets paid simply to *experience* life? Initially, I wondered if only artists and writers get paid to experience life, and they drag the rest of us into their experience. But of course, as any good philosopher will tell you, language is incapable of communicating experience.

All of us experience life (though many of us try to escape the experience. *"I want off the ride early. This vivacious and vibrant world isn't really doing it for me. Drugs, porn, or Netflix, please."*), but not all of us communicate that experience. Not all of us take the time to express our experiences in whatever medium we love. And I think that's toxic.

The very first thing we learn about God in Genesis 1 is that He is a Creator.

He is…creative.

Later, we learn that we are made in His image.[17] What does this tell us except that we also, at one level or another, are meant to be little creators? We take the lumpy clay He has given us and work to straighten it out into beautiful things.

The word for this is possibly my favorite Hebrew phrase: *tohu-va-vohu.*

Say it out loud. Do it now.

It means *wild and waste.* And it's how we find the world in Genesis 1. "Now the earth was formless and void *(tohu-va-vohu)"* and over the course of the next two chapters, we see God take joy in arranging it and breathing into it and crafting new things that weren't there before. He provides us the raw materials for our creativity.

---

[17] Genesis 1:27

And here I am once more, taking the raw materials of letters and words and arranging them into thoughts. What is their purpose? What are they here for? I don't know.

I've decided that whenever I get into one of these 'moods' where my inspiration is running high and my zest for life is untethered, I'll simply name the post after the day that caused the spike in passion. I've done it before[18] and I'm not scared to do it again. These posts, though free-spirited and often aimless, tend to be some of my favorites, and based on the feedback I've gotten, they may be some of yours too.

Isn't it funny that when our experience causes such an overflow of emotion that we simply feel the need to create in whatever way God has most gifted us, others benefit as well? I'm on some cooking kick tonight, so have you seen the film *Chef*? There's one scene where his life is falling apart and he is so overwhelmed and emotional he rushes to his kitchen and stress-cooks. And the food he creates is a) enough to feed the population of The Island of Man, and b) so good-looking your mouth won't only water, it will flood.

Others benefit when our creativity bubbles over.

So I hope these bubbles meant something to you. I hope they stir you to create something fresh and new and exciting! Don't just imitate your favorite celebrities or artists. Imitation means nothing except that someone has already done it before!

Take after the Lord, whose creativity is breathtaking and always new.

Psalm 103: Sing a new song to the Lord...

---

[18] See "December 27, 2016" or "April 3, 2018"

OCTOBER 22, 2017

on what is real

Margery Williams, in some of the greatest sentences of the past century, wrote,

> Real isn't how you are made,' said the Skin Horse. 'It's a thing that happens to you. When a child loves you for a long, long time, not just to play with, but REALLY loves you, then you become Real.'
>
> 'Does it hurt?' asked the Rabbit.
>
> 'Sometimes,' said the Skin Horse, for he was always truthful. 'When you are Real you don't mind being hurt.'
>
> 'Does it happen all at once, like being wound up,' he asked, 'or bit by bit?'
>
> 'It doesn't happen all at once,' said the Skin Horse. 'You become. It takes a long time. That's why it doesn't happen often to people who break easily, or have sharp edges, or who have to be carefully kept. Generally, by the time you are Real, most of your hair has been loved off, and your eyes drop out and you get loose in the joints and very shabby. But these things don't matter at all, because once you are Real you can't be ugly, except to people who don't understand.[19]

Who understands? Who can see outside the ceiling of visible reality? How real exactly is our physical world? I could reach across this small cafe table and punch my roommate in the head and he would feel some very real pain.

Months ago I kissed a woman in a thunderstorm and a week later she broke my heart. Only one of those things was visible.

Yet again, I find myself rambling in a non-linear direction in a coffee shop. I'd tell you to buckle up, but I had the seat belts removed years ago.

---

[19] Margery Williams, *The Velveteen Rabbit*

I mean, whose idea was frogs and fireworks? Who invented that tingly feeling when you push at the base of your skull? Or the similar feeling when your favorite song crescendoes and rolls over you like a tidal wave?

In the words of N.D. Wilson, *This is not a sober world.*[20]

Wilson goes on to describe this world, full of spinning spheres and dragonflies and Jerry Seinfeld and gravity, and how no sane person would believe this fantastical universe really exists.

We are born inside the roller coaster, so we don't know anything else. Nothing else makes sense, yet we often get bored on this spinning world, forgetting that orange leaves are falling from trees and we're in a hurry to get to work.

It makes me wonder: If the God who made *all this* made...all this, then what else does He have going on? What kind of crazy things has He dreamed up for when our eyes tire of the sun and we surrender to the grave beneath fluorescent bulbs?

A baby in the womb has about as much concept of the outside world as we have of heaven. In comparison to the world to come, this place is just clammy, warm and dark. We don't even know what's coming for us.

I think even if God did try to describe it to us, we wouldn't believe Him.

He says the new heavens and earth are going to be so freaking mind-melting that we won't even remember the former things. We won't remember volcanoes (creators of the loudest sounds known to man) or the whirring soundtrack of *Inception*.

My friend Tony, impassioned, writes,

> Certain scorpions, lassoed by a tight enough ring of fire, trapped and seeing no way out, appear to sting themselves to death in despair. (This proves to be an illusion. Scorpions are immune to their own venom. Surrounded by fire, they suffer asphyxiation and the muscles of their limbs and tails twitch and spasm from oxygen deprivation, giving the

---

[20] N.D. Wilson, *Notes From The Tilt-A-Whirl*

impression of suicide. Is it that we would despair, that we are compelled to imagine they do? Who among us, hemmed in by the Holy, could breathe? How could you not writhe or choke or roll over dead? Could you stand? Could you not only breathe but sing? Could you do anything at all? It is a wonder Israel made it out of Egypt, let alone a noose of fire — and how could it not be a noose?)

How tightly knit are holiness and reality?

As I contemplate the Holy, I cannot help but wonder if God is a lot nearer than we know. Is He akin to the idea of The Big Other, as suggested by philosophers, or is He more like one of us, lying in a trough for feeding animals, come into our very real physicality?

Mary, with her own skin and hands and lap, held God.

I'm tempted to wonder what reality really is, and if somehow I'm missing *it* by focusing on the physical world too much. Sunday school has taught me that too much love of money, power, sex or food is what leads to sin.

But can't we sin in the opposite direction as well? Can we imitate Buddhist monks who long to escape the trappings of this physical world by focusing too much on an ethereal 'spiritual world'? As if the two were so easily divided.

We've believed the same lie as the Greeks: "Everything evaporates."

We are not Pompeians, awaiting a dry destruction as we simply cease to exist. Our remains will definitely not be discarded by the gods along with their coffee filters and doggie doo.

Several months ago on a turbulent flight, I penned the words I want on my tombstone (You should try this too. It really helps to think through the weight of death and what really matters to you). I've memorized them:

Only laughter, never weeping
For I have only laid my head.
I am not dead, I'm only sleeping
Until the resurrection of the dead.

I don't know about you, but no freaking grave can hold this body down. If it couldn't hold Jesus', it sure as hell won't hold mine.

Our 6'x8' plot in the cemetery is not the final resting place for our bodies. I don't know where it originated, but American Christians have adopted this mindset where we think our spirit departs to go to heaven but our bodies just decay for all of eternity.

I mean, have you opened your Bible recently? It hasn't changed in almost 2k years...

My youth pastor growing up always pointed out that the Bible says the Sadducees did not believe in the resurrection of the dead, "so they were sad, you see."

Get it?

If this world is all there is, that's a major bummer.

On the flip, if this crazy, magical world that sometimes smells like lavender and always spins is not only real, but points to something even *more real than itself*, cut me off a slice of that. I want in. Hebrews says that this is just a hazy shadow of the real things which are to come.[21] The Higher Country. Our older brothers and sisters await us there.

A lump swells in my throat when I contemplate *the real* and how little this impacts my life vs. how much it should. Two heroes of mine died this year. Nabeel Qureshi and Haddon Robinson both met Jesus face-to-face, and they're no longer wondering about the Great Mystery. They no longer long to peek behind the curtain at the man pulling the strings.

I'm going to end this curvy-Pennsylvania-road of a blog post with a line from Rich Mullins, fitting for the time of year. This refrain is ultimately the only thing we can cling to; the only unchangeable constant in this rotating planet.

> ...So hold me Jesus,
> 'cause I'm shaking like a leaf...

---

[21] Hebrews 10:1

GO LIMP.
you can simultaneously love and be terrified of the same thing.

"Put the break of the wave on your shoulder as you turn with it," my dad explained how to bodysurf two decades ago in New Jersey. "You need to catch it right when it's beginning to peel. Then you just put your hands out, your head down, and fly."

Last weekend I was on a black sand beach in Tapachula, Mexico. I went into the hot Pacific to bodysurf as I've done for as long as I can remember, when my family would make our annual trip to New Jersey. You wait for just the right break to come your way before making the dive.

It was hot in Mexico.

As in, I tried to walk out to the end of the jetty without my Crocs, but didn't even make it halfway because the rocks were deep frying the soles of my feet.

As in, I had to hop from one wet patch of sand to the next because my feet were ablaze.

As in, I tried to go into the water to cool down, but the ocean was so warm it made me more hot.

But it was in that water, being tossed around by the waves that I remembered God.

I think if we're honest, it's incredibly easy to forget God. We get caught up in the minutiae of work, friends, family, and productivity that we neglect to focus on the intimate presence of God. And sometimes I'm reminded of that divine presence when I'm in the ocean. Its ferocity and terror have long served to reorient me toward Him.

See, I grew up on Cape Cod and never fully recovered from her beauty. The Cape still seems like a spiritual home of sorts to me, as I look back on my time there with a sepia-tinted nostalgia which only grows more intense with time.

My parents will tell you I hated the Cape the first few years we lived there, as I missed my Colorado life and refused to adjust to life in Massachusetts. It wasn't until about the fourth year there that I began to embrace the beauty of the forests, kettle ponds, bays and beaches of Cape Cod. At some point, my experience shifted from resenting the peninsula to loving it. The constant greenery was a stark contrast to the arid plains of my home in Colorado.

The island and ocean seemed to exude fitful life and endless mystery, inviting my friends and I to come and discover.

Last weekend, I tasted that again.

I was gliding atop the choppy breaks in the Pacific, but sometimes the waves would break before reaching me. Their foamy power rolled toward me, screaming like a freight train. A small voice in the back of my mind whispered to me that humans don't belong here. In this ocean. Humans are not made to experience such raw and untamed power. sometimes those waves rush at you and all you can do is go limp as they tower stories overhead,

lift you up,

and do what they want with you.

Sometimes when I go bodysurfing, rather than try to catch or fight the wave, I go limp. I submit to it. I give in to its power and let it spin me and throw me as it will.

I almost feel emasculated admitting this, but then I remember that the thing to which I'm submitting is a ferocious city-eater who has claimed millions of human lives over the millennia. It's bigger than anything else on the face of the earth, and there is, indeed, nothing wimpy about being terrified of the ocean.

It's odd how you can simultaneously love and be terrified of the same thing.

I sometimes think we should go to church with the same trepidation-mixed-with-affection that I do when I go in the ocean. Rather than fear and trembling, we tend to stroll into church with the same bored expectation my middle schoolers bring into history class.

Where in our own faith stories did we lose the awe and wonder about God? When did we forget to both love Him and be terrified of Him? For me, the periodic trip to the ocean and splashing about in something ineffably larger than me is what reorients my thinking about God. Maybe for you it's the mountains. Or the city. Or some other terrifying and foreign experience which refocuses your mind and experientially reminds you that you're *not* actually that significant or powerful.

Reading this post on your laptop, phone, or tablet probably won't do that for you. I hope you can power it down and go be reminded of the raw power of God; the intimate nearness and the terrifying strength.

Do you remember that?

Do you remember what it was that first brought you to your knees in repentance? Or, if you're one who has never had that experience but merely inherited your parents' experience, why haven't you sought it out for yourself? Ask God for it. Ask Him to show Himself to you and make you undeniably aware

of Him.

BEAUTY & THE MAD MARCH OF TIME
the progression of all things toward death is what makes them beautiful.

I watched out the window as the city of Philadelphia shrunk beneath us. No matter how many flights I take, there are still a few knots in my stomach which refuse to give up wondering

Will this be the one? Will this finally be the flight that ends it all?

Some of you may fly a lot, while others rarely or never. I used to love the romantic notion of flying. I used to write a dozen poems per flight, as the idea of flying thousands of miles in a mere few hours was (and is) truly magical.

Nowadays, I plug into my podcasts and try to fall asleep before we touch down.

I think all human beings find a lot of whimsy in novelty.

The first kiss is so much more magical than the 1,528th.

So is the first dance, or the first time in a new city.

I remember the first time I went swing dancing in an ancient castle in Chicago. It was October, 2012 and I will never forget that night as long as I live. The windows were open, allowing a crisp fall breeze to drift in and after a few songs, my friends and I retreated out to the balcony overlooking the city from behind a low stone wall. The entire night could have been straight out of an early two thousands chick flick; it was *that* magical.

But then we went a few weeks later.

And a few weeks after that.

And by the fifth or sixth time, the magic was slipping away. All that beauty of freshness and newness had somehow slipped through our fingers and gotten away from us.

Time marched madly on.

Now I'm flying home from a family vacation to New Jersey. I've been making this trip since I was born, so the traditions and memories from Ocean City run deep in my blood. However, the older I get, the more I see the same thing happening. The magic is slipping away from this tourist trap I once beheld as utopia.

When I was 4, the annual trip to New Jersey contained a sort of magic that has only been captured in pencil-illustrated children's books. But now that I'm older, I see the town as less magical and more money-grabby. Not that I don't enjoy the time with my family and the natural wonder of the ocean, but the trip itself is less…whimsical.

A few weeks ago, I was driving and listening to August Burns Red's song "Echoes." I think it may be their masterpiece. There is one part of the song, about a 30-second clip toward the end, which encapsulates all good things about the genre: Power, emotion, brutality, harmony, et al.

I found myself wishing I could just pause the song and somehow dwell in that moment of raw power and emotion. I wanted to stretch the feeling of those 30 seconds out into a shelter and build myself a home.

But of course I can't.

You have your own magical songs. There is a certain line or note that simply speaks to you in some way far richer than words. You wish you could simply put that hook or chorus on repeat and stay there. You just want to soak up the realness in her voice right there, or find a way to encapsulate the crescendo of this one song…but you can't.

And the reason we can't capture the beauty of those musical moments is that time is a necessary component of song. Without time, you don't have a melody, you just have one note. Without time, you don't have lyrics, you just have one syllable uttered eternally.

Without time, there is no beauty.

My aging grandfather drove me to the airport an hour ago. I remember when he used to play football with our family, and now he can hardly get in or out of his van—the one with the handicap plates. I think of his weakening body and the various ailments which have seized it and made his hands shake uncontrollably.

My throat swells at 30,000 feet.

A few months ago, my roommate from college explained to me why he cried at our friend's wedding:

"Some things are just too beautiful to behold and the only response is to weep."

My grandfather is aging and will not live on this earth forever. There is great sadness in that, but there is also great beauty. He is a great man and his life, as it rises and falls, will have been utterly spectacular.

Just as a song rises and falls, time leads its progression and there is beauty in this progression.

The natural progression of all things is what makes them beautiful.

This is why I still cannot get over the film *Logan*. While most of her superheroes exist in a timeless universe, Marvel chose to show the progression of time and the persistence of age in one of her brightest sons, Wolverine. The beauty of the film comes from the idea that all things age; all things die. And I think the reason this film brought me to tears is because it realizes this truth so graphically.

There is true, real beauty in this progression of time.

That is why the wisest man to ever live, Solomon, wrote that beauty is fleeting.[22] As I continue the endless search for my bride, it's hard not to be distracted by timely beauty: The look of her face or body as it rests in time *right now*. It's much harder to peer through the exterior and see the things that will truly last; the parts of her which will grow more and more beautiful with time. The things that I will want holding me when I weep or when my body begins to break down. The parts of her that I will want by my side even when all of her *present* beauty has faded.

Time kills all things,

but it also reveals their deepest, most painful beauty.

This is why certain parts of those songs are so freaking powerful. But then the song ends. The experience is over and we move on. And you go to bed and wake up in the slow silence of dawn into another day which has never happened before.

I wonder if a lot of the human struggle is a battle against this time. We try so hard to hold onto things in their present forms that we miss the real

---

[22] Proverbs 31:30

beauty of them—the fact that they are in flux and dying like us. The monstrous crescendo of your favorite song will eventually fade out, just like you will someday.

Maybe this is why we all love photographs so much: They hold the ability to freeze a split second of time in a manageable fashion you can always look back upon.

People in LA pay thousands of dollars to look like they did when they were younger instead of embracing the authentic beauty of age. We want to remember the magic of a concert by preserving it on our phones, but of course these tinny representations do little to convey the magic of the night's experience.

So what is the solution? It seems like we are fighting a losing battle as we wage war on the foe of time.

Perhaps the answer is not to battle time, but to find her beauty. Embrace that magical song as it passes by you in your headphones yet again. Enjoy your friends in their present state, instead of wishing they were the way they used to be *back then*.

Time marches madly on.

I wonder if heaven is the summation of all of these passing blips we experience when we hear a great song or hold a baby as it falls asleep. C.S. Lewis notes that these things are simply tastes of what is to come. The difference is, in this world, they come and go. They are not permanent. I can't help but think that heaven is simply an eternity of dwelling in those magical moments. The ones we only wish we could hold onto in this life.

May we be people who age well; a people who suck the life out of every passing second rather than longing for the past or diving into the future. May we learn to recognize the beauty of time as she whizzes past us; the slow-walking seductress leading us to our graves.

JULY 22, 2018: THE SOLIDNESS OF GOD

<u>you who dare God to reveal Himself: are you ready for what you'll see?</u>

Half a year ago I kissed a girl in her apartment at midnight. Her roommates had gone to sleep and she and I were left talking on the couch while Netflix's *House of Cards* flickered silently on the flat screen in the background.

It seemed to mean so much at the time, but now I can't remember the moment at all. Can't remember her smells or her motion. I don't recall very much; simply the fact that it happened.

It seemed to mean so much to me at the time, yet now the finer details of the episode evade my memory. What once weighed so heavily on my mind and my emotions now feels more like a dream from which I've awoken.

You live in a foreign country long enough and meaning will eventually come of the alien voices which were once mere babbling sound. Minds expand as they extend toward the infinite and I'm nervous about what awaits us once we become aware of it. Lewis says that once we reach that High Country, every ache and pain we felt in this life will seem like nothing more than a dream from which we were all too glad to stir.[23]

They say you can't take it with you, and I've realized something: I used to think it was because you can't carry your bricks of gold with spiritual hands; I used to think they would be too heavy for our ethereal hands to lift skyward.

Now I think it's the opposite.

Now I think our bricks of gold or silver aren't *real* enough to be carried to that High Country. Lewis also wrote that when Jesus passed through walls in His resurrection body, it wasn't because He was some effervescent phantom, but because He was more real, more solid than the walls

---

[23] C.S. Lewis, *The Great Divorce*

themselves. That Jesus walked through the walls the way a man passes through a fog.[24]

When I was a boy I had a dream that my parents bought me a .22 caliber rifle. I was ecstatic and took it to the woods to shoot. When I awoke, I was saddened to find that it was only a dream and I was still an unarmed 8-year-old. I had the same chance of bringing that dream-gun with me from sleep as we have of carrying anything from this life into the New Country where we are going.

You want to take your looks with you to heaven, so you can hide behind them from the fiery eyes of God? Or your bank account? Or your intellect?

Christ, the realest of the real, looks at us and asks, "How much longer will you continue to cling to these vaporous items—this sex and this money—before you begin to desire what is real?"

Last week I was on the phone with my friend Dalton. I asked him what he thinks of the invisibility and silence of God. "I believe that the hiddenness of God is one of the greatest gifts God can give to mankind."

Moses peeks at God's divine rear end and his face radiates with a blinding glow for days.[25]

You who dare God to reveal Himself: Are you ready for what you will see? Can you withstand the awful and excruciating glory of the Almighty?

It's a gift. It's grace. God hides Himself, not out of elusive menace, but out of incredible mercy. And I'm grateful. I'm glad I still get to see the beauty peeking through the blinds of the sunset or in the strange warmth of my cousin's infant daughter as she slept on my chest last month.

I've been overtaken by an overwhelming God.

Are you aware that you're born into a language? Whatever you grow up speaking, did you know your language reduces your opportunity for

---

[24] C.S. Lewis, *Perelandra*

[25] Exodus 33

knowledge to a fraction of a sliver of the universe? Our epistemology is confined to a ten mile radius around our house.

And yet we are bold enough to assume that we understand God.

What a crazy thought. We don't even understand ourselves.

Gregory of Nazianus wrote that at the baptism of Jesus,

> "Christ rises from the waters; the world rises with Him."

So may you rise.

May we rise from our collective sleep to a world much more real and much more alive that the one we've been inhabiting. May we not fall in love with this world of our dreams, but may we starve for the world to come. Uncurl us from our lifelong navel-gazing, O overwhelming God! May our eyes behold the real light of your presence, and may our skin develop to withstand its rays.

LOOKING FOR HEALING: MY LAST DAYS IN XELA
<u>time flies when you're having fun, but it crawls when you're suffering...</u>

I awoke to the sound of the world in Xela just like every day for the past year, only today it was different. Today the sun shone on me as I walked to my favorite coffee shop—the one where I wrote my first blog post in Guatemala, and now the place where I pen my last.

My life here has been chiastic: I think about my last night with Claudia, our last date at the same steakhouse where we had our first.

In a moment like this, you would expect some tried maxim like, 'man, my time in Xela just flew by,' but today, that would be a lie. I think it's been one of the hardest years of my life and I have learned something which logically makes sense:

Time flies when you're having fun, but it slows down when you're suffering.

I can't help but wonder if that's because God really wants us to pay attention in those moments. Like, to really pay attention.

The word 'suffering' also needs some explanation for those who don't know me too well. For the entirety of 2019, I have prayed the same prayer every day: "God, I just want one full day of being healthy."

As of now, it has yet to happen.

I'm 90% sure I had mono, which morphed into a plethora of fun co-infections. I was so sleepy it felt like I weighed a metric tonne. The worst part though, was definitely my throat, especially considering how my job was essentially to yell over the chaos of middle schoolers for 8 hours a day. It would start out sore and swollen in the morning, and be exponentially worse by the time school ended.

I also could not taste a thing, which may seem like a minor thing in the grand scheme of existence, but you quickly discover what a gift from God it is to be able to enjoy His creation with our tongues.

I visited five different doctors, each of whom danced around the fact that they had no idea what was wrong (compounded by the fact that we didn't speak the same language) by prescribing different drugs each time. Today, I have no idea how many chemicals are running through my bloodstream. On top of this, I had an extremely painful abscess in my—I'll just say it—bum, which recurred a few times as well.

I've told many friends that I now have a deeper appreciation for people who go through incurable, chronic afflictions. I used to look at them without thinking twice about it.

"Oh, of course that person has oxygen tubes! *C'est la vie!*"

"Ah, it's a real bummer that person is bound to a wheelchair."

etc.

After being sick for over four months, I now understand it on a deeper level. That's not to say I understand their experiences entirely, for I plan to get better and to return to full, active health eventually, but I do understand more than I did. I've learned the bitterly ironic pain of well-intended comments like, "Ah, that's a real bummer!" or even, "I hope you get better soon!" For some reason, they sting worse because you know the speaker has absolutely no experience or real interest in your pain.

Perhaps the best response I received was from a co-worker who, on our last day of school, genuinely asked me what I've learned from being sick for so long. I had to pause and think about it. Then I told him it damaged my faith because God was so far away.

It's easy to dance around and sing worship songs when you have the energy to do so. It's hard to do the same when you've been sick for months with no recovery on the horizon. Even harder when you've been sick for years, or your whole life.

I recently heard a story of an elderly woman who became very sick and being bedridden caused her to lose a lot of bloodflow. The doctors had to take one foot, then the other. Then one hand, then the other, then a leg, then an arm. All the while, her favorite song continued to be "Amazing Grace" and the nurses were astounded. This woman had no more limbs; would never do anything ever again, yet she resounded with joy and hymns.

The hospital chaplain came to visit her one day and asked how she had such joy in the midst of her tremendous suffering.

"If you don't know my joy," she told him, "you don't know my Jesus."

This story stuck with me because my symptoms pale in comparison to hers, yet I have trouble finding joy in the midst of my suffering. I imagine more lessons will be learned in hindsight, but one thing I can say is this: Until you go through an extensive season of suffering firsthand (and I don't mean a week-long cold), you cannot identify with those whose lives are suffering.

The Holy Spirit is referred to as our Comforter,[26] but what comfort can He give to those who already have it? You don't comfort the comfortable, you comfort those who suffer. Perhaps this pain really does bring us closer to Jesus of Nazareth in the end; how else will we identify with the Suffering Servant?

---

[26] John 14

I think about a different type of suffering, like the last night I was with Claudia. I walked her out to her dad's car, opened the door for her and said hello to her father. I squeezed her right arm with my left hand and closed the door behind her.

Time slipped by as I made my way back to the door of my house and suddenly, I was leaning on the table sobbing.

Then I was in the bathroom sobbing, wiping my face with TP.

Then I was up in my room, crying on the bed, both wanting to be alone and wanting to talk to all my closest friends at the same time. I called one when I thought I could hold it together. My voice was frail as I told him I'd just said goodbye to Claudia. He said a lot of nice and comforting things, but the one that stood out to me was, "tears indicate significance." The fact that I cried after saying goodbye to her—possibly forever—heavily indicated that she meant something to me. Evidently, she meant a lot more than I thought.

For such a small person, she sure left a gigantic hole.

If nothing else, Claudia taught me that I can be loved, no matter how I look, no matter how I feel. She taught me that I can be an object of desire and that, in a weird way, God can also love me. She has been an anti-narrative for a lot of rejection and pain from other adventures in unrequited love.

In essence, she helped me learn the lesson I've been learning from another person very familiar with suffering, the late Renaissance painter Rembrandt (via Henri Nouwen).[27] He was a brilliant artist, but much of his younger years were spent in monetary extravagance and gratuitous philandering.

The knowledge of his background only makes his latter years stand out more. He would lose four children and two wives in his lifetime, and after spending all his money, would die a poor man and be buried in an unmarked church grave.

---

[27] Henri Nouwen, *The Return of the Prodigal Son*

It was during his later years, however, that he would also paint perhaps his most famous work, *The Return of the Prodigal,* which shows the foolish younger son returning home, being held by his father. His life was stripped bare of the foolish, fleeting distractions until only the deep, significant

things remained. No longer is there meaningless fun or careless expenditure; simply an eternal loving embrace from a good father to a wandering son.

Most of us live our lives as this younger son while he is on the way back home: We feel broken, useless, like no one could ever love us again and weak. We may even constantly rehearse apologies/excuses in our head as we try to make our way back to God.

What Rembrandt's masterpiece reminds us, and what I have learned over the past several months, is that looking for reasons why we should be accepted is a fool's errand. If you cannot accept yourself, flaws and pain and baggage and all, then remember this: It's not your job to prove your acceptable-ness. Sometime it takes suffering and sickness to strip away all the things we use to try to hide our unworthiness, and it's not fun but it's significant.

As Jordan Peterson likes to say, there is nothing worse than meaningless suffering.[28] As Christians, we know that nothing is meaningless. We know that even our suffering has purpose, and I would contend that most of this suffering is to remove ourselves from ourselves in order to know Christ more deeply. Hopefully it won't take a year's worth of suffering for you to draw nearer to Him, but sometimes that's what it takes.

May we be people who suffer with purpose, finding comfort from our Comforter and healing from the Healer. May we suffer well. May we continually long for the day when our faith becomes sight and we no longer need to suffer in order to know Christ.

---

[28] Jordan B. Peterson, *12 Rules for Life: The Antidote to Chaos*

HOW TO BELIEVE

reflections on God, church, faith, and other trivial things

ALL THINGS NEW

this is what makes Good Friday so freaking good.

Last night, after our church's Good Friday service, we screened Mel Gibson's *The Passion of the Christ* for the youth group. Shockingly, some of the middle schoolers fell asleep because they said it was too boring (I think the subtitles got them).

It was only my second time seeing the film, and the first time I was unmoved. I had gone into it fully expecting to weep, but didn't. This time, I went in with no expectations.

I think it's the desensitization of seeing violence and gore on screens all the time that has caused me to barely react to the whipping of Christ, even when the Roman soldiers bring out the Cat of Nine Tails and pull chunks of skin from his ribs. Several of the girls in the group cried throughout the brutal film, but it was not the violence that caused tears to streak down my face.

I was lying on the ground watching the screen as Jesus pulled His heavy cross through the streets of Jerusalem. Blood covers every inch of His body. His mother is trying to push through the crowd to catch up to Him, and when she finally does, Jesus turns to her and says,

"See, mother, I make all things new."

I lost it. The tears poured down my cheeks and my chest heaved.

The power in those words reverberated through my body and my mind suddenly filled with a thousand thoughts about what it means for Christ—battered, bloody, and barely able to walk—to make all things new.

When I lived in Chicago, I attended a church whose motto was "Joining God as He makes all things new." I never gave it much thought until last night, but the more I meditate on those words, the more power they garner.

We follow in His crimson footsteps as Jesus stumbles to His death. We put to death our porn addictions and abuse we've received in the past. We look at Jesus, dragging His execution tool up the hill to Golgotha; dragging with Him our substance dependency and shame, our self-hatred and pride.

With Him, all old things are put to death.

And with Him, fresh life erupts from the grave as we also follow Him out of the grave and into

all

things

made

new.

I cried on the ground because I'm learning to apply the words of Christ to myself. And to the lives of my friends. And to the kids in my youth group. And to your life.

When Jesus says He makes all things new, I believe He means *all*.

Not *some*.

Not *most*.

All.

And how beautiful is this redemption! Do we believe the bloody Christ when He says this? Or do we doubt the extent of His reach?

Have you been an alcoholic for 40 years, or do you think you're too ugly to be worthy of love because of scars from the past?

Jesus makes all things new.

He does not do it in a cute, clean, pretty way. He opened up His own veins and sacrificed His own body so that we, the Beloved of the Lord, can be made new.

Do you believe it? Or is it just a nice sentiment?

(I'm in a coffee shop, wondering why I come to public places to write pieces like these. I keep shoving the lump back down into my chest because at any moment I'm gonna just collapse into a blubbering heap of sobs.)

Robert Smalls was born in 1839 as a slave in South Carolina. At the age of 12, he was sent into the fields as a laborer. In his twenties, he was assigned to a ship in the Civil War where he led a mutiny on the ship and commandeered the boat up North to gain his freedom.

Word spread about the slaves who bravely escaped their bondage and earned their freedom in the north, and Smalls grew in prominence and notoriety. A few years later, after the war ended, he returned to the plantation where he was born into slavery and bought it since his former owner had died.

But here's the crazy part.

Sometime after he had moved back into the plantation where he had been born a slave, a knock sounded on the door. There, standing on his porch, was his master's wife, now a helpless widow. She had nowhere else to turn.

Robert Smalls let her live with him and his family until her death.

This was the woman whom he had known his whole life as a master. A white woman who was 'higher than him' and likely even abused him. Smalls had every right to kick her off his porch and tell her to get lost.

But he didn't.

This is what grace looks like. This is what it looks like when Jesus takes your hurt, anger, bitterness, and hatred up the hill with Him. And kills them.

This is what it looks like when all things are made new.

A former slave takes care of his master's widow.

I think God has a distaste for old, stale things. Psalm 103 commands us to 'sing a *new* song to the Lord.' Get out of that tired place of hopelessness and depression and put it to death.

Die.

Rise.

Be made new.

"Jesus rises from the waters; the world rises with Him."
                    -Gregory of Nazianzus, on the baptism of Christ

That's what baptism is: All of you submerges beneath the surface, and all of you rises again. New. Clean.

Do you believe it?

Put those old things to death and join the God-man Jesus as He makes all things new.

All things.

All

things.

In case you've ever wondered, this is what makes Good Friday so freaking *good*.

HOW GOOD IS YOUR GOD?

As we find ourselves broken, Jesus simply asks one question...

Somewhere between our physical bodies and the Great Spirit, who is Yahweh the Eternal, is some kind of metaphysical connection. Lately I've been wrestling with where the small string is which I can pull with my fingertips and unravel this great mystery of how, exactly, the Transcendent interacts with us here on earth.

Last night I was listening to a podcast in which the preacher (who was hyper-charismatic and perhaps had a slightly over-realized eschatology[1]) said that he and his church spent time one Sunday meditating on the goodness of God. And as they did, people in the church began being healed.

He said something like, 'as we simply meditated on the goodness of God and worshipped Him and prayed, the goodness of God began to manifest itself in peoples' bodies. We simply don't realize just how *good* God is.'

I completely believe every word the preacher said, but I struggle with it. And maybe you do too.

I struggle to believe that God would show up and heal people simply because they were talking about how good He is. I struggle because I came out of a giant organization which would constantly pray for miracles and 'speak things over people' and claim to see a lot of healings and the like, which turned out to simply be mental persuasion more than actual miracles. I struggle because I was never once healed of any of my chronic health problems in my years in that organization. I struggled because there's a cynical mouth inside of me that's always saying 'bad theology always hurts people' (which is true) and then refuses to be stretched or to grow.

But then I realize that the root of this struggle is I don't really believe God is *that* good.

---

[1] For those of you who aren't huge nerds, that just means he leans more toward the line of thought that God will constantly provide miracles and show up in crazy, supernatural ways

I don't believe this eternal, glorious God cares enough to transcend whatever membrane divides the spirit from the flesh and touch our bodies with His fingertips.

Haven't you been there?

Haven't you dwelt in places where it seems like the goodness of God is nothing more than a nice piece of fiction?

Last night I was speaking to my youth group about sexual purity. We were looking at the story of Joseph, specifically the scene in Genesis 39, where he is seduced by his master's wife, but he flees from her, despite the consequences. I told my kids to also flee from sexual immorality.[2]

Because what you do with your body matters.

Our bodies are not mere intellectual conceptions which can be tossed hither and yon without consequences. They were made to interact with the beautiful creation of God, and with each other in beneficial ways, and when we use them in a way that makes beautiful things ugly, there are consequences.

As I spoke to these kids, most of whom come from broken families, and some of whom have been abused, I saw their faces begin to sink. I could see the thought bubbles hovering above their heads.

Welp. It's too late for me....Oh well.

And I saw myself leading these kids down the same path of shame and rebellion which was so pervasive in the 90's and early 00's. When you're simply told not to do something, you just want to rebel. And when a rule has been broken once, what's to keep us from breaking it again? And again? And again? Especially if it feels good. And then shame rushes in.

I was about to wrap up the message when I remembered I had thrown one more slide into the presentation. It was the photo from *The Passion*, showing the battered and solid red face of Jesus gazing into the morose eyes of His mother, with the subtitle at the bottom.

---

[2] 1 Corinthians 6:18

See, mother, I make all things new.

Of course I could barely speak because the lump in my throat was the size of a loaf of bread.

"This scene was while Jesus carried His cross up the hill to the place where He would be crucified," I explained. "He would take all of our sin and all of our shame and put it to death with Him. The question is, do you want to be made new? Do you believe that when He says *all things*, He really means all things? Or do you think you are too dirty and too far gone to be made new by Him?"

We are people of very small faith.

When I get lost thinking about deep philosophies and how on earth humans can transcend the thin barrier between us and the Invisible, it's easy for me to forget God's chosen method of revealing Himself and His goodness: Himself.

Jesus is the connection between humans and the divine.

His path to making all things new is one stained with droplets of blood.

His own.

What we do with our physical bodies matters because we too are persons comprised of spirit and body. We are remiss to divorce the two and use our body as a shortcut to satisfaction at the neglect of our spirit. It's the same as a man who waters his plants but forgets to feed his dog.

But we screw up.

And when we find ourselves in a place of sexual shame and brokenness, I think Jesus simply asks one question:

Do you want me to make you new?

I am a man of weak faith who daily doubts the goodness of God. I need Him to make me new several times a day. I don't know what happened in that one pastor's church; if those people were simply telling stories or if they were really healed by *Jehovah Rafa,* God our Healer. I don't know what the goodness of God looks like, or if you can bottle it up and spin a profit from it.

But I do know this: The goodness of God looks like the mangled and battered body of the God-man Jesus Christ while He hangs pathetically on the cross. The goodness of God is this carpenter from Nazareth making all things new while He collapses under the weight of His death trap.

The goodness of God is far greater than I can begin to comprehend, but I'm glad that preacher made me stop and think about it.

May we be people who wander around the corridors and archways in the cathedral of God's goodness; never exhausting its magnitude and always seeing it from a new angle. May we tire our minds thinking about the *big*ness of His *good*ness, and then think about it some more.

Because you never know what will happen…Perhaps those invisible fingertips will punch through the thin barrier once again and bring new strength to your bones.

EXPERIMENTING WITH GRACE
I found myself violently resisting what he was saying…

It seemed like every ounce of flesh wrapped around my bones pulled away from what my pastor was saying. I found myself resisting the truth he was speaking with the same furor as I resist putting my hand in a flame.

"Look, Ethan," he told me, "it seems like you don't have a relationship with God as much as you do with laws and rules."

What?

I internally recoiled from his words. I couldn't be one of *those* guys.

Could I possibly have become the pharisaical monitor of right and wrong? *I love God!* I thought to myself. *I'm, like, the opposite of a rule-follower.*

He proceeded to move forward and deconstruct many of my actions the past few months, for which I am now apologizing to you, my readers, for watering down the gospel of grace.

See, as insightful as I thought I was, I was still living in a place of labeling certain actions as 'good,' and others as 'bad.' Today I realized that's not true.

Because God is not about self-improvement.

He doesn't want us to slowly pick ourselves up by our bootstraps, and slowly, over the next fifty years or so, to crawl nearer to Him. He isn't sitting there, checking off columns as He observes our Good and Bad actions.

Robert Farrar Capon puts it more distinctly:

> Grace cannot prevail until law is dead, until moralizing is out of the game. The precise phrase should be, until our fatal love affair with the law is over—until, finally and for good, our lifelong certainty that someone is keeping score has run out of steam and collapsed.[3]

I realized that so many of my actions the past few months have been contrary to Christ-like living, even though they were praised as just that.

I went on TV 12 times in one week, nearly every time, mentioning that I am a Christian and I am grateful for what Christ has done for me. But what did this do? It made me more appealing to many Christians, and less appealing to non-believers. It didn't reflect the weakness that Paul showed, or the humility with which Christ conducted His ministry, but a braggart gospel of power and of myself.

A few months later, I announced a new campaign to talk about pornography, and specifically my struggles with it, which was also lauded with praises of being 'vulnerable' and 'encouraging.' But it really was just a careful packaging of my sins so as to just be appealing enough: Ethan the humble, broken hero.

---

[3] Robert Farrar Capon, *Between Noon and Three: Romance, Law, and the Outrage of Grace*

"That's not what confession is," my pastor told me today. "True confession should make everyone you confess to want to flee the room. Confession is a painful, self-deprecating, and nauseating exposure of our true selves. When confession is true, we *are* exposed; we do not *do* the confessing."

I am not a good person.

Therefore, every action I have ever done is not a good one. Confession is letting another human being catch a glimpse of this (because *OH!* how we use every mechanism in our arsenal to hide ourselves: humor, intellect, godliness and good looks, to name a few).

And if I am not a good person, and nothing I can do will make me such, what am I striving for?

"There are two types of repulsive sinners," my pastor continued. "Prostitutes and Pharisees."

It clicked.

"By fighting so hard to quit struggling with pornography, you're really just trying to convert from a Prostitute to a Pharisee. It's sin management. You don't have a porn problem, you have an Ethan problem."

God is not interested in self-improvement. He is interested in perfection. Anything short of perfection repulses Him.

So what is my option then? I wondered. *Surely God doesn't want me to keep walking in sin!*

"You're a whore right now. Don't aspire to be a Pharisee," he said. "The only option is death."

I nodded as I detected a whiff of grace in the air.

Grace is not a completion of laws and rules. It is not a mere forgiveness of wrongdoing, but it is setting ablaze the entire law book. It is violently demolishing the systems we have constructed to dictate how life *ought* to be lived. In grace, Jesus moves toward us and takes upon Himself our sin and shame. This was a trite phrase until my pastor put it this way: "Ethan no longer has a porn addiction. Jesus does."

What?! Jesus doesn't have a porn addiction! Jesus is perfect!

We so often talk about Jesus taking *all* of our sins to the cross, but when it becomes more tangible than abstract, we shudder. Surely Something so holy cannot move so near to us and take our burdens from us! Surely He can't be *that* good!

If Jesus truly comes to us with an offer to trade lives, the implications are huge. It means He takes ALL of our life, and gives none of it back. It means an utter destruction of sin.

It means we die.

Paul wrote, "it is no longer I who lives, but Christ who lives in me."

If Jesus takes our entire life, what do I get? I get Him. I get His perfect life.

Daily I am tempted to return to the Gospel of Good Works. Shame whispers into my ear that I'm not good enough, and if I just improved a little more, then I'd be okay. Shame calls us back to a god that says *just be a little better, then I'll chill with you.*

The voice of Jesus says, *I did not come for the healthy but the sick; I did not come to call the righteous, but sinners.*[4]

So, my friend, are you being scorched by the holy? Is He drawing so near to you that everything else you have bound yourself to has melted away, or are you still clinging to your handful of good deeds like a child holds a mound of sand?

We are a sinful people of weak faith.

And we are approached by a God whose terrible strength extends an open hand and invites us to let Him kill us.

And what a beautiful death it is!

> Listen carefully: Unless a grain of wheat is buried in the ground, dead to the world, it is never any more than a grain of wheat. But if it is

---

[4] Matthew 9:12

284

buried, it sprouts and reproduces itself many times over. In the same way, anyone who holds on to life just as it is destroys that life. But if you let it go, reckless in your love, you'll have it forever, real and eternal.[5]

ROTE THEOLOGY.
in theology, there are no airtight pipes.

I coined this term in my head several months ago. I think it's pretty simple and common, so I'm stoked to share it here.

Most of us are familiar with the concept of *rote memorization*. We all know that 2×4 is 8. We don't need to count out on our fingers how many 4's there are and what they add up to. We all probably know the capital of our home state without giving it much thought. We know how to drive from work to our home without much thought. These things all fall into the category of *rote* knowledge. The formula or path or idea is cemented into our minds.

The opposite of this would be a new or dynamic idea that requires thought and figuring out. Writing a research paper, navigating to a new place, or painting a portrait are things that require active engagement and creative thinking in their approach.

A while ago, I realized that my approach to God began to look more rote than dynamic. I realized that if someone asked me a question, I had pre-selected answers loaded into my canon of theological wisdom, ready to dispense at a moment's notice.

Hey Ethan, what's the trinity?

Well amigo, it's this eternal and pre-existent relationship between the Father, Son and Holy Spirit, one substance yet three persons. The Greek is *homoousion*, but we know them as co-equally God, yet different in work…

---

[5] John 12:24-25, *The Message*

285

I find myself doling out answers like this more often than I like. Rather than delighting (for instance) in the mystery and wonder of the Trinity, I have the answers condensed down into a few sentences. It's as if I have squeezed the entire ocean down into a few drinkable drops.

I've noticed that in spiritual growth, I have developed a pattern of coming to a conclusion on a certain topic, nailing it down, and moving on. *Okay, I now have figured out what I think about marriage and sexuality. Time to move on to eschatology.*

I think this is an incredibly toxic way to do theology and spirituality. It is different from nearly every other area of study, in that there is nothing rote about it. Doctors can memorize different bacterial strains and know that fruit is good for you and sugar is bad. Plumbers know that gravity always pulls water down, and a hole in a pipe means water will escape.

Yet in theology, if we are honest, there are no airtight pipes.

We have no more means of describing God and His kingdom than a baby in the womb has a way to describe the outside world. Someone could tell the fetal infant what it's like to be cold, or to taste a strawberry, or what color is like but he has no way of fully *knowing* those things until the eschaton, aka, birth.

For that fetal child to claim that he fully understands those things would be absurd. He can only describe sunshine while admitting that he is one who has not yet experienced it.

In the same way, when we talk about God, we should not claim to be ones who fully grasp Him or His awesomeness or glory. Our human languages are mere grasping at straws in comparison to the glorious reality which is Him and all things which we have not yet experienced.

For us to rotely claim that we have certain areas of theology figured out is to say that the god we believe in is incredibly small. He fits inside this little static box we've built for him.

Helmut Thielicke wrote of people like this, "I found in them no trace of life or truths learned by experience. I smelled only corpses of lifeless ideas."[6]

This is not to say that all theology and systems are flawed and awful. Rather, our approach to theology should be full of life and vibrant! We should approach God and His Word with the same attitude of David, who in Psalm 96 wrote, "Sing to the Lord a new song!" This command is actually repeated often throughout scripture. I think this is because God doesn't want us to fall into a pattern of rote recital of His word and His wonders. He wants us to know Him afresh every day, speaking (or singing) about Him differently every day, as we discover new aspects of Him and who He is.

Is your theology dynamic or stale? Have you metaphorically been singing the same old song to Him, or are you constantly in awe of Him, unable to fully put your knowledge of Him into words?

I think that as we mature as theologians, our answers to questions more often will be "I don't know, but this is some of what I've learned…" rather than assuming we have a complete grasp on our religion.

The more we learn about God, the more we realize how ridiculously huge He is, and therefore, how little of Him we actually know.

My final thought on all of this is, despite how big and mysterious our God is, He has made Himself known to us. He is the God who reveals Himself to us in a number of ways, including through the Holy Spirit, scripture, and most importantly, in the God-man Jesus Christ. He is a God who wants to be known because He is relational. He is both vastly unknowable, yet intimately close.

So may we be people who strive to know this incredible God. May our mouths constantly be filled with *new songs* to Him, as we come to know Him more and more. And may we rid ourselves of rote theology, as we serve a God who is anything but rote.

---

[6] Helmut Thielicke, *A Little Exercise for Young Theologians*

KALOPSIA, THE GREAT BLINDNESS OF GOD

they are just sitting on the edge of reality.

This summer a friend from college told me about a paper he wrote on an ancient Greek term called *kalopsia*. I was so fascinated by the term and its definition I tried to do some research of my own on the topic. However, the internet was oddly silent on this ancient term and I only found a few dictionary sites referring to it. No scholarly articles or anything. So in my own understanding:

Kalopsia: The condition of things being more beautiful than they are.

I thought about it for a while, because initially, that sentence doesn't make sense. I mean, how can anything be more...*anything* than it *is*?

But my friend gave me the example of a child looking at his parents. They seem perfect, impenetrable. When we're young, our parents are omniscient and unfathomably strong.

To the child, his parents are stronger than they are.

After more thought, I concocted another example: Lovers.

I wonder if, without kalopsia, the human race would even endure. I'll explain:

Have you ever seen a couple and thought to yourself, *How in the world is she attracted to him?* I know how awful it sounds, but I imagine we all have had similar sentiments at some point. Perhaps you see an old couple who is still madly in love and you wonder how they can still love each other, despite the wrinkles, sags, and medicine breath. Of course, we love to see those couples and respect and admire them, hoping to emulate their love someday, but have you ever wondered how they manage to see through the exterior beauty which is fading so quickly?

Kalopsia.

To him, she is more beautiful than the day they met.

288

She is more beautiful than she is.

I think back to the times I've been infatuated with a girl and it all makes a lot more sense. I've fallen hard and fast at various times in my life, and I know what it's like to completely ignore morning breath, birth marks and little pockets of fat. Even unseen things, like social awkwardness or interests that vary from mine fade into the fog. It's like I'm in another world where the atmosphere smells like lilacs and I'm 80 pounds lighter. She is the only thing I can think about, and songs pour forth form me like a burst dam. She awakens something in me that lay dormant for months or years.

And have you noticed that when someone is being admired so intensely, nothing can bring them down? You can't insult them. Their face is frozen into a perma-smile. When you know that someone loves you so blindly, you feel free. You feel unbreakable.

Kalopsia.

Even the film *500 Days of Summer* points at this. Toward the beginning of the film, the protagonist is falling for Summer like a ball of lead, and lists off a few of her attributes. The montage is composed of soft, intimate shots:

> I love her smile. I love her hair. I love her knees. I love how she licks her lips before she talks. I love her heart-shaped birthmark on her neck. I love it when she sleeps.

Time passes, and Summer inevitably breaks his little heart and reality flares up. The same montage, shot with harsher lighting and spoken with spite follows:

> I hate her crooked teeth. I hate her 1960s haircut. I hate her knobby knees. I hate her cockroach-shaped splotch on her neck. I hate the way she smacks her lips before she talks. I hate the way she sounds when she laughs.

I feel like those in the throes of kalopsia sit on the fringes of reality, where The Shins always play gently in the background and time passes in slow-motion. Life is cinematic and the lights in the distance become soft blurs that dot the horizon beyond your lover's head.

In the months since I first heard this word, I've wondered if it takes on any spiritual dimension. If, somehow, Jesus interacts with this ancient Greek term. I think the interaction is actually two-fold.

In a small way, I think Christians see something in Jesus that the rest of the world looks at and says *Him?? Really?? What do you see there?* Yet we, those who are on the inside of the relationship, understand. It makes sense to us to love this God-man, the carpenter from Nazareth.

Isaiah tells us that there was nothing beautiful about Him which should attract us to Him.[7] Of course, you and I don't know what Jesus physically looks like, but we still *know* Him. We see His actions and we see Him dangling from a tree on our behalf. His actions are beautiful. Who He *is* is beautiful to us.

The world looks on in bewilderment.

This relationship has gone too far. You're out of His league. Don't you know you can do better than some dude who lived 2,000 years ago?

Looking at our Savior, we are filled with the essence of kalopsia, and lose ourselves in admiration of Him.

But I think the second form is far greater.

I think that when Jesus looks at us, His bride to be, He sees us as perfect. He doesn't see us in the bathroom looking at porn, or under the covers cutting our thighs with a razor. He overlooks the anger we have at our sister as well as the times we've lied, stolen and cheated.

Jesus is infatuated with us. To Him, we are more beautiful than we are.

Just as a boy in love pursues a girl despite her flaws, and she reciprocates by ignoring his boyish immaturity and weaknesses, Jesus has perfected the art of ignoring the right things.

---

[7] Isaiah 53:2

I would go so far as to say that He has blinded Himself to our flaws.

In 1 Corinthians 6, Paul lists off a handful of terrible things people could be. He writes that many of us were slanderers, sexually immoral, thieves, greedy people, and so on.

"But," he writes, "you were washed, you were sanctified, you were justified in the name of the Lord Jesus Christ and by the Spirit of our God."

Do we still have sexually immoral longings and greed in our hearts? Of course. Yet Paul tells us that in the eyes of God, those things do not define us anymore. We were cleaned by Him because He loves us and sees us as spotless.

It is only the devil that wants us to think of ourselves as dirty and shameful. Jesus is too filled with kalopsia to worry about our past sins and shortcomings.

May we be those who see ourselves as madly beloved by a God who is too blinded by kalopsia to hold onto our sins. And in this kalopsia, may we delight, rejoice, and be freed from the guilt and shame which drive us back to our sin in the first place.

JESUS, THE EASY WAY OUT
she got down on her knees and prayed to Jesus right there.

A few nights ago, I couldn't sleep and headed to my favorite 24-hour coffee shop to write a blog. I was stoked to write one on the theological Father-Son relationship we are ushered into through Union with Christ, but there were no empty tables.

Being the ever optimistic bachelor, I approached the cute girl sitting alone and asked if I could share the table with her. She eagerly agreed and before I could get a keystroke down, we began chatting.

"Are you a lawyer?" she asked, pointing to my law book-sized Bible.

I told her No, I'm a Christian writer and this is my Bible.

The next three hours were spent talking about our religious differences, until 1am when I told her we should go across the street and I'd buy her an ice cream cone from McDonald's.

Over the course of our conversation, she verbalized most people's main struggle with Christianity. She was from a Muslim country, so she was accustomed to a religion *where* your *effort* earned you pardon in the eyes of an angry god: You sin, you repent. You do your daily prayers, you stay pure.

And *hopefully* your actions are good enough to earn you a spot in heaven.

But what if they're not?

I don't know…I just hope I'm good enough.

I spent a few minutes explaining what I believe: That Jesus is the one who repents for us. He is the one who lives a perfect life in our place. He is the one who was tortured and descended into hell so that we never have to. In that sense, Christians never have to wonder if *we* are doing enough to warrant God's favor. It's the difference between a God who is first and foremost a Father versus one who is an angry judge demanding punishment.

I recited one of the analogies I used with prisoners in Chicago when I used to work in the Juvenile Detention Center:

Imagine that you're on trial for murdering 100 people. The judge orders you to a life sentence of being beaten and tortured until the day you die. But then, something unexpected happens. The judge steps down from his stand and walks through the gate. He motions you to stand up, and the guard to unlock your cuffs. He then puts them on and sits in your chair. He tells you to go free, because he is going to serve your life sentence.

The girl responded the same way the inmates always did: "But that would never happen! You could just go back out and kill more people!"

"That's why I could never be a Christian," she added. "It's too easy! You take the easy way out!"

"Exactly!" I responded. "Jesus *is* the easy way out!"

She then got down onto her knees and began a relationship with Jesus right there.

Just kidding. I wish it was that easy.

As much as I pray for elements of our conversation to stick with her, I was certainly reminded of the good gospel of grace that night. I was reminded that I *have* chosen the easy way out. I have chosen to bind myself to Jesus, who makes my burdens lighter, because I am so so weary.

I have chosen the easy way because, as she said, I can go back out and commit whatever heinous crimes my mind can concoct and He will *still* welcome me back with open arms. Seven times seventy times. Such is the nature of grace.

I chose the easy way because, despite my constant sin and unfaithfulness, the mercy of God is new each morning. Because He still runs after *me*, the wandering prostitute, and showers His love upon me.

I think this is the gate through which all people initially come to Jesus: A man bending down to help up the adulterous woman, telling her that He does not condemn her (John 8).

And although this is the starting point, I don't think it is the ending point. I think those who choose to follow Jesus soon find that, while their sins are washed away and the punishment has been absorbed by Jesus and their minds have begun to be healed, life is far from easy.

There is an obscure word that many Christians today can't define, but understanding it helps unlock the Christian faith: *Cruciformity*.

It is the joining of the believer to Christ in His sufferings, being crucified alongside Him, putting our old selves to death. There are dozens of verses[8] pointing us to this idea that, with the benefits of knowing Christ also come

---

[8] See Philippians 3:10

joining in His sufferings. Jesus Himself tells us that following Him includes every part of His journey: including taking up our crosses and dying.[9]

Jesus never promised that our bodies will be immune to cancer, or that the baby will never die. He never promised that we won't be beheaded or lit on fire by those who don't know Him.

He didn't offer us a pardon from suffering and pain, but a way to walk through it *with* Him.

Jesus never promised us an easier life—in fact quite the opposite—but He did make us two promises which are worth mentioning here:

He promised to be *with* us

We will still have suffering in this life. Most likely, lots of it. But in this, we know that Jesus is with us in more ways than one. He is with us in the sympathetic sense, that He has already undergone suffering, and whatever we are going through is not foreign to Him. God the Father watched as His Son was tortured and pinned to a cross and died. Jesus endured the beating and the rejection and the shame.

Jesus is no stranger to pain and suffering. So as we walk through the valleys of our own lives, we can know that He has gone before us, but He also walks beside us through the Holy Spirit. He didn't promise an escape from the pain, but He offers to walk through it *with* us when it does come.

We have assurance of our salvation

For many years, I thought this term was such a grandma word. I didn't get why *assurance* was such a big deal. However, after a handful of conversations similar to the one I had the other night, my understanding of the word has changed.

We Christians don't have to worry if *we* are doing enough to satisfy God. We don't have to stress about where we'll wake up after our last breath is taken. There is no more mystery about whether our good deeds outweigh our bad deeds. Jesus has taken those scales and smashed them. He is the one who has satisfied the scales of justice once and for all, so that our puny 'deeds' don't even register on the meter.

---

[9] Matthew 16:24-26

The Bible says that the Holy Spirit operates as a down-payment, or a deposit[10] of our inheritance that is to come. We have assurance of our salvation, not because of anything we can do, but because of what Jesus already has done.

So yes, I have taken the easy way. And despite the fact that it is laced with continued suffering and pain, I hope you take it too.

COME & EAT
God loves to eat.

This post was originally published in the 'Food' issue of Humanity Magazine (which is edited by my talented friend Kailey Sullivan). Her magazine is a quarterly publication which focuses on a different theme with each publication.

Maybe you've noticed it too.

Once I began to notice the amount of intense importance given to food throughout the Bible, I realized that it's everywhere. In fact, you could even say that much of the Bible revolves around food.

Any elementary Sunday Schooler will be able to tell you what the first sin was: Eating. The wrong thing at the wrong time from the wrong tree. Eating is what led to 9/11, Columbine and Charlottesville. Eating introduced the human race to the sin which permeates every platelet in our bloodstream.

But it doesn't end there.

In the agrarian culture in which the ancient Israelites lived, eating was a central tenet of life. Therefore, many of Moses' laws revolved around what to eat, what not to eat, when, how, where and why to eat. Don't eat bacon, but do eat unleavened bread during Passover. Eat this bull in the presence of a priest, but don't eat clams.

---

[10] 2 Corinthians 1:22

The Bible is divine comedy: Eating is what doomed mankind to death, but it's also the means by which we are saved. First the serpent invited Eve to 'come and eat,' then it is the phrase Jesus extended to the sinners, prostitutes and tax collectors, and now to us.

Come and eat...me. My body and blood.

Do *this* in remembrance of me.

Eat.

Eat and remember me.

And if you're at all familiar with Christian eschatology, you also know how the Bible ends: With a feast.

I think God loves to eat.

It's not an accident food is so wonderful, especially when eaten with family and friends in community. But I want to zoom in on the first century culture into which Jesus entered and began shuffling things around.

An early church historian wrote that Jews did not take food from the same table as Gentiles (Non-Jews) "because they live impurely." There were all-male tables; tables for rich people and others for the poor, and so on.

Because in the first century, who you ate with mattered.

It was unlike our culture today in which one may waltz into a Chipotle and grab an open window seat one stool away from a stranger. In the first century, when it came to eating, everything was planned out and executed intentionally. In other words, no Jewish man—especially a rabbi—would grab a table at McHerod's and risk sitting near a Gentile for supper.

So when Jesus shows up, it's absolutely jarring for Him to constantly be seen at the table with 'sinners.' The cool thing is, this isn't just an isolated event that He did once to make a statement. We get the impression that Jesus made a habit of chilling with the societal outcasts. He likely even called many of them His friends.

Let's break down the three categories of people typically listed as eating with Jesus:

Sinners: Not much description of these people. Just imagine that you're part of a group of friends and the best way people thought to describe you was just as 'sinners.' Obviously not the top of their classes or the social elite. Just a group of no-good lowlives.

Prostitutes: Oh, you know…

Tax collectors: This group is interesting. These people were possibly the most hated group of people in the Jewish community at the time. They were Jewish men who worked for the Roman government collecting taxes from other Jews. However, they usually took extra cash just to fill their pockets and get rich from their own people. Think World War 2 Jews collecting taxes from fellow Jews, but working for the Nazis and also getting rich.

And these are the very people Jesus chose to dine with.

Repeatedly.

Even more fascinating, we don't get the impression that Jesus was an eyebrow-raising-chaperone or 'missionary' type as He hung out with these people. Luke 7 implies that Jesus was often mistaken for a drunkard and a glutton: He ate a lot and drank a lot. He wasn't a bore to be around.

Often the mental image we have of Jesus is a very tidy, clean and frankly, boring man who came and implored us all to be better people. The image painted by the Bible could not be more different. After all, there must have been a reason these notorious sinners kept coming back to eat with Jesus. (Hint: It wasn't because he just called them hoodlums and told them to shape up…who would want to keep eating with someone like that?)

He didn't wait for them to improve their lives or crawl out of their addictions before he sat and broke bread with them; Jesus moved into their space, where they were, and demonstrated to the world that they had value. That they were worth eating with.

So I ask myself: When was the last time I sat with a prostitute or inmate and ate a meal? When was the last time I exited my comfort zone to show someone I care about them, despite what society says? In high school, it was the lonely nerds isolated in the cafeteria. Who is it for you now?

Perhaps you're the one who feels like the outcast. Maybe you're the one who feels too dirty, unclean, and sinful to be wanted by the Lord. Let this be a reminder that especially to those of us who feel disgusting in the eyes of God that Jesus looks at each of us and says, "Come, eat with me."

He was willing to sacrifice His reputation in the eyes of the religious leaders to show love to the lowest of society. And He does the same to each of us.

I love the nickname often given to God: The Hound of Heaven. Because like a dog on the prowl, He is seeking out and chasing after the lowest, the farthest, and most overlooked members of the world. He is chasing after us with a bloodthirst the way a pup chases a fallen goose.

The most shocking turn of events though, is the table to which we are invited. We are not invited to eat gluten-free bread and grape juice, but the very body and blood of God Himself.

This is my body, broken for you; my blood poured out for the forgiveness of sins...

We do this symbolically in church today, as we anticipate the coming feast to end all feasts.

And we're all invited.

This invitation is not limited to those who follow a certain code or restrain from partying too hard. This invitation is for the sinners, the broken down and the unworthy, and it extends even to people like us, the addicts, the perfectionists and workaholics.

You may not have grown up in a family that sits down for evening dinner, and the feeling of invitation and nearness may be foreign to you. Fortunately, the family of God is enormous and welcoming. The food won't leave you wanting, nor will the drink leave you thirsty.

So will you come to the table? Will you come and feast on the Lord as He offers Himself to us? Will you sit shoulder to shoulder with the Least of These as we center ourselves around the table of the Lord?

Come and eat.

LETTER TO AN ATHEIST
You are loved...

After an hours-long e-conversation with a friend of mine who is an atheist, I decided the best way to continue the conversation was to sum up some of my thoughts in a letter.

Dear Friend,

I've been sitting in this coffee shop for about an hour trying to think of which articles or videos to send you that would really 'do the trick.' But nothing has come to mind and nothing really seemed to fit exactly what I wanted to say, so I figured, why not type up a letter that will say just what I want to say, in lieu of an in-person conversation?

You told me you've been an atheist for many years, and it has not helped you satiate the aches and pains within your soul. Therapy and medications, while they can be helpful, have not seemed to abate the void, or however you want to refer to it. C.S. Lewis talks about a longing for joy which is ultimately what led him to Christianity from atheism. It was not a longing for rules or for some false sort of religion that led him to seek out God, but the search for *joy*.

Contemporary pastor and writer John Piper strongly echoes Lewis' sentiments when he preaches, and in his monumental book *Desiring God,* in which he coined the term 'Christian Hedonism.' This refers to the fact that humans are made to seek out joy, happiness, and satisfaction (*eudaemonia*) at all costs. Christianity is, essentially, a human coming to realize that the greatest heights of joy and the ultimate source of satisfaction is to be found in Christ.

The Catechism states that the chief end of Man is "to glorify God and enjoy Him forever." This is the source of much of this thought. If we are not enjoying God, but are merely submitting to Him out of sheer will, or even worse—out of fear, then we are doing Christianity wrong. Hebrews 12:2 says that "For the joy set before him [Jesus] endured the cross, scorning its shame, and sat down at the right hand of the throne of God." Jesus underwent the most painful and humiliating death a human could endure for the sake of *joy!* It was not because God the Father told Him to, or that He would be in trouble if He didn't.

In the same way, we are drawn to God because of His kindness, because we see some sort of joy in Him. Men and women who stand on street corners and yell at people to condemn them are *not* reflecting the heart of God, who draws people to Himself because of His love and kindness. Psalm 37:4 says to "Delight yourself in the Lord and he will give you the desires of your heart." God calls to us and offers us joy and delight.

The biggest hurdle you seem to be at seems to be the first step, though: Believing that He exists. Hebrews 11:6 says, "And without faith it is impossible to please God, because anyone who comes to him must believe that he exists and that he rewards those who earnestly seek him." I've been at that place, looking for a god to relate to.

In Genesis, there is this story of Jacob wandering through the wilderness and one night a man comes to him and they begin to wrestle on the ground. They wrestle all night long and eventually the other man realizes he has been overpowered, so he touches Jacob's side and throws it out of joint. The man (who is God, it turns out) renames Jacob 'Israel,' which means "he wrestles with God." I think the best Christians are those who wrestle with God. I have little respect for those who believe whatever they are fed without wrestling with it and crying out to God, begging for an answer.

Of course, in the present secular atmosphere of our hedonistic culture, the hardest problem tends to be finding a god to wrestle with. And that is where I often find myself too. And I think the best things to do are these:

Pray. It sounds weird for me to tell you to pray, because to you, it may seem like speaking words into an empty room. But think about it this way: IF there is a God, and IF He really wants you to come to Him, doesn't this seem like a good place to start? I mean, what do you have to lose? The worst case scenario is you waste five minutes talking to an empty room. Ask Him to reveal Himself to you.

Join a community of Christians. I would love to take all my atheist friends to church. But many of them wouldn't go to an actual church with me, and if they would, we often live in different cities. Having conversations like this can help give you a taste of what it's like to be a Christian. Find people who will let you ask the hard questions and reply in a loving way. Christianity is not meant to be a solo endeavor where we just have some kind of ethereal connection to God and follow certain do's and don'ts. It is a life lived in a community that consistently shows each other grace because each one of us has received grace from God.

And I guess this brings me to the gospel. WHERE DO I BEGIN??

The gospel is not men working hard enough to earn favor from God. It is not a reward system of doing good things and 'getting' heaven. It's not something that is meant to enhance your life and make you happier (though that is essentially a result).

Jesus doesn't make bad people good; He makes dead people alive.

Each of us has screwed up. We have had hatred in our hearts toward others. We have lied. We have cheated. We have been greedy. This is not a matter of adding up our 'good deeds' and weighing them against our 'bad deeds.' Imagine instead that you're hanging from a chain that is connecting you to God. It doesn't matter which link in the chain you break; if one breaks, you're falling. And so has each one of us fallen.

This means that you, me, and Hitler are all on the same level. There are no degrees of fallenness when it comes to our standing before God. And no amount of giving to the homeless or petting impounded puppies is going to reverse that.

I learned a new phrase recently: *felix culpa*. It is Latin for 'happy fault.' I love it because it encapsulates so much of the gospel. Adam and Eve sinned in the garden of Eden. This was a bad thing. But because of it, the entire narrative of Jesus coming and dying for us, so that our sinful state may be redeemed came about. His body was beaten, broken and killed. Another fault. But how happy are we Christians that His body was broken! Happy fault. His blood poured out so that ours doesn't have to.

Buddhist monks sit in caves, striving for nirvana (self emptying), and when it is attained, they light themselves on fire to purify their souls. Catholic monks whip themselves bloody to punish themselves for their sins.

Jesus' blood fell from the fissures on His body so that ours doesn't have to. His blood has removed our sins because He was the only one who did NOT sin, yet was punished as if He did.

Felix Culpa. Happy fault.

And what did Jesus say as the soldiers were pinning Him to the cross? "Father forgive them, for they know not what they do."[11]

Jesus is the embodiment of grace and love. And since He was fully God, He shows us what God is like. God is grace and love.

I think you may see religion as people following certain rules in order to try to please some god. But Christianity is different from every other religion in the world, because we believe that our God came *to us*, while we WEREN'T seeking Him! Christianity is a free gift and all you need to do is accept it. It's like Jesus bought you a boarding pass and paid for the ticket and all you need to do is get on the plane.

Of course, these metaphors break down, but you get the idea.

The greatest gift in the entire gospel message is that we get GOD! In John 14:6, Jesus says, "I am the way, the truth and the life. No one comes to the Father except through me." Christianity is not about *using* Jesus to get eternal life. He does not merely point us the way to salvation. Rather, he says come *to me* to have eternal life. The greatest gift we can receive is God Himself!

Which brings me back to my first point: Joy. By binding ourselves to God, we find the greatest and deepest source of joy imaginable. Galatians 2:20

---

[11] Luke 23:34

says that "it is no longer I who lives, but Christ who lives in me." This means, yes, we will have our deepest desires fulfilled, but our desires will be changed! We won't look for satisfaction in things like money, fame, sex, drugs, etc. But we will delight ourselves in God! Because He will give us a new life.

Becoming a Christian is not self-help or life-improvement. It is getting a NEW life! It is being born again. You were born once, and the first life does not seem to have gotten you what you want, so coming to Jesus means being born again into a whole new life! It's far more than I can explain in this little letter so I'll leave it there.

There is so much more I want to say, and I wish this was a conversation not a monologue, so I'll end it here with how my dad ends most of his prayers:

I praise God that because Jesus walked out of His grave, we too will walk out of ours.

In Christ,
Ethan

MY NEWEST TATTOO: AN EXPLORATION OF HOLINESS AND TRANSCENDENCE

I'm only now am beginning to adequately know how to describe it.

The creation of this blog post involved me sneaking a picture of my tricep while in the middle of a coffee shop because I realized I don't have any other pictures of my newest tattoo. So here it is, stealthy as possible:

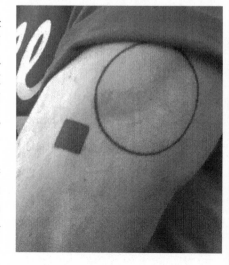

I honestly don't remember the exact moment I decided to get this tattoo, or even what sparked the idea in the first place. But I know what it means, and since getting it in October, I've given it a lot of thought and finally feel capable of writing about it in a way which (hopefully) won't sound trite and cliche.

The idea is simple, there are kind of two ways to look at it though:

#1. The big white circle is God, the Holy One, the Transcendent, and the small black square is the colloquial 'world,' including humans, the earth, our flesh, and our capability to understand things. Put simply,

> White circle=God
> Black square=us

Several years ago, I was in church when the pastor said something which has stuck with me:

> Sometimes, people will come to me and tell me that they're having a crisis of faith, or that they are losing their faith, or something like that. They sit in my office and cry and weep and wonder why they seem to be slipping away from God.
>
> After talking with many of them, I find that the opposite is true. They are not losing their faith. Rather, God is using this 'crisis' moment to smash the box they had previously held Him in. So in one sense, yes, the idea of God they had is slipping away and more often than not, this is a good thing! Because God is so much bigger and so much better than we usually imagine Him to be.

I wish I could remember verbatim what he said, but it was something like that. It was beautiful.

It made me realize that, as much as I hate to admit it, I am very good at constructing boxes in which to store my gods. I am good at building walls where He is not allowed to expand and stretch and reach his full god-ness in my mind.

I'm the guy with the freaking circle and square tattoo on my arm, yet I'm the one endlessly crafting boxes where I can store my convenient little god.

So, on the one hand this tattoo is a reminder of the infinite, incomprehensible nature of God. I think the best word to capture this is simply *holiness*. He is set apart and transcendent from us. Our chances of understanding and comprehending God is the same likelihood of a small black square understanding a big white circle.

I'm the type of person who can easily get entangled in a web of stale thoughts and rigid tradition, quickly forgetting the supernatural-ness of God. The fact that He is utterly other than us.

He is not like us.

Isaiah says His thoughts are not like ours, nor are His ways like our ways.[12] If we ever think God looks like a fellow little black box, we are in pressing danger of constructing walls for the divine.

One thing I've been pondering according to this interpretation, however, is something a friend pointed out. He said, "The way you have it now though, there is no reconciliation. There is no room for Jesus." Of course, to borrow the metaphor of my ink, that would mean the big white circle taking on the fullness of a small black square in order to rectify the relationship between the two. Still trying to figure out how that would look visually. I've toyed with adding a small white hollow square overlapping the two or something. Not sure. I know what my friend meant, but I don't know how it would be represented!

#2. Alternatively, the big white circle can be seen as the world (as in, Christians are in it but not of it...) and the small black square, then, is the Church; the elect of Christ Jesus. Those called by the small whisper of the Holy Spirit to come and live a life apart from the world.

This is inspired by lunatics like the prophet Ezekiel, who cooked his food over poop for a year. Or Elijah who was fed by ravens. Or Hosea who intentionally married a prostitute.

You see, to the world, these guys seemed like little black squares. They didn't look like the rest of the world because they weren't trying to be like it. I get the impression as I read through the Bible that many of the people

---

[12] Isaiah 55:8-9

who were closest to God a) suffered a lot, and b) looked absolutely insane when judged by worldly standards.

Peter talks about those chosen by God as being a holy royal priesthood, called to be set apart from the world; holy.

That's us. We are not meant to look like the rest of the world.

This affects the way we live, the way we use our bodies, the way we spend our money, the words we speak, and every other conceivable category of our lives.

It was said of the earliest Christians that they lived inverse lives of the Romans. Romans were stingy with their wallets and generous with their beds, while Christians were generous with their wallets and stingy with their beds. That's just a sliver of what it means to live a holy life. Looking 100% different from the way the world does business.

Another delicious example of this, which has obviously received heavy criticism for the way they do business, is the Christian-owned Chick-Fil-A. Despite the fact that they could rake in thousands, if not millions more dollars a week by opening Sundays, the chain has remained sound in their resolve to sanctify one day to the Lord.

May we be people who never seek to box in our Savior and restrain Him to our small squares.

THE HOLY PEOPLE

I'll never shake the image from my mind as long as I live.

Two days ago I was in a coffee shop in Denver. It was a nice, sunny day so the sidewalks were bouncing with people, enjoying the last stretch of this year's warmth. At one point, coming down the sidewalk toward the coffee shop, I saw a nun in full habit, rounded off with white New Balance sneakers.

It suddenly hit me: When you've devoted your life to the Lord through the expression of celibacy, you don't really worry about looking good or stylish. I envied that freedom.

As the nun drew nearer, I began to notice something fascinating.

Wherever she went, people fell silent.

Out of discomfort, some college kids she passed cracked jokes and giggled softly. Many people stared. She was the most beautiful thing I had seen all day.

There's this piece I've been working on for years and still can't seem to get it right. I may be drawing near, but the title is: DO PENANCE. Without giving too much away, there was a rainy spring day in Chicago several years ago. And I saw a holy man.

I'll never shake the image from my mind as long as I live.

He was wearing pale sackcloth from head to toe, and on the breast of the shirt, in bold red print, were two words: DO PENANCE. The man was in his 50's, and he was on his knees before a giant painting of Jesus. In the pouring rain.

He barely knew English, but even without words he painted an image across my mind I'll always return to.

In 2014, I attended a conference in Kansas City and one of the speakers was talking about 'holy men'. He mentioned a photographer who traveled the world, interviewing and photographing various expressions of the world's holy men.

It fascinated me.

It painted an entirely new portrait of the meaning of the word 'holy' and what it means to be a holy people. The men in these photos were nothing short of astounding and utterly different from the rest of the world with their facepaint and dreadlocks, longer than they were. They had chosen to pursue something invisible; something transcendent. To them, these invisible entities were somehow more *real* than the material things the rest of the world chases.

Looking at their faces, I was drawn into their world. It was obvious that they inhabited a different planet than the rest of us, their experience so vastly different from ours. I wondered if these images were not far off from what the biblical prophets in the Old Testament would have looked like.

Ezekiel was instructed to lie on his left side for 390 days straight. Then he had to bake his bread over his own feces.[13]

What do people like this look like, and what draws them to do such wild feats? Either they are truly mad, or they have come into contact with something so profoundly otherworldly that they are more sane than the rest of us.

Holy things stir us.

The word holy, most simply, means *set apart. Different from the rest.*

The small population inhabiting the sidewalk the other day fell silent in the presence of a 'holy woman', a woman who had devoted her life to the pursuit of the transcendent and would not be sidetracked. She said nothing. She did nothing but walk by.

But the world is hungry for holy things.

Whether we admit it or not, I think all of us are thirsting for more than what Hollywood and television can feed us. We are stuck in the same cycles of shopping for new clothes, trying to impress others, and building our own image.

Solomon wrote,

> All the rivers flow into the sea, Yet the sea is not full. To the place where the rivers flow, There they flow again. All things are wearisome; Man is not able to tell it. The eye will not have its fill of seeing, Nor is

---

[13] Ezekiel 4

the ear its fill of hearing. That which has been is that which will be, And that which has been done is that which will be done. So there is nothing new under the sun.[14]

We are hungry for more than all *this*.

We are hungry for the holy.

We reach a point where we've fed our addictions as much as they can consume; our eyes have become so numbed and desensitized that we don't even enjoy our hedonistic feasts any more. Our tongues have tasted every flavor known to man and our stomachs have plumped out in gross gluttony.

And where does this leave us? Hungry for more.

Yes, we are a culture starved for the holy. For something so much more *real* than what we can see and touch.

There are days I feel so lonely I want nothing more than a warm body to curl up with before a good film; someone to share my thoughts and frustrations with. Yet in my better moments, I remember that these longings, though not necessarily evil in nature, pale in comparison to the sweetness of Jesus. After all, the father of all playboys, Hugh Hefner, died recently and even 1,000 bedmates were not enough to satisfy his carnal ache.

There are times I assume I'll be satisfied once I sell my lemon and get a nicer car, or land a more respectable job.

But all of these things are dust on the sandals of holier men. Shiny cars, beautiful homes, and hot girlfriends do not cause crowds to fall silent the way the elderly nun did earlier this week. There is odd and quiet power in holiness, though it looks nothing like that of the world.

Men buy unnecessarily gigantic trucks and spend hours in the gym to become more 'powerful.' Women shop and diet to attract others. But to what end? How fascinating is another pretty face or swollen bicep?

---

[14] Ecclesiastes 1:7-9

I am fascinated by the holy; by those men and women who have decided that their lives will not look like the lives of the world. I'm amazed by people who forgo sex for 70 years in order to experience substantive ecstasy, or those who pilgrimage or preach. I'm fascinated by the stories of the prophets: Tortured, discarded and outcast. And WEIRD.

You don't need to alienate your friends and family to live a holy life, however. By no means am I a *normal* person, yet people are absolutely mind boggled that I am a 28-year-old virgin. We can pursue the holy in our daily practices and routines.

Do you use your body in ways that reflect a desire for the holy?
What about your money?
Your time?

Francis Schaeffer asks, *How then shall we live?*

God calls us to be a holy people. And I wonder if that means we will be weird. We will stand out. The world won't understand why we do what we do. It doesn't have to. It's glued to its material pursuits while we have forsaken them for something higher, something more transcendent,

something holy.

May we learn how to become more holy, more different, more weird. May we leave our lusts for material goods in the garbage and cling to the invisible. May we be led by the Spirit into poverty and brokenness so that we may truly be healed. May we reconcile our fleshly hunger with the Bread of Life, the Well who won't run dry, the Holiest of the holy.

DO PENANCE

he simply said, "pray to God. ask him to forgive your sins."

Josh and I screamed through the wet streets of Chicago on our bikes. Rain was dumping from the heavens. Not a pesky little misting, but the kind of weighty drops that punch your skin in a warm and refreshing way. The kind of rain that hits your head and runs down your nose and drips into your mouth whenever it opens.

It was the Thursday after Easter a few years ago and I was wrapping up my last year of college.

We rode up north and jumped into the lake. Then we rode down south and jumped into the lake. People stared at us as we pedaled by, confused by my lack of shirt and Josh's lack of pants. And we yelled as loud as we could everywhere we went.

Then we biked to the Loop, the absolute center of downtown Chicago. We landed in Daley plaza, which is basically the center of the Loop, and the rain continued pounding us. It was the kind of rain that runs down your brow and drips off your eyelashes so you can't see clearly. It was the kind of rain that pommeled the pavement so hard mist rose up from the streets.

Everything was gray and nothing was dry.

When we rolled into Daley plaza, we found a huge painting of Jesus standing in the middle of the expanse, with a giant cross several feet away from it. Since it was shortly after Easter, I was not surprised to see religious imagery still hanging around the city.

What really stood out, however, was the man kneeling before the painting.

Josh and I walked around the painting (it was Jesus with red and white lights shooting out of His hand[15]) and saw an older man on his knees. He was

---

[15] This is called the Image of Divine Mercy, from a vision seen by Saint Faustina. The red and white represent the repeated imagery of water and blood in Scripture: Baptism and Eucharist; the liquid from Jesus' side on the cross, et al.

about thirty feet from the painting, wearing sackcloth and staring at the painting.

As we walked our bikes closer, I was able to read his sackcloth shirt, which had two bold words printed on it in red: DO PENANCE.

It's an image that won't soon leave my head.

This man was probably in his 50's or 60's. On both knees before a painting of Jesus. In the pouring rain. In the center of Chicago.

He was cycling the rosary through his soaking fingers as he prayed, whispering holy words to the Creator of the universe.

Once he finished, I tried to speak to him, but he barely knew English. In a thick Eastern European accent, he simply said, "Pray to God. Ask him to forgive your sins."

Then he said, "I have to go. My parking meter is almost up."

There are few scenes in my life that stand out as moments I will always look back on with some sort of transcendent curiosity. That man earnestly loved the Lord and sought to please Him. I know nothing about that man other than what I wrote above. I never will. I couldn't pick him out of a one-man lineup at this point.

But the vivid image of an older man in the rain praying to Jesus. That will stick with me.

To be sure of what I'm writing, like any good scholar, I Googled the definition of *penance:*

> *n. voluntary self-punishment inflicted as an outward expression of repentance for having done wrong.*

It seems to line up exactly with what the man was doing. While Josh and I were out in the rain to intentionally have a blast (I love being in the rain, in case you haven't noticed…), this man went out to punish himself. To atone for his sins. To beg for mercy.

Many have whipped themselves raw to make up for their transgressions. Many have forgone food, sleep or other comforts to earn a rightness before God. Brennan Manning even voluntarily locked himself away in a Swiss prison to try to earn his forgiveness.[16]

As beautiful as these actions can sometimes be as raw expressions of worship, they neglect the One who has already been whipped raw for our transgressions. We forget that someone has already been striped that we may be cured.[17]

We don't need to punish ourselves because the Penitent One has already come and taken the punishment.

Throughout the Bible, we see the consistent image of the grape being smashed to create wine. Wine, a symbol of joy, necessitates that something be crushed for its existence. We believe this too.

We believe in the One who was crushed for our joy.

But if we think we need to take some of the punishment for our sins, we are telling Jesus that He is not strong enough to carry them Himself. It's a subtle way of saying to Him, "Yah, your crucifixion was pretty good, but it could still use my help…"

How arrogant are we to suggest to the Creator of the Universe that He needs our help?

Now, none of this is to suggest that spiritual disciplines like fasting and vigils do not have their place; nothing could be further from the truth! But the purpose behind them is never to take upon ourselves the punishment we deserve. It's to create spaces for hunger and satisfaction in the presence of God. It's to find our pleasure in Him above all else, not to suffer because we are trying to 'make it up to God.'

Later in his life, Brennan Manning came to the conclusion that the only possible end of all things was the grace of God. Without this all-

---

[16] Brennan Manning, *The Ragamuffin Gospel*

[17] Isaiah 53:5

encompassing grace, no amount of his own pathetic penance would suffice. He wrote,

> God loves you unconditionally, as you are and not as you should be, because nobody is as they should be. It is the message of grace…A grace that pays the eager beaver who works all day long the same wages as the grinning drunk who shows up at ten till five…A grace that hikes up the robe and runs breakneck toward the prodigal reeking of sin and wraps him up and decides to throw a party no ifs, ands, or buts…This grace is indiscriminate compassion. It works without asking anything of us…Grace is sufficient even though we huff and puff with all our might to try to find something or someone it cannot cover. Grace is enough…Jesus is enough.[18]

Do you truly believe that Jesus suffered enough that you don't have to, or are you still trying to earn His mercy with your church attendance or Bible-reading record? Are you willing to cast yourself into the net of His grace, or do you still think you could be doing more to absolve yourself?

If you're not sure, ask yourself: Do you feel like the man in the rain in Chicago is somehow more right with God than you are? There are no levels of forgiveness or rightness with God; the ground is level at the foot of the cross.

Let us be people who repent and turn away from our sins without feeling a need for extra penance. May we not whip ourselves raw because we believe in the One who was whipped raw for us; the One who took our sins against Him and destroyed them on a hill outside Jerusalem.

Once and for all.

---

[18] Manning, *Ragamuffin.*

COME, BE CLEANED

reflections on Good Friday, cherries, and cockroaches.

"A bowl of cherries is ruined by the presence of one cockroach, but a single cherry does not improve the allure of a colony of cockroaches. It is always easier to turn something disgusting than beautiful." The podcast host continued to describe the psychological roots of disgust; What makes things tainted or impure?

I realized that this motif is true pretty much across the board. There is nothing beautiful or pure which is not immediately ruined by the presence of something gross. An entire meal is ruined when someone finds a minuscule hair (and hair is also ruined with a little bit of food in it). A pinch of dirt ruins a perfectly white counter top, but a pinch of white countertop doesn't cleanse a whole field of mud.

And a hint of sin ruins an otherwise beautiful and whole relationship between God and His people.

Add all the good deeds you want to the heaping pile of lusts, crooked desires and hateful thoughts, and you're left with more or less the same thing. And I think that's where people start to go astray in their thinking: when they think that adding more "good" to their thoughts, actions and words will actually make a difference in the overall quality of their soul.

All they're doing is adding more cherries to the infestation of cockroaches, hoping it will look more appealing.

And we're all guilty of it, right? This is why we strive to be *good people* (as vacuous a term as that is), and beat ourselves up when we fail. So then the question becomes, What would Christ have us do? And I can't help but wonder if realization and acknowledgment is key. You start out by agreeing that you are utterly incapable of cleaning yourself up, but accepting that Someone has loved you enough to do it for you.

Tim Keller summed it up succinctly: "The Gospel is the realization that you are more sinful than you ever dared imagine, and more loved than you ever dared hope."[19]

Today, on Good Friday, we recognize that the Ultimate Good has moved in and lived among us. Today, we can acknowledge that we are the collection of cockroaches, but there is hope because we have met something SO good and beautiful that it cannot be tainted by us.

Rather, not an 'it' but a 'He.'

The beauty,
goodness,
and power
of Christ are strong enough to move into the unclean and clean it, rather than become contaminated by it. We are the unclean; we are the pile, the infestation, in need of restoration. You add anything else to your heaping tower of sin and I promise you, it will just be lost in the swirl and ruined by it. No amount of good deeds, donations, kind words of encouragement, or community service can make clean what you have made broken (And yes, I mean *you*, as we are all participants in the destruction of our own lives and our world).

There is no good thing you can add to a pile of manure to make it *good.*

This is why we confess that Christ, who knew no sin, became sin; taking it up into Himself that it may be destroyed once and for all. He didn't just polish the pile of feces; He destroyed it Himself and instead gave us something wholly beautiful, clean, and pure.

Nothing else would suffice.

Today we recognize and remember the utter destruction of our sin and shame in the Man, Jesus Christ from Nazareth (A crap hole of a town..."What good can come from Nazareth??" they used to say) as He nailed it to a tree.

---

[19] Timothy and Kathy Keller, *The Meaning of Marriage: Facing the Complexities of Commitment with the Wisdom of God*

It was taken up *in Him* so that we may live forever *in Him*.

The divine exchange.

The *felix culpa*: The fortunate fault.

The only hope of being washed and made new.

So the question falls to you, my friend: Will you acknowledge that your life is un-cleanable without help more powerful than yourself? Will you agree that adding your own measures of 'good' is as useful as putting a rose on a city dump?

And will you accept the gift given today: The cup of Christ, which He drank down to the final, painful dregs, in order that we may be made clean? That we may not even bear a trace of our former contamination, returning to full, unbroken relationship with Him?

Come, be cleaned.

THE GOD WHO ACHES WITH US

maybe all those emotions were put there for a reason…

I once lay on the floor of a Cape Cod basement, hugging a leg of a coffee table for an hour when I thought my girlfriend at the time was cheating on me. She had gone on a midnight fishing trip alone with another guy and my innards were wrenched. I was young and didn't know how to react or process, so in the presence of all my friends, I curled into a ball on the floor, wrapping myself around the leg of the table.

Was it a prayer or an emotion? Was it both?

How does one carry the rich platter of emotions which burns within us to the Transcendent? I praise God that He often speaks in tongues much deeper than language can convey, as he knows the groanings and growlings of our innermost being. Sometimes my prayer is the act of lying on the floor, unable to move because my grief has laid me down and pinned me to the floor; sometimes my worship is jumping up and down and screaming out of excitement from atop a cliff.

"The body responds well to metaphors," my friend Elliot once told me.

Sometimes the words won't come, but the language comes dripping from my posture, from the weight in my eyebrows or my sedentary days on the couch. The Lord is not removed from these actions, these movements. He not only gave us language and mouths with which to formulate our thoughts, but bodies with which to communicate our emotion.

We jump and dance in joy and mope and weep in loss.

Why are we so quick to assume the Transcendent knows nothing of our weariness and pain? I've loved and lost more times than I can count and though Shakespeare would be proud, it's a hell of a lot of baggage to carry.

But then Jesus says, "Hey, my burden is light. Give me that…

That too.

Even that little carry-on you're hiding behind your legs, I want that too."

It's a wild God who looks at us and says he wants us; an absolutely insane God who wants all of our baggage too. All of our shortcomings and weaknesses. Our sorrows along with our joys. Perhaps His joy is not in which emotion or feelings we carry, but in the fact that we are willing to relinquish them into His eager arms, to let Him feel them with us.

Like a boyfriend taking on the role of Mr. Hero, He is excited to take from us our burdens and walk alongside us. The difference is, He is strong enough to carry them, and carry them well.

In Chicago, a friend whom I had fallen in love with told me she didn't feel the same way. I didn't know what to do so I walked up to my dorm room and sat on my bed. I didn't write or cry or punch anything, I just sat there.

I didn't even pray, I just sat there.

And then I sat there longer.

It was at least an hour until I rose from my bed, having accomplished nothing but to *feel* the feelings.

And I don't think that was an hour wasted. I think that in feeling whatever it is we feel, we worship the One who put those feelers in there in the first place.

It is no sin to feel anger or sadness. Nor is it a sin to rejoice and celebrate.

Perhaps we only walk waywardly and stray from the path of the Lord's intentions when we try to numb these feelings by acting out. By punching walls. Or people. By looking at porn, because at least *those* girls will love me. By shooting up on heroin because at least *this* friend will hang out with me for a while.

God did not give us emotions, or the ability to feel them, only so we could escape them and not process the reality of our lives. My friend Liz once told me "emotions are the way we interpret reality and the things that happen to us."

Tears are the body's way of adjusting to reality.

Emotions aren't bad, but how we deal with them speaks volumes. Your sadness can turn inward and self-centered and your anger can coagulate into a lifelong grudge.

But it is no sin to feel. Jesus was a man alive to His emotions; the entire spectrum is on display in the New Testament. When his friend John the Baptizer died, He went out to a solitary place to be alone, to weep and grieve.[20] And when His friend Lazarus dies, we get the shortest verse in the Bible: "Jesus wept."[21] When the Jews had kicked the Gentiles out of the temple and used their lot to set up sales booths, Jesus' anger flares and He goes nuts and whips people for being so stupid.[22]

I love how the Hebrew word typically translated 'heart' actually means 'guts.' As in, they understood that there are emotions so deep and rich that you feel them in the deepest bits of your body. There is an ache in your

---

[20] Matthew 14:13

[21] John 11:35

[22] Matthew 21:12-17

guts. So when the Psalmists write about grief and broken hearts, they are writing from that deep place within them.

From their guts.

When I enter a season of deep emotion, I often turn to music or poetry to help cope with the mountains of emotion which rise from the earthquakes of my soul. I typically have to force myself to return once more to the Lord or to His Word, because I tend to think of it as dry or irrelevant. But when I do, it usually involves a series of words flowing out of me—not unlike these—and I am reminded once more of the intimate nearness of the Lord.

I'm reminded that there is no emotion or feeling or thought foreign to Him.

I'm reminded that He is near to me while remaining ineffably large enough to handle my anger, my sadness, or my grief.

May we be a people of tears and of laughter.
May we be a people who lament and rejoice.
May we be a people whose anger flares and joy soars.
May we sit still, and may we rise from our beds.

YOU CAN BE HAPPY WITHOUT JESUS
I kept finding myself on couches with women, searching for meaning...

"It's like I keep trying to scratch some deep, existential itch with these women."

I sat across from my good friend on the restaurant patio eating our carrot-topped Asian fusion burgers. He was telling me how he couldn't stop going back to Tinder in order to meet women to mess around with. "It never goes quite *too* far," he informed me, "but after each time I just feel gross, like I've just used her and it was meaningless and futile. Sometimes I may edge the boundary in order to try to *feel* a little more by going further."

I listened intently to his confession, knowing full well the feelings he was describing. My transgressions may wear a different skin than his, but I was no stranger to the feeling of after-the-moment remorse. Whether it was hours-long binges with pornography or making out with girls I should not have, I know how it feels to search for meaning in these ecstatic sensual highs.

Several years ago when I was in college, I remember a moment in Systematic Theology class which pivoted my worldview. As someone raised in a Christian home with mostly Christian schools and church several times a week, I was raised with a rich soteriological paradigm. I was under the assumption that everyone who was not a Christian was crawling around in some sort of arduous wasteland, just waiting for someone to introduce them to Jesus.

I was accustomed to the stories of Christians whose coworkers asked them, "What's *different* about you?" The person then shares the gospel with them and their world is enlightened upon their receipt of salvation (aka, ultimate satisfaction).

My world was also riddled with rockstar salvation stories: "I used to do drugs and sex and alcohol but then I became a Christian and now I just want to read my Bible."

Nevertheless, my paradigm was gently shattered in Dr. Clark's class when he was talking about the life of the non-believer. Granted, as a category, this is enormous and cannot be summed up simply, but his words did euthanize many of my naive assumptions.

"Some of you may think non-Christians are out there just in agony, waiting for someone to share the gospel with them," he explained. "You may think that they keep trying thing after thing to try to salve their existential ache and once you introduce them to Jesus, they'll be overjoyed and all their problems will vanish.

"While this may be true of some non-believers, it certainly does not describe the majority of them. There are plenty of people out there of all religions (or lack of religion) who are perfectly happy going about their lives without Jesus. They do not feel an absence of joy or peace or happiness. They are not just 'ignoring the void' so to speak; they are genuinely happy."

The little box in which I held my missiology was shattered. As I said above, I was under the impression that everyone was storing up their pain and confusion until Jesus could come to them and help make sense of everything.

How could someone legitimately be happy without Jesus??
What is the point of being a Christian then?
What's more, how will I ever convert anyone to be a Christian if they're already happy?

I remember being shocked and deflated.

A few days later though, it clicked in my mind and rather than inducing fear, my professor's words brought me profound comfort. Think about it: Being a Christian doesn't make you happy. I've preached that message for years, often with a tagline about how being a Christian often brings *more* hardship into your life. If that's the case, then the opposite must also be true. Non-Christians can be very happy indeed.

A deeper thread seems to undermine a lot of this line of thinking though. There *should* be some sort of existential discomfort to those who do not know the Maker of existence, no? This is where the second half of my epiphany comes in:

The purpose of you, your body, your senses, and your life is not to make you happy. Your sensual pleasure (brought about by marriage, sex, drugs, masturbation, alcohol, money, the rush of investing and entrepreneurship, or skydiving) is not the point of existence.

That's why my friend in Chicago and I found ourselves on couches with women, searching for some sort of meaning in our kisses. That's why Instagram promises us better lives if they were only filled with travel, adventure and more followers—just like the celebrities we follow.

But lo, the meaning of it all is not sensual pleasure. That's exactly why we cannot count on the empty feelings within non-believers to push them toward salvation. If that were the case, would it not also say something about the nature of God Himself? That He tricks us into salvation the same way you direct a donkey with a carrot on a stick? That He's nothing more than one more balm to our raging desires—another meal for our hungry tummies?

The message of the Bible is not broken when people achieve happiness outside of God.

Perhaps it is proved all the more right. If you think about it, what is the gospel message? That we are unhappy and Jesus comes to make us happy? Even if this is preached across the stages of many megachurches in America today, it is not the gospel.

The gospel is that we are dead and waiting to be brought to life. The gospel is that we are sinful and our sinful selves need to die in order that Christ can bring to life the New Man, the Spirit-filled man within us.

The gospel is far bigger than mere happiness or satisfaction. This is why my friend and I continually run back to the empty wells of pornography and hook ups. This is why we go further and further with our sensual boundaries, thinking that just a *little further* will satiate the ache within us.

The answer is not to pursue happiness, but *life*.

The billions of non-Christians who are happy outside the sphere of salvation may feel content and happy, but they are still sinful. They still continue treading the hamster wheels of systems which oppress millions for the satisfaction of the few. They still twist God-given desires into strange and bent means of gratification.

Put simply, they still sin.

And as the tattoo above my heart serves to remind me, the mission of the Christian is to advance God's kingdom on earth as it is in heaven; to join Him as He makes all things new. Sure, non-Christians may be participating in non-profit volunteer work and donating to charities but their penance doesn't make up for the depth of their sin against a holy Creator. They may be happy, but they still need Jesus. We all do. We will endlessly need Him.

I think I would go so far as to say that any sort of Christianity which promises satisfaction, happiness, or a better life (in this life, of course) is a twisting of the truth of the gospel. The happiness of the pagan masses is not a problem for the believer, as the good news of Jesus Christ is not that you can come to Him and be happy. The promises of Christ are often quite the opposite: "I did not come to bring peace, but a sword." Or, "if you want to follow Me, you must deny yourself and take up your cross daily…"[23]

Of course, the implication is that what we give up and the suffering we endure are mere shadows of what await us in Christ Jesus Himself. You cannot achieve that level of pleasure in nudes exchanged with supermodels or hookups with Bumble dates. No matter how much meaning you try to extract from a drunken night with friends, or the identity you try to extract from the purity of your childhood memories, you can't heal yourself. You may reach some sort of personal utopia or a myopic nirvana, but have you healed the world or merely made yourself happy? Have you atoned for your sins or just pleased yourself?

May we be people who live in a constant awareness of our sinfulness. May we look to the cross of Christ, not for the sake of being shamed, but forgiven. May we love our neighbors—Christians and non-Christians alike—in order that they too may come to know the source of all life, the man Jesus from Nazareth.

THE HOLY HUMILIATION
Don't just be humble; be humiliated.

I have seen the gospel smash violently into a human being like the Titanic into the ice. How sweet is the song of that message: The declaration that "you are loved" has a way of plowing into those who have never before heard it. Can you hear it again for the first time?

God gave Himself for you.

---

[23] Matthew 10:34-38

The God-man Yeshua was robbed of His skin and dangled like pulp from a tree. Because He loves you.

This message is global and requires little context for the thrust to overtake someone. For millennia this simple yet planet-shattering news has moved people to every extreme of love and sacrifice imaginable, offering themselves up to torture and death for the name of Christ.

So why do so many of us get bored with the church and drift away like a summer cloud? Why did my cousin decide that he wasn't necessarily angry at God; he was just bored of doing Christian stuff, and hasn't returned to church since high school?

We were born to pastors—great ones at that—so the words 'Jesus loves you' basically were our second, third, and fourth words after 'mama.' The jarring and beautiful message which is the gospel of Jesus Christ never moved us because we were born with an understanding of this love. It wasn't foreign to us, therefore it was not monumental.

When loving parents constantly communicate the love of God, it can easily become nothing more than recited words in the mouths of our mothers. We are like babies born in velvet sheets when someone tells us the wonders of what it's like to sleep comfortably—we already know. We have already experienced it.

Last night at youth group, I held one of my freshmen boys as he wept violently, his tears puffing out his eyelids and painting pink spiderwebs across his cheeks. I had just finished a message on dying to our old selves so that we may live again with Christ; there can be no resurrection if there is no death. Most of the youth group was in tears, but this one boy wept especially bitterly.

"I—I just can never be good enough," he sniffled into his sleeve. "My older brother is so much smarter than me and my mom likes him more. The only person who actually likes me is my dad's girlfriend, but they live 45 minutes away…"

Over the past weeks, I have been getting peripheral insight into Chris' family layout. In addition to the weed- and alcohol-fueled parties his parents throw weekly, they seem to care very little about their children, as if the kids came into existence and started living in the same house as them like a stray cat—they're around but they're not paramount.

As a result of Chris' background, I have seen the declaration of the love of Jesus wash over him. He is beginning to toe the waters of this love and slowly wade into the shallows.

I'm praying for a tsunami.

To Chris, love is a foreign object. It's something to be strived for rather than freely given. It's something you earn with good behavior and better grades. The context he has known for 15 years has set him up for a concussive shift when he collides with Jesus.

He is about to enter a world where love is freely granted, especially to the undeserving. It's a paradigm where the prostitutes are praised and the holy men are reprimanded. Chris is entering the gates of a kingdom that wraps the beggars in fine linens and puts the wealthy outside its walls; those who think they deserve entrance are the very ones who are shunned.

So then the question arises: How does someone like me enter this kingdom? Someone who grew up so familiar with the Bible I could recite the book of Lamentations backwards, making it a Shakespearean comedy instead of a tragedy? Where is there room for the proud and comfortable in this upside down kingdom?

There isn't.

And the solution I've arrived at is this: Humiliation.

It's easy to ask for humility. All virtuous people strive to be humble. But what we don't realize, what we are not brave enough to ask for, is humiliation. It's the deconstruction of our individualistic contexts and it is the only sure path to humility.

If we truly want to be like Christ, we must be humiliated.

We must join Him in His kenosis, His self-emptying, to such a degree that we no longer seek to impress others. We no longer seek to impress God.

We no longer try to earn our way into the kingdom because, as empty cups, we have nothing to offer. Our knowledge of facts and Bible verses earn us no credit in this paradoxical kingdom. We have no tokens with which to pay the gatekeeper and gain passage into this high country.

Only those who acknowledge their own wretchedness, their own unloveableness and undeservedness can gain entry. Only those who empty themselves of all their hard-earned merit badges and participation trophies can enter. The only requirement is brokenness and a desire to be healed; dirtiness and a willingness to be washed.

So examine your context. Are you someone who expects to be ushered into the kingdom because you're a pretty good person and you're accustomed to being loved? Or do you realize your own filth and come to God begging to be made clean?

In many ways, we should assume the mindset of Chris the Freshman. We should be surprised that God would shower His love on worms like us and even make time for us in His busy schedule. It should catch us off guard when he drapes His finest linens over us and calls us Son and Daughter.

I think this spirit of surprise and excitement is what He loves. This is the childlike context with which we enter the kingdom.

So may we too replace our pretense with curiosity and our comfort with humiliation. May we be people who examine our context, that the gospel may smash into and topple us. May we enter into the mysterious paradox which is the kingdom of God.

HANG IT ON THE TREE

it's not just ornaments we hang on the tree every year...

Every Black Friday my family has a tradition of getting together and doing family-ish holiday-ish things. This means ushering Fall to the exit and welcoming in the Christmas season by gobbling up the Thanksgiving leftovers, getting a tree, setting it up and decorating it.

Now, decorating our tree does not mean simply adorning it with generic store-bought orbs and candy canes which have about as much sentimental value as a handout from a sidewalk petitioner. Each Christmas morning, my brother and I must go to the tree and find that year's ornament. It's getting harder and harder the older we get, as there are more places for it to hide and blend in among the overflow of decor.

Each year's ornament has something to do with a big event which happened in our lives that year.

Each year, we take our memories and hang them on the tree.

I pulled from my ornament box a little hammer and looked at the bottom of it. In Sharpie:

Ethan 2005

I started my first job at ACE Hardware that year. I remember the miserable nights vacuuming all over the old shop on Cape Cod. I took that year and hung it on the tree.

The next ornaments I pulled out were a papier-mâché elephant and a miniature globe. Oddly, they both had the same thing scrawled across their bottoms:

Ethan 2010

That was the first year I was with the missions organization YWAM and hit up Australia, India, New Zealand and rode elephants through the jungles of Thailand. I vaguely remember my mother saying something about how she couldn't decide so she just bought me two that year.

I think about the adventures of that year as I hang them on the tree.

Then there was '07—a car—for the year I got my driver's license. And I hang it too on the tree.

There is the construction paper star, slopped with glitter and a round polaroid picture of me in the middle from Sunday School.

I hang *Ethan '92* on the tree as I think about those innocent years so long ago.

It's fascinating to have each one of these years summed up in a single object, light enough to hang from the branch of an evergreen. So much happens over the course of 365 days, yet it seems like every year my mother and father were able to sum them all up perfectly in these ornaments.

Today as I piled these little objects packed with so many memories onto the tree, I marveled at how incredible it is that each year, rather than diminishing, my connection with them seems to grow. Each year, I open up the same cardboard box filled with my little handfuls of memorabilia. One (or two) for each year of my life. I slide backward and forward through time. In some ways, it's one of the best and most consistent documentations of my life.

I take these reminders, hold them in my hands, and hang them up. If I let my mind wander too much into the fog of nostalgia while adorning the tree, I begin to recall more about each year:

The moves across the country,
the friends gained and lost,
the introduction of a new addiction or insecurity,
the spark of a new hobby,
and I hang them on the tree.

It's a way of remembering and recognizing the past. The American version of an Ebenezer or cairn.[24]

Just as God instructed the Israelites throughout scripture to make altars so that they would *remember* the past, my family's Christmas tree serves as a reminder to me of His faithfulness to us over the years.

Because each year was marked with just as much bad as it was good. Each year contained some events we'd be better off forgetting, but haven't been

---

[24] Throughout Scripture, God commands His people to pile up rocks so that they, as a people, remember certain events from their history, or times they saw God deliver them. These are called Ebenezers or cairns.

able to shake. Sins and pains. Deaths and illnesses. And as I adorn the tree, I symbolically hang those events on the tree just as much as the happy ones.

"Remember," God says to the Israelites, "what I've done here this day. Tell it to your children and their children." But like us, the Israelites often forget. They lose faith and wander astray from the One who brought them out of Egypt and worked wonders for them.

They sin and chase other lovers. Just like we do.

So, roughly 2,000 years ago, God came down to set things straight. To help us remember and to take the events of the past, the good and the bad,

and hang them on a tree.

Moving into this season, we remember the One who descended to us so that we may ascend to Him.

We remember the One who forgets our pasts.

He takes not only our bad and wicked deeds, but even the good ones we do to try to impress Him, and hangs them on a tree.

And as we progress forward in time, to future Christmases and Thanksgivings and Halloweens, He has already hung them on the tree as well.

He takes *Ethan 2008* (the year I taught myself guitar...but also the year we moved from Massachusetts to Colorado and I had my heart broken because of it), and hang it on His tree. All the pain of that year, along with all the sins and twisted desires, are now hung on a tree outside Jerusalem.

Because somewhere along the line, God decided that it wasn't good enough for us to simply *remember* His faithfulness, but He wanted to take action. To get some skin in the game.

So He took our entire lives. The good, the bad, and the ugly, and He hung them on a tree.

They are still there, but He's not. This God of ours is big enough to take our pasts and crucify them, to destroy them and leave them there on that tree after taking them into Himself. But He didn't stay there with them. He left them in His divine rearview mirror and forgot about them.

So as we move into this Advent season, when God entered our physical reality, let's not only remember our own pasts, the good and the bad. The things we miss and the things which bring us down. As we decorate our own evergreens, let's remember the One who traded places with us and hung on a tree in our place.

THE BORING & THE HOLY

take off your penny loafers and bow down.

In 1983, U2 played a concert at Red Rocks Amphitheater where they recorded the live concert video *Under a Blood Red Sky.*

They never played another show there again.

In interviews since the shoot of the video, U2's singer Bono has said they could never have a better concert than they did the night of June 5, 1983. The seats were only one-third filled due to the pouring rain and mist that had invaded Colorado the entire day leading up to the show, yet U2 refuses to ever play there again for fear of ruining the holy night they once experienced.

I regularly run at Red Rocks Amphitheater, pacing back and forth across the stone seats, or jumping up all 60-something of the rows. As an outdoor exercise spot, it is absolutely unbeatable. I've also seen a good amount of shows here, and they never fail to disappoint. The natural acoustics of the gigantic red rocks cause a surreal intimacy between the massive audience and the performer.

I've had a lot of good days at Red Rocks, but I wouldn't call any of them holy, per se.

Then there are the janitors. The people who literally vacuum the miles of seating before each show while being baked in Colorado's summer sun.

There are the beer vendors and the lighting technicians, all just showing up for work.

But there was that day back in 1983 when this ordinary land became holy.

& & &

For about two years, I worked with an organization called YWAM, which stands for Youth With A Mission. Or, if you've ever known a YWAMer, it stands for Yes, We Arrange Marriages. Today, in thinking about this post, I realized it also stands for Yes, We're After Miracles.

I love YWAM with everything in me, and have nothing but love and respect for every single YWAMer. But during my time there, I got this idea that my Christianity was nothing unless crazy miracles were happening and people were leaping out of wheelchairs left and right as my shadow grazed them on the sidewalk.

This led to a lot of discouragement in my life, as people rarely kept out of wheelchairs for me, even after hours of prayer. I got it in my head that my faith was too weak and I needed to try harder. I thought the Supernatural was avoiding me for some reason.

YWAMers also have this unspoken rule that you've got to travel. A lot. Or else your ministry is 'too comfortable' and not affecting the needy people of the world. So in my landlocked seasons when I was forced to stay stateside, I also felt somewhat bummed out, as I was unable to be where God was doing the *real* action.

& & &

Earlier today I was thinking about the story of Moses, especially the part where 40 years pass and he has done nothing but herd sheep in the desert. We kind of glaze over those years to get to the good stuff like freeing millions of slaves, as if there isn't anything for us to learn from his 40 years of monotony.

But then one day, as he's watching his flock in Midian, he sees a bush on fire but it's not burning up. The coolest thing I realized about this story is that he wasn't in a foreign land. He was in a place he had been passing by for the last 40 years, and NOTHING had ever happened.

In your life, it would be equivalent to the water cooler in the office or the elevator to the third floor. A place so mundane or ordinary that you don't even realize when you pass by it. Now imagine you've been passing that same water cooler or riding that same elevator for 40 years. I can't even comprehend this, as I'm not even close to 40, nor have I even stayed in the same place more than a few months at a time!

The point is, the place Moses was was more boring than beige. It was very, very natural; nothing super about it.

Until one day, it was holy. It was related to the divine.

It was so holy God spoke to Moses and said to take his sandals off because the ground he was on was so holy.

The water cooler speaks to you and says this office space, this faded blue carpet, is now holy.

Take off your penny loafers.

& & &

The other day I was driving on Santa Fe, a road I have to take to get anywhere, so it's become sort of drab to me. It is my 'water cooler,' or 'desert of Midian.' I was listening to a random playlist when a song came on. I can't even remember which song it was, but I know it was a Christian song, and suddenly my car traveling across Santa Fe became a holy place.

Usually my music, Christian and secular alike, just crackles through my speakers as background noise while my mind races on. But that day, the sun set in a misty haze over the nearby purple peaks of the Rockies. I caught glimpses over the factories where the yellow and red treetops were beginning to pop among their greener brethren, and the entire scene just leveled me.

I don't know how to describe the emotion aside from a holy moment. It was a brief glimpse of the Almighty.[25]

God used the view from a very ordinary road, as I was driving in my very ordinary beater, and even a song I had heard many times before. My speakers were no longer coiled springs interacting with silicone cones, they were something more than that.

The supernatural reached through my very natural environment and poked me.

I had this friend in college who used to keep a little brown notebook in his breast pocket. On the front of the small, beat-up booklet was written in ballpoint pen *Glimpses*. He opened it for me and flipped through full pages of one-line entries where he saw the supernatural peek through his natural days; where he saw God reveal Himself in the smallest ways.

One of the entries was just something like, "the rays of sunlight through the skyscrapers."

They were all that small, or smaller.

I wonder how much of the world we take for granted, dismissing opportunities to witness the holy in the ordinary.

I can't help but wonder if God more often works through seemingly 'natural' means to work in transcendent ways. Look at communion: A loaf of bread is suddenly Christ incarnate, and some fermented juice is the blood of the Creator.

Baptism is a person falling under some water and coming out. But it's also more than that.

It's the dead come to life. It must be.

There is a holy movement in the rhythms of communion and baptism, and I can't help but think that this rhythm underscores more of our day-to-day lives than we think.

---

[25] See Exodus 33, where Moses is essentially mooned by God.

So keep your eyes open.

Seek out the holy, even in the natural, even in the boring and mundane. Even after 40 years in the same place, walking by the same water cooler.

"CHRISTIAN" IS A NOUN, NOT AN ADJECTIVE
"The music is not saved. It is not a Christian."

It's a staple of American culture:

"Christian music"
"Christian movies"
"Christian rap"

There is a strict dichotomy drawn between the art of most Christians in the public sphere and the art of non-believers. TobyMac makes Christian music, but Drake does not. Darren Wilson makes Christian movies, but Chad and Carey Hayes (screenwriters of *The Conjuring*) do not.

Ever since an interview[26] I read with Jon Foreman of Switchfoot, something has bugged me about this binary. Jon said, "I am a Christian and I make music. The music is not saved. It is not Christian."

In other words, Jesus did not come and die to save songs. He did not suffer in order to bring *Oceans 11* out of the flames of hell. "Christian" is a noun, not a verb.

It refers to a person who has put their faith in the man Jesus of Nazareth. Acts 11 points out that the word was first employed in Antioch, and it was an insult more than a descriptor. The accusers said of the Christians, *you just want to be like your master, Jesus Christ. You are Little Christs!* And the term was born.

---

[26] The website which originally hosted this interview shut down and no longer exists, so this may not be word-for-word what Foreman said, but the idea is the same.

For the first 300 years of her existence, Christianity suffered brutally at the hands of the Roman Empire until 313 AD, when Constantine declared Christianity legal. Soon after, the persecution let up and the empire converted to Christianity. You may have heard of a little thing called The Holy Roman Empire. This was a marriage of religion and politics in 800 AD, from which the Western church has never fully recovered. In fact, Voltaire said of it, "The Holy Roman Empire was neither Holy nor Roman nor an empire."[27]

We see signs of its recession now, but we are very much still in the paradigm of Christendom. Christendom is a fancy word for a "Christian culture." It accurately describes things like the Bible Belt, and the fact that politicians still appeal to Christian values when making speeches, or why Oscars winners thank "God." Christianity is not persecuted in the West because of what Constantine did 1700 years ago, and we are only now beginning to see signs of its fading.

When Christianity became widely accepted across western culture and Christendom became the predominant form of belief and action, this made room for "Christian things" to emerge.

For instance, in the 13th century during the fourth crusade, there are stories of western marauders breaking into eastern churches and stealing holy artifacts and relics. Were these things actually 'holy' and did they contain special power from the divine? Perhaps, but probably not. They were merely "Christian things." They were elevated to a position of holding some sort of essence borne of man's perception more than divine origin.

And we fall into the same traps today.

I catch myself creating this false dichotomy between Christian things and secular things; holy spaces and unholy spaces. How many times have you heard someone crack a dirty joke only to have someone else say "Dude! You can't say that in a *church!* Not in *here!*"

It's a *Christian space.*

---

[27] Voltaire, et al., *The Works of Voltaire*

Contrary to everything the Bible teaches, we believe that there are places where we can go to meet God, but the rest of the time, He's pretty far away. He's trapped in a cathedral somewhere or attending a council in Jerusalem. He's not in my car on the highway, or in the movie theater.

Another implication of Christendom is that, in this culture, nearly all the art created was sacred art. Handel's *Messiah*, the Sistine Chapel, and every triptych in Italy was commissioned and created by the church, for the church. The cutting edge of art and music was in the church, and nothing existed outside of it. Even the architecture of churches was meant to inspire awe in visitors. Anyone who has set foot in an ancient cathedral can attest. What we have see in the dissolution of Christendom is a reduction of support for quality art from the church, and a focus on creating private art, exclusively for the enjoyment of Christians.

What originated as an insult to highlight the early believers striving to be like their master over time became a descriptor of various merchandise and media in order to boost sales. The word has become a marketing ploy.

The sad thing is, we Christians have gobbled up this Christian marketing scheme. As if the word held some promise of *This album is imprinted by the divine and will change your life (And of course, the lyrics are squeaky clean).*

I love seeing Christians fudge this boundary wall. For instance, worship band King's Kaleidoscope dropped not one but two f-bombs in a recent song, which the singer said came straight from the pages of his journal as a prayer to God. He broke free from the typical restraints of what Christians should and shouldn't have in their work.[28]

Then you have Christians on the other side such as Kendrick Lamar and Chance the Rapper who run in secular circles and use their platforms to raise awareness about things like social injustices and struggles with God. (And with them, the writers of *The Conjuring* films who wanted to remind people of the presence of the spiritual world)

---

[28] "Kaleidoscope Controversy: Use of f-Word in Song Brings Kings Kaleidoscope Criticism." Cross Rhythms.

I think that the more we can dissolve the barrier between "Christian stuff" and "secular stuff," the more we will be able to make a difference in our culture. If the gospel is universally appealing and is meant for the redemption of the whole world, shouldn't our creations be equally accessible and relatable? How many times have you sat through a 'Christian film' and thought, *Yah...life is definitely not like that...*

I am a Christian. Many of you are Christians. Don't be fooled into thinking that your music collection, DVD sets, or certain stores are also Christians. They are not. They are works made by Christians, hopefully with the same care and quality non-believers put into theirs.

The sooner we can simply live as Christians, do good work, and speak well to the world in which we live, the more effective we will be as *Little Christs*. So may we do so. May we work hard, love well, and not construct false descriptors to segregate our art from that of the world. I think changes like this can begin by monitoring the way we speak about certain things. If we could erase the adjective form of "Christian" from our vocabulary, I think we would begin to think differently about how we are to live and create in the world, and relate to those who are not believers.

"HAVE YOU EVER SEEN A REAL MIRACLE?"

short answer...yes.

I got this email last night as I was going to bed and as I was replying, decided that this should be a blog post because I know Josiah and I aren't the first to have these questions.

> Hey man. Dude I gotta say, I love your writing. Been a huge blessing reading it. I read *Leaving Weather* and had a good moment with God after. You voiced a lot of thoughts I was having, it was awesome to see someone else saying it. I'm 19 and finished my Discipleship Training School [a missions school with Youth With A Mission] a month ago. You're ahead of me by a few years and I'd say I look up to you. I have one question. It's simple but I'm asking because you seem like a honest guy, and I trust your response. Have you seen any miracles, like for real?   -Josiah

Hey man!

Thanks so much for reading and for taking the time to reach out! That means a lot. To answer your question, I'd say two things:

1) We need to define what we mean when we say 'miracles' and

2) Yes.

I think when most people use the word "miracles," they are referring to what the Bible calls 'signs and wonders,' or things used by God to show people who He is. Things like healings, demon possession, nature miracles like water into wine, etc. are what I'm guessing you're referring to when you ask that, and my answer to those things is…yes.

But what's more important is the kind of miracle which is not 'significant' nor is it very 'wondrous.' Things like my parents staying together and being awesome. Or how about the fact that we get to fly through space on a world lousy with sunsets, lasagna and road trips? That may sound basic, like the colloquialism "life is just a miracle" sung by bored, chipper housewives or knitted into your grandma's quilt, but I think that if we read the Bible we should come to see pretty quickly that the entire universe is rich with the fingerprints of God; His presence and glory. What are the first two chapters about? He's making trees and bushes and flamingoes, so if we dare say that those things are not miraculous (and by extension, that they don't bear a direct compass hand pointing to their Maker) then we almost seem to give Him the middle finger.

What I'm trying to say is, when we draw a line between something being 'miraculous' and 'not miraculous,' we set ourselves up for disappointment.

I had a friend in college who always carried a little brown notebook in his pocket. On the cover, in small handwriting, it just said 'Glimpses,' and he recorded the small ways he saw God appear throughout the day. I flipped though it once and most of them made no sense to me. They were things like, "the sun in the leaves by Wicker," or, "that sidewalk spot outside work."

They were utterly insignificant things, but they were placed and times where for whatever reason, He felt God was grabbing hold of his attention, even just for a moment.

When I was in YWAM, and for several years after, I was what I call a 'miracle hunter.' I was so hung up on seeing big miraculous things that I would be really disappointed when they didn't happen. I was more into the miracles themselves than I was the One performing the miracle. It's kind of a volatile recipe there.

Do I think I've seen genuine healings, demonic liberations, and other dramatic miracles? Yes. The first was in Thailand when a man severely crippled by a legion of demons was freed after ten minutes of prayer.

The real questions, which I'm guessing you're really after though, are:

Did it cure my faith once and for all?

Have I believed perfectly since seeing a manifest episode of God acting within creation?

No. Far from it.

Jesus said "blessed are they who have not seen and still believe,"[29] and it's so true. I was someone who had to see in order to believe, yet even AFTER I saw, I struggled with believing!

Think of the Israelites after leaving Egypt: they had just seen some of the most intense displays of God's power ever witnessed by human eyes (plus there's still a huge pillar of smoke and fire near them), yet they quickly FORGET those things and start to doubt. Hundreds of thousands of them.

Miracles don't cure your doubt.
Miracles are no shortcut to faith.

By definition, faith is trusting in something you cannot see. And that's why I've saved the most important miracle for last: Salvation.

---

[29] John 20:29

All other miracles fade away but only one is eternal. Suppose you saw someone's severed leg grow back. Fifty years from now, that same leg will be decomposing in a coffin six feet underground. Or suppose God cures someone of cancer. Cool, but seventeen years later they get hit by a bus and die. The miracle was cool but it was basically just an extension of this life for a few short years.

All miracles are temporary, save the one that extends their life *forever*. Introduce someone to the Author of human existence and you'll witness a miracle which has more longevity and joy in it than anything else you could experience. Plus, you reap the peripheral benefits as well. You get to see their slow progression over time and walk with them as their faith develops and they move from 'milk to meat' as Hebrews says.[30]

Another thing to note is that almost every sign and wonder miracle is meant for the purpose of leading to the Big Miracle (salvation).

Suppose someone's back gets healed. How much more likely are they to listen to the Gospel about Jesus Christ and put their faith in Him at that point? Miracles are not ends in themselves; they are meant to lead people to Jesus.

The Spirit may have temporarily healed their body, but it's for the purpose of having Christ heal everything else indefinitely. Miracles are fun and exciting, and we have a right to rejoice when we see them, but they're not eternal. One thing is.

I know that's probably not at all what you were asking for, but there's my very longwinded response!

Halfway through, I realized that you're probably not the only person wondering about miracles so I'll probably end up blowing this up into a full blog post. Let me know what you think though, and I hope it helps!

---

[30] Hebrews 5:12; also see 1 Corinthians 3:2

"CHRISTIAN ART"

Christian media is safe, not necessarily good...unlike God

Recently I was sitting with a friend and the subject of music came up. I asked him what type of music he listened to and he told me he loved "Christian music."

I hadn't realized that was a genre.

Christians can and do make music all the way across the spectrum of musical genres, and many of my favorite metal bands are Christians. However, I love what Jon Foreman once pointed out about that phrase:

People are saved. *People* are Christians. Music is not Christian. Jesus did not die so music could go to heaven; He died for *people*.[31]

Lately I have been thinking a lot about the topic of Christian art and how we interact with the creative endeavors of the world.

Michael Gungor has said that he and his friends could tell, without fail, which songs were 'Christian' after only hearing the first five seconds of them because they sounded more fake and plastic than 'secular' music.[32]

Bono said that Christian art ironically lacks the honesty which is so evident in the Bible's own songbook, the Psalms.[33]

I think the Christian media scene has carved out for itself a unique niche. Speaking generally of the past decade or two, it doesn't create the best

---

[31] The website which originally hosted this interview shut down and no longer exists, so this may not be word-for-word what Foreman said, but the idea is the same.

[32] Jacobs, Hervict. "MICHAEL GUNGOR On The Problem With The Christian Music Industry." AWAKEN GENERATION, 9 Dec. 2013, awakengeneration.wordpress.com/2011/11/16/michael-gungor-on-the-problem-with-the-christian-music-industry/

[33] Fuller Studio and Bono, directors. "Be Brutally Honest" YouTube, 26 Apr. 2017, www.youtube.com/watch?v=8V0QiX8zJmQ.

films, the most original music, or the most unique books. There tend to be boundaries within which it works, and these boundaries give a lot of people comfort.

In other words, people perpetually subscribe to Christian media because it's *safe*.

We can be sure that by shopping at Hobby Lobby, we may be buying some mass-produced original-seeming kitsch piece of art or a quote painted on 'vintage' wood, but at least it won't have any cuss words or nudity.

Many American Christians have become attached to this universe in which safety and shelter is prized above honesty, authenticity and risk.

We would rather something be safe than good.

Ironically, this is the exact opposite of C.S. Lewis' description of God via the character of Aslan in his Chronicles of Narnia:

> "Aslan is a lion, the great Lion."

"Ooh" said Susan. "I'd thought he was a man. Is he...quite safe? I shall feel rather nervous about meeting a lion"

"Safe?" said Mr Beaver. "Who said anything about safe? 'Course he isn't safe. But he's good. He's the King, I tell you."[34]

This is one of my favorite ways to think of God. He isn't safe...but He's good. Like the beautiful power of a tsunami or the destructive slithering body of a tornado, God isn't safe. Not at all. But He is good. He is beautiful.

American Christianity has created a space where certain things are allowed, others are questionable, and others are completely forbidden. I laughed when I saw the film *Blue Like Jazz,* which sought to be a more 'edgy' movie...for being a Christian movie, because they allowed a few uses of *damn* throughout the film, but nothing worse.

---

[34] C. S. Lewis, *The Lion, the Witch and the Wardrobe*

I walked out of the theater and was asked what I thought of the film. My answer, as with all Christian media, had to be caveated: "It was pretty good...for a Christian film."

Why can't Christians just make all-around good films? Or music?

I am encouraged, however, to find out about more Christians working in secular creative spheres. For instance, the creators of *The Conjuring* films are strong Christians who wanted to awaken sterilized Americans to the reality of the spiritual world. The creator of Marvel's *Doctor Strange* had a similar mission by using magic as a symbol of invisible forces at work around us constantly.[35]

For quite a while now, many of the leading metal bands have been made up of Christians, such as August Burns Red, The Chariot (long live), and The Devil Wears Prada. I've often wondered why this genre specifically has thrived in Christian circles, while others have not seemed to be able to keep up with mainstream media. (I wonder if this is because hardcore is a genre in which openness about struggles and anger is encouraged?)

However, as it stands now, these creatives seem to be more of the exception than the rule. Christians seem to seek shelter within walls and boundaries for fear of judgment from other Christians.

"Am I allowed to say that? But what will people think of me?"

I wonder if Christians think those thoughts more than the rest of the world, and this is exactly what hampers our work, and in turn, our witness to the world for Christ.

By establishing walls to work within, we may effectively cater to a handful of Christians, but fail to reach the rest of the world. In Jesus' words, we

---

[35] Asay, Paul. "Doctor Strange Is The Most Religious Superhero Movie Ever." Watching God, Patheos Explore the World's Faith through Different Perspectives on Religion and Spirituality!, 7 Nov. 2016, www.patheos.com/blogs/watchinggod/2016/11/doctor-strange-is-the-most-religious-superhero-movie-ever/.

have the 'innocent as doves' bit down, now we just need to work on getting more clever and original.[36]

Earlier this year, Christian rapper Lecrae took a lot of heat when he began to speak up against racial injustice in America. The pushback changed him and how he went about creating his craft. It seemed like people wanted him to be this picture of a 'good, Christian rapper who raps about Christian things,' but when he began to speak up about real issues he was facing and struggles he was having, many Christians took up arms.

When Lecrae began to wander outside the bounds of what Christian artists are allowed to speak about, others got nervous.[37] There have been many times I've hit 'Publish' on my blog, nervous about what I was revealing to the world. *Was that too much?* I'd often ask myself. *Did I share too much this time?*

Yet every time I've taken a step in the direction of honesty and vulnerability, the feedback has always been positive. I think Christians are wearying of pseudo-niceties and polite conversation and we are ready to address the more warped things in this world, in our own souls.

For too long, most of us have pretended that being a Christian means living in a nice, easy world in which there is no pain, anger, grief or conflict. The more we wake up to these realities, the stronger our art, our voices, and our witness will be.

So no longer will I pretend I have it all together. No longer will I mask my anger, my loneliness, or my brokenness before a world that needs more Christians who are honest.

And I hope you won't either.

May we be Christians who reach out and touch the broken and hurting place in the world with our vulnerability. May we be people who share our stories as testimonies of what Jesus has done in us, using honesty rather

---

[36] Matthew 10:16

[37] Boorstein, Michelle. "This Rapper Is Trying to Get His Fellow Evangelicals to Talk about Race. Not Everyone Is on Board."

than plasticity. May our art penetrate the bubble which so often retains Christian art from reaching anyone outside our comfortable communities.

THE NAKED JESUS

at first glance, it seemed like a typical crucifix painting...

In 2014 at Moody Bible Institute, a student group put on an event to educate students about pornography and the sex industry. I paced through it, thinking I had already seen all this before. The exhibit opened with scientific facts about the chemical effects of pornography on the brain, showing how it rewires our mental pathways to crave porn.

Heard them before.

Then there was a room of testimonies, people shared how porn had damaged their lives and relationships. As sincere and moving as these stories were, I had heard others like them before too. After all, these addiction stories were basically my own.

But then we moved to the last room.

On the wall was a painting. Eye level. About 4×3 feet. At first glance, it seemed like a typical crucifix painting. There hung Jesus on the cross, bleeding and ashamed.

But then you looked a little lower

and then you realized that he was not wearing any garment to politely cover the Savior's genitalia. There was no loin cloth to protect the Lord from disgrace.

It was jarring to realize I was looking at a painting of Jesus' penis.

In many ways, the fact that artists have typically covered Jesus up while hanging on the cross has done a disservice to our perception of His scope of atonement. We are used to seeing Him, battered and bloody, yes, but at least with a shred of decency left and a towel wrapped around his midsection.

One of my theology professors would always say we postmodern people do theology like this—and then he would crouch and cover up his crotch, like an embarrassed child who had jumped out of the bath and been caught by the babysitter. We will talk about God in relation to anything but our genitals.

We try to 'clean up' the crucifixion.

Today I got curious and checked for myself. Sure enough, all four gospels tell the same story:

> Matthew 27:35—When they had crucified him, they divided up his clothes by casting lots.

> Mark 15:24—And they crucified him. Dividing up his clothes, they cast lots to see what each would get.

> Luke 23:34—Jesus said, "Father, forgive them, for they do not know what they are doing." And they divided up his clothes by casting lots.

> John 19:23—When the soldiers had crucified Jesus, they took his garments and divided them into four parts, one part for each soldier; also his tunic.

Historians have pointed out that crucifixion was not only a torturous execution, but also a shameful humiliation. That's why victims would always be crucified naked: one last insult to injury.

Now, why is it important to us that Jesus was crucified naked?

Throughout the millennia, artists have tried to restore to Jesus His dignity by covering up the shameful bits. They have censored the truth of scripture in order to protect young eyes.

The reason my school displayed the painting was to remind us that, while Jesus has absorbed all our sin and wrongdoing, He has also absorbed all of our shame. He was not covered up in order to maintain His dignity while dying on the tree; He was stripped and exposed, so that even until the end His atoning work would be victorious, even over our sexuality and shame.

J. Vernon McGee writes:

He was crucified naked. It is difficult for us in this age of nudity and pornography to comprehend the great humiliation He suffered by hanging nude on the cross. They had taken His garments and gambled for ownership. My friend, He went through it all, crucified naked, that you might be clothed with the righteousness of Christ, and so be able to stand before God throughout the endless ages of eternity.[38]

I too am guilty of dichotomizing my sexuality from my spirituality. As American Christians, I feel like this is the norm. We go to church over *here* and think and talk about sex over *there*. And if I looked at porn, I hide it from God until enough time had passed that I could go and safely confess.

But what I have realized recently is that this is wrong. When I begin to see my sexual desires as something *good,* something given to me by God, it is easier to align them with His will. When I realize that I don't have to hide my desires from Him, but rather give them over to Him, it becomes easier to escape temptation and have peace that I can trust Him with my desires. I can trust Him to bring me a wife in His timing, and I don't have to fear that He'll never give me one because I have these *bad* desires.

I think many of my struggles with pornography came from this thought that 'sex is bad, dirty, and shameful. I need to hide these thoughts from God.' A lot of them came from a fear that my desires for sex were bad, and therefore I was a bad person. But God loves healthy sexuality. In reality, Jesus has taken all of my shame and all my twisted views of sex to the cross and destroyed them when He was crucified naked.

He has redeemed our perverted views of sexuality. He has taken every last centerfold hanging on the walls of our minds and torn them to shreds. He was crucified naked so we need not be ashamed anymore.

---

[38] J. Vernon Mcgee, *Thru the Bible: Genesis through Revelation*

THREE DEATHS

is death something to fear, or something that's already been defeated?

Yesterday I woke up to one of my best friends sobbing, cussing, and punching the wall.

Josh never cries. He is one of the funniest humans I have ever encountered. It was a surreal way to wake up.

I was on the top bunk while he was on the bottom, occasionally pounding the wall by our bed.

I continued listening to him as I waded further from the shallows of my subconscious and into the reality of the day. Josh was on the phone in the bunk below me, and I soon pieced together that his friend Dan had died in a car accident the night before. As I continued listening, it became clear that Dan had been married just a few weeks prior, and his wife Kayla was also in the car accident. She was in critical condition. A driver had slid in the snow across the center of the road and hit them head on.

I crawled down from my bunk and sat with Josh on his bed, holding his shoulders. He called another friend to tell him the news. In the middle of the call, he got a text, paused to read it, and sobbed back into his iPhone,

"Kayla just died too."

I sat with Josh a while longer as he made a few more phone calls to inform friends and family of the death of his friends. It was a very surreal morning.

& & &

Today I saw on Instagram that a young Ugandan boy had died. I had been following his story for a few months now, as his medical condition continued to baffle doctors and his health waned. A friend of mine had moved to Uganda solely to care for him, and posted updates periodically. Today's photo on my feed was a flower and a polaroid portrait of the boy. The caption stated that early this morning, he departed to be with Jesus.

It really did not fit in with the stream of selfies, mountaintop adventurers, and latte art surrounding it.

& & &

Saturday evening I delivered a message to an auditorium full of high schoolers. I had a message written up, but I felt like the Lord kept pressing one word into my mind for the event: *Weight*.

I talked about how we have become desensitized by media to the point that nothing really has weight. Everything is fluffy, funny, and ironic. It is rare to be scrolling through my newsfeed and find something of real weight, like I did today. My brain has become used to the constant input of noise that ends up becoming a shallow buzz, removing me from what is really important.

And that surreal morning with Josh, I awoke to a jarring reality that didn't make sense to my cluttered mind. Dan and Kayla would never again wake up together and get coffee. They wouldn't drive to their church or meet up with friends.

I realized that I have become extremely focused on things that do not matter, things that do not last. Things that, when I get a phone call saying a friend of mine has died, will not matter at all and I will be sorry to have wasted so much time on them.

I like to think about the word *glory* as equivalent to *weight*. Like a giant rock in a river, the weight we give to things helps to shape our lives. The more glorious something is, the more it will inform the way we live, just as the bigger a rock is, the more it will form the shape of the river. But I feel like lately, I've been trying to stack up a bunch of pebbles and demand that they withstand the flow, but when the tides surge, they are quickly swept away. What has the most glory in your life? What most shapes the way you live and the way you spend your time? Is it truly glorious?

I have been wrestling with how exactly I want to conclude this post. It is incredibly heavy and indelibly important, but the only thing I can say after witnessing all this death is this:

Jesus hates death.

He hates it more than we do. God didn't create humans in the hopes that they would one day die. He made us to have life, and life to the fullest. When His dear friend Lazarus died, all Jesus could do was weep. So what I want to say, dear reader, with all the gravity I can muster, is that experiencing the love of God is the fullest life imaginable. It is the only preparation for death.

Moody once said, "One day you will read in the papers that D.L. Moody has died. Don't believe a word of it! For at that very moment I will be more alive than I have ever been in this old body." Right now we can rejoice that Dan, Kayla, and the young Ugandan boy are more alive than we could ever dare imagine. One day it will be true of me and many of my friends. And I hope with all my heavy heart that it will be true of you.

Jesus has swallowed up death, and drank every dark drop down. He has taken it into Himself that it may be destroyed and done away with. He has made it possible for us to chant in its awful face,

Where, O death, is your sting? Where, O grave, is your victory?

Is death something you fear, or is it something that has already been defeated?

Come and find life where it may be found, in Christ Jesus, and in Him alone.

THE DEATH OF DEATH

"tomorrow I am going to find out the grand mystery."

You know that thing no one talks about? The taboo which is politely removed from conversation? That thing that haunts the darkened corners of your mind like a ghost in a Louisiana mansion?

Death.

I once watched an Australian film in which two prisoners were sentenced to death by firing squad. On the eve of their execution, one writes a letter to his beloved which opens, "Tomorrow I am going to find out the grand mystery."

And it is a mystery, a secret left primarily to plague the minds of theologians and morticians because no one else wishes to get the hands of their minds dirty with such unpleasant thoughts.

Death. And what follows.

Tonight I sat in Chick-Fil-A with my parents as they told me about a man who took his own life last week. He sat on a park bench and shot himself. His body was discovered by a jogger. My dad did the funeral, and despite the protest of the late man's wife, my dad preached the gospel.

"When it comes to death, you have three options," he explained to me in the fast food franchise. "You can avoid thinking about it with distractions and endless entertainment; you can try to fight it with plastic surgery, money, and anything else that promises to give your life youth, or the third option..."

I waited.

"Listen to someone who has died and come back to tell about it."

"Like that kid who went to heaven and back?" I joked. He chuckled but we both understood what he was saying.

N.D. Wilson wrote in *Notes From The Tilt-A-Whirl*, "Do not fear the shadowy places. You will never be the first one there. Another went ahead and down until He came out the other side."

One man has descended to the depths of *sheol*[39] and returned to tell us. One man descended from His place on high to tell us what it's like.

One man has disclosed The Grand Secret.

Jesus said to Martha, "Your brother will rise again." [40]

---

[39] 'Sheol' is the Hebrew word for "the grave"

[40] John 11:23

My mom cut in to tell me that the funeral was unlike any she had attended before. She described the presence of the Holy Spirit in the room that day, as my father eulogized to the primarily secular attendees about this Man from heaven. This God-man who hates death so much He underwent it, so it would be destroyed once and for all.

Jesus said to her, "I am the resurrection and the life. He who believes in me will live, even though he dies." [41]

Then my mom told me that the next day was Sunday and several of the families from the funeral returned to my father's church to learn more about this carpenter from Israel—that guy hanging on a tree, beaten to a pulpy collection of tendons, most of his skin ripped from him.

I explained to my high schoolers this past weekend that when we think of life and death, we should think about them in relational terms. Those who are most truly alive are *known* by God, while those who are dead are those cut off from Him. *Depart from me,* He says, *for I never knew you.* [42]

It's not about belief or doing just the right number of good deeds; it's about knowing the Holy One and being known by Him. And those who don't want to know Him, those who hate Him, don't have to spend all of eternity with Him. They will depart from Him, and it will be their own choice.

There is a weight to conversations about death. You can talk about celebrities, post offices, and sauerkraut and make jokes the whole time. But when your friend tells you their mom died from cancer last month, the conversation suddenly sinks to a richer depth. There is weight in death, and with this weight comes opportunity.

What better place is there to preach hope than a funeral?

As my dad also said at the ceremony, 'the statistics on death are pretty good...just about everyone dies.'

---

[41] John 11:25

[42] Matthew 7:21-23

So my friend, are you looking for hope? Are you looking for the answer behind The Grand Secret? Or do you prefer ignorance? Do you prefer broken relationship with the Creator of life and the Destroyer of death?

Christians die expectantly. We die with the excitement to someday pop up from the ground and walk this earth again. Our burial plots are nothing more than what a toaster is to a slice of bread: A place to be shoved down for a few minutes and later emerge enriched, improved and completed.

I once heard about a man who was in a car accident. As he sat in his driver's seat awaiting death, a pedestrian who witnessed the accident ran to his window and talked to him. He was with the victim for his last minutes on earth. The witness later talked about how much peace the man had on his face as he slipped out of his broken body.

The pedestrian later showed up at my pastor's office, terrified because he realized that if he were to die that day, he would not have that same peace about his departure.

He was terrified of death.

But O, how we have hope!

Where, O death is your sting? Where, O grave is your victory? [43]

One day every one of you reading these words will be dead. I will be dead. The question is, are we going to walk out of the grave again, or will we stay in the earth while everything around us springs back to life?

The other day I was on a plane thinking about death and began writing my epitaph on the drink napkin. What I came up with was,

> Only laughter, never weeping
> for I have only laid my head.
> I am not gone, I'm only sleeping
> until the resurrection of the dead.

---

[43] 1 Corinthians 15:55

Have you thought about your own death? Is it with hope and peace that you approach your final day, or is it with fear and anxiety?

May we be people who embrace death because we know the One who has been there before. May we have peace because He took death into Himself, destroying it once and for all. And may we have hope because Jesus walked out of His grave so one day, we will too.

WE'RE GOING TO DIE.
you are not the exception to death.

2,448,017 Americans died in 2005.

652,091 were from heart disease; 559,312 from cancer; 117,809 were from accidents. Gun deaths were interesting: 12,352 people were murdered with a gun, while 17,002 people killed themselves with one.

Every month, roughly 20 women in Papua New Guinea are accused of being a witch, tortured, and publicly burned alive.

In 2017, Chechnya began exterminating homosexuals within her borders in "Gay Concentration Camps."

To us, these are not human beings (mothers, brothers, best friends, co-workers, etc.), they are numbers. They are statistics. And like it or not, no matter how hard you try, you will someday join the ranks of those calculated integers.

"It's hard to be optimistic when you know you're going to die," wrote Neil Strauss in his book *Emergency* after spending years discovering how to survive nearly every possible situation known to mankind. He had faced natural dangers, human dangers, toxins, et al, and gives detailed accounts of how to overcome and survive them all.

The book ends somewhat bluntly with an account of a nineteen-year-old girl getting hit by an SUV while crossing the street. Her body goes flying yards into the air. No amount of survival skills can prepare you for freak accidents. You can't outrun the reaper forever.

When I saw the film *Annihilation,* all of which is a metaphor for cancer, I was hit by the fact that I will die someday and whatever comes after is *it*. Like, that's all. I cannot do anything else that I had once planned on; I can't fulfill unrealized dreams or say a last goodbye to my loved ones. I can't go out and have another meal or sit in another coffee shop. When that moment comes, when my SUV finds me on my crosswalk, that's it. Period. End of sentence.

I realized how desensitized we've become to death the other day when I opened up the newspaper (it's like Twitter but made out of big pieces of paper) and this was one of the top stories:

Who's going to die in "Avengers: Infinity War"? Here are the candidates

By Michael Cavna
The Washington Post

perhero players won't live to see the final credits, will they? Here is our breakdown on

The attention-grabber in this story is the death of a [yes, imaginary] person. You can see that the author mentions that whoever the unlucky candidate is "won't live to see the final credits." No, Michael, they won't live to see *anything* else, will they?

I know that this article was about fictional characters, yet I think Hollywood's constant formation of our thoughts on death treat it so casually. A thousand buildings explode and bodies litter the post-battle streets, but then we get up and throw away the half of our popcorn barrel we didn't eat.

Do you realize that one day, YOU will be one of those bodies? That one day, YOU won't get to get up and say a few more things to your bestie, nor will you get to change your mind about *this* topic or take a trip to *that* country?

Perhaps one of the scariest things about death is that you go into it naked.

Whatever it is you believe lies in wait for you on the far side of the curtain, you don't get to dress up to impress them. You don't get to hide behind your money, your job, or the grades your kid got on his high school transcript. Or your transcript. Your intellect won't wow the Judge, nor will your toned body woo the fellow dead in the cemetery.

We spend so much of our time (aka, our life) constructing walls behind which to hide. I can't tell you how many days of my life have been spent worrying about my looks or shopping for clothes which will hopefully take me to that next 'level' of society.

Impressing people earns you no merit postmortem. You walk through that door buck naked, with no meritorious degrees, exotic cars or fashionable clothes.

Too often, this line of thought becomes distilled into the coy maxim *You can't take it with you*, but far too rarely do we think about this and meditate on it. If you think this post is too dark for a Christian writer, look no further than the Bible to remind us of our own mortality. The psalmist instructs us to number our days; to remember that each one has a number and that number only goes up, never back down. You can only live it once and you have a finite number of days allotted. Maybe your number goes up a little when you eat more kale, but that SUV is coming for you. And it will not miss.

There is a cow skull on the wall of this bar. I don't think it was put there as a *memento mori,* but it's working. Even animals are made uniquely. That bull was not the same individual as his sister. James Cromwell, who played the farmer in the film *Babe,* said that he became a vegetarian after making that film because he realized that he had participated in the deaths of these animals which he had come to care for. Their unique 'personalities' will never again be realized on this earth.

Regardless of your dietary habits, whether you're a pig or a human, you're going to die and there will be no more. Your effect on earth will conclude, and 99.9999% of us will be forgotten within a generation.

Yesterday I asked my parents if they remembered their great-grandparents and they spouted off a few facts, but for the most part, not really. Their great-great-grandparents? Nothing. "My dad's side was from France, but I forget where my mom's side came from."

One day, that will be you: your offspring unable to articulate one iota of affection toward you and the majority of your carbon will have been recycled by that time. If you're lucky, someone will have a book of yours or a work of art you made on their wall, and say "Oh, Ethan? Didn't he pass away a couple years ago? Oh, he's still alive? No, I think he died in '23..."

And that's about all you get. That's it.

I've spent 1,000 of my words attempting to get you to think about your own mortality—about the fact that you are not the exception to death—and for what purpose? I think that gaining this perspective helps us move to a place of unpacking the bigger questions. Centrally, What *does* happen to us after we die? Then, in light of this, how then shall we live?

If, upon dying, you enter a nihilistic vacuum and cease to exist, your life has two options: Hedonism or suicide. It truly was meaningless and none of us deserve more than to be discarded on the side of the road and neglected eternally.

If, however, you believe that there may just be something—or Someone—awaiting you, then that changes things. D.L. Moody once said that "One day you will read in the papers that Dwight Moody has died. Don't believe a word of it! For at that moment I will be more alive than I ever have been in this feeble, miserable life..."

And if *that* is the case, then shouldn't that affect how we live our lives? Shouldn't it make us want to bring people into *that* life? I don't see the Bible as a restrictive set of rules or a dogmatic system of beliefs. Right now I see it as an invitation to *eudaimonia*, Greek philosopher-speak for "the good life." Jesus said that He came so that we may have "life and life to the fullest," and I want a taste of that. I want to draw others into that.

Not only do I think that people will rise again from the dead, but I think the earth will undergo a restoration. I think that there will be a world without litter, deforestation and a depletion of our atmosphere. And I think we can begin to participate in that now.

That's why what we believe about the *next life* should change how we live *today*.

Jesus breathes meaning into matter.

Jesus heals reality.

Colossians refers to Him as the firstborn of creation.[44] Paul goes on a multi-paragraph rant on how everything that there is exists because of, through, and for Him. This is not a threat or a mere doctrinal statement. This is living, breathing reality. This is an invitation to come know, and be known by, Life Himself.

Personally, I believe that every one of us will rise from the dead. The only difference is how we will respond: You will either rejoice at the idea of spending endless days with Jesus the Nazarene, or you will continue your rebellion and hatred of Him indefinitely.

Think of it like a wedding party: We're all invited and we all show up. You can choose to join the dance floor and party, or you can spend the entire evening pouting in the corner because your ex showed up. See that? Two people at the exact same event having wildly different experiences.

I need to stop here or I'll think of more anecdotes and metaphors until the sun goes down.

May we be people who learn to number our days. May we be people who are conscious of the next life and let that affect this one. And may we daily grow in our realization of Christ's love for us and let that overflow into the lives of others.

---

[44] Colossians 1:15

WE WILL BE FORGOTTEN.

you die twice: the day you die, and the last time your name is said.

A small number of people ask big questions.

Lately I've been attempting to figure out what would constitute a life of purpose, doing anything in order to leave a lasting mark on the world. There is almost nothing you can do which will be remembered in 100 years.

Do you remember your great-great grandparents? Have you given them much thought lately? I'm pretty sure mine came to the USA from France, but I'm not sure. The Renaults are long gone and there's a good chance they will never be thought of again.

Ever.

I recently heard it put this way: Everyone dies twice. The day your heart stops beating, and the last day anyone ever says your name.

Ultra-famous YouTuber Logan Paul has millions of followers—over 30 million worldwide—and an interesting slogan: "Dent the universe."

He wants his legacy to be one of debauchery, wild fun, and "doing it differently." When I watched his videos, I couldn't help but think how myopic his perspective is. Sure, he's a big deal right now. Everyone is talking about him…right now. And he has all the money, fame, cars, and girls he could ever want…

right now,

but what about in 100 years? Will Paul still be making headlines from the grave? Will his great grandchildren even know who he was? Will his colloquial 'denting of the universe' have been anything more than a hyped-up line to peddle hoodies to middle schoolers?

It seems like this sentiment has been chanted before from the pages of Ecclesiastes: "No one remembers the former generations, and even those yet to come will not be remembered by those who follow them" (1:11) and again in chapter 9, "For the living know that they will die, but the dead know nothing; they have no further reward, and even their name is forgotten."

How terrifying it is to realize that we will be forgotten, no matter how grand a stage we currently have or how many followers digitally chase us around the globe. You can be president of the United States and still be forgotten. I mean, we've had 45. How many can you name? Give it a few hundred more years. Look at Commodus.

"Who?"

He's the emperor of Rome most historians point to as signaling the collapse of the empire (which was much more powerful and long-standing than the United States), yet most of us wouldn't bat an eye at his name, save the few who remember it from the film *Gladiator.*

You will be forgotten.

So today, I dangled my arm out the window of a bus hurtling through the Guatemalan mountains, soaking in the fog-capped hills and antique buildings as they whipped by. I was asking myself what the point of it all is; why do I go on existing if the only thing I'm guaranteed is that I'll be forgotten? The answer where I tentatively arrived as the tropical palm trees gradually changed into deciduous foliage is this: Affect your generation.

If you're watching for it, the Bible frequently uses the term 'generation,' and I think I'm beginning to understand why. You can't affect the generation which will live in 2300 AD, but you can affect your own in 2019. In many ways, how we affect this present generation *will* affect future generations.

Both as a teacher and a pastor, I've felt that my impact on the world has been incredibly small. I've even fallen into envying Logan Paul and his ilk with their massive followings and abundant resources, because I'm only affecting about 40 kids…and most of them aren't even paying attention.

But which is better: To entertain 30 million kids with obscene antics and terrible morals, or to [try to] lead 40 kids closer to Jesus?

But what about guys like Francis Chan and Tim Keller who write best-selling books and speak to millions of people *and* lead them closer to Jesus?

That's where it really hurts, but I have to trust something Chan said recently. He prayed that there will be an end to the culture of celebrity pastors and speakers and that the emphasis of church will return to local congregations and small-time pastors.

This is a guy who speaks all over the world to crowds of thousands—and he's wishing for that culture to *end,* so we need to take a cue from him. We need to acknowledge that a lust for millions of followers is really sinful at its core, even if you say you want it to lead people to the Lord.

If this desire sounds familiar to you, ask yourself this: If you want a platform so you can 'lead people to Christ' with it, how many people in your own life have you led closer to Christ? If you have influence over, say, 10 people and you're half-heartedly discipling them because there aren't that many of them, why the hell would God trust you with 10,000?

"He who can be trusted with little can be trusted with much."[45] -Jesus

This line of thinking has helped me refine my purpose in two main ways: In time and in scale.

In time, because no matter how hard I try, I'll be forgotten soon. And in scale, because as long as I'm trying to do the best with what God has given me *now*—a following of 40 kids or 40 million kids—I'll be alright.

I can't help but feel a certain sort of rage at the temporal nature of this world, but there's also nothing I can do about it.

This morning I woke up in a paradise called Irtra, but I left to return to polluted Quetzaltenango. All good things will end, but so will the bad. So will all your work and effort. So will all your pride and the things you're most proud of.

There's a dog next to me in this cafe and I'm looking at him while writing this piece and trying to swallow the fact that he doesn't know he's going to die. He also doesn't fret about his purpose until then. Maybe that's why we can justify killing animals: because they are largely unaware of their own

---

[45] Luke 16:10

362

existence and are driven by their stomachs. It's only us humans who are plagued by awareness.

I'm reaching into my shallow well of hope in order to end this post. I'm trusting that even though my name will soon be absent from the lips of future generations, it won't slip the mind of the Almighty. I'm trusting that what I will inherit in the High Country will surpass this fleeting notion of remembrance.

In essence, I guess there has been only one human who has done anything worthy of remembrance. Perhaps that's why, on the night He was betrayed, Jesus said to take bread and wine in remembrance of Him.

Even if we neglected our sacraments worldwide, He wouldn't be erased from the history books.

He is He who cannot be forgotten.

Jesus, the ugly carpenter from Nazareth who crapped Himself in the manger also holds together the atomic fabric of the universe and actively restores all things. Jesus, the pulp of a man who hung on a cross is the dark energy supergluing the mist of molecules together, allowing us to go on existing.

It doesn't matter if my name is forgotten in a few years, as long as His isn't. And it won't be.

The bigger risk is that we forget Him.

THE SEARCH FOR SIGNIFICANCE
the end is near.

Do you miss your great-great grandparents? Or their parents? Or anyone before them?

It's eerie to look into the not-too-deep past and realize what a small impact those not-too-distant ancestors have on us. We don't miss them; we barely even think about them. But isn't that what any of us want—to know we will be missed when we're gone? Because being missed means we have made an impact in the world and in the lives of the few, or the many, who do the missing.

Yesterday I got a phone call from my mom that Onyx, our 9-year-old pup, has been having seizures. He's never had them before, but apparently he was thrashing around and losing control of his body and then didn't recognize my parents for an hour after each episode; he had 4 in 2 days.

I found that this usually means they have a tumor and the end is near. My parents—whom I agree with—won't pay thousands of dollars for surgery, so I don't know how much time he has left. Nine isn't even THAT old. I thought he had 5 years left in him, but we will find out in the next few days. My mom asked me to come be with him today while they were at work, just to be sure he doesn't have any more seizures and hurt himself. He didn't, fortunately, but it was still bittersweet, knowing the reason I was there.

It also became more bitter when I realized that 4 or 5 people MAX will even miss him, despite how massive his presence is in my own life. I began asking questions like, Because his existence affects so few people, does that make it insignificant? Do numbers determine cosmic importance?

Cosmically speaking then, even if my funeral pulls 200 people, what is that number against billions of humans over millions of years in a universe millions of lightyears across?

I will barely be missed; I will surely be forgotten.

When things like this happen, it causes my life to pull into focus. Even though he's 'just' a dog, it's a reminder of my own mortality, and that of my parents, and essentially, everyone I know. Then I think about my own funeral and hope there will be more than 4 or 5 people there, but then wonder why that would even matter. Everyone at my funeral will also one day die, so why would I strive to have a big funeral as opposed to a small one, when just 100 years from now, that won't matter at all? Big or small funeral, I'll be forgotten.

In most of my blog posts, I would turn this into a triumphant declaration of the gospel and Christ breathing meaning into matter, but on a personal level, that's harder to believe when I'm facing my own mortality and significance. Do I want to matter after I'm gone? Do I just want to be missed when I'm gone?

Do you miss your great-great-great grandparents?

The other day my throat hurt so bad I thought I may have reached my own end. I began imagining what would happen if it was somehow the end of Ethan M. Renoe and I didn't wake up the next day. It was strange, even if I was pretty sure it wasn't realistic.

Not yet, anyway.

If you're anything like me, you may lose your temper at small grievances like getting a speeding ticket, or become impatient with some annoying person on the bus. But you expect that when something big; something real happens, you'll react like a saint. Like if a family member passed away, or if you got cancer, you expect that you'd somehow transform into a world-class poet who graces the world with her smile and exemplifies grace in the face of agony and doom.

After the non-stop Kick Ethan's Nuts Festival known as 2019, I have only learned one thing:

I am no saint.

After being sick for 8 months, 4 sinus infections, 2 anal abscesses (which I never admitted publicly before, for obvious reasons, but they were in the top 3 most painful things I've experienced), one heartbreak, one wristbreak, one toothache, and now a sick dog, I'm about ready for this year to end.

Did I accept my crap pile of a year with grace and pensive reflection? Of course not! I complained and tried to learn some profound lesson from it, but nothing has yet come. Nothing, save, perhaps a closer examination of my own mortality.

Perhaps all God was trying to do this year was put me in my place.
Perhaps He was just trying to prick a needle into my inflated head.

In that case, it has worked. Not being able to exercise or socialize as usual has certainly pulled my self perception into a slightly more realistic perspective. I've been reckoning with my coming demise and the debris I will have left the world in my wake.

But maybe, just like Onyx, I will have mattered deeply to a very small number of people. And maybe, though making many mistakes in those relationships, I tried to love them well, and that's about all we can hope for.

But there's more, isn't there? There always is.

We have become familiar with the rhetoric of Christ taking our sin and trading it for His righteousness, right? His good stuff for our bad stuff. He died our death and gave us His life. But what if there's more?

What if, in addition to giving us His life, He also gave us His meaning, His purpose? What if, without Him, we have no purpose but to exist and vanish, but with Him, we are handed infinite worth, value, and meaning?

What that means is, you get to see your life two ways, with or without His imparted significance. Without Him, you're a pawn in the machine of nations and your most sincere prayer must be, "Bury me in an unmarked grave, another casualty to the vanity of history."[46]

But with Him, with His imparted purpose, you can simply exist and know that you matter. Those who dwell in the sphere of His love also inherit His significance. Any attempt to earn this will surely be in vain. Otherwise, we would have no explanation for the value of human life, especially those who are handicapped or sick or weak.

I guess I have learned something from this season of suffering: Work to prove my worth less; enjoy my imparted worth more.

May we be people who recognize our inherent value given to us by Christ, and live out of that first and foremost. Before we try to validate ourselves or prove our worth, may our undeserved significance be a sign to the world that Jesus is the Giver, not only of life, but of meaning.

---

[46] Silent Planet, "Northern Fires (Guernica)"

THE DEAD & DREAMING

it's like waking up from a long sleep, but without the morning grog.

And then one day, it all goes black.

All the stories you've held in your chest are released to fly into the night. It's kind of like waking up from a long sleep, but instead of morning grog, you are met with stunning clarity. It's like you've been living your whole life under the cover of a shadow and the canopy has been removed. People living in darkness have seen a great light.[47]

We really can't comprehend it. We really can't know what to possibly expect. You awake to glory or oblivion, but either way, it's more real than the addictive fever dreams we've had down here,

down where it's gray,

down where there's fog and haze.

My soul shudders at the thought of the light. At the thought of this far country to whose shores we will one day drift.

I have come to grasp the meaning in the myriad songs that talk about living life as if through the thick filter of a dream state, and longing to wake up into reality, to shake the rote haze from my bones and stir them to vivid life.

Because one day this will all end and we will meet the Light. We will encounter this ferocious flame face to face and all the unsecured flotsam and jetsam will burn away. All the fantasies which never came true; all our aches for *eudaimonia*[48] which were lost in our respective translations of the world will no more haunt our memories than an ant I killed when I was young haunts my conscience.

---

[47] Isaiah 9:2, Matthew 4:16

[48] A Greek philosophical term for total happiness, satisfaction, etc.; 'The Good Life'

I want life like that day in Las Vegas: We were in a suburban neighborhood outside the city and found a couch on the side of the street. In front of a house. So we sat on it. We posed on it and took pictures. We played and felt alive.

Today I drove by 4 couches on the curbs of my own neighborhood and was not amused.

It's not the object, it's how you see it. The couch in Nevada was exciting because we were on a road trip and everything is exciting. The couches I saw today are not exciting because I'm driving familiar streets. I'm trapped in an excruciating routine I can't shake from my bones and I've never felt more asleep.

Another time we were in Brasil and had made it to Rio. A week of backpacking along the coast had landed us at our destination. Every bus we boarded and ride we hitched; every ferry we awaited from the docks and every hostel we crashed had led to this one location. Our hostel had an antique shop in the basement and a window overlooking the Copacabana. I saw more than a couple beautiful Brasilian women pass by.

I was alive. I was awake. I was alert to the moment and the location I was in, and that was enough for me. I wasn't trapped in the mundanity of routine and dying for an escape to come and lift me from the dream.

But I ask myself: Is this a dream from which there is waking, or does it dissolve with the morning light, along with the rest of my understood reality? Does the Christ come and remove it from me as well, or does He come to breathe into me the fullness of reality itself?

We Christians do not long for a dream from afar: we encounter reality firsthand. In the communion table we are not told to "stand by and watch," but to "*come* and *eat.*"

Our dreams are realized in the body and the blood.

Our dreams took on flesh 2k years ago and gave Himself to us and for us.

You know how there are those passages in certain books which make your arm hairs stand up and cool shivers run from your neck down to your tailbone? There are a lot of those lines in my all-time favorite book, Lewis' *The Great Divorce,* but one seems most relevant in our situation.

> "Hell is a state of mind - ye never said a truer word. And every state of mind, left to itself, every shutting up of the creature within the dungeon of its own mind - is, in the end, Hell. But Heaven is not a state of mind. Heaven is reality itself. All that is fully real is Heavenly. For all that can be shaken will be shaken and only the unshakeable remains."

Those who desire things other than Christ are left asleep while the rest wake into fitful life. Life more real and more near to the individual than can be comprehended in this life—in this state of stupor and guessing.

Now we see as through a glass darkly, but soon we will know in full.

Soon we will be like Moses, who saw God face-to-face on the mountaintop and there will be no more speculation about this god or that. There will be no more epistemological disagreement about the proper way to *know.*

Because we will not only know, we will see. We will touch. We will run and breathe in the fullness of Life itself; Life Himself.

I—the eternal bachelor—have realized this many times. I can close my eyes and dream all I want while alone in my house, but imagining another person there with me isn't remotely on the same plane as being in the presence of another human being. If you haven't done this before, here's a little experiment: Sit by yourself for ten minutes and just imagine scenarios happening with you and other people as if they were there with you.

Then go hang out with other people and see how vastly different it is.

The difference between dream and reality.

In some ways, many of us are living in a dream world right now, yet think we're awake. Many of us think that our breath means we're alive.

Someone once posited to me that when it comes to theological definitions, life and death is a matter of relationship. Those who are alive are those who are known by God. Those who are dead are those to whom He says, well,

"You're dead to me."

So, in asking someone 'Are you alive?' I may really be asking them, 'Do you know Jesus? Do you know *The Life?*'

And I hope you do, my friend. I hope you know Him and are known by Him, that you may come fully alive.

HOW TO THINK

you would think thinking would be easie

THE DIFFERENCE BETWEEN PEOPLE & IDEAS

seems like a pretty simple dichotomy...

Lately I've been giving some heavy thought to something which should seem obvious to everyone. It's the notion that people (human beings) are not the same as ideas (abstract belief or thought structures).

Seems like a pretty simple dichotomy, right?

Perhaps it's not quite as clean cut as it first appears. For instance, a few weeks ago I had a conversation with someone who was raised in a Presbyterian church which leaned more conservative and held to orthodoxy. To me, those all seem like good things and I would likely agree with everything proclaimed at this church.

However, the people who were leaders in his particular church abused their power, hurt congregants, and rather than purely teaching Christ and Him crucified, used the Bible to control, manipulate, and take money. What was the person's response? He decided that orthodoxy was a repressive system of belief and if that was its logical end, he wanted nothing to do with it. He developed a view of the Bible which was substantially lower than someone who clings to orthodoxy and became much more progressive, postmodern and universal in his thinking.

This makes a lot of sense though, right? If someone uses a certain idea—or rather, a twisting of a good idea—to hurt you, you're probably going to run the opposite direction of that *idea*.

Here, however, is where my friend neglected to differentiate between people and ideas. Rather than recognize the beauty of orthodoxy and the power of Scripture, he associated it in his mind with the abusive people from his upbringing and discarded both. This is what happens when emotions blend with epistemology (the way we construct what we know and believe to be true) and it blinds us.

Because my friend experienced a good idea via bad people, he ran from both when he got the chance. Sadly, his is not an isolated story. I've heard this time and time again, and it's easy for emotional wounds from people to cloud our beliefs, and I can't hold this against anyone in the least.

This works the opposite way as well. Take, for instance, a bad idea which affects billions of people worldwide. I have no problem declaring that Islam is a *bad idea* no matter how it is applied and from its foundations, it has no good to give to the world. I can freely discuss Islam as a bad idea without a second thought.

However, this does not mean that I think all Muslims are bad people. The trouble is, in our current eggshell-sensitive moment, to say anything against a religion (except Christianity...) is considered hateful against Muslim people. Here again we find ourselves at a place where we need to be able to freely deliberate between the two. I am not harboring hatred toward Muslim people, but I am aggressively against the ideas they believe. I have met numerous kind, lovely Muslim people all over the world. All this can be summed up simply:

Be gentle on people and hard on ideas.

Modern conversation seems to be hyper sensitive to the notion of anyone being hard on ideas, for fear that people will be offended. As a Christian, I invite people to be hard on my beliefs. I myself am hard on my own beliefs, hammering them like a blacksmith in order to root out any impurities and make them stronger. I am not one to blindly believe something that sounds or feels good—I would wager people like that are the same ones who become offended when anyone critiques their beliefs.

Do I want people to come out and attack me as a person? Of course not! But when someone comes with genuine questions or critiques of my beliefs, it's a chance for both of us to learn and grow and, as YHWH says in Isaiah 1, reason together.

In the gospels, I see Jesus being gentle with most people, save the ones who thought they were more righteous than others, and quick to correct crooked beliefs. Just open to nearly any page of the gospels and you'll see people spouting off superstitious or heretical beliefs and Jesus simply responds with truth. It's almost like He's playing Whack-a-Mole with lies. They keep popping up and he keeps slamming them back down.

Finding this balance of grace and truth as displayed by Jesus[1] is much easier said than done. I think they key is to always be aware of when you are talking about a person or people, and when you are talking about ideas. Often, this differentiation will be harder than it seems. Learning how to love people who think differently than you is difficult, but not impossible. When disagreements arise, always remember to root out the ideal differentials rather than attack the person (in philosophy, this is called the Ad Hominem Fallacy).

If more people in the world adopted this dichotomy, I think there would be much more peace even in our disagreements. We need this in mind when discussing current topics like abortion or homosexuality. For example, I am staunchly Pro-Life, but would never alienate or shame a woman who had an abortion. When discussing any topic, especially deeply personal ones like these, it's important to not forget the humanity of all people, regardless of how your beliefs or lifestyles differ. Alienating or dehumanizing anyone is absolutely contrary to the heart of God, going all the way back to Genesis 1: We are all made in God's image.

One caveat I'll make, though, is this: Christian leaders form a unique category here. I have a hard time accepting people like Creflo Dollar, Joel Osteen and Stephen Furtick because of their leech-like abuse of Scripture. Because they rob people in the name of Jesus. Their ideas are harmful and toxic, and I don't know if merely critiquing their ideas is strong enough.

We see Jesus and Paul coming down hard on religious leaders who were misleading people in His name. Paul went so far as to wish they would emasculate themselves, and Jesus called them 'whitewashed tombs.' I would have a hard time extending grace to my friend's pastor from the beginning of this post because of the damage done in the name of Christ.

Of course, if they were to repent and acknowledge their missteps, all would be forgiven, but as long as a Christian leader goes on deceiving and stealing from people, they need to be confronted.

---

[1] John 1:17

Outside of that, and especially with those outside the Body of Christ, we need to be loving, gentle, and seek understanding. Let's build bridges to people while seeking to spread truth in what we believe.

May we be hard on ideas and gentle on people.

THE DUMBING DOWN OF CHRISTIANITY
I mean Joel Osteen doesn't even have a freaking Bachelor's degree.

The other day I was (surprise, surprise) in a coffee shop in the mountains, seated near the counter. A guy in his early 20's walked in wearing a TOOL shirt and a long ponytail. I could overhear his conversation as he approached the barista and they began chatting. Somehow it came up that she attends a Christian university and he clearly didn't approve.

"Do they incorporate religion into all the classes there?" he asked. "Even the science classes? How does that work?"

She valiantly began explaining how they pray before every class and teach from a Christian worldview, but it soon became evident that she was being crushed in this conversation. He was well schooled in the writings of Dawkins, Hitchens, and Nye and began doling out the punishment.

I use the word punishment because this poor barista has herself been punished by a church system which, for the past 200 years, has begun discarding intelligence within the church in favor of emotion, conversion experiences, and passion. Ask most American Christians today any question deeper than "Does God love everyone?" and you're bound to get some sort of response suggesting that that sort of discourse should be reserved for theological universities.

The other day a friend of mine said that he sees no merit in understanding Calvinism or Arminianism because he just wants to *Love God and love people*. And it seems that the ball stops there for most Christians today. No need to know any more than that.

I would go so far as to say that there is even a *fear* in evangelical Christianity of knowledge. In my experience, this fear comes from one of two sources: People are scared that if they come to know too much, they'll be like the Pharisees and will just become haughty and judgmental to others, thus weakening their love for God; or they're afraid that they'll learn too much and go off the deep end of liberalism and swim in the risky waters of universalism and other heresies.

We have replaced rich, robust theology in the church with emotional music and constant reminders that "God is love and loves you and He's your personal Savior and loves your soul..." These words are great at bringing outsiders through the doors (because they're true by and large) but poor at growing believers into mature witnesses with rich understanding of the deep things of God.

I have found the opposite to be very true in my own walk. I have found that the more I learn about God, His Word, and theology which describes Him, the more I can love and worship Him, because now there is that much more to adore and be amazed by. If my ability to worship God is a fire, learning more about Him only adds more wood to the blaze. After all, if you really loved God, wouldn't you want to learn as much about him as possible?

Our logic is pretty backward here.

Quite honestly, I'm exhausted by Christians who don't want to learn more. It's one thing to not know much about our faith, but another to have no desire to grow.

I'm saddened that atheists are so passionate about what they believe that they will read stacks of books in order to define their beliefs, while we are happy to float along the surface with a (no offense) 'Hillsong-deep theology' and call it good. And we wonder why people are leaving the Church in droves! A church that offers only emotional, squishy feel-good theology is going to lose the long-term wrestling match to a well-read and convincing atheist nearly every time.

Puritan Cotton Mather wrote, "Ignorance is the Mother not of Devotion but of HERESY" (caps lock his).

The mushy-gushy can only last so long.

Just as a marriage cannot be sustained by the tumble of infatuation, a life of faith cannot be sustained by passionate emotion. Yes, it may be a wonderful (and necessary) entryway, but without depth of knowledge and understanding, it will be "blown here and there by every wind of teaching and by the cunning and craftiness of people in their deceitful scheming."[2]

One of my theology professors is so passionate about this issue that he has brought up the same metaphor at least three times this semester. It goes something like this:

> "Why do people say they want to 'know God, but not know *about* Him? That is absolutely ludicrous! Imagine if I told you 'I love my wife, but I don't know anything about her.'
>
> You could ask me where she was born and I would shrug.
>
> What type of music or food does she like?
>
> I don't know.
>
> What color are her eyes?
>
> No idea. But I love her.
>
> See how insane that sounds? The more you come to know *about* someone, the more you are able to *love* them."

Yet we have no problem floating on the surface of our knowledge of God. And then we wonder why we have such trouble witnessing to others or describing what we believe, or why we believe it, to others.

J.P. Moreland, in his book *Love the Lord Your God With All Your Mind*, demonstrates how the Second Great Awakening led to the beginning of emotional preaching and impassioned calls to a quick conversion experience, as opposed to a period of contemplation, learning, and discovery of the Christian faith and doctrines. We live in the fallout of that style of thinking. Moreland writes, "the intellectually shallow, theologically

---

[2] Ephesians 4:14

illiterate form of Christianity…came to be part of the populist Christian religion that emerged."

I was fascinated to learn that the Church was once the place where believers came to learn deep theology and robust doctrine, but now that seems to be reserved only for Biblical universities. Nowadays anyone can start a church, and as long as it's engaging and entertaining enough, people will show up. Never mind if it's true or not. (Case in point: The pastor of the largest church in America, Joel Osteen, doesn't even have a Bachelor's degree, much less a seminary degree and look where that leads…) This all helps me realize why people are seeing less and less need for the church. After the initial emotion has worn off, what does it really have to offer?

It should not only be pastors, authors, and theologians who study what they believe, but all believers. Jesus Himself stated that the greatest commandment is to love the Lord your God with all your heart, soul, strength and MIND,[3] yet we tend to overlook this last one and focus on the heart and soul.

God paints an intense fate for those who neglect to grow in their understanding in Hosea 4:6 when he writes, "My people are destroyed for their lack of knowledge. Because you have rejected knowledge, I also will reject you."

So let's not get destroyed and rejected, eh?

It's not too late for Christians to grow in their understanding of the holy. It's not too late to learn the meaning and value of our creeds, doctrines, and systems. There is merit in learning and understanding the deeper parts of our faith and I say we start sooner than later.

If you're reading this and thinking, *Gee, I would love to come to a deeper understanding of God but don't know where to start,* I'll give a few great starting points here. Additionally, if you're reading this and thinking, *Gee, I don't really learn that much about the Bible or God at my church, it just kind of hypes me up,* it may be time to change that. Begin by talking to your pastor about it before going church shopping!

---

[3] Luke 10:27

Here are some books which are very easy to read and introduce us to cursory facets of the Christian faith:

Delighting in The Trinity: An Introduction to the Christian Faith by Michael Reeves

Desiring God: Meditations of a Christian Hedonist by John Piper

Mere Christianity by C.S. Lewis

The New Lonely by me

(The last one isn't entirely theological, it's just a really, really good book. ;})

THE CHURCH & THE SINGLE PERSON
"no more segregation."

The other day an acquaintance from college messaged me out of the blue, asking if I'd ever written about single people in the church. I was kind of taken aback, as he's one of those guys who became fluent in Greek and Hebrew and listened to about 14 sermons and Church History lectures a day in his spare time. Not only that, but he has been married as long as I've known him and has a bundle of kids. Right after we graduated, he became a pastor in the midwest. In other words, this is a dude who has it all together on the ministry side of things.

So of all people, I was surprised that he would ask me for input when it comes to practical ministry in the church. Granted, it may have been a while since he *was* single and having to deal with the pressures and awkward conversations we face as singles in the church, but nonetheless, I have given a lot of thought to his question.

More specifically, he asked how churches can best minister to the single people in their congregations. I gave it a lot of thought and, though this post is far from comprehensive, this is what I have come up with:

No more segregation.

For some reason, the popular practice in the past decades in the American church has become to separate people by the season of life they are in.

Many churches sequester the 60+ crowd into their own Sunday School classroom, while the Young Marrieds are in another. The youth group and children's church have their clubs of course, which often leaves that awkward gap for us single people to mingle in whichever classroom we happen to drift into.

I don't think the answer to the question is to create "Singles" or "Young Adult" classes or groups. Assigning people a place to be based on the season of life they inhabit is not as helpful as overhauling the entire system of apartheid.

What I mean by that is, What good are we doing the members of our churches by separating them? Shouldn't the oldest people who have been walking with God the longest be the ones mixed into small groups with younger people, mentoring them and helping them to walk in step with the Lord? And can't the middle-aged couple pour into the newlyweds as their marriage builds muscle in its thighs and begins to walk?

One of the most unappealing things to me is the thought of going to a "singles mixer" at a church. I mean, how desperate am I? (Pretty desperate, honestly) But the idea of going to this meeting where the entire premise is all these lonely souls searching for our better halves just grosses me out. I mean, talk about awkward pressure and forced conversations. Is this all the church is to single people? A mixer?

The issue is not with churches "doing singles ministry better," but uniting their entire church as one, a family where all age groups and statuses interact. Isn't that something Paul was adamant about across the pages of the New Testament? There is neither Jew or Greek, slave or free, man or woman, old or young, single or married, but all are united in faith in Christ.

After mulling the question over this past week, I reflected on which experiences have been the most fruitful as a single person in the church. I think the answer is, I grew the most by being in close contact with those who were not in the same *category* as I. How much can I really learn solely from other single people in their 20's? What can they learn from me? (A little, sure, but you get my point…)

Many of the most formative hours of my life have been spent eating with college professors or meeting with influential writers or pastors decades older than me. There are the meaningful conversations I have with people my own age, but of all places, shouldn't the Church be a place for the coming together of people of *all* ages and seasons of life? Why do we feel the need to divvy ourselves up rather than come together?

Maybe what the lonely single person needs more than other lonely single people is to be poured into by older folks who have moved through where they are, and can give them hope and wisdom.

This past summer I was part of a class on addiction, put on by my church for people of all ages who wanted to learn more. Due to the nature of the course, we all became very close and intimate very quickly. The nice thing is that the others in the class ranged from college students to 60-year-olds, and across the entire spectrum of marital statuses. And because of that, I got to hear firsthand accounts of porn and drug addiction from married couples, divorced men and women, and of course single people like me.

The beautiful thing about this class was that it was a holistic representation of the Body of Christ, from young to old, not just a segregated slice of it sitting by itself and spinning in circles.

So how should churches go about doing singles ministry better? I think that's the wrong question, and if we find ourselves asking it, we are probably already heading down the wrong path.

A better question is, how can we cultivate a church that simultaneously ministers to the 70-year-old couple and the 25-year-old-bachelor? What good is the church if it does not bring together the widow and the newlyweds and enable them to love one another uniquely in Christ? If grandparents want to hang out with people their own age, they can go to the YMCA or a bridge club. If I want people my own age, I'll go to a coffee shop or join a sports league.

But we should go to church to interact with people with whom we have *nothing* in common except our union with Christ. As a single person, I don't want to be stuck with other single people, but with a variety of people in a collection of life seasons. This is closer to the picture of unity Paul longed for, and the best place for real growth to occur. Not only that, but it makes the single people feel less dissociated and awkward.

There isn't anything wrong with us. And I think the last thing we want from a church is special treatment. Or "singles groups."

Let's work on returning our churches to places of inclusion and invitation. Places of unity. Let's make them places where Blacks chill with Whites, old folks hang with hooligans like me, and single people spend meaningful time with couples

and it isn't weird.

THE EPIDEMIC OF MALE LONELINESS
why do close male friends seem so WEIRD to us today?

I recently began reading Doris Kearns Goodwin's monumental biography of Abraham Lincoln, *Team of Rivals,* and within the first couple chapters, noticed a theme which kept popping up.

Goodwin begins by giving a thorough background to each of Lincoln's rivals for the presidential seat, and nearly every description at some point mentioned a close male friend of theirs. Writes Goodwin:

> Such intimate male attachments, as Seward's with Berdan, or, as we shall see, Lincoln's with Joshua Speed and Chase's with Edwin Stanton, were a common feature of the social landscape in nineteenth-century America...In the absence of parents and siblings, they turned to one another for support, sharing thoughts and emotions so completely that their intimate friendships developed the qualities of passionate romances.

To highlight the extremity of these relationships, Goodwin recounts the story of William Henry Seward who met a young man named David Berdan while they were both in school together. They shared everything together, including theater, books, songs, and vocational aspirations. Tragically, Berdan contracted tuberculosis while traveling overseas and died on the ship back to America. "Seward was devastated," writes Goodwin, "later telling his wife that he had loved Berdan as 'never again' could he 'love in this world.'"

Let's just take in the obvious fact that that's not something you say to your wife.

That aside, I've been wondering why these deep male-to-male friendships seem so odd to me as a 21st-century reader. I think the idea is related to another chapter of mine regarding men and their lack of physical touch, but it's also a different issue. I mean, guys don't necessarily have to touch in order to be close and brotherly.

Personally, I feel like I have been blessed to have known (and to continue to know) a slew of really, really great men. The first being my father, which the older I get, the more rare I realize this is. Growing up, my best friend for as long as I can remember was Dave, and he is still my best friend to this day. In college and my travels abroad and my intermittent seasons of homelessness and vagabonding, I have always come across men with whom I can share everything.

I can't help but wonder if many heterosexual men veer away from such relationships as they may be perceived as homosexual or *weird* in some way. What this leads to is an abundance of loneliness, causing men to satiate their loneliness with more insidious salves.

How many fathers have been caught in a pornography or alcohol addiction, despite having a relatively enviable, stable life? This is conjecture, but I can't help but wonder if addictions like these arise because men think that their wives and kids *should* be enough human connection to satisfy them, never thinking their souls may be craving more *friend* connections. How many men feel this loneliness but feel weird about seeking out male friends, so they settle for the false intimacy of porn or the artificial ecstasy of substances?

I know men who—like Paul Rudd's character in *I Love You, Man*—prefer the company of female friends, because they may be intimidated by other men. Others find themselves a girlfriend and cut off communication with all other friends indefinitely. I also know those who simply opt for very few or no friends at all, believing any sort of vulnerability or emotional nearness to other men to be un-masculine.

I would argue that the opposite is true.

Take a look at King David from the Bible. This is a dude who killed lions and bears with his bare hands while growing up as a shepherd. This is a dude who lusted after and married several women (not a *GOOD* thing, but it proves that he was quite straight...). This is a *masculine* dude that any man would be wise to look up to.

And this is also a dude who had a close friend named Jonathan. And we get this verse after Jonathan's death where David says, "I grieve for you, Jonathan my brother; you were very dear to me. Your love for me was wonderful, more wonderful than that of women."[4]

As a very heterosexual man, this makes me feel a little weird. I mean, here is this emotion toward another man which seems like it has no place being in the Bible! I mean, aren't men only supposed to love women or else things get weird?

No.

Our perverted culture has twisted up the word 'love' to a very base and carnal definition which can *only* be interpreted sexually. In other words, we cannot hear that "David loved Jonathan" without immediately thinking *"David was gay??"*

I do not think that's what this passage is saying at all. There is so much more to love than the mere act of sex. I think he was deeply grieving for a very close friend of his. I would certainly express a similar sentiment if Dave or any of my other close friends were to pass away, because I really love my guys a lot.

And I tell them that often.

And I am quite straight.

---

[4] 2 Samuel 1:26

I think this problem has arisen out of fear and a misled perception of masculinity. Our culture subliminally preaches the idea that *real* men are lone wolves who do not need help or close friends. They need a wife and they need to be a good father and good worker…but friends?? There's not really a category for it anymore.

In my experience, the breakdown of close male relationships has led not only to a breakdown of male friendships, but of other man-to-man relationships like mentoring and accountability. I can count on one hand the number of guys I know who have intentionally sought older men for the sake of growth and wisdom. For millennia, there was a system in place for younger men to be raised up and encouraged by older men, but that seems to have disintegrated with a culture telling us that we can do it all on our own.

So what do we do about this? How do we begin to address a culture which informs us that male friends are weak or weird? I think the first step is to name it. Identify that our culture (especially Christian culture in America) gets weird about men being too close.

If you're a man and as you read, you're thinking to yourself *Gee, I don't have that many close dude friends!* it may be time to change that! It is not healthy to have a life devoid of testosterone. If your only friend is your girlfriend/fiancée/wife, or you have a host of female friends without any guys, you are missing out on brotherly fellowship which, I would argue, is necessary for a healthy and holistic life.

If you're a woman reading this and a particular guy keep popping into your mind as you read, perhaps it's worth gently bringing up the topic and encouraging him to find men to do life with. I do think it's toxic when a man only has female friends and confides in them things which should be reserved for other men or a spouse.

Obviously I'm not pushing for an extreme here, where we should *only* have male friends and *no* female friends. What I'm pushing for is balance. We (men) are often averse to intimacy with other guys, and I would love to see that change. We need not continue living under the stigma that men don't need male friends, so let's strive to repair this. Let's reignite the bromance.

MEN & THEIR EMOTIONS

why is it so rare to encounter a man in touch with his emotions?

We tend to speak the language of desires and emotions as if they did not directly affect every element of our lives. By 'we,' I'm sure the maxim applies to women too, but men are especially alienated from our emotions and feelings. We deny the deepest longings of our souls for the sake of surrender to the cultural notion of 'lone wolf masculinity,' which litters every square inch of our society.

Yesterday I listened to an episode of the podcast Hidden Brain entitled *The Lonely American Man*. Lo and behold, the podcast echoed some exact sentiments I had been thinking recently, but went further as it interviewed men and researchers who have been studying this trend for a while.

The thing that struck me the most, and dialed up sharp pangs of nostalgia as I listened, was when they interviewed teenage boys, some of whom were in middle school, others were seniors in high school. The younger boys talked about how much they valued their best friend and always got excited to have sleepovers and be with them, sharing their most intimate secrets... and *feelings*.

This is something that struck my ears as most unusual. Not because it's bad in any way, but because it's odd to hear a male of any age talk so openly about his feelings. The boys were young enough that they hadn't been programmed to hide their feelings, shoving them down into a stale state of apathy and stoicism. One of them recounted how his best friend had helped him when someone in his family had died and he was able to go to his friend and pour out his grief and cry before him.

Sadly, by the time these boys had gone through high school, the shift had happened. There was a sharp retreat from feelings and emotions; these were replaced by toughness and confidence and the pseudo-ability to not reveal any feelings teeming beneath the surface.

At some point in their developmental years, these boys intuited the notion that having feelings is weak and unmanly. It's really no mystery where that stereotype came from: Look at our culture at large and tell me where you see a strong, emotional man with a healthy rein on his feelings. We have Thor-types, the man who is so macho and courageous that he is relatively oblivious to the weather happening within his own heart (if there is any… See also: Cowboys, James Bond, and basically any Brad Pitt character). This toughness is also seen in music, as rappers and rockers alike are too tough to do anything but get money, conquer women, and be more tough than anyone who would threaten his clique.

Alternatively, men are often portrayed as aloof and idiotic. Think Homer Simpson or literally any family sitcom where the father bumbles through life, unaware of his family, his kids, and most of all, himself. Funny? Sure. But deep….? That's an entirely different question.

The emotional man is almost always painted as an outlier: The emo teenage boy or the homosexual. Tom Hanks seems to cry a lot, but he is assuredly the exception and not the rule.

My point is, the male influences seen across the board in media is anything but emotional, and these influences have spilled over into the day-to-day life of boys and men. The problem with quenching our own feelings, though, is that they may be shoved down in one area, but arise in another like an internal version of Whack-a-Mole. You may shrug off your loneliness and act like you don't need fellow human beings, only to have it arise late at night in yet another episode of pornography and masturbation. You may say that your parents' divorce or the names the kids at school called you don't affect you, only to have the roots of your adult alcoholism trace right back to those very events.

We have the option to either embrace our emotions or escape them, drowning them in a flood of numbing agents and superficiality.

I'll never forget a conversation I had with a classmate in Chicago years ago. I asked him what he was learning from life lately, expecting him to give me some trite Christian-ese phrase. Instead, he looked back at me and sincerely said, "I'm learning that it's okay to be broken and vulnerable. It's okay to let the Lord and other people love me as I am." I was taken aback by his honesty and openness with the very deep things he was experiencing in that season. My respect for him, rather than diminishing, shot through the roof.

Ironically, many of the manliest men I've known have been ones who have gone through similar seasons of humility and awakening to the emotions raging inside of them, as they learned to sort them out, order them, and experience them both with the Lord and with others. Some people call it 'soul work,' while others consider it 'self care.' Whatever you call it, the important thing is to rightly recognize that the things you feel, good or bad, are very real. They are meant to be experienced and not drowned out.

Isn't this what we see all throughout Scripture? I mean, the Bible's book of prayer, the Psalms, is lousy with emotion. Men soak their couches with tears,[5] or experience such rage that they want to smash the infants of their enemies against a rock.[6] And these are not limp-wristed milquetoasts writing these lines, either. These are songs penned by men who killed lions and bears with their bare hands, and fought in battles. Yet how odd is it to picture a Braveheart-like character writing beautiful poetry like we find in the ancient texts? Why is this so foreign to us today?

Some of it, men, comes from a right understanding of our God. He is not a stale and emotionless being, stoic and flat in the sky. We see our God as one who is alive and active, and His emotions are no different. He is grieved and He is hurt. He delights and is filled with joy. He weeps and He sings. (We are so quick to forget the shortest verse in the Bible: "Jesus wept."[7])

To deny ourselves the experience of our own emotions is, in part, to deny our own humanity. It is also to deny the fact that we are made in the image of a very vibrant and sensitive God. (Of course, the opposite extreme of being overly emotional is viable, though this is vastly the minority when it comes to American men specifically.)

My friend Frankie wrote this beautiful post, and I tried to trim it down but there's so much good stuff in it I left it pretty long:

> Emotions are important. Emotions are intrinsic to what it means to be a person. It is impossible for a person, a human, to think, live, act, exist,

---

5 Psalm 6

6 Psalm 137

7 John 11:35

without emotion. If I devalue emotions and feelings, then it has acute ramifications for my theology at large. Our theology proper will begin to envision a deterministic god who's stripped of a heartbeat; our anthropology will envision humans as functionally a-emotional, capable of removing feelings from the fabrics of our beings (and surely nobody will like being around us, since we can't take a joke, can't cry for the sake of crying, can't be silly for the sake of being silly—indeed we will look more like Spock than the Suffering Servant); our ethic will logically lead to a strange, unrealistic, impersonal law that makes absolutely no sense with experience and can't satisfy the longings for justice, love, goodness, or any actual desire in the human heart.

If you get emotions wrong, you get personhood wrong. If you get personhood wrong, don't bother talking about God, humans, love, mercy, goodness, fear, or anything else. American Christianity is filled with people who look more like the Pharisees than joyful poets. This strange view of emotions is not Christian. It's not even human. It's just absolute falsity.

It's time to be done with bad theology. It's time to view emotions rightly. It's time to live life to the full. It's time to weep; its time to laugh; it's time to hug and kiss; it's time to fall in love; it's time to love so much it hurts; it's time to love like God has loved each of us; it's time to "live to the point of tears."[8] Emotions are important to my view of life, my philosophy, and my theology. Emotions are intrinsic to how humans know. We cannot know or be known without emotions. My exhortation to each of you: Let yourselves feel. I know it's the scariest thing in the world. But it's what it means to be human. If you want to cry, cry. If you want to yell at God, yell at God. If you feel scared, tell somebody, and maybe, I pray, let yourselves be comforted. If you want to live, risk. There's no other way to live.

I don't know what this looks like, particularly because there is likely no solve-all solution for every man in the world. I think some key elements are openness, honesty, vulnerability, and friends with whom to share our

---

[8] Quote by Albert Camus

feelings. Often, we cannot begin to feel things and be real with ourselves without the help of others to walk with us through those places.

May we be men who are honest enough to emote fully. May we learn to be vulnerable and expressive, rather than distracted and off-center. May we not become carried away on the tides of our feelings, but be sensitive when the time calls for it and in control of ourselves when other times call. May we experience life fully, as our God feels His emotions fully.

ARE MEN STARVING FOR PHYSICAL TOUCH?
why are men so afraid of physical contact?

Yesterday I was in the mall with some friends. As we cruised the walkway, all the girls suddenly linked arms and began skipping. To make fun of them, Casey and I (the only two dudes) also linked arms and began skipping. That's how we discovered the sad truth: Casey never learned how to skip.

Everyone laughed, mainly at Casey not knowing how to skip, but also at the fact that two heterosexual guys would link arms to walk around the mall. This observation continued a line of thought I had been pondering for a few weeks:

Why is it that men are afraid of physical contact?

Most women seem to have little problem touching each other in gentle, platonic ways, and the general public has no problem with it. It's not abnormal to see two girls linking arms or holding hands in public. But with men, it's another story. Mark Greene points out that a rise in homophobia in response to the cultural shifts has done as much damage to heterosexual men as to homosexual men.[9] We have become afraid of touch from other men, largely for fear of being seen as gay or un-masculine.

As a single man in his mid-20's, touch is not a common occurrence in my life. I can specifically remember a handful of meaningful moments in my life where another man went out of his way to show physical affection. A

---

[9] Mark Greene, "Why Men Need Platonic Touch."

few years ago, I was visiting home and saw my old youth pastor, a big, burly mountain man with a big beard and a hulking frame. I went to him with my hand out, which he promptly ignored and spread his wings for a suffocating bear hug.

A few months ago, my current pastor did the same thing, likely unaware how momentous a hug it was for lonely ol' me. I went home and tweeted:

@EthanRenoe: Next time you see a single person, give them a big hug because it's likely been a while since they've had human contact outside of a handshake.

As a young man who has struggled with pornography for half my life, it's easy to whittle away time daydreaming about being touched and held, but to really touch another human is far, far different from the imagined sensations.

We are starving for touch.

When I was in college, we regularly had fight nights on my floor, where two men wrestled to the death…or at least to submission. Whichever came first. I still have a scar on my elbow from one of these nights, and I remember who gave it to me. There's a good chance I would have no recollection of this man had we not went flesh-to-flesh in attempt to prove our merit. Anyone who has ever wrestled will tell you how close you feel to your opponent during and after a wrestling match. The prolonged skin-on-skin contact, where your sweat blends together can be—in a platonic, heterosexual way—a very intimate experience.

It's odd that one of the only times it's not 'weird' for two men to touch like that is when they are battling each other.

This dilemma seems to be an exclusively Western (maybe even American) issue. When I was in India, it took a few days to become accustomed to the groups of young men who would walk down the streets with their arms around each other to express their friendship. Many Eastern cultures see no problem with male platonic touch, and one has to wonder how the dynamics of those friendships are different as a result.

Even the Bible shows a physical nearness between male friends. In John 13:23, Jesus is eating the Last Supper with His disciples and John has his head on Jesus' chest. Does Jesus cry, *'Ew, gross! Get offa me!'*? No. He accepts the gentle demonstration of friendship.

One of the closest friendships in the Bible is between Jonathan and David. They made a covenant of friendship, and the Bible tells us that "Jonathan loved David as himself."[10] At the end of the chapter, "they kissed each other and wept together—but David wept the most."[11]

Now, these are not two slobbering milquetoasts; these are two men who had already fought in wars and demonstrated their boss-ness. David is even called 'a man after God's own heart,' so clearly his friendship with Jonathan is a good thing.

Compare this to our culture. Beside the fact that they wept together, they embraced and kissed! They weren't making out, but the expression of a kiss on the cheek is a common expression of closeness in a myriad of cultures.

But many of us were raised far differently.

I have seen many men and boys in my life whose fathers never touched them or hugged them, instilling into their minds that male-to-male physical contact is a *bad* thing. Because their father's father probably didn't touch their father, and on and on up the family tree. In addition to homophobia, Mark Greene points out that men also fear being seen as sex offenders and child molesters, and that the slightest sign of physical affection will label them as a pervert. To them, all touch is either sexual or aggressive.

I have struggled with this as a youth pastor as well. It's hard in our culture to walk the fine line of showing healthy contact without wandering beyond the border into *creeper territory*. So how do we fix this problem of a generation of men who are starved for genuine physical contact? Greene concludes that when he became a father, much of his time spent with his son was very healing for him.

---

[10] 1 Samuel 20:17

[11] *Ibid.*, 41

392

"As a stay at home dad, I spent years with my son. Day after day, he sat in the crook of my arm, his little arm across my shoulder, his hand on the back of my neck. As he surveyed the world from on high, I came to know a level of contentment and calm that had previously been missing in my life.

The physical connection between us was so transformative that it changed my view of who I am and what my role is in the world. Yet it took having a child to bring this calming experience to me because so few other opportunities are possible to teach men the value and power of gentle loving touch."

But what about those of us who are still years away from becoming fathers? How do we come to find a healthy experience of physical touch, and live it out in authentic community, raising up a new generation that isn't afraid of over-sexualized physical touch?

It begins with becoming comfortable with ourselves and bodies and seeing them as *good* things. Too many of us withhold healthy physical touch out of fear of being gross or out of shame, rather than trying to embrace healthy touch (which is really miles from creepy, perverted touch).

Pray that God will lead you into security about yourself and teach you what healthy touch looks like, so you can love others as best you can.

Spend time with little kids. They are too young to have inherited our shame and sense of social awkwardness, so they just crawl all over you and constantly demand to be picked up.

It's a hard thing to discuss because of all the stigmas that physical touch has inherited in the past several decades, but this overlooked topic is worth exploring and amending.

I hope that we as men can work toward being masculine men who genuinely and appropriately express our affection for those in the various spheres of our lives. And that the men in your life can work toward the same thing, seeing physical touch as a form of healing and deepening intimacy, rather than sexual, aggressive, or gross.

MEN, MASCULINITY, AND MEEKNESS
is gentleness the opposite of strength, or her twin sister?

Gentleness is not a strength of mine.

I'm sometimes referred to as 'blunt' and 'harsh.' The Bible says that Jesus was full of both grace and truth;[12] I tell people that the truth comes easy for me, but grace is tougher. For some people it's the opposite, but not me.

I read books like John Eldredge's *Wild at Heart* and get really pumped up about being a manly man. A man who is not afraid of anything or anyone; who never loses in a fight, and who is on a mission. It's hard to rectify the typical American hero who is tough, strong, and courageous, with words like 'gentleness' and 'meekness.'

The notion of being meek or gentle is something that has never appealed much to me, until I reframed my working definition of the terms. I remember being in college and doing an exegetical paper on Philippians 4, and verse 5 seems to come out of nowhere and sit there awkwardly on the page. Paul is wrapping up his letter to the Philippian church and is shooting some closing exhortations at them. Then he writes, "Let your gentleness be evident to all. The Lord is near."

It sat somewhat uncomfortably with me, because I looked at myself and did not see a gentle person. Yet this command is situated directly next to the line "The Lord is near." As in, because Jesus is near; because the Holy Spirit is within you, the world should see you as a gentle person. The body of Christ should be gentle to one another, and to those outside the Body.

How un-manly.
But then a number of things happen.

You turn the page backward and read Philippians 2, which describes Jesus' *kenosis,* a fancy word for self-emptying, and realize that the manliest man who ever lived was gentle to the point of death. He emptied Himself for

---

[12] John 1:14

394

the sake of those He loved, allowing Himself to be crushed by the hands of other humans.

Now let me ask you a question: Was Jesus weak? Was He weaker than those who crucified Him? Or in many situations, does it take *more* strength to restrain our impulses?

Think about a father wrestling with his toddler son. They fight, the dad falls down on his back and allows his boy to stand atop his belly, triumphant. The father does not employ his full strength to wrestle his son. That would be ludicrous. But is the father weak because he does not utterly destroy his son in the wrestling match on the carpet?

There is a gigantic chasm between weakness and meekness. The best definition I've ever heard for gentleness is from Elizabeth George, who said

"gentleness is strength under control."

I think that for many men, we think of gentleness as a sign of weakness. We think that if we are soft-spoken and light-hearted to those around us, we will be seen as weak or timid. I think that the exact opposite is true. If we intend to follow in the footsteps of the One who allowed Himself to be beaten to a pulp and hung on a cross, then we must adopt a mentality of meekness.

It does not reflect a weakness, but rather, a confidence; it projects a comfort within our own skin, saying "I don't have to be bold and harsh and impose myself upon others in order to be seen as strong."

When I think about men in my own life who have helped shape or form me, none of them (none of the constructive ones, anyway) were harsh or demeaning to me. None of them urged me to be a better, more manly man by being blunt and hurtfully critical.

Rather, they were gentle. And not once have I thought of any of them as weak or un-manly. Just a few days ago, a mentor of mine called me out for a few foolish things I was doing. His words cut deep as he called me out for instances of being too full of myself and for some other areas in my life where he thought I needed improvement.

It hurt, but the way a muscle hurts as it grows stronger. Why? Because he approached these things gently. He did not come down harsh with only *truth, truth, truth!* but he brought up the topics with gentleness. For that reason, I received his criticism and will hopefully grow as a result. Was he manly, firm, and constructive? Yes. And although he was equally soft and gentle, I did not once think he was effeminate or weak. Quite the opposite.

And I can tell you that it feels good to be on the receiving end of gentleness. We all want to be around those people. The harsh, quasi-manly people turn out to be the ones who are typically insecure and lonely.

So let's work on gentleness. Let's work on becoming softer alongside our strength. Let's refine our definition of meekness so that it is not a twin of weakness, but of control and strength.

WHY CHRISTIANS NEED TO GO TO CHURCH
she rolled onto her side and kissed me...so go to church.

Because I'm a hopeless romantic (and because a theology teacher of mine once said "You can't have a good theological conversation without talking about sex"), this post necessitates some fanciful anecdotes.

I've been single for a long time. Like, a long time.

And with singleness comes a starvation of sorts. For someone like me who is a huge people-person, loves physical contact, etc., being single for that long means going without a lot of these meaningful gestures. So, in 2016 it had been roughly 4 years since I'd had a good kiss.
Or a bad one.
Or any at all.

As a typical American, I see kisses constantly, primarily on TV and in movies, but of course those do not compare to putting your lips on those of another real, living, 3-dimensional human being.

Many midnights ago, I found myself whipping through the mountains of South Carolina with a beautiful woman, feeling more alive than I had in a long time. I abruptly yanked the car to the side of the road and grabbed a blanket from the back of my car and we ran out into a field beneath the stars.

We talked for a while and then she rolled over onto her side and said, "I want to kiss you."

And she did.

And it was nothing like watching a kiss between two actors on a screen.

I think part of the issue of talking about church to people my age is that it is nothing like describing a good kiss. Our eyes don't light up. If anything, it's more like describing the experience of putting rash ointment on your butt. *It's effective and it cures the problem, but that's about it. Nothing to write home about.*

But church should not be old and stale.

Church is the place where Christ comes to us in the form of one another, ministering to each other as 'Christ with skin on.' It's the place where theoretical theology becomes beautifully tangible and real. It's the place where we literally 'taste and see that the Lord is good' when we come to the communion table.

It's the place where we stop thinking about a good kiss and feel the warmth with our own lips (especially if your church has a good singles ministry…).

Watching church happen online provides almost none of that. Yes, we can learn about the Bible a bit, but we are not *participating* in the life of the church by doing so. We are effectively watching *others* participate. Besides, if everyone had that mindset, eventually all pastors would just be preaching to empty rooms with a camera!

I think one of the most consistent and clear images the Bible gives us regarding the church is that of a body. In 1 Corinthians 12, Paul describes each member as having a different role to play, just like a finger, a spleen and an ear. The body struggles without each and every part functioning well as part of a unified whole.

And that, in essence, is the church. A body where people come together and belong and have a function and are cared for, the same way you care for your teeth.

A professor once told my class that to segregate yourself from the body is like cutting off your pinky. You can hold it, severed, in your hand, and try to reattach it. You can rush to the emergency room and have it set back on, and for a time, there is a good chance it will be accepted back.

But say you leave that pinky in your basement for a day. A week. A month. Try reattaching it then. At a certain point, the digit is just a rotten piece of ex-flesh. It is rancid and useless. My professor was describing Christians who try to maintain their faith while cut off from the life-giving community of Church, the Body of Christ. Sure, you may retain a flicker of warmth for a season, but ultimately, you are cut off from the source of life, the Body.

There is a lot of debate among American Christians right now over whether church attendance is really important for spiritual growth or, according to Donald Miller, if walking in the woods could serve the same purpose.

I'll spare you the technical details of running through the sacraments, fellowship, the mission, the justice and redistribution of wealth as God's vehicle to heal the world, communal worship, and the teaching of the Word. Can you get some of these things online with the advent of sermon podcasts, or worship music? Of course! And they **are** great things!

But they are not church.

Rich Mullins, one of the greatest Christian songwriters to ever live, once said, "Come to watch people like me for entertainment, not spiritual nourishment. If you want spiritual nourishment, go to church."

Here are some of the main reasons to get involved, summed up.

It is selfish not to.

Being a part of a local body means you're receiving worship, sermons, sacrament, etc., but it also means you are *giving* to the other members as well. We all have different gifts and are all able to serve in one way or another. Your severed pinky didn't just receive nutrients from your body without giving anything back; it was necessary to rock climb, play football, type, count to 10, and a dozen other daily tasks! To call your digital pastor's sermon 'church' is selfish, because it suggests that church is simply *what it can give me.* This does not look at all like the give-and-take relationship described in Acts 4, where the members had this beautiful community where everyone was cared for.

The church is the only place in the world to receive the sacraments.
You may have grown up in a denomination like me, where this was not really taught or understood very well. I always thought the act of communion was pretty expendable and life would go on if we stopped doing it. Wrong. You may not understand the mystical transaction that happens at the sacramental table, but it is more real and central to the Christian life than we know. Same with baptism.

Community > Individualism.
We live in a ME-culture. We are not brought up to think of collectives, tribes or families, but of individual people. Church is one of the richest expressions of fellowship and raw honesty in the world. It's a place where elderly widows come and sit side-by-side with tattooed millennial boys. It's a place of coming together, eating potlucks, helping others move, and encouraging. We profoundly miss this community (in which we give *and* take) by skipping church.

Come and be fed!
The last thing I would say to a Christian questioning the validity of church attendance is simply to ask, 'why *wouldn't* you come to the source of life every week?' Would you stop eating and let your body disintegrate? If not, why do that to your spirit and soul? We go to church because it is nourishing and filling to us, and reminds us of the abundant grace we have received in the Person of Jesus Christ. Why would you want to cut yourself off from that??

And lastly, a caveat.
Many of you may have found yourself resisting certain parts of this chapter, as if it seems legalistic or that you will be damaged if you continue at your current parish. If that is the case, it may be time to look around for a new church to be a part of. Yes, there are some unhealthy and lifeless churches out there, and yes, some churches may be a better fit for you than others. *But!* Don't expect any church to be completely perfect. every one is

imperfect and every pastor needs grace just like the rest of us. Wrestle with your issues with church attendance to determine if they are more selfish in nature, or if you are in an unhealthy body and it's time to look for another church to attend.

Just like every spouse has his or her flaws but you love them anyway, no church is perfect. That doesn't mean you marry everyone you meet, but commitment and contribution to a church is not only valuable, but essential in the life of a Christian, and beneficial to the Church worldwide.

May we be Christians who love our churches and brag about them to others. May we accept them despite their flaws and love them for the unique expression of Christ they present. May we come to them both to be filled and to pour into others. And may we encounter Christ richly in our churches, that we may be lighted and become a light to the world.

Let's be Christians who contribute to a solution rather than complaining about the problem. And that won't happen simply by ceasing to show up.

MANY ARE LEAVING THE CHURCH; FEW KNOW WHERE THEY'RE GOING
you've deconstructed your faith, but where does it take you?

I don't need to tell you there's a trend of Christians—especially famous ones—loudly leaving the faith and exiting stage left through what appears to be a curtain of liberation and pink-painted atheism. Or agnosticism. Or most likely, "I don't like labels, I just want to love people and delight in the divine wherever I meet her…"

This isn't necessarily new, but with the recent announcements by Hillsong leader Marty Sampson, writer Joshua Harris, and the Gungors, it seems like the very Christian religion is on the line. If you step back, however, and look at these events in light of 2,000 years of Christian history, it seems awfully trivial.

After all, a handful of people leaving the faith against the billions of Christians worldwide shouldn't really be earth shattering, so why can it feel so scary when someone public renounces their faith? Some, like the Gungors, leave angrily and try to tear people away with them, inviting them to a freer existence; one that supposedly makes more sense and is scientific and 'real.'

The irony, which very few people are pointing out, is that while it may be easy to deconstruct evangelicalism, or Christianity as a whole, none of these people are deconstructing the 'faith' to which they are fleeing.

You may highlight the crusades as a massive blight on the history of Christianity all while ignoring all the violence done by atheists (or other religions) and the hopeless existential dread which necessarily follows atheism.

You may point out that science undoes the millennia of religious ignorance, but what, then, does science offer you? Does it provide a moral system of ethics, or the chance at purpose? The same could be said of amorphous, undefinable New Age spirituality, which can be formed however the practicer wishes. It's the Build-a-God Worskshop. And often, these gods look a lot like you.

It is, dare I say, sexy to deconstruct your Christian faith right now, but to what are you running? Why have you not done the same work to deconstruct that structure of belief to ensure that it will hold up? If you have searched the depths of the Christian faith and found her lacking, have you done the same homework to ensure that your new system won't let you down in the same way?

I know many, many people who have been wounded in deep ways by their church or some Christian organization. This is not the heart of Christianity, yet it is often blamed for peoples' departures. These wounds are legitimate and not to be overlooked. They do not, however, provide one with a clear alternative. One may say they are leaving the Church because of abuse, or a myriad of other reasons, and their disgust is warranted. What it does not do, though, is offer a meaningful place to turn. Because of this, I have seen many of these same people leave the Church and spin in circles because of a lack of an alternative. The Church, of course, needs to be doing her part to reach out and help heal these wounds.

When someone leaves their Christian faith, even on these grounds, the question must be asked: To what are they running? Does it offer purpose and morals? Is there a genuine connection to the Transcendent, or are they just making up their own rules and calling it god?

One avenue I have seen doing great work on this 'deconstruction of secularism' is Mark Sayers via his books and *This Cultural Moment* podcast. You may also look at *How (Not) To Be Secular* by James K.A. Smith. These pieces all look at what factors have brought us to this moment where we see Christians flocking away from their faith because they have deconstructed it (or at least, their experience of it), without doing much work in sensing out where they are going instead.

Christians and non-Christians alike need to become more aware of the secular culture in which we live; becoming experts in deconstructing atheism the same way many have named themselves experts in dissecting Christianity. We are leaving the age of Christianity being the dominant cultural force and moving into a post-Christian world in which we will once again exist on the outskirts. Much of the hatred of the Church has come from its abuse of power and legalistic dogma. Once it is a minority position however, it can once again shine as the beacon of hope, purpose, and healing it is meant to be.

WHY THE CHARISMATIC MOVEMENT BURNED ME

passion at the neglect of truth results in cults and damage to outsiders.

"For years now, my sinuses have been really messed up," I told this friendly stranger after the service at a church in New Hampshire. "I can barely taste, I have constant pressure headaches, and frequently get sinus infections."

With a confident smile, he laid his hands on my shoulders, though over the course of the prayer, they would migrate across my cheeks and nose. He began, "God, you have given us authority over the sicknesses that infest our bodies. In *Jesus'* name, I *COMMAND* this illness to get out of this body!"

He pressed on my nose.

"OUT!"

He declared some more healing at me and then told me that by the time I left the church doors, it would have started healing and all my nasal issues would be better. "The healing is beginning now," he said as we departed. "It may take a few minutes but it's healed now."

It wasn't.

That was in the spring of 2012, and my sinus issues wouldn't be resolved until January 2017 when I had surgery to correct my deviated septum.

The sad thing is, that was not one isolated incident. I was with a hyper charismatic missions organization for two years from 2010-12, and over those two years, I cannot count how many times my sinuses were prayed over and "declared" to be healed, every time leaving me disappointed and questioning God's healing power...or my own faith.

If I just had more faith, my sinuses would have been healed months ago!

Its worth noting here that I'd consider myself a charismatic believer. I believe God still works and heals and does crazy stuff. I've seen it with my own eyes. I had a professor in college who once told me that any miracle I'd ever seen was just my imagination playing tricks on me and I was misremembering everything, because God doesn't do that anymore.

That is not me.

I'm more akin to Tim Keller, who once said that he considers himself an 80% cessationist: 80% of the time, people are being dramatic or being deceived by their own minds, but there is still that 20% of times that are truly unexplainable and supernatural. (I may be more like 60/40, but you get the point...)

I saw a herd of demons cast out of a man in Thailand and nothing can convince me that that's not what I saw. I saw a man's hand healed in Brazil while I held it. I helped run an organization in Nigeria which reported people born deaf or blind receiving their senses for the first time ever. These were evidences of God moving and transforming peoples' lives in explicit, undeniable ways, unlike things I experiences stateside at the hands of overzealous pentecostals.

I remember one instance at a church in Boston (where I also received prayer for my sinuses after the service...*maybe THIS time it'll do the trick*) when the pastor stood before his congregation and told them, "I've been in so many churches across America, and you know what the problem is? God isn't there." The audience cheered.

What he meant was, people didn't dance around the aisles and go crazy and passionately *declare* healing over hopeful visitors. If that pastor were to attend the church where I currently work, he would probably have the same critique: God is not in the building.

It's as if the zeal and passion of the worshippers indicate where the presence of God is and is not. Like, if you weren't dancing crazy enough, you weren't really worshiping. Nevermind stillness and waiting upon the Lord in contemplation and silence, like Christians have done for millennia.

There were countless times I was in charismatic worship services and felt the pressure to dance around and smile a lot because that's what everyone else was doing. If I wasn't [awkwardly] dancing, I was doing it wrong.

The pentecostal/charismatic subculture has a lot of great things to offer the church today. In a recent seminary class, we discussed the different emphases of various congregations, and Pentecostal churches focus on the *Power* and *Presence* of God. They are aware of these things in proportions the rest of the church can benefit from.

That pastor was right to a degree, in that many churches and pastors *have* neglected the power and active presence of God in our midst, and that is something we should work to recover. However, somewhere between doubting the active work of God and telling someone they're healed when they're not is a healthy balance.

Most of Christianity is finding the healthy balance between two extremes.

In this case, I like to pull from John 4:24, where Jesus tells the woman at the well that true worshipers worship in spirit and truth. Many charismatics are heavy on the *spirit*, but light on *truth* (Yes, of course many tribes are heavy on truth while neglecting the Spirit, but that's for another time). Both spirit and truth are necessary for a thriving faith and active growth.

Truth at the neglect of the Spirit dries up faith, creating an evaporated and crumbling Christianity.

But spirit (passion/zeal) at the neglect of truth to anchor it results in cults, unorthodox sects, and a lot of damage to outsiders (like me).

It took years for me to recover from thinking that my faith was lacking because no matter how many people prayed for me, my nasal passages were still screwed up. There were other times I was practically forced to speak in 'tongues' by babbling incoherently, but nothing ever emerged from it.

The F is wrong with me? Why is my faith so weak? I used to wonder.

Rather than seeking out what the Bible really says about these things, and developing a healthy, realistic and holistic theology of miracles and healing, I believed the culture I was submerged in at the time. (Paul explicitly says that not everyone can speak in tongues…so why is it forced in so many pentecostal gatherings?)

I was in one charismatic service where a guy went up to the microphone and announced that he had a dream about the Ninja Turtles, and that was an indicator about the spiritual climate of the church. In other words, his fantastical amphibian dream held more weight than the words of Scripture.

The point I'm trying to make in all of this is, find balance. Know the truth of scripture as it is illuminated by the Holy Spirit. Pray often. Pray for one another often. But beware of the language you use and the beliefs you hold, as they may be damaging to others.

Watch out that you make things like healings and miracles the *ultimate* things, rather than subservient to the one most important thing: Knowing Christ. Without a doubt, we are to pray for the sick and injured. But there is a huge difference between *asking* for healing and *demanding/declaring* it. The words we use matter.

Watch out that we do not pressure one another to worship in one certain way. We are free to dance and go wild, but we are also free to sit and be still.

I hate the idea of someone in my shoes wandering into one of those pentecostal churches with some ailment, being *declared* healed, only to leave the church the same as they entered. I hate the idea of this earnest seeker rejecting Christianity as a whole and never coming to know Christ because of the misleading and destructive language used. Fortunately, that was not the case for me, though as you can see, damage was still done.

May we continue this conversation as people who seek to know truth and commune with the Spirit, neglecting neither and always growing in both. No church is perfect, but there is a time and place to call out unhealthy and toxic behaviors.

IT'S (PROBABLY) A GOOD THING EVANGELICALISM IS DYING

you can't judge systems by how their participants live.

I don't remember which year of college it was when a little lightbulb went off in my brain about the future of American Christianity. Just as the middle class is evaporating in the American economy, so is the 'middle class' of nominal Christianity—in the words of Jesus, people are becoming either 'hot' or 'cold' rather than 'lukewarm.'

Evangelicalism has served a good purpose for many people in recent centuries, but just like all manmade movements, it has run its course and the good it promises for the future may be dim. You can Google 'evangelicalism is dying' and find a plethora of articles defending that claim as well as rebutting it using statistics and surveys, but what I want to do here is present more of a personal reflection than an analytical prediction.

One thing I have discovered as someone who grew up in the evangelical circle is that there is a lot of good to be gleaned from it. There is a lot of good to come from encouraging people to be born again, read their Bibles, pray often, and maintain a loving relationship with the man Jesus Christ. However, over the past several decades, the word has slid into a season of upheaval, and it is more of a weaponized put-down than a descriptor of people doing those things.

I recently talked with someone who also grew up in evangelical circles but had a vastly different experience than my own. I grew up the son of a 'non-denominational' pastor and had a wonderful experience of grace, love, acceptance, and seeking the truth of God's Word. Turns out this is not the story for everyone, which has morphed the word 'evangelical' into a slight against a certain group of people, usually on one side of the political aisle. This person pointed out that in pursuit of truth, his pastors and other leaders neglected Christ's teachings of love and grace in favor of theological dogmas. He was treated badly in the name of evangelical doctrines—not because the doctrines themselves were corrupt, but because the humans who applied them were sinful.

Pain causes all of us to think irrationally and twist our vision of truth or reason, and that's a very valid reason to leave a relationship or abusive local church. But more often than not, I have seen people use pain or abuse as a reason for Christianity to be an awful, terrible system.

I work at a school which had to fire its English teacher last year because he was flirting with middle schoolers. Does this mean that the entire school was founded on principles encouraging pedophilia back when it opened in the 60's? Of course not! Yet this is the logic often applied by people leaving the church in favor of a more accepting theology. Someone mistreated them, and rather than acknowledging that it was an individual, or a small pocket of people, acting harmfully, they throw the baby out with the bathwater and assume that the entire system was corrupt from the start.

In the same conversation with the progressive person, I brought up Islam, and how from its inception, it is a religion predicated on violence and therefore, (to put it lightly) a bad system, period. What was his response? "Yah, well Christians have also done violence in the name of religion like the crusades…" This is the exact same logical fallacy as assuming my whole school is abusive merely because one teacher was. It's a logic which assumes that back in the 1960's, the founder created it in the hopes that the teachers would hit on the students. Sounds ridiculous, right?

When we talk about Islam vs. Christianity, we can't judge them by how the practitioners live, but by their founding principles. Look no further than their founders: Muhammad led 86 battles in his lifetime to expand his Muslim empire by bloodshed. Jesus led 0 battles in His lifetime and the only blood He ever shed was His own on behalf of His persecutors. The differences seem obvious.

But back to my point.

Several years ago, I was talking with a friend who told me I'll have to lower my standards for a spouse because—in her words—no one was 'as Christian' as me. It grosses me out to type that, because there is nothing special about me as some sort of super-Christian. I read the Bible, I pray, go to church, and I sin a LOT. The fault in my friend's thinking is that there is some spiritual hierarchy in which we participate based on our merits.

In other words, the majority of people in America who call themselves Christians are less 'Christian' than they are 'moralistic therapeutic deists.' It sounds complicated, but it's simple when you break down those words:

> **moralistic:** There is some sense of morality associated with your behaviors. You need to do *good* and avoid doing *bad*. The more good you do, the better your chances of reaping rewards, either now or in the eschaton (next life).

> **therapeutic:** It *feels* good to do the right thing, and you can pat yourself on the back when you do something good. Your conscience is clean and you can look around (or down) at your fellow man, happy that you are a doer of good.

> **deism:** You associate all of this with some sort of transcendent entity (but most of the effort to better yourself is done by you).

Sound like the majority of 'Christians' you know? When evangelicalism began in the 1800's, its goal was to love people, especially the poor, promote biblical literacy, and genuinely point people toward deeper relationship with Christ. Now, however, the term has been wed to political platforms and become an umbrella for any group of Christians seeking the comfort of a denomination without the restriction of oversight.

When my friend said I'd have a hard time finding a spouse if I didn't lower my standards, she may have inadvertently revealed the truth about a lot of people in America calling themselves Christian: That they don't even adhere to the basic tenets and practices of Christianity. According to one study, the number of self-proclaimed Christians who do the basic practices (Bible, prayer, church, adhere to creeds, etc.) can be whittled down to 3.7% of the American population.[13]

The word 'evangelicalism' is not found in the Bible, so I don't feel remorse over its decline. The New Testament uses two words primarily to describe genuine followers of Christ: Christians and 'followers of The Way.' I like these because they are generally vague and demand definition from outsiders. In other words, they invite conversation, whereas 'Evangelical' automatically boxes you in, aligning you with a now-dogmatic string of beliefs. Not to mention, evangelicals put Trump in office which assumes the elevation of his political party to that of the kingdom of God. If the kingdom of God is truly transcendent and not of this world, no political party can hope to so widely align with it.

For instance, republicans tend to hold fast to the pro-life platform. I'm heavily pro-life and believe humanity begins at conception, but find that often, republicans ignore basic facts, like how outlawing them will not reduce the number of abortions performed, it will only make them more risky. There are also studies which reveal that legalizing abortions actually reduces the number performed each year. As a category, evangelicals seem to resist ideas like these and (ironically) cling to their version of safe spaces, which are pro-life candidates, the political right, and so on. (The bottom line is, many people don't like to think too much on either side of the aisle…).

I see the decline of evangelicalism as a system to generally be a good thing, and here's why. It eliminates the middle class, so to speak, therefore forcing people to choose a side. Either you are a Christian who knows God's Word, wrestles with it, and tries your best to live it out; or you are not. You are secular or you are Christian. There soon will not be the gray, amorphous umbrella term of 'evangelicalism' to hide under, forcing people to think

---

[13] Trevin Wax, *On The Imminent Collapse of Evangelical Christianity*

more dynamically, define their beliefs, and either live out their faith or abandon it.

Christianity thrives in the counter-culture, and the coming years may press it back into that form, likening it more closely to the Christianity witnessed in the Bible. A Christianity which stands up to oppressive power and gets people killed; a Christianity people are actually willing to die for.

PROGRESSIVE CHRISTIANITY ISN'T ABOUT HOMOSEXUALITY

many people are having this conversation, quite frankly, wrong.

I just finished skimming an article written by a right-wing writer who was combatting progressive Christianity by pointing out its 'moral and spiritual bankruptcy.' A couple people had shared this article with me, likely because of my recent video ranting some of my frustrations about the incoming progressive wave of Christianity.

While I do think there is a lot to be concerned about with the influx of progressive Christianity, many people are having this conversation, quite frankly, wrong. The writer of the above article spent the entire span of his content combatting one thing: homosexuality. It seemed like there were dozens of little fires popping up about this one topic and it was his job to quickly extinguish them with his memorized scripture, as if homosexuality is the sole cause and issue of progressivism. In reality, it's merely a small room in a giant house of ideas.

I would argue that his article has much more to do with 'why homosexuality is bad' than actual progressive Christianity. For some reason, that's become the first thing to come to mind whenever the topic is breached. It's as if the sole reason Christians are progressing is to accommodate the LGBTQ+ community. In reality, what I've seen happen is the LGBTQ+ community has not only become the whipping boy for the conservative right, but also the golden child of the liberal left.

In other words, this group of people has been objectified by both sides for the sake of making arguments. Both sides' arguments may be summed up rather simply, and redundantly repeating them won't change anyone's mind.

Left: "They are people with deep desires and we need to respect that. Imagine if you were as attracted to men as you are to women and someone told you it was sinful to be that way. We need to embrace and affirm them after years of hatred and exclusion. God doesn't think they are gross and twisted, but beautiful."

Right: "God has made the natural world to operate in a certain way: Male with female. To fight the natural order of things is to fight God, and therefore, sinful. (Yes, there is homosexuality in animals but there is also cannibalism of their young, so that's not the best comparison...) To love someone is to not let them go on in their sin, but to do this lovingly and relationally."

Years ago, C.S. Lewis said that if the devil can push a believer to either extreme—the Left or the Right—then he has succeeded, because from there he can push us to sin in that direction.[14]

Both sides (ideally) approach the subject with love and hope for the best in the world and in their community (including the LGBTQ+ community). For this article, I'm going to assume both sides have the best intentions in mind, even though in reality, either one can come off as pretty repugnant. After all, if the only alternative to 'progressive Christianity' was that article above, I'm not so sure I'd want to stick with that side either.

The problem with hinging the entire conversation on what someone thinks about gay people is that it's missing the forest for the trees. More accurately, it's like missing the entire country of Brazil for a single tree.

Whenever a conversation turns an entire group of people into a point in an argument, we need to pause and look at the ideas being presented beneath the surface. In this case, the variance in opinions has much less to do with one's attitude toward homosexual people and much more with their views of God, the Bible, theology, anthropology and philosophy. That's exactly

---

[14] C.S. Lewis, *The Screwtape Letters*

the reason I have never openly written about "Ethan's views of homosexuality" because for one, that doesn't matter; and two, that's not really the main issue…is it?

Our beliefs about certain categorical pockets are not necessarily indicative of what we think about that specific thing, but about something much larger going on behind it. As Rob Bell says, *this* is really about *that*.

People ask me what I think about homosexuality either because they want affirmation in their ways, a conversational sparring partner, or an ally against gay people. They don't ask me my views about Jesus or scripture, or theology, which is really where the conversation begins.

Over a decade ago, I watched the film *Flight of the Phoenix* in which a plane crashes in the middle of the desert and the crew must find their way back to civilization. The only part I remember is the captain saying that if their aim back toward civilization was off by just one degree, they would all be dead in the desert. That's exactly the case here too. Both sides have slightly misaimed their trajectory and missed the mark by miles.

The author above claimed to be addressing 'progressive Christians,' but simply popped out a bunch of verses from scripture which condemned homosexuality. Is that really the method we are employing to draw people to the beauty of Christ? Perhaps a better analogy is that of the tree and the forest. He set out to uproot the tree but ended up simply hacking away at a single leaf.

So what am I getting at here?

The conversation doesn't hinge on homosexuality, or homosexual people. In fact, it doesn't even have to do with sexuality at all: That's merely the result of Christians stooping to do combat on the level of our over-sexualized culture.

The conversation needs to zoom out to the level of how we read the Bible. How we grow spiritually and how we know Jesus. We need to understand both postmodern thought and Gnosticism to have this conversation well. Because it has far less to do with sexuality than it does with thoughts, beliefs, hermeneutics, and conviction.

True believers won't be distracted by debates about who's allowed to do what with their bodies. I think true believers are more focused on their own sins and are actively humbled by the Gospel. The Gospel reminds conservative people that they are not the judge of other peoples' actions, and it reminds liberal folks that there is a holy God who will deal justly with mankind.

When it comes to the wave of progressivism in the West, we need to zoom out from the myopic topic of sexuality and look at why and how we think the ways we do in the first place. This is far easier said than done, since it's much easier to pick a side and drive our stake in the ground there than attempt to strike a healthy balance of—as Jesus had—grace and truth.

Here are some thoughts to hopefully challenge you whether you consider yourself more conservative *or* liberal.

If you find yourself leaning to the right, ask yourself why you're so quick to rail against this one specific group of people (or their actions). Is it because you, yourself don't struggle with that? Is it easier for you to stand for the integrity of Scripture than it is to love people who are different from you? Does your sense of 'rightness' outweigh the love you show to those in the LGBTQ+ community? Do you see them as humans (do you even know any gay people?) or as argument points? WWJD?

If you're a left-leaner, ask yourself where you get your sense of truth. Take some time to honestly figure out what you root your beliefs in: Is it your own feelings, desires, or gut impulses, or do you have something larger than yourself to inform your ethical code? You argue for the rights of people wanting to do a myriad of actions, but do you draw the line somewhere? Is incest between a brother and sister permissible if they *really love* each other (Of course, they wouldn't have kids, they'd adopt…just like a gay couple), or is all love not *really* equal? Is it hard for you to concede that there may be a larger scale of right and wrong than what you agree with? WWJD?

As Christians, I don't believe our job is to choose political, or even theological sides, but to love people, love God, and do our best to not screw up. We all sin in one direction or another, so let's try to reorient ourselves toward Christ and not toward a winning argument.

May we be Christians who pray, love all people, and strive to read God's Word accurately and carefully, recognizing that our thoughts inform our beliefs and our beliefs inform our actions. And may we never use humans as pawns in the chess games of our moral debates, regardless of which side we are on.

RACE IN THE KINGDOM OF GOD

the Bible tells us there is something thicker than blood.

"I don't think it's a football movie," said Denzel Washington in an interview about his film *Remember the Titans*. And he's right. We recently watched the film at my church and (big surprise) I found myself choked up at one specific scene toward the end.

The high schooler Gary starts off about as white and racist as they come. He hates rooming with his black teammate Julius, but over the course of football camp and the intense team bonding sessions pushed by his black coach (Washington), he flips and ends up becoming best friends with Julius, even at the cost of losing his girlfriend.

The two friends become even closer throughout the film, until one night after a football victory, Gary gets into a car accident. He's rushed to the hospital and soon the whole team is in the waiting room. When Julius arrives, he discovers that he's the only one Gary wants to see. He rushes back to the room where Gary lies bloody on the bed.

"Out!" the nurse shoos Julius out, "only kin's allowed in here!"

"Alice, are you blind?" Gary yells from the bed. "Don't you see the family resemblance? That's my brother."

A deep-south white boy scolds his nurse for missing the 'family resemblance' between him and a dark skinned teammate.

And that's **exactly** what family looks like in the kingdom of God.

Throughout the gospels and into the rest of the New Testament, Jesus emphasizes the value of spiritual family over biological family. For instance, in Matthew 12, his mother and brothers come to see Him while He's surrounded by crowds teaching. Rather than rush out and embrace them, He says, "'Who is My mother, and who are My brothers?' Pointing to His disciples, He said, 'Here are My mother and My brothers. For whoever does the will of My Father in heaven is My brother and sister and mother.'"

He puts so much emphasis on His spiritual family over His biological one that He postponed seeing them in order to drive home this point.

Later, while He hangs from the cross,

> Jesus saw His mother and the disciple whom He loved [John] standing nearby, He said to His mother, "Woman, here is your son." Then He said to the disciple, "Here is your mother." So from that hour, this disciple took her into his home.[15]

Bringing Mary the mother of God into his home may seem like an extreme move on John's part, but it's heightened further by the fact that this is a tribal, family-driven culture. Your family was *your family*. Nothing is thicker than blood, etc.

Except, says the Bible, there is something thicker than blood.

In 1 Corinthians 6, hidden in a discourse on sexuality, Paul uncovers a key truth about biological families. In essence, He writes that a man and woman may become one *flesh* via marriage and sexual intercourse, but according to Paul, there is a deeper level, which we are all invited into as the body of Christ. "Whoever is united with the Lord is one with Him in spirit."

Your biological family may unite you to your relatives by *flesh*, but even deeper than that is this mysterious union with Christ in which we are all united by *spirit*.

This means two things, the first of which may be hard for some of us to swallow, though the other is incredibly beautiful:

---

[15] John 19:25-27

1   If you are a Christian and a (biological) family member is not, you are more closely related to all other Christians in the world than you are to that member, according to the Bible. After all, you'll be spending all of eternity with them, but only this short life with that family member.

2   You are spiritually connected to them through our union with Christ at such a deep level that it surpasses that of family bloodlines. You can find Christians of every color, ethnicity, language, age and gender and automatically have a rich connection with them through your shared union with Christ.

Have you ever wondered why Paul ends so many of his letters with some kind of exhortation to not disrupt the bond of peace, or to be at peace with one another, and so on? I think this is why. As believers, we must recognize the example we set, not just as members of our own families or churches or groups, but as members of the worldwide family of God. We are adopted into *His* family in such a deep and mysterious way that we can't even understand it!

It means that an elderly black man and a young Asian girl are brother and sister. Same with my widowed grandmother and the young Hispanic family in her church. That's the beauty of the church which is found nowhere else on earth: the unity we have in Christ is greater than our differences in age, race, gender, personality, and whatever else would normally divide us.

Paul writes in Galatians 3, "There is neither Jew nor Gentile, neither slave nor free, nor is there male and female, for you are all one in Christ Jesus."

Our position as sons and daughters of God exceeds all other attributes or identities we may ascribe to.

That which unites us is greater than that which segregates us.

Like Gary in *Remember the Titans*, we can look at every other believer in the world and say, "That there is my brother (or sister)…don't you see the resemblance?"

COMFORT, LENT, AND THE PERSECUTED CHURCH

how do you commune with the Transcendent?

For a quarter of a century my faith has been defined by coffee shop conversations and the occasional argument with other Americans whose lives look pretty much the same as mine. Regular church attendance and a slew of sermon illustrations. My Bible studies are cute and Instagrammable.

I think the biggest issue to emerge from my comfortable religion is that I struggle to recall times where I've had interaction with the Transcendent I claim to grasp so intimately. Jesus referred to the Holy Spirit at our *Comforter*, but most Americans are already comfortable. Who needs a comforter when you're already cozy? It's like offering a duvet to a guest in the summer: Unnecessary.

How do you interact with the Transcendent?

He is the God whose bigness escapes the confines of language and whose essence knows literally no boundaries. We may try to box Him in with systematic lists of 'He wills' and 'He won'ts', but I think even those get shattered and left like flotsam in the wake of His ship. We may have narrowed down one aspect of His character, only to crack open another story from the Bible which reshuffles our deck of theological playing cards. Just when we were starting to get the spades separated from the clubs, He slips more jokers into our hand.

I once posted on Facebook that in 2016, one Christian was martyred every six minutes for a total of roughly 90,000 martyrs. That number makes Christians *by far* the most persecuted group in the world. In fact, Christians make up roughly a third of the world's population, yet they account for 80% of its violent persecution.

So why was it that my post received negative feedback so quickly from Christians and non-Christians alike? Americans tend to see Christians as merely entitled whiners who do little but stand in the way of 'progress.' We are seen as the oppressors far more than the oppressed.

Our babies are not born with eight arms because we suffer from radiation poisoning. Our playgrounds are not haunted by the ghosts of communism, nor are our herds cursed by local witchdoctors. My wife will not be raped for being a Christian, nor will our baby be held by the legs and smashed against a bus.[16] My prayer life is more often a string of niceties that sounds nothing like the violent dreams of the imprecatory Psalmists, nor do I make rash vows[17] like Ezekiel who lay on his left side and cooked his food over his own poop for a few years.[18]

How do *you* interact with the Transcendent?

Transcendent: Existing apart from and not subject to the limitations of the material universe. From the Latin *transcendere,* meaning 'to climb over.'

Kantian ethics describe the Transcendent as 'not realizable in experience.'[19]

In other words, how do you experience the unexperiencable?

If everything we know is simply a gleaning from our experiences, how do we come to know God, the grand Other? My epistemology is optimistic at best, but I'll leave the philosophical ranting to smarter people.

I've come to find the key to unlocking the Transcendent is simple: Jesus.

Plato (that ancient pre-Christ Christian…kind of) talked about the invisible and ethereal *forms* which were represented by the lower, tangible physical world. Jesus is the union of the two. Jesus is who you get when you smash together the Divine and the visible.

Jesus is the reason matter matters.

He is the *form* become flesh.

---

[16] This is from an account in the film *Furious Love*

[17] Please do yourself a favor and read "In Defense of Rash Vows" by G.K. Chesterton. It takes <10 minutes.

[18] Ezekiel 4

[19] Immanuel Kant, *Critique of Pure Reason*

Jesus breathes meaning into molecules.

I've been rereading David Platt's book *Radical,* and he shares an anecdote about a conversation he had with a Hindu and a Muslim. He told them that most religions of the world see God on top of a mountain, and the various religions are simply taking different paths to the top. The men nod in agreement. "Yes, that's exactly it!"

"But what if God came down to the base of the mountain because none of us could even make it a few steps up the mountain?" Platt replied. "Let me tell you about Jesus..."

Jesus is the top of the mountain come down to our place at the bottom. Jesus is the king of the upside down kingdom; the defier of the rules of mathematics. He could have invented the show *Jeopardy* with how backward His answers are.

You want to love your life? Lose it.
You want to be great? Be the servant of all.
You have enemies? Serve them some food & eat with them.

I think the idea of inversion helps to explain why we as Americans struggle so much to connect with the Divine. If Jesus came for (and as) The Least of These, it makes sense why we Americans—aka, The Greatest of These —have so much trouble resonating with Him. We've turned our faith into trite captions for our filtered photographs rather than a means of sacrificing ourselves daily. We prefer entertainment to disciplines such as fasting, prayer and silence. Many of our churches preach about how God wants to enhance our lives and make them better than they already are, which only adds to our societal confusion about Christianity.

We don't long for the Word of God because it has never been taken away from us. Believers in other nations, meanwhile, rip Bibles into different sections because there is only one for a dozen people to share in their jail cells. Then they memorize their entire section.[20] We are a people of weak faith and weak wills.

---

[20] Check out *The Heavenly Man* by Brother Yun for more of these crazy stories.

I don't want this post to be one of those American guilt posts, but I hope it calls you to examine your own context. Raise awareness about the persecuted church worldwide, and stand with them in prayer. There certainly seems to be some correlation between the persecution faced by Christians and their experience of God.

Some years ago, a group of Koreans were being held captive and awaiting their deaths, but miraculously they were rescued and released. Months later, they all reported that they longed to be back in that jail cell because they had never felt so close to Jesus as they did there.

I think experiencing the Transcendent has to do with removing the comfort we receive from anything other than Christ. Fasting is the removal of the comfort of food in order to be satiated with Christ; chastity is the removal of sex in order to experience the pleasure of Christ. Silence is the deprivation of music and noise in order to hear the gentle whisper of Christ. And so on.

J. Muyskens points out that Christian growth is not a matter of addition, but subtraction.[21]

You want to connect with the transcendent? Subtract.

The timing of this post happens to be a great segue into the upcoming church season of Lent, when the Church worldwide gives things up for the sake of joining Jesus in His poverty. What will you subtract from your life in order to have that void filled with Christ? What will you sacrifice to know Him better?

There are Christians right now around the world who are being tortured and slaughtered for the name of Christ. They do not have the option to give things up for Lent, as everything is forcefully being taken from them.

May we join them in this season by voluntarily giving up some of our own comforts. May we not forget our brothers and sisters in Christ who are daily persecuted around the world, but may our mindfulness lead to prayer and action. And may we be people who relinquish our rights to comfort and

---

[21] J. David Muyskens, *40 Days to a Closer Walk with God*

entertainment in order to commune with the Transcendent, who gave up all of His rights to commune with us.

MOTHER TERESA'S DARK NIGHT OF THE SOUL
there is a huge element of her life which most people tend to overlook.

Whenever you want to talk about a stereotypical 'good person,' there are a mandatory few people who come to mind: Ghandi, The Pope, or Mother Teresa. Few people have made such a mark on the world using humility and grace as she, yet there is a gigantic element of her life which most people tend to overlook.

In the 16th century, a Spanish monk named John of the Cross penned a poem entitled "The Dark Night of the Soul," which introduced and gave shape to this concept of the dark night. In essence, it is a time of feeling distant from God for the purification of the believer's soul. Few pieces of writing are so intense and deal so squarely with feelings of abandonment from God. John records his battle with divine exile as he battles his demons and attempts to put to death all earthly desires of his flesh.

Since the inception of the idea, plenty of Christians have recorded their own dark nights of the souls, to varying degrees and lengths. In the 18th century, a man named Paul of the Cross reportedly had a Dark Night which lasted over 40 years. More recently however, Mother Teresa reported her own Dark Night of the Soul which lasted roughly 50 years.

For 50 years, Mother Teresa endured "Such deep longing for God, so deep that it is painful, a suffering continual, and yet not wanted by God, repulsed, empty, no faith, no love no zeal," she wrote in a letter.

For 50 years, she lived in what she called "the darkness."

For 50 years, Mother Teresa forced herself to smile toward God, writing that her smile was "a big cloak which covers a multitude of pains."

She went so far as to say that she often felt unwanted and unloved by God.

I want to remind you who we're talking about here. We're not just talking about a woman who showed up to church on Sunday and went through the motions. This is no lukewarm quasi-religious person who talks about God despite no relational depth with Him.

This was a woman who committed her life to the poorest of the poor in India. She lived with orphans. When a new shipment of shoes arrived, she made sure to get the first shot at it...so she could dig through them and take the worst shoes available. She didn't want anyone to wear worse shoes than she did, and as a result, her feet were mangled and misshapen.[22]

Her spiritual writings have influenced millions and led them into a closer walk with God through humility and sacrifice. Yet this woman, to whom the Catholic Church awarded sainthood in 2003, seemed to have an intense struggle with darkness for the majority of her life.

Too often, we as American Christians portray our faith as an ever-increasing journey in which we only improve and grow. Peppy megachurches spew positive messages about God's favor, as if the Bible were chock-full of stories of flawless people living happy lives. Yet when a contemporary figure as notable as Mother Teresa releases letters in which she admits to struggling with darkness for most of her life, we tend to look away.

That won't make anyone's day or put a skip in your step.

When we are honest and articulate our own walks with Jesus, how many of us can really attest to a nonstop happiness-fueled life, derived of pain and suffering? That's not my experience, and I would wager it's not yours either.

I imagine that when you think about your own walk with the Lord, there tends to be more silence than revelation. I can usually relate more to Psalm 22's refrain, *My God, My God, why have You forsaken me?* than I can to the songs of rejoicing and celebration because the Lord has delivered me.

---

[22] This is from a story told by Shane Claiborne who lived with Mother Teresa for a year while she was still alive.

I think there is enormous value in honestly sharing our stories and our experience with the Lord, rather than shining it to a blinding polish that hides all our blemishes. From outside of Christianity, I imagine this collection of people pretending to be perfect and pain-free would be more repulsive than attractive.

It is important to note, however, that Dark Nights of the Soul, including Mother Teresa's, are not purposeless suffering. John of the Cross, when he first articulated the concept, spoke of the night as a time to purify the soul, robbing it of its desire for earthly pleasures.

For example, in my own life, I can pinpoint several points of feeling very distant from God and alone. Most of the time, I have fled from the feelings of abandonment and loneliness with the escape hatches of Netflix, Facebook, or pornography. But when I think about God using these times to purify me, I should see them as times to eradicate sinful desires from my life. I should come to terms with singleness to the degree that my desire for a wife is eclipsed by my desire for nearness to God. I should see it as a time to chop away at my pride in order to live a more humble life.

For some odd reason, it brings me comfort to know that one of the greatest contemporary saints, Mother Teresa, wrestled with the same feelings of darkness and abandonment I often find in myself. I feel like we modern people tend to be so distracted by technology and noise that we don't feel this disparity to the degree that she did, but if we were to strip away all the distractions, we would likely be scared of what we would find.

We wear the masks of 'pretty good people' most days, and this is what is addressed by the Dark Night of the Soul. The Dark Night is a reminder that we are utterly in need of God and the redemption of Jesus Christ.

May we be people who, when feelings of darkness arise, see them as opportunities for purification rather than escape into the world of noise and distraction. May we be honest about our imperfections, struggles and pain. May we humble ourselves like so many saints before us, embracing our experience with the Lord as unique. And may we be faithful to Him to the end, despite the hardships, trials and darkness that come against us.

THE NEW LONELY

we are terrified of silence.

Last night I was at a restaurant with a friend of mine. We were on the patio having a great conversation when a married couple sat down at the table next to ours. We were bewildered as the husband took out his smart phone, began playing electronic music on the phone's tiny speakers, and set it on the table for the remainder of the meal.

We are a people terrified of silence.

I often bemoan to my friends and family about how lonely I am. The irony being that I am complaining *TO* my *friends and family*. I think our culture has twisted up this word, loneliness. We can each name half a dozen songs about being alone in a crowded room, or maybe while sitting next to a lover, but is that really loneliness?

Tom Hanks was lonely in *Castaway*.

Will Forte, in *Last Man on Earth*, is lonely.

My guess is, you are not lonely.

I think what we confuse for loneliness today is actually some modern unrest inside of us. We have this lack of peace within ourselves that calls for constant noise and distraction. And when no one can hang out on a Friday night, we call ourselves 'lonely' because that void inside of us is about to act up. We're about to have to face ourselves.

Thank God for Netflix.

I watched a movie recently where this Middle Eastern Christian monk is talking about silence. He says "Sure, you can go to a quiet place like a forest or a desert and it will be quiet for a while," he says. "But there is another kind of silence that is much harder to attain. And that is the silence within yourself. A stillness in your soul."

My guess is we're not lonely, we have a lack of peace within ourselves.

So I came up with a term for this, and to be honest, I guess it's not that original. I was thinking about how this feeling we associate with loneliness really comes from somewhere else, perhaps an overload instead of a lack. We are always connected digitally, and therefore, more disconnected personally.

We have noise coming into our bodies constantly, so why would we expect there to be silence in our soul?

It's the New Loneliness.

We are the New Lonely.

I think the more we try to fill our heads with music, podcasts, Netflix, social media, sports, news, or whatever your drug of choice is, the less we will be at peace with ourselves. And therefore, the more 'lonely' we will feel.

Our loneliness is not one induced by too few friends, but by too much noise. Too many flashing lights and screaming sirens.

Take away the noise, the friends and the distraction and it's easy to feel the angst rush back in; a feeling we often call loneliness. When was the last time you sat in silence and meditated?

I live in Chicago, where I am *always* seeing *a lot* of people. And most of these people are distracting themselves. They have their earbuds in, their head sunk onto their chest, gazing into their device. Or maybe they're tourists, snapping a steady stream of photos and selfies just so they can look back on that time they went to Chicago and took a crapload of pictures.

Why are we so discontent to be where we are? With the people we are with? What are you so scared of missing online that is not present where you are?

I'm tired of the angst social media has created in my life along with most of my contemporaries. We are more distant from ourselves, more reserved from those around us, more polished online than in person, and we are very very lonely. Social media creates and plants within us desires we didn't previously have. It's a cruel loop.

Perhaps the way to escape the New Loneliness is to trim down the input we take. Turn your phone off and go for a walk.

Don't take a picture of it.

Pray.

Talk to yourself.

Think.

Talk to a friend.

Don't take a picture of your hangout.

Have any of my Christian friends actually obeyed Psalm 46:10, or have you just posted it to Instagram?

"*Be still and know that I am God.*"

DEAR INTERNET,
today they just send nudes.

I just got back from a week in the mountains with my beloved children. I'm a youth pastor without any kids of my own, so when I talk about "my kids," I mean these teens and tweens whom I love with all my heart. We had a phenomenal trip, but the more time I spend with them, the more my heart breaks as I get to peer deeper into the culture in which they dwell.

And that culture is shaped in large part by you, Internet.

When I was in high school not that long ago, girls would wear the sports jacket of the boy they adored. They would fill their notebooks with his name, and perhaps her own name followed by his last name.

But today, to catch the eye of the boy she likes, a teenage girl will just send naked pictures via Snapchat or any other myriad apps designed for just that kind of lewd communication. Today, in order to impress her boy, she has to strip down and reveal her body just to keep a guy interested for longer than a few minutes.

So thank you for that, Internet. Thank you for disrobing my kids just to let them feel a little bit of value or beauty. Thank you for putting into their pockets unlimited connectivity and unrestricted access to the world.

Thanks to you, I walked in on three of my 8th graders talking about sexual acts I didn't know about until well into my college years. So thanks for spreading your wealth of information.

Thank you for stripping down and beating to a pulp any hope my kids had of holding an attention span longer than 14 seconds. They have become addicted to your apps and videos like a drug addict to his beloved heroin.

When we first arrived at the cabin, we made a rule that during group activities, discussions and meals, your phones were to be nowhere near you. That rule lasted about five minutes before my kids were pasted to their screens once again, unable to enjoy the company of the friends and leaders present with them.

And I know this is no accident, dear Internet. I have read article after article about how you rake in the profits the more time my kids and I spend on your apps. Not only do you beckon them back to your beloved apps with push notifications and unique sound effects, you want to keep them there as long as possible. You have countless little algorithms in place to ensure that my kids will whittle away their time (aka, lives) glued to your precious screens, unable to break from their devices longer than a few minutes.

Unable to sit in silence, their minds unstimulated.
Unable to be with their closest friends in a mountain cabin for a week.
Unable to read a book (those heavy paper things) because 'it's too boring.'

You hide behind the cloak of 'connecting us with our friends,' when just the opposite is true. You don't want to connect us; you want our time. Because the more time we spend on your slice of the web, the more money *you* make.

Dear Internet, you are heartless and cold; a vacuum cleaner sucking not only our time but our money as well. You don't see us or feel warmth; you only see dollar signs and addictive triggers in our brain chemicals.

My kids are less healthy because you have glued them to beds and couches.

My kids are less secure in themselves because you flood them with images of far away models flaunting as much skin as Instagram will allow.

My kids are less at peace because you have programmed them to crave your constant stimulation and to wonder who has contacted them in the last 3 minutes.

My kids don't see their bodies as things of value; they see them as a means to some kind of cheap digital affection.

My kids are more exposed, not only to sexual and pornographic content, but violent and gory images as well. One of my students is addicted to looking at snuff films and pictures of humans who had died brutal deaths. Did he wake up one day and decide to look at these? Or were they served to him on one of your popular websites?

You may have done a lot of good for the world, but most of what I see is destructive and uninhibited. You don't care about the souls of my kids, you care about dollar bills. Perhaps if you were only aware of just how much damage I've seen you do in the lives of my students, you'd at least try to make an effort to improve things.

Please leave my kids alone and stop berating them with your addictive tactics and ruthless dopamine stimulation. I love them more than you ever will, so the least you could do is make an effort to change.
...or just go die.

YOU MUST TALK TO YOUR KIDS ABOUT SEX.

my dad gave me The Talk in a Chinese restaurant

My dad gave me The Talk in a Chinese restaurant when I was 8 years old.

I was playing in a little league game and after our victory my dad took me to lunch and gave me The Talk. I have discovered that most of my students' parents never gave them The Talk at all and that breaks my heart.

Worse, many parents give such little preparation to their children that some experience sexual abuse and no one finds out until they're in their 20's and it finally explodes, all because their parents never opened up these channels of dialogue or created a space for their children to talk about these things.

If your role as a parent is to lead your kids into wisdom, to scaffold their transition into the real world, shouldn't one of your most important duties be to explain the beauty of intimacy and the danger of unhealthy attachment? Danger doesn't necessarily mean something is bad: Fire is both beautiful and dangerous.

Sex is beautiful and dangerous.

Like a stallion whinnying to run free, handing your child the reins involves built-up trust, and the willingness to say, "Wow! What a beauty! Be careful now. Control him and he will serve you well."

I wonder if these parents think they're doing their kids a favor by sheltering them from the dirty, dirty S-Word, and that their lives will be better if they never discover it. The problem is, all kids will find out about sex. Parents are the ones who can decide how and when. If I ever have kids, I intend to get the first word in before the world has a chance to. When parents decide not to teach their kids about sex, the world is more than happy to.

I remember being in middle school at a friend's house, watching MTV in his bedroom (which I was not allowed to do at home; nor could I, since we grew up cable-less). I vividly remember a commercial in which a famous rapper spoke directly to the camera: "Remember dudes, no matter how banging her body is, you gotta strap up. Don't risk it."

I recall seeing that commercial through the filter of the wisdom my parents had already implanted in me. My dad gave me that first talk over Egg Drop Soup, but many more followed it. There were check-ins and updates and open communication about sexuality. Because of my parents, I could see a commercial like that and interpret the message as worldly more than biblical (or true), even if I wouldn't have used those words.

I can't imagine how many others in my generation saw the same commercial but without the preparation. Perhaps that commercial was the closest thing they ever had to The Talk, so to them, the only sexual ethic was to not get or give an STD and you're good.

Strap up and you've done the right thing. Simple.

I was recently talking to someone about this and he said his parents never gave him the talk either. He's my age. "Why is it," I asked, "that some parents don't give that talk to their kids? If I ever have children, we're going to be talking about it constantly!"

"Simple," he said. "Shame. Their parents probably didn't give them the talk, so the idea of bringing it up to their kids seems terrifying. Or they have some sort of trauma or sexual wound, so talking about it with their kids would be incredibly painful. So they just don't."

But you know what happens when those children grow up and pass through puberty with the internet as their primary sexual education? They go out and create their own sexual wounds, passing them down to their own children. The cycle continues from generation to generation as long as parents live by fear more than wisdom and love for their children.

If it seems like I'm being especially hard on such parents, it's because I am. After being a youth pastor for three years, and now a teacher for one, I have seen that the majority of parents are failing. Whether they are drug addicts, abusive, apathetic, or simply not trying very hard, I have developed a thin patience for parents who don't care for their own children. Sure, they all *say* they do, but where is the evidence?

It's easy to tell when a student has loving parents. Not only are they far more well-behaved, but they seem to operate from a sort of comfortable confidence which can only come from a place of having received love. But when they don't receive rich, quality love at home, and their sex education is Xzibit telling them to strap up (or worse: pornography), where do you think they'll turn to find that love?

For this reason, I adamantly place "The Talk" with your children under the umbrella of loving them. You can't say you love them and then shrug and say 'they'll figure it out for themselves.'

In the film *Lady Bird*, when the eponymous protagonist asks her mother about sex, her mom reluctantly shivers and falls silent. She wiggles her way out of the conversation as quickly as possible and as you can guess, the high schooler ends up losing her virginity to a jerk. "You'll have plenty of un-special sex in your life," he tells her immediately after revealing that she wasn't, actually, his first.

Is this really what we want for our kids? To be throwing their bodies around to a plethora of suitors who may not even see them as special? Perhaps a scarier question to ask is, do most parents even care enough about the bodies and souls of their children to prepare them for these situations?

Teach your kids or the world will teach them. Love your kids or the world will love them—and this love is hollow, foolish and destructive.

WHY I AM PRO-LIFE

this may sound a little extreme, so I want to begin with an apology...

Abortion kills twice. It kills the body of the baby and it kills the conscience of the mother. Abortion is profoundly anti-women. Three quarters of its victims are women: Half the babies and all the mothers.　　　　　　　　　-*Mother Teresa of Calcutta*

I want to begin with an apology. Far too often, Pro-Life people come out swinging *against* Pro-Choice people, rather than loving them and offering sympathetic dialogue. We have condemned mothers who have gone through with abortions instead of coming alongside them and helping them find other options. And for that, I am sorry.

This post is not intended to put down or shame anyone. In fact, quite the opposite. It seems ironic to me that someone claiming to be Pro-Life would resort to tactics of shaming, belittling, and hating other humans. Talk about a self-defeating argument. I've seen far too many "interview videos" where the Pro-Life interviewer poses questions to intentionally and sarcastically embarrass the interviewee, so I'll do my best to avoid that tone.

Instead, I want to simply give some reasons for why I personally continue to hold my Pro-Life stance, as it applies to all humans on earth, whether they agree with me or not. So please do not take my reasoning as any kind of assault or tactical maneuver *against* you, because that is not my goal.

It's also worth mentioning that as a Christian, I am aware that I write heavily from a Christian worldview, and therefore some of my reasons are based on scripture and God's love for all people.

God Loves Everyone & Hates Death

So I think the place to start is there. In God's love. He loves the unborn children just as much as He loves the mothers in whom they dwell who are debating what to do with their *surprise*. He loves the Liberal and Conservative alike. He loves the woman who would never dream of having an abortion, and He loves the woman who has already had two dozen.

And because of this love, not a single person is meant to be wasted.

God hates death.

We see this in the life of Jesus, as every time one of His friends died, He either wept or retreated to a lonely place. God did not make us with the hopes that we would all die, but that we would all have life and life to the fullest, but death is the direct result of sin.

Josh Howerton points out that while Jesus laid down His life for all, abortion does the opposite: "Abortion is the evil reverse-image of the gospel. Instead of 'I'll die for you,' it says, 'You die for me.'"

The Language of Abortion

Many of my Pro-Choice friends contend that the heart of the issue is really about deciphering where personhood begins. They contend that the tissue inside a pregnant woman is not, in fact, a person, but simply a collection of

432

cells which will *eventually* grow into a person. Yet because I believe the Bible is true, I look to it for the answer (And yes, I realize this will do little to persuade my non-Christian friends but like I said, I'm explaining why *I* believe what I do).

David writes in Psalm 51, "In sin did my mother conceive me." He does not say that she conceived a lump of tissue which later became me; he says that his *personhood* was developed in the womb.

Throughout scripture, we see writers employ phrases such as "She was with child." It doesn't say that she was with a *fetus*, but with an actual child. If this argument is too semantic, look no further than the media and their liberal use of language describing pregnancy.

When a celebrity is pregnant, she has a "baby bump;" but when the child is unwanted, it is referred to as a fetus, cells, tissue, or just a part of the woman's body. The language used is malleable depending on what the reporter wants to convey.

Another common argument is that the fetus is not an individual human as long as it is dependent on its mother's body for life. Yet how many of us could sustain ourselves sans parents at the age of 1? or 2? 3? 4? If a child is born with health defects and needs machines to survive its first weeks, can we kill it because it is not independent of its life support?

I do not believe there is a justified age or level of dependency at which ending a life is permissible.

Pro-Life Versus Pro-Birth

There is a difference between being Pro-Life and simply Pro-Birth. Many people put a lot of effort into getting the baby born, but care very little about what happens after delivery. Being Pro-Life involves a plethora of multi-faceted issues, such as battling the death penalty or doctor-assisted suicide. Someone who cares about fetuses but wants to "bomb the hell out of terrorists' families" is not Pro-Life. I believe God loves all life, not *just* the babies in the womb.

This, however, is easier said than done.

I think Pro-Lifers have a responsibility to work toward creating alternatives for mothers in crisis, such as making adoption, pre- and postnatal health care, and emotional support more readily available. If we really care about these children, we should do more than simply protest Planned Parenthood, but take active steps toward being the solution, even going so far as to adopt unwanted children into our own families. When we claim to be Pro-Life, but do little to support the continuation of that *life*, we are defeating our own stance.

Abortion is Racist

From its inception, the abortion industry has targeted minority groups. Whether or not Margaret Sanger was a racist is a hotly debated topic, but regardless, she said some highly disturbing things. In spite of what Stranger (or any Pro-Choice person) actually believed, historic numbers have seen abortion target minority groups.

Abort73 points out that due to abortion, the black population has dropped 30% from 1973 to 2012. It also points out that in 2014, abortion killed more black humans than all other causes combined. It concludes, "To put it bluntly, abortion has thinned the black community in ways the Ku Klux Klan could have only dreamed of."

Again, the call lands on the shoulders of Pro-Life people to rise up and offer alternatives. Abortion clinics are incredibly easy to find in lower-income urban centers, but where have we offered alternatives? How often have we come alongside single pregnant mothers and offered our hands instead of pointing fingers and hurling shame?

I am not a racist, nor is God, and if we want to encourage flourishing for all of our brothers and sisters of all skin colors, we must speak out against abortion and offer help wherever we can.

Rape, Poverty, and Disability

Conversations about abortion often lead to a slew of hypothetical questions, one of the biggest being *What if the mother was raped?* Aside from the fact that less than 1% of abortions are due to rape or incest,[23] what I am about to say may sound extreme.

---

23 www.operationrescue.org/about-abortion/abortions-in-america/

Even in the case of rape, I think the mother should carry the baby to birth.

If we truly believe that God loves *all* life, we must believe He loves it regardless of how it was created. Just because something horrible occurred, does that mean something beautiful cannot come of it? I believe God is in the business of redemption, and loves to take hideous, ugly things and turn them beautiful. It is easy to find accounts from women who were raped but chose to keep their child, and not one of them regrets it.

Similar arguments that arise have to do with poverty and disability in the child. The simplest question to ask is, would you consider the same solution if the child were already born? Would we try to kill a 5-year-old simply because his family was poor, or because he had Down Syndrome? These sorts of questions all loop back to the nature of the fetus itself, as addressed above. If we believe the being inside the pregnant woman is actually a person, we cannot justify any reason for its termination.

Conclusion

I realize that this brief post is far from conclusive and will probably do little to change anyone's mind. I hope to have conveyed some of the major reasons why I hold the stance I do on abortion, though I realize it is a complex and emotionally-loaded topic. I do not shame or condemn anyone who believes or acts differently than I, but I hope that at the very least I have made you think.

I also hope that this post will spring some of my fellow dormant Pro-Lifers into action, not to fight the Pro-Choice agenda, but to offer love and aid to those in the throes of crisis. I think the way to end abortion is not to merely battle the entity itself, but to construct healthy and fruitful alternatives.

HOW TO QUIT

porn, drugs, sex and doughnuts

WHY I'M THE D-BAG IN THE GYM

a quiet voice whispered to me, "Ethan, you do the same thing."

I like to lift weights in the evening. It's a more subdued atmosphere with a unique energy to it. Tonight I was at 24 Hour Fitness going through a chest routine when a cute girl caught my eye. I watched as she walked over to two guys on the bench press, one was evidently her boyfriend. I was about to return to my exercise when I noticed in the mirror that he was yelling at her.

I paused the music banging through my headphones.

From where I was, I could hear: "Get the fuck away from me! Leave me alone!" He then returned to spotting his buddy on the bench press, as if she was a nuisance who had finally buzzed away.

I continued observing and the exact same thing repeated itself several more times. She quietly approached him to ask a question or show him something on her phone, only to be met with, "No! Leave us alone! Get out of here!" She sunk her head and retreated.

Anger welled up inside of me, and I silently calculated how hard I could throw a punch in the middle of chest day (fellow lifters will understand).

As she returned again to her boyfriend, only to be met with anger and the feeling that she was bothering him, I began praying for the opportunity to interject. I didn't want to fight anyone, I just wanted to tell her that she deserved better; that there are men out there who don't treat women like mosquitoes. I was furious.

How could a man treat a woman so expendably? How could he steal all the benefits of a girlfriend, yet tell her to f-off when he didn't want her? How could he objectify her in such a pragmatic way?

It was in the midst of my anger in the gym that a silent voice spoke to me. He said, "Ethan, you do the same thing."

I resisted this thought. The thought that perhaps, when no one is looking, when the door is closed, I am the same as him. But the Lord persisted.

I am a porn addict.

I employ the language common to many substance users: That I am *presently* in the throes of battle with my poison of choice (Regardless of how long I've been free of it), rather than assuming a triumphalist attitude that I have somehow *beaten* my addiction and now live free of it.

There in the gym, I was humbled as Bible verses sunk in in the most piercing way.

Why do you look at the speck of sawdust in your brother's eye and pay no attention to the plank in your own eye? For in the same way you judge others, you will be judged, and with the measure you use, it will be measured to you.[1]

In the dark of my room, I too have taken women when I wanted, and left them when I was finished, shooing them away like fruit flies from a melon. I too have objectified and used these digital mistresses for my own pragmatic gain. My sins are more secretive though, allowing me to polish a chromed veneer to the public while I crumble behind closed doors.

There in the gym, my resistance slowed and I humbly understood what the Lord was saying. If I condemn this boy for his actions, yet do the same thing when eyes are turned away, what right do I have to judge him?

If he is condemned then I am as well.

The Lord knows my sins, yet for some ridiculous reason, has removed them from me. He has washed me spotless of my iniquities. He loves this dude in the gym too, and understanding this is the root of showing grace.

I've been reading Philip Yancey's latest book, *Vanishing Grace,* and have been simultaneously broken and amped up at realizing the depths of the love God has for us. For me.

But tonight, this concept of grace put skin on and abused his girlfriend in the gym. Tonight I was forced to look into a mirror and extend grace to someone who does not deserve it, just as it has been extended to me.

---

[1] Matthew 7:2-3

If I am to compare myself to someone, it should be Christ—the image of perfection and love. The ground is level before His cross and I am no better than the abusive boyfriend, the rapist, or even the murderer.

Tonight I joined in the chorus with the Apostle Paul as we bellowed, "Christ Jesus came into the world to save sinners—and I am the worst of them all."

Tonight I am once more grateful for the gospel of grace.

Tonight I am grateful for Jesus: That He died for abusive boyfriends and porn users alike, and that He walked out of His grave, so that we someday may do the same.

THE QUIET ANESTHESIA (PART 1)

I didn't cry for seven years.

I cannot count the number of worship services I've stood through unmoved. Others around me were weeping, dancing, or shouting their passionate cries to the Lord while I stood there wishing I felt something.

Anything.

The Catechism states that the chief end of man is to glorify God and enjoy Him forever, but most of the time, if I'm honest, there has been little to no enjoyment of Him. In fact, in the midst of my addiction to pornography, there was often no enjoyment of anything at all.

I've been thinking about this post for a while, and how exactly I want to say this. Because what I have found to be one of the absolute worst effects of porn is that it numbs me to reality. To the good and the bad. It files down the sharpened points of agony when suffering comes into my life, but it also curtails the heights of joy when there is reason to rejoice.

I feel like men and women turn to porn because something is lacking in their lives. They want to escape the bad and painful bits, but end up escaping the good too.

Sometimes it would be so bad that I could not enjoy sunsets
or hikes in the mountains
or board games with friends
or sitting by the sea
or any of the small things that simply enrich our lives
because my mind was elsewhere.
It was as if the volume was turned down on reality.

It's similar to the way C.S. Lewis described grief:

> At other times it feels like being mildly drunk or concussed. There is a
> sort of invisible blanket between the world and me. I find it hard to
> take in what anyone says. Or perhaps, hard to want to take it in. It is so
> uninteresting.[2]

I didn't cry for seven years.

Not because I resisted it by any means. The tears just never came. My wells
were empty. My emotions had evaporated.

I even wondered, in the throes of my addiction, if a family member or dear
friend were to die, if I would have cried. Or if I'd be the one at the funeral,
sitting stoically silent, my face dry as the western plains.

Addiction is *that* powerful.

Even a 'non-chemical' addiction such as pornography has the ability to
rewire our brains to the extent that we don't feel. (And of course, any
learned person knows that there are *plenty* of neuro-chemicals involved in a
pornography addiction.)

In David's great psalm of repentance after he had committed adultery with
Bathsheba, Psalm 51, he continually calls for God to return and awaken
emotion within him. He prays, "Let me hear joy and gladness...Restore to
me the joy of your salvation." Part of repentance is returning to a delight
in the Lord; it is also mourning the places we have grieved Him.

---

[2] C.S. Lewis, *A Grief Observed*

When I look at the person of Jesus, I see the polar opposite of numbness. I see someone who was entirely alive to His emotions, the full spectrum. I see a man who wept at the passing of his dear friend. In the Christian world, I often hear the verse thrown around as a bit of trivia: *Do you know the shortest verse in the Bible?*

Jesus wept.

Do we ever take time to think about the implications of these two words?

God wept.

God…..cries.

If we are to be like Jesus, then we are to be alive to our emotions.

Seeking to escape the hard times and numb the pain is not what God wants in us. The enemy may lure us in with the promise of a pain-free life, but what ends up happening is reality becomes dimmed.

To be like God is to embrace the reality around us with the emotions He has wired into us, not to escape it. I picture Jesus on the mountain, crying out to the Father for guidance. I see Him in the temple courts, fiery with rage at injustice. And there He is in the garden, nervous and terrified of the suffering He is about to go through.

And as He hangs on the cross, shattered and dying, He is offered a drink to ease the pain. This cocktail was designed to reduce the agony of those suffering torture, so they could slip into death with some amount of comfort.

But He turned it down.

Jesus refused to partake in anything that would reduce His experience, the good and the bad, in life and in death.

Saint Irenaeus said that "the glory of God is man fully alive."

Jesus was fully alive. From the moment he emerged from Mary's womb til' the blood dripped from His toes onto the dirt beneath the cross, I see a man who embraced every ounce of His life, and continues to from His place on high.

To embrace pornography is to escape life.

So let us cling to Jesus. Let us cling to the One who gives to each of us *life, and life to the fullest.*

PORN MAKES YOU NUMB (PART 2)

if there is one thing which unites all of humanity, it's addiction.

You've been there. We all have.

Regardless of which addiction has taken you as its prisoner, you've experienced the numbing agent it provides. My pastor in Chicago once said that if there is one thing which unites all of humanity, it's addiction.

In the words of Saint Peter (and Bob Dylan), we are all slaves to something. We are all the proverbial dog returning to his vomit. Eventually you become used to the flavor because at least your stomach is being filled with *something.*

We tend to look at the more blatant effects of a pornography addiction, like the marriages it ruins and the relationships it alienates; we look at how it fuels global sex trafficking or creates highly unrealistic expectations for how a human should look. But we overlook one of the most basic and common effects of pornography: Desensitization.

I was once on a spontaneous date in California with a beautiful woman which ended up going well. Very well.

She and I took off from In-N-Out Burger through the serpentine mountainous road outside the city and found a field from which to stargaze in the crisp spring darkness. It was nearing midnight and the clouds only let us see half the stars in the sky.

In other words, it was a really, really beautiful date.

We were lying on the 'emergency blanket' I keep in my trunk for such situations, when she rolled onto her elbows, looked at me and told me she wanted to kiss me.

Then she did.

I remember the thought running through my mind as it happened: *I feel like I should be feeling more than this. I feel like I should be more present. More blown away by this moment.*

Earlier today I was talking with a college friend on the phone. He recounted times he had held his girlfriend as she wept, but he was removed. Detached. Emotionless. He said he felt nothing watching the woman he loved weep about what weighed on her heart. He was physically holding her, but he was somewhere else.

As he described the moment, he laid the blame for this removal from reality directly at the feet of pornography.

As men (and women I'm sure), we are robbed from much of the ability to feel feelings when we struggle with an addiction. It removes us from ourselves. One writer describes this as 'the man who walks beside himself.'[3]

We are experiencing our lives from somewhere outside, rather than from within, from our center.

The more I learn about feelings, the more I realize how many of us are uncomfortable with our feelings. As I've said before, I once went nearly a decade without crying. The more I grow, the more emotional of a man I become. And I've found this to be more in line with how God intended us to be: He did not create us to be binary robots with no emotions or impassioned reactions to our lives. The God of the Bible is one who is adamantly alive to His emotions, the entire spectrum.

We are quick to run to the lighter emotions of laughter and happiness, but anything that dives beneath the surface of weight or reality we are quick to wash away.

---

[3] George Hobson, *The Episcopal Church, Homosexuality, and the Context of Technology*

If your girlfriend leaves you and the pain is too much to bear, are you going to patiently *sit* in that feeling, or try to quell it with your vice of choice? For an addict, the choice is obvious, even if we don't want it to be.

The problem with using substances (pornography, alcohol or otherwise) to escape the painful feelings is that, yes, they make the lows less low, but they also make the highs less high.

They rob us of the ability to deeply take in the power of beauty.

They may take the tears away, but how often are those tears necessary to experience life well? What kind of son wants to sit in his mother's funeral with dry eyes? What kind of Christian wants to hear a powerful representation of the gospel and be unmoved? I certainly did not want to lie in that starlit field in California holding a beautiful woman and *feel nothing*.

Being fully human means being fully awake to our emotions, not distanced from them. God never intended to give us shortcuts when we grieve a loss or feel rejected. Nor did He want us to pacify the beautiful feelings of falling in love or watching your son take his first steps.

But pornography robs us of these beautiful moments by removing us from the present moment. It takes us to a place where pain and rejection don't exist, but neither does beauty or intimacy.

Yesterday my church was performing baptisms and I was asked to share a few words beforehand. I stood up and, strange as it may sound, talked about a personal hero of mine, Nabeel Qureshi. I had just found out the day before that Qureshi had finally died at the young age of 34 after a long battle with cancer. He left behind a wife and daughter, but he is now reunited with another daughter they had lost to a miscarriage, and most importantly, with his savior Jesus Christ.

I had followed Nabeel's videos the past year as his face and hair grew thinner and he became emaciated from his treatment. His last video update was an announcement that he was being moved to palliative care in order to make him more comfortable until he slipped away. Even now a lump rises in my throat.

As I spoke before my church and recounted the story of the brother we lost, a similar lump rose. My eyes filled with tears and I had to stop talking.

"Yesterday, our family lost a member..."

Silence filled the room.

"...but......but today we celebrate new members coming into it."

I then entered the water with one of my middle schoolers and we baptized him. The beauty of the action is unspeakable. Something sacred happens as we observe certain family members moving on while new ones are ushered in.

And you know what? That moment choking up in front of my church was not *bad*. It did not make me feel like less of a man, nor was it painful, in the negative sense. It was a beautiful moment which I was able to experience in the presence of my community and my God, and if there is one thing the enemy wants to take from us, it's that.

It is these moments of intense beauty which get stolen from us the more we numb ourselves with pornography. The enemy doesn't want us to feel. I think he would be much happier if he could rob us of our ability to feel and worship God with a healthy and full emotional life.

But may we be like Christ, whose rich and vibrant emotional life should teach all of us to feel things to the fullest without taking shortcuts and numbing the pain. May we suffer well and rejoice well. May we grieve deeply and laugh loudly. May we loose the chains which keep our emotions subdued and drugged in the dungeons of our souls.

DISCOVERING THE HIDDEN ROOTS OF ADDICTION
addiction begins long before you actually act out.

Several months ago, some of my friends pointed out a subconscious habit of mine. I was teaching Sunday School one morning and afterward, two friends of mine started making fun of my hands.

I had known for years that I have a problem with biting my nails, and have halfheartedly been trying to quit. That Sunday morning, my friends brought something to my attention that I had been doing during the entire lesson. It seemed insignificant at the time, but as time went on I realized that it was key to breaking the habit.

They pointed out that I was feeling my fingernails with my other fingers. I vehemently denied it as they began doing the "live long and prosper" hand sign from Star Trek with each pair of fingers rubbing against its neighbor, exaggerating my habitual finger-feeling.

Over the ensuing weeks, they repeatedly pointed out how often I felt my fingernails without realizing it. I continually denied it until I made a harrowing discovery. I happened to glance at a triptych my brother shot of a workout photoshoot last summer and made a fatal discovery.

Do you see it?

I sent that to my friends and they laughed. It was enlightening to suddenly be made aware of something I have unwittingly been doing which has contributed to my nail biting. It works like this: I unconsciously made a habit of feeling my nails with their adjacent finger, and when the edge was too rough or sharp, I'd end up bringing it to my mouth for a nibble.

Gross, I know. (Did you know that biting your nails is technically a form of auto-cannibalism? Eating yourself??)

My friend recommended that I buy a nail file rather than clippers, as it would help create smooth edges all around, thus when I felt them, there would be no sharp edges and therefore no need to bite them.

In order to quit my habit, I had to examine what happens before the action itself in order to see where the act stemmed from. Addressing that root made it much easier to quit biting my nails.

This solution I discovered can inform how we address more insidious habits and addictions. Look at a pornography and masturbation problem: By the time you've reached the point where you're acting out, it's typically too late to stop. You need to observe what was happening the previous hours and maybe even days leading up to that point in order to identify patterns of addiction.

With porn specifically, the roots are manifold and diverse. It could be any number of factors, including shame, inadequacy, stress, loneliness, wounds, and so on. It has become evident to me that when I'm in public, what I do with my eyes heavily affects the behavior which follows when I get home later. If I allow my eyes to linger on a beautiful woman, that has direct consequences later in the lonely hours. If I neglect to fill my mind with Scripture and choose to surf Facebook instead, this directly affects what happens in my thoughts throughout the day.

Often these early stages can go undetected and we unconsciously fall back into the same patterns and wonder why we can't just quit the action. It can help to make a mental (or written) inventory of everything that happened that day. Doing this consistently can help uncover hidden patterns and things which act as triggers for us to get drunk, high, and the like. An addiction doesn't start the second you bring the bottle to your lips, or open up your laptop; it started hours or days before that moment.

Solomon addressed this method of prevention, rather than reaction, in Scripture. In Proverbs 5, he commands his listener to not even go down the street where the adulteress lives. He doesn't just say don't go by her *house,* he says to not even go down the *street* where her house is. He wrote that, knowing the closer we allow ourselves to get to temptation, the harder it is to deny it. But if you can prevent it earlier than later, it's easier to navigate the mores of desire and addiction.

So plan ahead. Don't wait until you are in the midst of your addiction to look for a way out. Return to the root of your habit or addiction and dig it out. Just as I had to do with my nail biting dilemma, figure out what *really* causes the action and start there. Figure out how you can 'smooth out the edges,' so to speak. Eliminate the earlier patterns and habits which lead to acting out later on.

Most often, breaking a bad habit requires instituting new habits to replace them. For instance, I need to file my nails at least twice a week (new habit) to keep them smooth enough for me not to feel them and then bite them (old habit).

For sinful habits, it means creating patterns of worship and thought-formation to replace former thought patterns. This is the idea behind one of my favorite words, *liturgy.* Liturgy basically refers to a formative pattern which shapes our habits and thoughts *toward* God, transforming our minds which, by nature, are oriented *away from* Him.

For example, making a habit of filling our minds with scripture every morning will slowly replace lustful thoughts of body parts with goodness and truth. It will daily remind you how much you are loved and forgiven, replacing feelings of shame and insecurity, which often lead to acting out sexually or with substances.

Transforming your mind, as Paul put it in Romans 12, requires consistent patterns and habits, not a one-time event. There is so much to be said about habits, liturgy, and thought formation which I'll have to save for another time!

Fighting any kind of addiction is difficult. It requires persistence and most of the time, feeling like you're being defeated. But that doesn't mean it should continue to thrive in your life and run rampant like a western wildfire. Fortunately as Christians, we believe there is grace when we return to our habits and forgiveness when we screw up. Just as I still catch myself bringing my fingers to my teeth, recovery is a journey, not a light switch.

May we be people who work to identify the roots of our addictions and cut them off at the source. May we strive to live in freedom, accepting grace when we fail. And may we institute new habits in order to do away with the old, for the new has come and the old is gone!

PORN AND THE DOUGHNUT MAN
Jesus doesn't just want you to quit looking at porn.

I used to work at Chicago's #1-doughnut-shop-4-years-running and I ate far more doughnuts than any human should.

Sometimes I would get to close up the shop, which included one of my favorite parts of working there (aside from…did I mention free doughnuts?). The location had a little window which opened to the sidewalk, where a constant stream of pedestrians passed by. In the last 15 minutes or so of business every day, I started boxing up the doughnuts in 6 packs to give them away.

There were few things I loved more than popping open the window and leaning out to yell "FREE DOUGHNUTS!" to people as they passed by.

"Wait…they're really free?" was the most common response.

I shoved the box into their hand and their day was instantly made. Their face brightened and they were *bursting* to tear that box open and dig in.

One evening I was closing up shop and slid the window open to see a man digging through the trash can a few yards from me. Without hesitation, I held up the big box of Chicago's favorite doughnuts and said, "Hey man, I've got some fresh doughnuts for ya!"

He looked at me, shook his head, and tossed out a limp *'nah.'* Then he went back to picking through the garbage.

I was blown away.

Who, when offered the best doughnuts in the city, turns them down in favor of rummaging through a public trash can??

Not a minute later I realized I had just witnessed the gospel. I saw myself in the homeless man.

I would be remise not to mention C.S. Lewis' famous quote here:

> It would seem that Our Lord finds our desires not too strong, but too weak. We are half-hearted creatures, fooling about with drink and sex and ambition when infinite joy is offered us, like an ignorant child who wants to go on making mud pies in a slum because he cannot imagine what is meant by the offer of a holiday at the sea. We are far too easily pleased.[4]

I realized that I am constantly trying to find my own path to pleasure. I am always trying to satisfy myself, be it with pornography, girls, money, etc. The reason we can't simply sit and let the Lord satisfy us is that we don't trust Him. We don't think He'll really come through for us, therefore, we feel this need to provide our own satisfaction…which never really works, does it?

Part of the problem is this: Whenever I have messed up, with pornography for example, I immediately begin to pile the shame and guilt upon myself.

---

[4] C.S. Lewis, *The Weight of Glory and Other Addresses*

However, I don't think Jesus is standing there wagging a finger at me the way a master stands over her dog after he pooped on the rug again. In fact, I don't think He even wants us to feel *bad* about screwing up again and again and again and again.

But I do think He is sad for us.

Instead of condemning us, I think Jesus is a few yards away hanging out a window offering us free doughnuts while we dig through the trash.

He has so much more to give us, so He stands there and watches us dig through the garbage, hoping to find something of worth. *Maybe this year I'll find that job that will really set my life up right…Or maybe next week I'll garner the courage to talk to that cute girl at the coffee shop. Then…THEN I'll feel whole!*

He wants so badly for us to see Him, and what He is offering us. Jesus addressed this Himself in John 6:35-36:

> Jesus answered, "I am the bread of life. Whoever comes to Me will never hunger, and whoever believes in Me will never thirst. But as I told you, you have seen Me and still you do not believe."

We keep hearing Him calling to us and return to sticking our noses in the trashcans. We can't imagine that Jesus could possibly have something better for us than what we could scrounge up for ourselves.

Jesus doesn't want you to quit looking at porn, or whatever your habit of choice is. He doesn't want you to simply resist this one urge so much that you are beating yourself up. He wants us to realize that the pleasures He is offering us make everything we could find for ourselves look like trash.

When we accept that He has pleasures stored up for us beyond our wildest dreams, we will no longer *want* to return to those old habits we've been trying so hard to kill. They'll simply fall away like powerless dead leaves.

They'll start tasting like garbage.

THE UNBEARABLE LIGHTNESS OF PORNOGRAPHY

Even pornstars wake up with bad breath.

I'm 26 and single, but not for lack of trying. Several months ago I met a girl in a coffee shop and we had instant chemistry. We sat in the same booth from 10pm until the shop closed at 1am, supposedly getting work done but really just talking late into the night.

I came home that night and couldn't sleep. The creative and emotional side of myself was awakened, and on nights like those, it seems like every sentence from a poetic podcast and every note of a song is heightened exponentially. Something about the way this other human sees the world makes me come so much more alive.

That night I felt like I had known her for decades.
She made me feel nostalgic.
I wanted her, bad.

Despite the apparent feelings of nearness and intimacy I felt with this girl, in reality, I had known her for three hours. My mind was high on the possibility of what may someday be a reality. I didn't know the secret, intimate bits of her, but that didn't stop me from making them up for myself. As time passed, I realized I didn't really know her as well as I thought (Naw, *really??*). What had seemed like such immediate intimacy was really projection of myself, and what I wanted her to be like, into the mysterious parts of her person.

To be honest, she really just reminded me of someone I used to love. I had filled in all the pieces of her I didn't actually know so that in my mind, she was exactly what I was looking for.

Time will cure you of this.

The longer you get to know someone and their weaknesses and their small, icky bits and the nooks and crannies of their soul which reek of selfishness and ignorance, the more you realize the *realness* of their humanity; the weight of their brokenness.

Last night I was with some friends in a pool and had a revelation of sorts. We were splashing around and wrestling, 'drowning' each other, and just having a blast in the chlorinated water. It was in this small neighborhood pool that I realized the vast difference between real humans and the two-dimensional images of them which seem so arousing on a screen.

Every so often I'm reminded of this: How vastly different the people portrayed in pornography are from real, stinky, heavy human beings. It's a difference so large that mere language alone cannot convey the disparity between the two.

Pornography robs not only the actors of their humanity, but the viewer of theirs too.

Sometimes we think of pornography as a substitute for a real man or woman in your bedroom when you're alone at night, yet when you're actually in the presence of another person's body it is so unlike the two dimensional images that the two are not even comparable. The word 'substitute' implies that there is some similarity or correlation between the two, but in this situation, the two aren't even on the same planet.

Even pornstars wake up with bad breath.

My pastor once told me that "You're longing for this beautiful four-course meal of marital intimacy, but you've gone and acquired a taste for crap instead. It's literally like you're trying to fill yourself up on this handful of feces instead of this delectable, satiating meal of real love."

The more I think about it, the more I realize how weightless and flighty pornography is. It is faint and ethereal. Not only does a real human body have weight and smells and smoothness of skin and roughness of whiskers, but the intense presence of other humans is richly intimidating. Being around friends in person carries with it weight which runs deeper than a mere sensory, voyeuristic perception.

When we are with other people, we are, to some degree, exposed and watched in ways we never will be by our screen-centric relationships.

Every relationship is essentially an experiment in how real, raw and honest you can be in front of this other human.

One time someone asked me how I would describe "feeling the presence of God." I thought for a second and said, "It's like this. You know when you're in the same room as someone but you're both reading? You're not looking at them or hearing them or interacting with them in any way, but the room is still different because they are there and you are aware of it. The air shifts when they walk in or leave. That's how it is with God. There comes a point in solitude when you just become aware of His presence in a way you can't describe."

When we are starved for human contact of any form, we tend to try to find replacements. We try to make up for this lack of human intimacy by acquiring a taste for crap rather than pursuing deeper intimacy with others and with God.

As a single person it's easy to forget the rich beauty of being in community and the realness of being in the tangible presence of others.

One of the first times I realized this was when I went to see the film *Noah* in theaters with my friend Lila. I had spent the last year and a half getting to know her pretty intimately as a friend, but that night something seemed to shift. In my eyes, she was slipping from the friend zone into a place of deeper beauty and richness as a person because of how well I was coming to know her.

Now, Emma Watson starred in the film and she had long been a celebrity crush of mine. I would sometimes see films of hers and leave sad because of how beautiful she was and how I would never know her. That night when we sat down in the screening of *Noah,* I expected the same thing to happen. Yet when she came on screen I internally shrugged.

Because what does this two-dimensional character have on this beautiful woman seated next to me whom I've come to know at a deep level and who can actually love me back?

It wasn't her photogenic beauty or the measurements of her body that drew me to Lila, but the richness of pleasure I experienced just by being around her. In time I found myself wanting to be around her no matter what. Even if she grew old and saggy. Even if she got sick and all her hair fell out.

I just wanted to be with her.

But our eyes are deceptive and it's easy to forget the depth of this intimacy and how much more satisfying it is than simply looking at girls on screens and pleasing ourselves in isolation. How hollow!!

In many ways, I'm coming to see the work of God in our lives as one of unfolding us from ourselves. Lifting us up from being people who strive to pleasure ourselves into people who are patient. People who find true joy in the presence of others, in His presence.

May we be people who seek to please ourselves in the rich presence of others rather than the fleeting and imaginary presence of pornography. May we come to appreciate the weight of those around us in place of the unbearable lightness of distant 2-dimensional actors. May we pursue intimacy at all costs and retrain our taste buds to crave wholesome meals more than the flavor of feces.

DYING TO QUIT
he did a very stupid thing because he was turned on.

I recently wrapped up Stephen King's book *Duma Key*. It was a fantastic read and no one writes like King. He really is a master storyteller and managed to keep my attention through 700+ pages which flew by like a children's picture book.

The plot focuses on a man, Edgar, who suffered a construction accident which lost him his right arm and damaged his hips. As a result, his wife divorces him and he moves down to an island off Florida called Duma Key. Here, he finds that things are not as they seem and some ancient spirit which has lay dormant for decades has been stirred and begins oppressing the characters. She possesses people in some way and causes them to do destructive, murderous things against the protagonists and their families.

It makes a lot more sense when you're reading it.

In one scene, Edgar is sure his wife is about to be killed by their attorney, Tom Riley. Minutes later, the phone rings and he expects to hear the news that his ex-wife has been slain. However, the voice on the other end of the line is that of his former lover, in tears because she has just received news of Tom's death. He was in a car accident, but it was odd: He had driven straight into a brick wall. He was not intoxicated and there were no signs of foul play; he seemed to have just driven straight into a brick wall.

Edgar pieces the puzzle together: Tom was possessed by the evil sea spirit and sent on his way to kill his ex-wife. For a split second though, he had a glimpse of clarity and made the snap decision to veer his car into the wall rather than go through with the murder.

As I thought about this anecdote the past week, I realized there is a bit of wisdom we can glean from it as it pertains to sexual temptation. As a counter example, let's look at a much different episode from scripture.

In Mark 6, King Herod is throwing a big party with dancing, drinking, and revelry. He sees his niece dance and is so pleased with her dancing that he promises her anything, up to half his kingdom. She made the grotesque request for the head of John the Baptist on a platter, which he obliged. Growing up, I always interpreted this as a little 7-year-old girl doing some cute dance which tickled him and he made a rash vow.

However, when I looked into the passage more deeply, I realized a number of things. For one, his niece was probably a grown and developed young woman, and the type of dance she was doing was not that of a toddler at a family gathering. Put frankly, Herod was turned on by his niece, and in his trance of lust, made a promise to give her anything she desired.

It's easy to dismiss this event as disgusting and proclaim that we would never do anything *that* repulsive. But if you've ever been ensnared in a web of lust, you know the feeling of "I would give *anything*" to the object of your affection in order to satiate your desire. Hopefully not the incest part, but the offer of half his kingdom because of how blinded he was by his turned-on-ness.

Just like Tom Riley, Herod was in a trance, possessed by a force much larger than himself, only he was not able to break free and as a result, a prophet of the Lord was beheaded. When we are under the control of our sin, unable to break free, we will always wound others or ourselves.

In the fictitious account of Tom Riley, he was able to break free only for a few moments and save the lives of others, though it cost him his own life. I think this is what Jesus meant when He talked about chopping off various body parts if they cause us to sin.[5] It's better to suffer wounds on ourselves than to do damage to others while under the power of sin.

So what do we do with this?

As a porn addict, I can point to very specific instances where the trance lifted long enough for me to make a hard decision; to chop off the hand, so to speak. Shut the laptop and walk away.

If you're anything like me, you know what it's like to live under this fog for days at a time, and when it relents, we are able to catch a glimpse of clarity and make a decision to effect change. In college, I confessed my addiction to a friend and made the decision to turn over control of my phone to him. He put a passcode on it so I could not access the internet at all via my smartphone.

Years later, in a bold move of frustration at my struggle, I told my dad, who decided to pay for counseling and accountability software. Similarly, I occasionally take time away from Facebook, Twitter and Instagram by having a friend change my passwords.

There are times when, in the words of Sexaholics Anonymous, you have lost control and your life has become unmanageable. You may think you have autonomy over your struggle, yet there is a reason you keep returning to it like a dog returns to his vomit.

My urge to you, brothers and sisters, is to take advantage of those moments of clarity when the fog lifts and you're able to see clearly for a few minutes. Make the hard choices to swerve into the brick wall, or chop off the hand which causes you to sin. Make changes that will affect your actions when the trance returns and the fog settles over your mind once more and you are driven to act out.

Go to a meeting,
confess to a friend or parent,

---

[5] Matthew 5:30

put a password on your phone or laptop,
fellowship with other people who are in recovery,
install the software you keep putting off,
etc… (I'm sure there's something popping into your head right now. Do it.)

Addiction is a singular and inescapable focus on the object of your desire. You cannot make the decision to walk away from it when you are under its spell, so make the move that will prevent your fall *ahead* of time, rather than acting responsively.

Whether it's alcohol, sex, porn, drugs, or any other unhealthy habit, be proactive. Don't wait for the temptation to return before you take action because by that point, you will most definitely give in again. It is worth suffering a wound in order to save your life and the lives of others. After all, addiction does not just affect the life of the addict, but all those connected to him or her. Spouses, children, families, friends. Everyone suffers the longer we choose to dwell in our addictions.

So may we be people who, in moments of lucidity, can choose to make changes to our lives which will prevent our addictions from consuming us. May we make decisions in the light, rather than in darkness. May we act in wise activeness, rather than passive response, waiting for our addictions to magically drift away on their own. If it hasn't stopped on its own yet, chances are it's not going to.

But most of all, may we never forget the grace which is offered to us every time we give in to the trance of addiction. May we live with a constant awareness of Christ and all He has done for us that we may be free from the destructive power of sin.

A PASSION WASTED
"did he have passion?"

According to legend, when an Ancient Greek died, his friends and relatives did not examine his possessions or his wealth. They did not judge his life based on his merits, his achievements, or his social status. They asked only one question:

Did he have passion?

Whether or not this is historically true, I love the idea behind it. In a sense, it gave the man the freedom to fail. It gave him the liberty to attempt great things he was passionate about, and even if he failed, what mattered was that he tried at all; that he was passionate. It wasn't about the money he made or the legacy he created.

Imagine if we didn't judge anyone by their social standing, or the cards in their wallet, but by how passionate they are about things their hearts pulled them toward.

For instance, my friend Harris is passionate about good coffee, so he decided that's what he wanted to do with his life. It won't make him rich, and it won't afford him a Beamer, but it will keep him genuinely happy because he loves it. I love spending time with Harris because his zeal and zest for life is contagious.

But don't we all know people that *don't* seem to have any passions? They may have the money and the house and even the looks, but they lack some sort of tangible passion.

One film that will always stick to the inside of my brain is from *American Beauty*. Lester is a middle-aged suburban cubicle drone, and the opening scene depicts a day in his life. It opens with him in the shower, dryly narrating, "In a way I'm dead already. Look at me. Jerking off in the shower. This will be the high point of my day. It's all downhill from here."

Is viewing porn the highlight of your day?

Does it give you the rush of downhill skiing, or the thrill of chasing a tornado? Perhaps your greatest desire is to be an award-winning chef, or write a best-selling novel, but instead you have settled for porn, for a 20-second dopamine rush that both gratifies and quiets the deeper longings within your soul.

One of the biggest mistakes people make when addressing a porn addiction is assuming that the problem is purely sexual.

For much of my own life, I assumed that once the wedding day arrived and the rings were in place, this struggle would magically evaporate.

I'm still not married, but I have discovered this is a myth. (If it were true, why would we see so many marriages destroyed by pornography?) Addressing a porn addiction starts by zooming out and examining every aspect of our life, and one of the most important areas is our passion.

Our American society has given us permission to live lives devoid of passion. Advertisers want us to think that their products will make us happy. Movies offer a momentary escape from our boring real lives. TV shows tend to offer us interpersonal connection with the characters for a season at a time.

All this ends up doing is polishing our exterior and distracting us while the real *me* withers away inside. When someone suppresses his or her passions, be they hiking, exploring, making music, writing, or any of the other million things to do on this earth, they will quickly go looking for a substitute.

Several months ago, I sat down to lunch with a friend of mine who is one of the foremost experts on sexual struggle. I brought up that I was struggling with porn at the time, and he asked me what seemed like a random question:

> "If you had all the resources in the world, all the time in the world, and you couldn't fail, what would you do?"

I thought for a second, then said something about traveling and writing and teaching, quickly followed by *but that won't ever happen for me.*

In two seconds, I had quenched my soul's permission to dream. I had, in essence, told myself that my dreams and goals will never be realized, so I should buckle up for a life of slaving away at things I hate doing.

Who *wouldn't* want an escape from that kind of life??

My friend was not asking me what I want to do on the weekends to escape from my real life, or what I could dream about doing for the next fifty years, while sitting in a cubicle. He was trying to invite me to *life*. He was saying, O*kay, so you know what you're passionate about, now why aren't you doing anything about it? Why aren't you out there working toward that?*

God doesn't call us to a bored life.

I love how Eugene Peterson translates Romans 8:14-16:

> **God's Spirit beckons. There are things to do and places to go! This resurrection life you received from God is not a timid, grave-tending life. It's adventurously expectant, greeting God with a childlike "What's next, Papa?"**

My dad sporadically disappears for a day and resurfaces later, telling us about the 14,000-foot mountain he just summited. My mom spends her free days gardening in the yard. My friend Neil had a 48-hour layover in Peru, so he spontaneously decided to hike a 40-mile trail in his penny loafers. Laura is a nurse who thinks delivering babies is the most beautiful thing in the world, so she does it every day.

These are not perfect people, but they are people who have examined themselves, discovered what they are passionate about, and then do those things. You won't hear a passionate person tell you porn is "the high point" of their day.

Why would they need a substitute for their passion?

Are you struggling against porn, but it doesn't seem to be going anywhere fast? Quit looking at the problem itself, because chances are, the roots are much deeper than an unfulfilled sex life. Ask yourself, *What makes me feel alive?* and go do it.

Live in such a way that at your funeral, your friends and family will gather round, and in one unified sigh declare,

'he (or she) lived a passionate life.'

LOVE YOURSELF

he hit himself in the head and yelled, "I'm such an *idiot!*"

Every Thanksgiving, my family hosts our annual football game and we invite friends and neighbors to come play. I specifically remember a few years ago, a little guy named Mike was playing. He couldn't have been more than ten or eleven, so playing with the adults was a bit above his skill level.

Unsurprisingly, he dropped the occasional pass or got tackled after only a few steps, as would be expected from any prepubescent boy playing with grown-ups. What I noticed about Mike though, is that whenever he would drop the ball or mess up a play, he couldn't seem to get over it.

He would hit himself in the head and yell, "I'm such an *idiot!*" as if he had just dropped a baby instead of a football.

Over the course of two hours, Mike continued to beat himself up relentlessly, despite the encouragement from the rest of his teammates. No one else was pointing fingers at him or telling him he did a bad job, in fact quite the opposite. We would encourage his good plays and if he dropped it, shout *It's okay, Mike! Don't worry about it! Good hustle!*

Here's the interesting part: by beating himself up and putting himself down, Mike did not become a better football player. His constant self flagellation didn't make him catch more balls or run faster.

You could say his shame was unproductive.

You don't become a better football player by telling yourself how awful you are at it.

I saw a lot of myself in Mike. Whenever I screw up, I tend to bash myself in the head and tell myself how awful I am, as if this will make God or my pastor happy.

Don't worry, God. I screwed up but I can punish myself. (Stupid! Stupid!...)

I realized that when I take it upon myself to make myself feel bad for screwing up, I really am not that productive. I don't become a better Christian by beating myself up whenever I fall down.

In regards to pornography, Michael Cusick calls this "the shame cycle."[6] You screw up; you feel bad and beat yourself up; you feel worse; this shame leads you to believe you're not good enough for a real spouse; you escape the pain with pornography; and the cycle repeats…

When we beat ourselves up for any sin, we are not living out the gospel. The gospel tells us that all of our sin *and* shame have been taken to Golgotha and pinned to the tree with Jesus. When we try to take some of the punishment for our own sins, we are in essence telling Christ that He is not strong enough to bear all of it Himself. Not only that, but beating ourselves up does nothing to help us quit any sin or addiction.

A few weeks ago, my pastor gave a great message, and toward the climax, he ended with this line. "The key to being a good Christian minister is to learn how to be gentle with yourself."

I was kind of surprised, as most of my life, I had been told that Christianity is learning to put others before yourself. I think that while this is true, we also must recognize that we cannot effectively minister to others if we are not being loving to ourselves.

Jesus said to love one another as we love ourselves. The problem today is, many of us do not love ourselves. By that, I do not mean a sort of egocentric, narcissistic bloated sort of affection for our own reflection. I mean that we genuinely must love ourselves and be gentle to ourselves. When we love ourselves, we cultivate a deep well from which to pull in order to give to others; when our cup is full is when we can pour into other people's cups.

---

[6] Michael John Cusick, *Surfing for God*

Shame doesn't allow for this. Shame convinces us we have nothing to give to others and ironically keeps us very self-centered. People who are full of shame can only think about themselves and how bad they are.

I've spent a lot of time telling other people Jesus loves them without believing it to be true of myself.

Today I was washing the dishes and had a related thought. I am very tough on myself when it comes to sin and trying to keep a rigid set of rights and wrongs. Then I realized that because I am this way with myself, I often act this way toward others. Because I cannot give myself grace, I have a hard time showing it to others.

People who can learn to forgive themselves and grow from their mistakes end up being more gracious to others. They become human magnets who draw others to them because grace is a magnet. It reminded me of a passage from one of Henri Nouwen's books:

> We spend countless hours making up our minds about others. But imagine your having no need at all to judge anybody. Imagine having no desire to decide whether someone is a good or bad person. Imagine being completely free from the feeling that you have to make up your mind about the morality of someone's behavior. Imagine that you could say: "I am judging no one!" Wouldn't that be true inner freedom? The desert fathers from the fourth century said: "Judging others is a heavy burden."[7]

When we carry around guilt and shame, that's what we 'send' to others. But Jesus said that He takes our burdens and struggles and replaces them with His: "My yoke is easy and my burden is light,"[8] He tells us. This doesn't mean our lives are pain-free or that we will never work hard. It simply means that we get to exchange our shame for freedom. We trade Him our guilt for joy. We trade Him our sorrows for lightness, and our sin for grace.

---

[7] Henri J. M. Nouwen, *Life of the Beloved*

[8] Matthew 11:30

When we experience these transactions, we become more gracious and loving people, and that is the whole point of the gospel. To become people who realize we are loved so that we can show that love to others.

May we be people who love ourselves in order to love others. May we forgive ourselves in order to show grace to others. And may we give up the burden of judging ourselves in order to give up the burden of loving others.

A POETIC REFLECTION ON PORNOGRAPHY
the bedroom shrine and the bathroom liturgy.

Cognitive dissonance so thick you've convinced yourself you're *actually* that hot doctor from Grey's Anatomy. I'm familiar with porn: That thing that reduces you to a little boy nervously wringing the church bulletin into a telescope over and over again in the presence of a real woman. It makes you insecure; it shatters your manhood.
Or womanhood.
Or humanhood.

My friend Dave says everything is psychological. He asks me why I rest my head on my palm when listening to him speak and says it's from social anxiety. I say it's because my scruff feels nice, but he's probably right.

Porn has robbed me of a lot of confidence.

Pornography is: That focus so singular everything else pulls into the background and ceases to exist. It's just you and your desires. In that one moment, it is the biggest thing in the universe. I know what it's like to have no alternative and you have one extant purpose in your life: To swipe open your phone or crack your laptop and type in that one phrase; to view that one video which will bring relief. That one image that will save your soul. Scratch that one itch so it will *never* itch again (or so it promises).

The bedroom shrine and the bathroom liturgy.

Our idol now comes in pocket size.

The ancients built their three-dimensional gods out of wood, metal and stone. They constructed the Tower of Babel to touch the heavens. Humans once said, "Come, let us build ourselves a city, with a tower that reaches to the heavens, so that we may make a name for ourselves; otherwise we will be scattered over the face of the whole earth."[9]

America decided to do them one better: "Let us build a two-dimensional idol that will enslave the population. It'll keep them in their dark rooms. Look how flat we have formed this ruling god. Come and worship."

A scorpion, when surrounded by a ring of fire, senses its imminent doom and begins stinging itself to death.

We have become the arachnid.

We have attached our instruments of death to our own palms and remain unaware of the destruction they promise.

Like the song of the archetypal bully: *Stop stinging yourself! Stop stinging yourself!*

The worst sinner of them all, a.k.a. the Apostle Paul, knew addiction. I call it 'the do-do chapter': *I do not do the things I want to do, and I continue to do the things I don't want to do.*[10]

Sound familiar?

Chicago, five and a half months ago. My pastor stands in this little exposed-brick room on the west side and says that if there is one thing that unites every human, it is addiction.

> Roses are red,
> violets are blue.
> I was born an addict
> and you were too.

---

[9] Genesis 11:4

[10] Romans 7

Let's learn the language of addiction since we all have it in common. It'll come slow. You live in a foreign country long enough, meaning will eventually come of the alien voices babbling nonsense.

The more I realize the counterfeit nature of pornography, the more excuses I make for not quitting *yet*. It's bizarre. Porn is a counterfeit adventure, so once my life looks like an Indiana Jones movie, I won't struggle with it anymore. Porn is a counterfeit intimacy, so when I star in the sequel to *The Notebook*, I won't struggle with it anymore.

Once _____ happens, I'll be able to stop.

I've got a stack of postcards in my room and no one to send them to. I can't seem to shake the loneliness out of my bones.

"I'm still single so I've got time to quit."

f that.

Porn burns you bad. It burns you so freaking bad.

Sometimes you look at a sunset but it's as if someone poked it with a thumbtack and drained all the color out of it.

You ever find yourself wrapping your fingers around the very thing causing you so much pain and refusing to let go? I have this recording from the turn of the 19th century and it's one of the most beautiful songs I've ever heard. An old black man named Washington Phillips croons,

> Leave it there,
> O, leave it there.
> Take your burden to the Lord
> and leave it there.[11]

A Denver mentor of mine recently told me I've fried my taste buds by eating so much $#!t that I no longer have a palate for delicious things. You were made for intimacy but you fry your brain with this hollow substitute.

---

[11] Look up the ancient recording of *Take Your Burden to the Lord and Leave It There* by Washington Phillips and you won't regret it.

Jesus offers us the Bread of Life and we turn it down in favor of internet doo-doo.

And He is God, that thing which is bigger than all things.

God, who, when porn seems like the biggest thing in the universe, remains bigger.

God, who patiently waits until our acting-out session has ended and once again extends His almighty hand to help us up.

I've been overtaken by an overwhelming God and all my sermons about mercy have come true, unlike my dreams about becoming an astronaut. (Guess I can still write about heaven from down here.)

A God who turned water into wine can surely turn our years of lust into songs of victory. The same God who raised His friend Lazarus from the grave can surely stir to life our numb hearts.

Alcoholics Anonymous says that the first step on the journey toward recovery is to admit your own powerlessness to help yourself.

So quit trying.

Let yourself be brought back to life by the Resurrector.

WHAT TO SAY WHEN SOMEONE CONFESSES THEIR PORN STRUGGLE

we knelt side by side, our elbows sinking into the cushions, and prayed.

In my years of struggling with pornography, I have had dozens of friends with whom I share my slip-ups and struggles. Some were better than others.

Many of you at one point or another will have a friend come to you and confess that once again, they have given in to the destructive machine of pornography, and it helps to have a response ready. Here are some traits I have seen that helped me when I confessed to others. They did not shame me, but they did not let the sin go unacknowledged either.

I will recount some of the best and worst traits to have in receiving a confession, with the aid of Psalm 51, David's song of confession after sinning with Bathsheba, which I consider to be the best source for grace after a sexual sin.

Don't say nothing.

Some of the most awkward times of confession were when I confessed to an old roommate of mine in college. He would silently listen and nod, then when his turn to speak arrived, he said nothing. Perhaps a 'thanks for sharing,' and that was all.

One time, I asked him about why he responded like this. He said he was silent because he didn't know what to say. I think silence was his response because it seemed the most graceful. In his mind, he was acknowledging that sin had no power over me by not 'tearing his robes' to grieve my sin, and his silence showed that my sin was not a big deal.

But to me, his silence did two things: It gave me permission to continue to sin, and it made me feel awkward and dirty because he could not even come up with anything beneficial to say. Additionally, sin *IS* a big deal, so letting it go unacknowledged is not beneficial to anyone.

> 8 Let me hear joy and gladness;
>   let the bones you have crushed rejoice.
> 9 Hide your face from my sins
>   and blot out all my iniquity.

Bring it to the Lord.

Another roommate from college had a much different response. When I confessed to him, he would simply turn to the couch in our room, kneeling before it as an invitation for me to join him. We would kneel side by side, our elbows sinking into the cushions, and pray together for forgiveness and deliverance.

Although he had similar struggles to me, he was much more mature and farther along than I was. His response to me did not make me feel alienated or awkward, because he knelt *with* me. He joined my side in the battle as we brought our sins to the Lord. His was not a finger pointed at me, but a hand coming alongside me in the fight.

> *12 Restore to me the joy of your salvation*
>   *and grant me a willing spirit, to sustain me.*
> *13 Then I will teach transgressors your ways,*
>   *so that sinners will turn back to you.*

Stay far away from shame.

Perhaps the most important thing to remember when a friend confesses to you is that they have already acknowledged that they have screwed up. When I go to a friend to tell them about my misstep, I do it out of an awareness that I have done wrong and need grace. (If a friend does not see a problem with it, the conversation should be much different from the outset.)

Therefore, the *last* thing to do is emphasize the wrongness of what they have done. They probably already know this. There is fine line between shame and guilt. Guilt tells someone that they have *done* wrong, but shame tells them that they *are* wrong—that they are a bad person and don't deserve good things.

It is right to acknowledge that they have messed up, but move on to grace. Do not dwell on their sin. Do not let their sin define them.

> *3 For I know my transgressions,*
>   *and my sin is always before me.*
> *4 Against you, you only, have I sinned*
>   *and done what is evil in your sight;*
> *so you are right in your verdict*
>   *and justified when you judge.*

Dispense grace.

Possibly the best person I have confessed to is my friend Elliot. Though we are the same age, I feel like his wisdom and capacity for grace are eons ahead of mine. When I confessed to him, he was not surprised or *scared* of my sins. He would not recoil or be off-put by my admission. He would simply continue the conversation in his normal tone of voice and offer constructive questions and observations.

He would ask things such as, "What's going on in your life (or missing from your life) that led you to this?" Or, "What exactly happened last night?" He wanted to fully comprehend what I had done, not out of a nosy curiosity, but so that all my sin could be brought to light and he could adequately speak grace to me.

Elliot consistently preached the gospel to me in these times of confession. What this looks like is a clear communication to me that I am washed and made new. I may have stumbled last night, but to Jesus, it is in the past, and through Him, I have complete forgiveness and acceptance. Elliot would tell me that my sins do not define me, and I am still lovable and whole, despite a slip in character.

He would also usually begin one of his sentences with, "You know, something I was thinking about the other day on this topic was…" and then proceed to share some insight on waging war on our flesh or receiving mercy. Dispensing grace is the most important part of receiving a friend's confession because it is what breaks the cycle.

Grace is the antithesis to shame.

Shame is what keeps a man in the cycle of pornography because it is a voice telling him he is not worthwhile and no real woman will ever love him. Therefore, he turns to digital women. This, in turn, causes more shame, and the cycle only worsens as it sends him in a helpless spiral deeper and deeper into the pit of addiction.

Grace needs to replace shame by saying, *Your sins do not define you. Through Jesus, you can be made whole and clean. You are worthy of a real woman (or man).*

> 1 *Have mercy on me, O God,*
>   *according to your unfailing love;*
> *according to your great compassion*
>   *blot out my transgressions.*
> 2 *Wash away all my iniquity*
>   *and cleanse me from my sin.*

Be patient and consistent.

Most likely, this will not happen in a day. I cannot count the number of times I have gone to Elliot or my roommates to tell them of my iniquity. Each time, I feared that *this* would be the final straw. That *this* time they would be tired of hearing of my slipping up and I would finally be beyond repair.

But each time, they listened and offered me grace, putting me back on the path toward healing. You probably won't heal them in one day, and this is not your fault. It's a journey more than an epiphany. Each one of us should persistently be preaching the gospel to one another to be reminded of who we are, and what has been given us in Christ.

> *8 Let me hear joy and gladness;*
> *let the bones you have crushed rejoice.*
> *9 Hide your face from my sins*
> *and blot out all my iniquity.*
> *10 Create in me a pure heart, O God,*
> *and renew a steadfast spirit within me.*[12]

PORN AND THAT PLACE IN THE DISTANCE

I ran five miles barefoot and collapsed on the front steps of a cathedral.

I have a journal filled up with dozens and dozens of pages recording the most epic episode of my life: The time two friends and I backpacked along the coast of Brazil. We began in Sao Paulo, mapping out our route, arguing about whether we should plan it out or simply play it by ear.

Of course, the entire voyage ended up being played by the seam of our pants because there was no way to plan everything that happened over the ensuing voyage. Throughout it all, there was one distinct attribute of that season which loomed large over the entire expedition. One thing was different than anything else I had experienced or have experienced since.

---

[12] All verses from Psalm 51, written after King David's extramarital affair.

From the morning the three of us walked out the front door, Rio de Janiero was on the horizon. It was a mysterious destination we were working toward with every step we made and every bus we boarded.

There was one night we earned some cash on a ferry by singing kid's songs with Joel's guitar and dancing with the kids. Afterward, one of the families invited us into their home for the night.

There was the wild night in Ubatuba, and the wilder night at Paraty dancing behind the Gecko Chill Bar, which ended with me running five miles barefoot along the river and collapsing on the front steps of a cathedral on the edge of town.

All of these episodes were overshadowed by this singular goal which drew nearer to us every day. Or rather, we drew nearer to it:

Rio.

It had some legendary quality to it as we made our way there. Every local bus and ride we hitched brought us that much closer to our destination. Lucas had a girl waiting for him in Rio, and Joel and I were excited to arrive and take our boots off and simply sit on Copacabana Beach having finally arrived. We knew Corcovado (The giant Jesus statue) would welcome us atop his hill with open arms, and we were eager to arrive.

That time was so unlike any other solely for that reason. There was a destination toward which we strived every hour of every day. I grow nostalgic for that trip because when I look at my present life, it pales in comparison. There is no city in the distance toward which we sojourn; I simply go to work and make enough money to pay rent and the heating bill. There isn't really momentum as much as there is stagnation and routine.

So it makes sense that I would seek out alternate forms of adventure. Like pornography.

When we lose sight of the mission we are on, and the country that awaits us beyond the horizon, the tedium often drives us to what Michael Cusick calls "counterfeit goods."[13] Porn gives us the same rush as an authentic

---

[13] Michael Cusick, *Surfing for God*

adventure, but it burns out quickly and leaves us feeling more empty in the end. Cusick says it's like going to Thailand and buying a knockoff Seiko watch because it looks and feels the same as the real deal, but the quality is a sliver of the authentic thing. The counterfeit—though it makes you feel cooler for a few days—ends up in a drawer after a few weeks because the wrist strap broke or the mechanics gave out.

It's easy to see how we could turn to porn as a counterfeit for intimacy, love, and approval, but I think adventure is one of the most overlooked thirsts in a man's soul. We were all created with a longing for adventure—whatever form it takes in each individual—but we have lost sight of our destination. Whether you're a white collar cubicle employee or a vagabond elephant wrangler, it's possible to neglect the larger adventure you're on. Even on days when life feels like the opposite of an Indiana Jones film, we must remember that there *is* a home that we've never seen; there is a city where we're headed and every day brings us one step closer to its gates.

Most days I don't live like I'm moving toward my true home. Most days feel rather bland and boring, which often leads me to find adventure in more nefarious forms. Of course, the 'adventure' is nothing more than a rush of chemicals to my brain promising to be fulfilling and exciting but ends up leaving me emptier and more ashamed than before. The 'adventure' is actually a form of denial in which I deceive myself into thinking I'm not just at home in my bathroom, but am actually with a beautiful woman.

But we are hungry for *real* adventure.

So how do we conjure up this sense of expedition and keep our minds set on the destination resting on the horizon? I'm still working on that part. But I know it begins internally before externally. I don't think a plane ticket is necessary for us to be reminded that nowhere in this world is our home, or our ultimate goal. After all, when we finally did arrive in Rio, we were mugged at gunpoint on the northern edge of the beach.

Nowhere in this world is our ultimate destination.

It's important to keep in the forefront of our minds the fact that we are moving. Philosophically speaking, our lives are *teleological,* or, they are heading in a direction whether we realize it or not. We are on the move constantly as we pass through time, and for those of us who are hidden in Christ, our home is that beautiful country on Mount Zion; the New Jerusalem where once and for all, peace will prevail and we will live in the light of the Lord.

As we journey toward this nation, shouldn't we be inviting as many people as we can to come with us? Whether we like it or not, we are on a mission. And there is a destination. As it relates to addiction, I've thought a lot about how this distant place can help set us free now, and it comes down to adjusting our mindset.

Does your future shape your present? Do you anticipate a destination more glorious and beautiful than you can comprehend today? This is why hope plays such a central role in Christian theology: Without anticipation of a better world, we only have doom and depression to accompany us.

So may we be a people with hope for a glorious future; people who eager long for the coming of the kingdom which brings with it peace and joy. May we keep our eyes on that country in the distance, nestled just beyond the horizon, and constantly be reminded that we draw nearer every day. And may we happily bring many people through those gates with us, inviting them into joy and out of despair.

THE HIDDEN SELF

it has been one of the deepest roots of my addiction...

"And you're wondering why you felt like you weren't good enough?" my friend Dave said. "You were literally conditioned to think that way!"

I had just finished telling him about an exercise I had been doing for a class on addiction in which I created a timeline of my life. In doing so, I realized that there was a lot of rejection in my younger years. Prior to college, nearly every girl I had been interested in either dumped me after a few weeks, or flat out rejected me from the start.

I hardly dated anyone after that.

It's taken me a while to admit it, but one of the deep roots of my addiction to pornography has been feeling that I'm not *good enough* for a real woman.

You see, in middle and high school, I was not the oxen of a man you see today. I was not the "Shirtless Runner."

I was a nerd.
A geek.

Whatever label you want to stick on the kid that moved a couple times, went to three high schools and two middle schools, and had a collection of 500 comic books. The kid who had every detail about Middle Earth memorized and longed to become Batman (truth be told, that's part of the reason I started working out...I guess comic books were good for *something*.)

After a number of failed relationships (or whatever you call two 9th graders going to a movie), I came to think that the problem was me. That I was the undesirable one.

So I worked to change it.

I chopped my Beatles-era haircut and hit the weights. I bought nicer clothes and dropped the Star Wars t-shirts. I did everything I could think of to change people's perception of me into a man who *was* worthy of dating. The problem with these things is that they do nothing to heal the wounded heart of a person.

Dr. Dan Allender says that men today are broken hearted. "Not broken hearted as in sad or full of grief," he writes. "Instead, we are broken into fragmented selves that are unable to do much other than posture and pretend we are someone whom we know we are not."[14]

At an early age, my heart was broken into a dozen different pieces. Some of these pieces ventured to the identity of a nerd while others worked at getting into better physical shape. Some tried to earn value in artistry, while other fragments delighted in being the class clown.

---

[14] restorationproject.net/interview-with-dr-dan-allender-pornified-masculinity-and-hope-for-restoration/

All of these "identities" were only parts of a shield, though. Like a turtle shell I could tuck into whenever someone looked my way, while the *Real Ethan,* the weird, eccentric, tender-hearted self stayed safe inside.

John Eldredge echoed this sentiment when he wrote,

> This is every man's deepest fear: to be exposed, to be found out, to be discovered as an impostor, and not really a man…We are hiding, every last one of us. Well aware that we, too, are not what we were meant to be, desperately afraid of exposure, terrified of being seen for what we are and are not, we have run off into the bushes. We hide in our office, at the gym, behind the newspaper and mostly behind our personality.[15]

The sad thing is, most of us go on living like this and wondering why we feel so severed from our *real* self. Why there is no peace inside us. Why we feel splintered into so many pieces. Social media doesn't help because we can look any way we want online.

I maintained the charade for many many years until recently when I decided to do the tough work of examining myself and taking a good, hard, honest look in the mirror. It was like pulling a hermit crab from his protective shell: It was ugly and it snapped and fought like hell against being exposed, because the work of healing is not easy.

Several years ago, I was on the bus in Chicago with a Moody student who was an acquaintance of mine. He began sharing what the Lord was teaching him in that season, and the only part I remember was one line: "The Lord is teaching me that it's okay to be weak, to be broken."

I don't think I've ever had so much respect for another human being in my life.

It's as if he was standing before me as the bus tilted and rocked, holding his palms open to me saying *Look, this is me. I'm not that cool. I'm hurt and broken. But God's cool with that, and I'm learning to be cool with it too.*

So I'm attempting to become like that. It's incredibly hard for a man to admit that he is weak and broken, but I think that is the first step in healing.

---

[15] John Eldredge, *Wild at Heart*

Women don't fall in love with how many pounds you can put up on the bench, or that sweet new shirt from H&M. They can't even love the jokes you make or the intelligence stored in the folds of your brain. People love other *people*, not the things they try to wrap around themselves as a disguise.

Learning this is hard, because ever since we got the boot from the Garden of Eden, we've been trying to cover ourselves up, trying to look better than we actually are.

Underneath all the fancy fig leaves and one-liners, we are all pretty ugly and weak, but that doesn't mean we're unworthy of love. God doesn't stop chasing you because you woke up with bedhead, or you can't curl 5 pounds.

It's hard to examine myself and see that there are a lot of things I don't like about myself. But it's even harder to accept that despite them, God still loves me. And hopefully, there's a woman out there who will too. But living with a splintered heart and trying to be a dozen men at once is exhausting and will keep us returning to the fire hydrant of porn to try to nourish our broken heart.

My friend Michael Cusick points out that the word "integrity" comes from the word "integer," meaning *whole*.[16] A person of integrity is a whole person, not a shapeshifter who modifies themselves to fit the scene.

So may we be a people who give up disguising ourselves and trying to be more impressive than we are. May we seek wholeness, root ourselves in quietness and peace and know ourselves as we are known by God, recognizing that God loves the weak and the broken; He lifts up those who are low.[17]

> "But [Jesus] said to me, My grace is sufficient for you, for my power is made perfect in weakness." Therefore I will boast all the more gladly about my weaknesses, so that Christ's power may rest on me. That is

---

[16] Michael John Cusick, *Surfing for God*

[17] Psalm 145

why, for Christ's sake, I delight in my weaknesses...For when I am weak, then I am strong."[18]

LETTER TO MY YOUNGER PORN-ADDICTED SELF

you think the struggle will fade away on its own eventually...

As a 25-year old college graduate, I have been battling pornography for half my life. The fact is, more young men and women than ever are growing up with this struggle against pornography. I decided to write a letter to a younger version of me, sharing some of the things I wish I'd known when I started looking at porn and what I've learned.

Dearest Ethan,

As you enter the tenth grade you're going to be faced with many challenges. You're going to be hit smack in the face with a new set of struggles and the navigation won't be easy. But you're going to make it.

There will be insecurity – mostly around the pretty girls. This will happen for a few reasons—one being that half a dozen of them have turned you down already. I want to tell you that your value doesn't come from being accepted by them...but I'm not sure you'll believe me.

You'll feel different. You'll start to feel an apparent distance from every other person on earth, and the looming sense that you're the only one of your kind; that you're the only one who gets you. You'll feel alone on a very crowded planet and you won't understand why. I want you to know that you will eventually find people like you, people who understand and get you. I want to tell you to hang in there.

It'll happen.

I want to warn you—most of all—that you're about to begin the battle of your life. The struggle with pornography.

Younger Ethan, you're going to live for quite some time in a dangerous place; a place where you feel like the struggle doesn't really matter because

---

[18] 2 Corinthians 12:9-10

marriage is a long way off. I mean, you're still in high school, and no one else is being affected by your little secret, right? You couldn't be more wrong. I know you expect that the struggle will simply fade away eventually. I know you expect to finally reach a point where you can just stop and live life to the fullest. I know all of your excuses. The one that says it'll stop when you meet the right girl or get the right job. Or maybe just when you find the right circle of friends so you don't feel so alone, then the struggle will just fade and you'll carry on with life.

You need to know that it doesn't happen that way.

Pornography doesn't simply fall off or fade away, but clings tighter the longer you let it invade your life.

Your secret sin of pornography is going to follow you. It's not going to go away on its own. It can't. You need to stop and do something about it.

Find help,
tell someone,
but you aren't going to. You're going to let it hang on, and it will stay just as long as you let it.

Pornography will follow you into your first year of college. It will tag along as you travel around the world and do international ministry for a few years. The sin and struggle will hide itself in the shadows, in the corners and crevices when you close the door. It will follow you to your third year of college, the place where you expected to meet the girl who would become your wife.

But here's the thing with this porn 'habit': without working through the insecurities and pain from the past, you will only be more tightly tethered to it. This addiction—and I hate to break it to you but it is an *addiction*—will prevent you from making any real move toward an actual woman. Your brain has been altered, the lines between pornography and reality are blurred. You will graduate as single as ever, and the struggle will only continue.

You see Big Guy, porn has a way of sticking around. I know in the beginning it creeps up so slowly. It lies to you with its sultry voice telling you it's no big deal. It entices you with its deceptive ways and makes you believe it'll go away on its own later on.

That's the lie pornography wants you to believe—
it's fine.
It's temporary.
You can quit anytime.

Pornography is like a weed in your garden: The first one shows up and it seems like no big deal. You simply ignore it because one little weed poses no real threat. Five days later, you return to the garden and things have changed a bit more, now there are a bunch of weeds. Three weeks later the garden is being overrun and you can't stop thinking about the weeds. 6 months later the weeds begin to choke the very life right out of your plants. Pornography is a weed in your life. Don't wait to fight it. Take action against it now!

I know what you're thinking: What do I do? How do I stop this habit that has barged into my life rather uninvited? The truth is, it won't be easy. Remember I said you were about to enter a battle? Battles aren't won easily and they certainly aren't won overnight. And honestly, there is no clear-cut simple path to freedom from pornography. But that doesn't mean you shouldn't start.

Start now. Start today. Start before you wake up 10 years from now and find yourself in deeper than you ever thought you could be. And once you start, keep up the fight—never letting your guard down.

And most importantly, remember that when you mess up, there is grace. When you feel down, the Lord can lift you up. And when you feel dirty, it is Jesus who makes us clean. But more on this in the next letter.

Be cool, Little Guy.

Sincerely,

25-year-old you

#METOO, FETISHES, AND JESUS

there was not enough of an edge.

I just finished reading an incredibly interesting article[19] from one of my favorite investigative journalistic sites, HuffPost's Highline. Despite the typically liberal slant of the organization, I was happy to find that they did a balanced examination of the material related to Weinstein, Bill Cosby, Larry Nassar, and other exposed predators from the #MeToo movement. By that I mean, rather than simply label all the perpetrators as terrible humans who deserve to rot, author Emily Yaffe researched the roots beneath the abuses.

An investigation like this leads rather quickly to the notion of sexual fetishes and the desire for a very pointed and specific outlet for sexual desires. Research in the article claims that if someone possesses a unique sexual fetish, it is rooted in something that happens in their lives before puberty hits, typically between the ages of 6 and 8.

The author cited examples of men (the number of men with sexual fetishes is roughly four times higher than the number of women) who had a 'rubber fetish' due to watching a babysitter wash the dishes with rubber gloves on. Others reported fantasies of acting out scenes from movies or shows they watched frequently as children, even harmless material such as *The Andy Griffith Show.*

The piece then painfully moved onto the story of a man referred to as Michael. He is a man who is listed as a sexual predator in California. The only difference between him and the ilk of Weinstein is that Michael did not have the same level of *power*. Michael was arrested eight times for exposing himself on public transport, but the story behind the actions is what is really heart wrenching.

Michael grew up in the Midwest, a Native American-Black blend in a school full of white children. He entered high school with the full knowledge that no girl wanted to date him because of his heritage. His one 'sensual' outlet as a teenager was going to a friend's house where the mother would walk

---

[19] Emily Yoffe, "Understanding Harvey (And Bill. And Larry. And Charlie. And...)." The Huffington Post

around scantily clad. And because he enjoyed it so much, he assumed girls would enjoy seeing him like that an equal amount. From there, his propensity toward exhibitionism sprouted until it was a daily routine.

As I read the story, I began to see Michael as more than just a 'sexual deviant,' and more as a wayward child seeking intimacy in a twisted way. To be clear: I am not condoning or applauding the behavior of sexual predators or abusers. However, examining the roots of their…(what is the right term now? It changes by the week) psychopathology is fascinating in terms of regarding these men. It helps us see them as fellow fallen humans rather than beasts.

The notion of a fetish is in and of itself a fascinating entity. As stated above, they develop early in life and anyone familiar with elementary psychology knows that things carried over from childhood are *very* deep indeed. I'll be frank with you and say that, as I read that article, I kept wondering if I have any sexual fetishes. To the best of my knowledge, the answer is no. In my years as a porn addict, the thing I continually sought more than a specific physical element was simple intimacy. Emotional (and yes, physical) nearness to another person.

To be real personal, I still remember a dream I had when I was probably in first or second grade. In the dream, I was at recess at my school and was sitting on the playground next to a girl in my class. I remember the feeling of intimacy toward her, and I feel that that longing is something which has followed me for decades. Of course, that desire in and of itself is a good and healthy longing, but the way I go about satisfying that desire can quickly become polluted when pursued down the wrong avenues.

Happy as I am that I personally don't have any fetishes I'd be embarrassed telling others about, I can certainly sympathize with the notion of bearing the weight of an uncontrollable desire. I'd wager that most of us are familiar with this to some degree, and that's the part that probably scares us about the entire #MeToo movement. We may think thoughts such as *If I had as much power as Harvey, would I have done the same thing? Am I privately acting out in some way, just with less luxurious access?*

A song by my favorite metal band, August Burns Red, puts it so perfectly:

I'm just as much the problem as the man behind bars
He did with his business what I do in my heart[20]

The reason the #MeToo offenders can be easily categorized as men with fetishes rather than some other form of sexual dalliance is simple: With the amount of money they had, they could have easily gotten a high-end prostitute or escort to satisfy their whims. But evidently, that wasn't enough. There was not enough *edge* or risk of being caught. The acts had to be personal and to the point that the woman could say no, thus presenting an element of risk rather than mere purchase.

Louis C.K., for instance, repeatedly masturbated in front of female coworkers, or simply exposed himself to them. In retrospect, he acknowledged it was wrong, yet could not explain why he had to do it, rather than simply move it to an environment where that type of behavior is societally acceptable.

These sexual drives, fetishized or otherwise, are all-consuming and intense. In the heat of the moment, they feel unbearable. Lust seems to come to us, offering a release for the pressure, yet once the deed is done (whatever it is), shame and guilt rush in, which in turn create more of a desire to return to our perversions. It's a brutal cycle, familiar to addicts of every stripe.

Perhaps you read this as someone with a fetish and are nervous for the coming condemnation. Well, fear not. One thing I have learned about Jesus is that He can handle our desires. He is capable of understanding them. We need to remember that we do not worship a God who is distant or unfamiliar with our deep longings. We worship a God who *desperately* longs for all of mankind to return to Him.

For comparison, think about the last time you had your heart broken and how desperately you longed for that person to reciprocate your feelings. Now multiply that by the number of humans who have ever lived.

No, our God is not unfamiliar with our deep desires. He was there when those things were planted in us. He lived through my 2nd grade dream with me, and he was there when that other man initiated his 'rubber fetish.'

---

[20] August Burns Red, "Provision" from Rescue & Restore.

I remember being at a church in Chicago and was so beaten down by the weight of my lustful desire that I went forward during communion to pray with a deacon. I told him what I was experiencing and very gently, he put his hand on my shoulder and said, "You know you can hand those to Jesus, right? He is able to hold your desires. Are you willing to trust Him with them?" As he said it, he motioned holding an invisible egg before his chest, then offering it over to Jesus. "He is big enough to hold your desires if you are able to let Him."

It's not easy, giving up our deep-seated desires to an invisible and often-quiet God. And as Christians, I don't think it's healthy to pretend that we do not have them. In fact, bottling them up and keeping them a secret from our trusted brothers and sisters may only result in more damage later on, just as it did with the now-ashamed men of MeToo. Rather than pretending they don't exist *or* acting them out, can we be people who offer them to the Lord, knowing that He is gentle and good?

This is done through prayer and silence as well as fellowship with other believers we can trust. And it is certainly not easy. But I believe it will be fruitful in the end.

May we be Christians who don't ignore these awkward and uncomfortable things, sweeping them away and pretending they don't exist. Rather, may we address them, both in ourselves and in those close to us in ways which are gentle, true and full of grace. And may we always remember that Christ, who is full of strong desires Himself, knows and understands our lusts and longings.

"4 REASONS YOU SHOULD KEEP LOOKING AT PORN"
there's a weight to our sexual brokenness which cannot be trivialized.

Last night I tried to write a sardonic satire piece on pornography entitled "4 Reasons You Should Keep Looking At Porn." I got through the first 3—

Avoid the unnecessary pain!
You'll never get rejected!
Provide jobs for struggling actors!

—but then I got to the last one, *Provide jobs for people worldwide*, and I simply could not maintain the satirical tone.

The piece wasn't meant to be a funny satire, but simply a "Hey, these are true facts about pornography that I want to write in a different way" type piece, but I realized that there is a real weight to the sexual brokenness of our world that should not be trivialized.

As hard as I tried, I could not come up with a satirical way to present (even in a somber, sardonic tone) a child being taken from her family and forced to commit sexual acts with strangers, all before the age of a Kindergartener. Or women who, when the PornHub camera stops rolling, burst into tears because any real sense of personhood they held onto has evaporated.

When I was in junior high, I got caught by my parents looking at porn on our family computer. They sent me to chat with my youth pastor, who explained that although I messed up, there is grace and forgiveness for me, and that everyone struggles with it.

Over the next couple years in youth group, I would find porn to be the subject of many of our jokes. We would break up into our high school boy's group and spend half the time making jokes about masturbation and porn. I don't think this was my youth pastor's fault, as I grew up in the era when pornography was exploding onto the digital scene and leaders in the church hardly knew how to react. Certainly, making light of the subject was easier than delving into the darkness we were dealing with.

So that's what I knew. Growing up, it became normal to joke about porn and masturbation, and I carried the tradition long into my college years, and even recently, I find myself making jokes I immediately regret.

Because there are things we just shouldn't joke about.

I think this may have been what Paul was referring to when he wrote that there should be no "foolish talk or coarse joking" (Ephesians 5:4) among the people of God. I think God calls us to be better than that.

Look at Jesus as He talks to the woman at the well in John 4. He could have easily cracked a few one-liners about her being married five times ('Hey, you know what they say! Sixth time's the charm!'), but He doesn't. He addresses the deeper issues within her soul that she was neglecting to address, and got to work healing her.

I think when we encounter Jesus, we have to make a decision. Are we going to keep making light of things that hurt us, and our world, or are we going to speak of them seriously and address them in a life-giving, healing way? Are we willing to apply pressure where it aches, or just keep inhaling the nitrous oxide and forgetting the injury is there?

So in place of my satirical piece, here are the same three facts (I combined the last two) about pornography, presented with the gravity they warrant.

Quitting Porn Hurts

Most of us came to pornography out of innocent curiosity, sensual desire, or accidental exposure. Maybe you even had a family member who thought it was cool to show it to you before you even hit puberty. But all of us *stay* with pornography because it takes away the pain. Pain from broken relationships, abandonment, rejection, and a whole novella of other sources. It keeps us in its grip because the numbing agents get straight to work, helping us to escape the harsh reality of life. Maybe your marriage is a let-down and you want a quick upgrade. Maybe you're tired of being overweight and never being asked out.

There is almost no itch pornography cannot scratch.

But for some reason, I expected my life to be easier and more pain-free when I quit. I quickly found that's not the way it works. If you struggle with porn and masturbation, don't *quit* trying to *quit* because the familiar pain from your life returns. And it will return.

Expecting pain to evaporate when you remove porn from your life is akin to expecting the agony of an amputated leg to magically disappear once the morphine wears off. That's just not how it works.

When you take away the numbing agent, everything is going to hurt *more*, not less. Expecting this is helpful, because if you expect everything to feel good when you quit, you'll be surprised by the pain and eventually rush back to your source of comfort.

A friend of mine recently compared porn to a cozy recliner. "When you have a bad day, all you want to do is get home and relax in the comfort of your La-Z-Boy. But it doesn't feel good to get up out of that chair, and then to keep standing. You have to get stronger at standing, not just return to comfort."

Invite Jesus into your life, and even into your past to walk through these painful places *with* you. Embrace the pain. Embrace revisiting painful moments in your life in order to properly heal from them.

Scars make us stronger, laughing gas does not.

You won't be rejected

One of the appeals of pornography is that it never says no. It never rolls over in bed, or walks away from you at the bar. The women and men on the screen are always smiling, happy to see you, and eager to do exactly what you want.

John Eldredge writes, "The dangerous thing about porn is it allows a man to feel like a man without requiring anything from him."[21] In other words, there is no risk of rejection with pornography.

And I think this has raised up a generation of milquetoasts, myself often included. I see a lot of men and women who lack confidence in themselves because they have become accustomed to this risk-free outlet. Why talk to a real girl when I have my laptop at home?

People often ask me why I'm single, and if I'm honest, I think porn has a lot to do with it. I have avoided the risk of asking out a woman because the safety of my web browser beckoned louder. There are times when a situation calls for us to be bold, but we choose the route of passivity because porn has conditioned us that way. It conditions us to avoid risks.

You are perpetuating the sex trade industry

How could I possibly be helping the sex trade industry? I've never even paid for porn!

These same sentiments echoed through me for years until I began to understand the way the internet works. Traffic is what drives a website to

---

[21] John Eldredge, *Wild at Heart*

success, because the more clicks it gets, the more companies will want to advertise on it. And the more advertising there is, the more money the website is getting.

Like it or not, by visiting pornographic websites, you have funded the sex industry.

Sadly, this does not just include voluntarily actors, directors, 'writers', and cameramen. It also includes the people who are victim to human sex trafficking. If pornography creates the desire, the sex slave industry is the ultimate outlet for those urges, against the will of the victims.

The two are intricately connected.

Children as young as 5 are forced into the sex industry by the thousands every year. Some counts position the current sex slave population—these are people who are forced into being sex slaves; they did not choose it, are not being paid for it, and they have severe emotional, mental, and physical problems as a result—at around 4.8 million.[22]

4.8 million human beings.

It breaks me down to know that I have unwittingly contributed to this number with my porn addiction.

Somehow, in all of this, Jesus still wants me. He still wants you. He still walks over to us and says, "They do not condemn you? Then I don't either" (John 8:10-11). He still draws near to us, no matter how fast we try to run from Him. He still washes us and makes us clean.

I want to close with a piece from the great Puritan prayer, *The Valley of Vision*:

> Lord, in the daytime stars can be seen from deepest wells,
> and the deeper the wells the brighter thy stars shine;
> Let me find thy light in my darkness,
> thy life in my death,

---

[22] *"Forced Labour, Modern Slavery and Human Trafficking"*, International Labour Organization, www.ilo.org/global/topics/forced-labour/lang--en/index.htm.

thy joy in my sorrow,
thy grace in my sin,
thy riches in my poverty,
thy glory in my valley.

THE VIOLENT PROGRESSION OF PORNOGRAPHY
how your secret porn problem is fueling global human sex trafficking...

I don't write this post as an authoritarian expert on the ins and outs of addiction or sex trafficking. Nor do I pose as some sort of holy man descended from the mountain with a word from the divine.

I write as a porn addict.

I've sat in the basements of downtown cathedrals with the other perverts and sex offenders, confessing my week. Some of the other men at the Sex Addicts Anonymous meetings have a legal mandate to declare that they are registered for their addiction. They've done illicit things with children or the helpless elderly and been caught. In our imaginations, we tend to paint these men as wicked and sinister, endlessly plotting out when they will pounce on their next victim.

But that's not what I see in the basement of the church. I see remorseful men, apologetic for their actions, and trying to break free from the desires which enslave them. The scariest part of attending S-meetings is the realization that I could be on the same path. These men did not wake up one day and decide to molest the innocent. Nearly every case began with a pornography addiction.

But sin has a bottomless stomach. It will eventually tire of digital images and want to move on to more tangible outlets.

The irony of me—a 25-year-old virgin—sitting in an SAA meeting is that I haven't even come close to this sort of offense. My thorough Christian upbringing hasn't even let me get past first base with a woman. So what was it that led me to attend my first SAA meeting all those months ago?

A big part of it was realizing that my addiction no longer affected just me.

Before I dive in, I want to address something: If you struggle with pornography but refuse to label yourself as an 'addict,' you are most likely wrong. For the majority of my life, I raged against the notion that I am actually an *addict*. The term seemed so dirty and helpless. *You're only an addict if it ruins your life,* I thought, totally neglecting the fact that every alcoholic is an addict well before their life is ruined. Imagine how grateful a drug addict would be if they were able to kick their habit *before* it destroyed their life. So when it comes to pornography addiction, why do we assume that someday the problem will magically flutter away as a butterfly leaves a branch? Sin is hungry. Get help before it gets worse because it will *not* go away on its own.

Not only does a pornography addiction affect your friends, family, self worth, romance, and practically every relationship in our lives, but it fuels global sex trafficking.

As a blogger, my money comes from people visiting my website. The more clicks I get in a given month, the more money slides into my bank account. Advertisers pay for that precious space between the content, and they're willing to pay more the more visitors per month a site has. The same is true for every website on the internet. The more visitors they get in a month, the more money they receive *even if those visitors are not paying to be on their site.*

So when it comes to pornography sites, they make money from all the men and women visiting their site, even if they don't spend a dime. And as these porn sites earn more money, they are able to bring in more 'talent,' or actors and actresses to star in their videos. And while many of these actors are consenting adults, many are not. In fact, 49% of women who are rescued from sex trafficking say that at one point, pornography was made of them against their will.[23] Additionally, about 90% of American porn websites buy their content rather than making it themselves.[24] What this means is that, as much as they promise that their products are above board, they really have little to no way to verify the actual age and consent of the people featured in their videos.

---

[23] According to Rescue:Freedom; rescuefreedom.org

[24] According to CovenantEyes

What this means for us is that we do not have to spend a penny to help fund human sex trafficking. It breaks me down to think that I have unwittingly contributed to the trafficking of real human beings in other parts of the globe simply by spending time on certain websites. In essence, we who look at porn are no better than the men in the SAA meetings who lay their hands on children and force them to do unspeakable things. Our rampant desires have continued the trade of videos which subject people to dehumanizing actions and terrible conditions. There really is no way around it. We cannot pick and choose which pornography sites are 'ethical' because the waters are so muddied.

However, the point of this post is not to point fingers and bring shame upon your head just because you have watched pornography. This post is an encouragement to people in the same position as me: Get help. Fight your addiction. Tell a friend, pastor, or spouse and begin to make efforts against pornography addiction, and by extension, human trafficking.

I have reached places which felt absolutely hopeless. I have felt like there was absolutely no good outcome for me, my future marriage is already doomed, and the slavery to my desires was eternal. But this is not the case. I have come to realize that there's nothing Jesus loves more than taking broken and twisted situations and making beautiful things out of them.

Nothing and no one is beyond redemption.

You can help take a stand against this today. If you are also a porn addict, get help. Go to SAA meetings. Download filters and accountability software. If you know someone in the throes of a pornography addiction, offer them help as well. Do not pile up shame and guilt, because that is the most counterproductive way to go about helping an addict of any kind.

Together we can take steps to combat the behemoth of sex trafficking, and it can begin by realizing that our 'harmless porn habit' is actually taking a toll on other people's lives.

YOU CAN'T SAVE YOURSELF
it takes a total paradigm shift.

I have a friend named Brandon whose story goes something like this: He used to party and do a lot of drugs. He slept with a lot of girls and watched a lot of porn. But about two years ago, he became a Christian. At that moment, he stopped EVERYTHING. He hasn't watched porn in two years. He hasn't been drunk or abused substances. He hasn't slept with anyone. He just works hard at his job, loves Jesus, and enjoys his friends.

If your story is anything like mine, it's way different than Brandon's.

If I'm honest, I'm a little jealous of how Brandon just cut all his bad habits out of his life and set his eyes on Jesus, because if it was that easy, I would have done it years ago. My story looks a lot more like feebly praying to the Lord a long time ago, then falling headfirst into a battle with pornography in 7th grade, and not really making much progress since then.

My story looks more like a roller coaster, where *I've got it under control!* swiftly drops into a binging streak and free falling plummet, and I ask myself the question many of you have probably asked yourself a thousand times: *If I'm a Christian who takes Jesus at His word, shouldn't I be free from all my sin?*

I mean, that's what the Bible says, right?

The answer is a firm *eh.*

I've been taking this class on addiction at my church, and a big part of the curriculum is examining the methods of Alcoholics Anonymous, one of the most successful addiction recovery programs in history. The first week was one of those jarring classes where a lot of what you believed about addiction got flipped on its head, and I made a big realization in my approach to my own battle with porn.

Jesus promises us freedom from sin. The question is, what does He mean by *freedom?*

I realized that it doesn't always mean quitting. In fact, sometimes the opposite. Long-time addicts of any kind will agree that the only way to begin healing from an addiction is to hit absolute rock bottom. To reach the point where you can finally say, "If I have any hope in repairing my life, it must come from a source outside of myself. Because I am empty. I am spent. I am unable to help myself."

So maybe, when Jesus says He will set us free from our sin, it means pushing us even further into an addiction so we reach that place. Perhaps He wants us to get to the point where we must say, "Jesus, I cannot help myself. I need you. There are zero other options."

And then after that point, you'll never look at porn again, right?

No.

Not at all. Recovery is a long process, and I think in many ways, seeing recovery in this light makes the gospel even more real and more wonderful. Because then, every time we slip up and sit before the dim light of the laptop, having just screwed up *again,* its a reminder of our own helplessness.

It's a total perspective change. I tend to fill up with shame every time I screw up with pornography, and picture myself drifting farther away from God. But when we think about the gospel as a compass to our helplessness, each screw-up should only point us to how much we need Jesus; how we cannot do it on our own; and how His grace expands even more every time we fail.

We talk about the gospel as Jesus saving us, then get confused when we can't save ourselves from sin, as if we are the ones who should be doing the saving.

I'll paraphrase a story from John Z's book *Grace in Addiction:*

Imagine that you're on the deck of a cruise ship late one night and somehow slip off and fall into the water. It's dark and you can't swim. You try to yell, but water is filling your mouth. Somehow, someone on board sees you and tells the captain. He slowly turns the ship around, but your arms are getting even more tired. The liner finally gets close enough to you to throw a life preserver near you. With all your remaining strength, you cling to it as they reel you in. Men at the base of the ship haul you over the rails to safety. Your first words after being saved are:

Did you see how I grabbed onto that life preserver like an expert?? Did you notice the strength of my biceps and the dexterity in my wrists? I was all over that thing!

Everyone would think you lost your mind! You just got saved from a situation that surely would have left you dead if not for everyone else on the ship. You were rescued, plain and simple. Z writes:

> Sadly enough, some form of the above tends to be our own response to most of the good things that happen to us...While Christians often talk loudly about God's power and grace, their rhetoric just as often betrays a secret belief that their own initiative and willpower has played a decisive role.

Don't underestimate Jesus' power to use your addiction for good. Remember that you're still in the middle of the story, not the end, and (cheesy as it sounds) it's never too late to move from a state of hopelessness to a happy ending. More often than not, your story won't look like Brandon's, where Jesus magically zaps all your struggles out of your life. But He is good. And He is always moving.

Perhaps freedom in Christ is even deeper than simply *no longer committing a certain sin*. Perhaps it means that when God looks at us, He no longer sees alcoholics and porn addicts, despite how long it's been since their last relapse. Maybe freedom means we don't have to bear the weight of our own sins, even if we are *presently* battling them, even daily giving in.

Next time you mess up, remember that Jesus is present in your struggle. He's not there pointing fingers and condemning you, but He is inviting you to Himself.

Inviting you to give up control and let yourself be saved by Him.

WHY PORN IS BAD: I DON'T LIKE WOMEN.

porn has made me not want women, but their pieces and parts.

I grew up in the church all my life. With my dad being a pastor, I grew up knowing the evils of the lust of the eyes and the treachery of adultery. After high school, I worked with several missions organizations before attending Moody Bible Institute. All that is to say, I was shocked to read some of the comments on many of my blog posts.

There are people who DON'T think porn is bad?

I mean, I knew millions of people struggled with it, but didn't realize there were people who genuinely didn't see anything wrong with it. I got comments telling me to mind my business, it's not hurting anyone, and it's just a natural part of life. One friend even told me that "there is no universe in which I don't watch porn every day."

As a good Christian boy, the argument is much easier to build. Simply pull from the Sermon on the Mount, where Jesus declares, "if you even look at a woman lustfully, you have already committed adultery with her in your heart." I wholeheartedly agree with Jesus. Because He's Jesus. But some people see it differently.

There are plenty of great resources out there to describe the abuse women in pornography receive, its connections to sex trafficking, and the years of recovery after escaping the industry. But with this post, I want to briefly share three unscientific negative effects it has had on me as a viewer.

It distances me from my friends and family.
Porn is far more exciting than our normal, quiet, everyday lives. These hyper-beautiful, hyper-sexualized people are walking around and hooking up every couple minutes, and that simply does not happen in real life.

As a result, there have been many times I have felt far away and removed from those around me. Porn curbed my emotions and made me apathetic to those dearest to me. I didn't *want* this to happen, but it was the natural outcome of filling my mind with all these exaggerated scenes that were so much more *exciting* than *real* people in *real* life.

496

I would be in the same room as my friends, but my thoughts would be elsewhere.

The distance makes you lonely.

As a result, we lose connection with real people. We lose intimacy and this causes severe loneliness. This is part of what causes the cycle of addiction, because what is the fastest way to get rid of our loneliness?

More porn.

It is a shortcut to intimacy, but it is hollow. We do not get to *know* the people in these films, we only see one side of them. They are not complete humans to us. Pope John Paul II put it well:

> There is no dignity when the human dimension is eliminated from the person. In short, the problem with pornography is not that it shows too much of the person, but that it shows far too little.

The cycle is cruel, because it creates feelings of loneliness, then promises to heal them, all the while digging a deeper hole in which to bury you.

I don't like women.

After the viral video of my shirtless run in the rain blew up, a number of people asked how I could *possibly* still be single. Naturally, a number intimated that *there must be something wrong with him if he's still single!*

I've been telling everyone that I'm very picky. And this is entirely true. I am very selective with the women I choose to pursue and date. But largely, the way I view women as a whole has been impacted by pornography.

No longer am I satisfied with the cute girl next door. No, I need a strong Christian woman…with the body of a Kardashian and the smile of Melanie Laurent. And if she could have the lips of Emily Ratajkowski and the eyebrows of Cara Delevigne, that would be nice too.

Porn has made me not want women, but their pieces and parts.

I want all the 'benefits' without the effort of actually getting to know someone. To hear her deepest fears and insecurities, as well as her favorite movies and books. To cook up some inside jokes and share some memories. To get lost together in a big city, or run out of gas somewhere in the badlands.

Without my permission, porn has set the standard of beauty impossibly high, far too high for any *real* woman to attain. And therefore it has effectively prevented me from having any kind of romantic relationship the past several years.

There are studies proving that porn increases domestic violence, and I think this why. It trains us to not want humans, but body parts. And when these *body parts* are having a bad day, or *aren't in the mood*, or don't agree with us, violence ensues.

When we don't see people as humans, it's easier to treat them as objects... like punching bags.

Isn't that what Hitler did to the Jews? If you dehumanize someone enough, anything is permissible. And porn is doing the exact same thing to men and women by way of our sexuality. It has dehumanized it and reduced sex, this God-given gift, to body parts on a screen.

I end not with doom, but with praise to God, who makes all things new, all things beautiful, all things clean. Even if our addiction seems cyclically hopeless and deathly permanent, He is greater and has overcome.

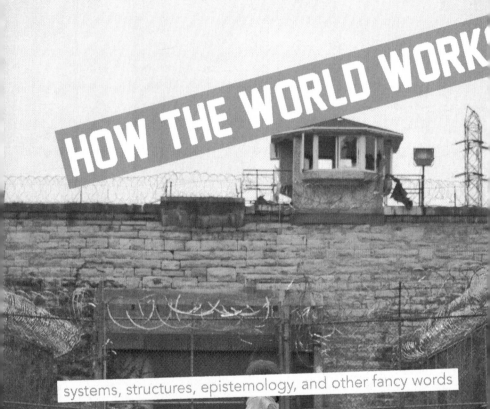

HOW THE WORLD WORKS

systems, structures, epistemology, and other fancy words

ZOOM OUT

'cause when you zoom out enough, you'll always reach the same thing.

I still feel like I'm not ready to write this piece. It's something I'm still learning which applies to every aspect of our lives.

It's the art of zooming out. How the heck do I describe it?

Last night I was playing frisbee at a park in Denver right when the pink sun set behind the Rocky Mountains. It was a beautiful night: Just cool enough to run around shirtless and not overheat. The game was great; the teams were split evenly and we went back and forth on the scoreboard for a while, until my team made a number of blunders and the other team shot several points ahead of us.

I started to get upset.

Then, I went to block this one pass and was successful. Unfortunately, he was whipping it across the entire field and I was point blank in front of him, catching the frisbee directly in the wrist. It hurt. A lot. I couldn't use my right hand for several minutes. It's still swollen.

I began to get angry. I stopped running for the disc and just walked, while the other players ran all around me. After a few minutes of moping, I started to tell myself,

zoom out.

I wasn't mad because we were down a couple points and I had made a (beautiful) block and hurt my wrist. I wasn't mad at my teammate's blunders, or even my own for that matter.

I was upset because my car broke down a few days ago and I'm deep in debt. I was upset because I'm not a huge fan of my new job (even though no job is good in the first week), and because the kids in my youth group are little termites whom I want to set on fire, and have really been testing my patience and wearing me down the past few weeks.

I was upset because I just want to hold someone's hand. It's been over five years since I've had one to grasp and the thundering pain of loneliness has been shivering up and down my spine lately. More so since I passed the midpoint of my twenties almost a year ago. I was upset because I'm battling my necessary millennial quarter-life crisis and the existential pangs of God's silence has been wearing heavier than usual on me lately.

That's why I was upset.
See what happened there? I zoomed out.

Suddenly I wasn't as upset about the score of the game or my throbbing wrist. Suddenly a lot of smaller things got out of the way and made room for bigger things to occupy my thoughts. I think this applies to every area of life. Everything that makes up your whole, entire life should be zoomed out. Your bank account, your anger and sadness, your addictions and vices. Your entertainment and friend group.

Zoom out.

Because if you zoom out far enough, you always get to God.

What's bigger than Him? How can you zoom out beyond Him? How can you see far enough to look past Him? How can you think hard enough to describe Him? What kind of mechanism can dissect Him?

Derrida would call this deconstruction, but I think it's the opposite. We are not zooming in so as to lose the picture in favor of the colorful blobs like the lilies in a Van Gogh. We are stepping back. We are seeing ourselves in light of a bigger picture. We are seeing ourselves—our current situation—through the eyes of Someone infinitely bigger than we are.

So zoom out.

The art of zooming out reminds us that everything is theological. I may be upset that my clutch blew out and I'm down $800, but what good is worrying about that when I remember that Jesus had His skin ripped off *for me?* Suddenly my issues become much smaller when they're held against the work of God.

In the words of Rob Bell, *this* is really about *that*.[1] Your anger at your wife isn't really about how she puts the dishes away; it's about something deeper in you. His cutting episodes aren't really about enjoying the feeling; they're about something else. We don't watch porn because we prefer 2-dimensional screens to actual human touch. We don't fall into substance addictions because we like putting foreign substances into our arms.

This is really about *that*.

What's happening in this bigger picture? You may not see it unless you...

zoom out.

When you think about God, do you think small thoughts? Do our perceptions of God Himself need to be zoomed out? Are we confining Him with our narrow lenses? Is He truly transcendent, or is He simply another addition to our lives?

I was chatting with my counselor an hour ago and he used a fitting analogy. He likes cooking, so he told me that our lives are like stews. We put in things we like, such as hobbies, jobs, friends, families, and interests. These are the meat and veggies in the stew. But God? God is the broth. God is what makes this stew a stew. In Him do the rest of the ingredients come together. He, like the broth, infuses the rest of the ingredients and binds them together, infusing them with flavor and life. Without Him, you just have a random pot of loose, dry ingredients.

He is in all and through all.

He is not just an ingredient in your life; He is the source of all things. Zoom out far enough from anything and you will always find Him and what He is doing. You will see Him making all things new and invading every area of your life.

We are stressed out people. We tend to only see ourselves. In the words of my theology teacher, 'we are very folded in on ourselves.' We are people who get hung up and distracted by small things, forsaking the bigger picture for a small detail which isn't going our way, so

---

[1] From his book *Sex God*

zoom out.

May we be people who know how to unclench our fists, let go of our preferences and opinions and learn how to see things and people other than ourselves. May we be people who can

zoom out.

ZOOM OUT: WASTE
there is this gigantic pile somewhere...

The other day I was at the gym. I never take a pre-workout before I workout unless it's offered to me for free, and this day it was. My gym had a rep from a supplement company come in and offer free pre-workout drinks, so I took one when I walked in, gulped it and threw the little plastic cup away.

Halfway through my workout I started to slow down so I went back to the table at the front and got another cup, filled it with the blue liquid, downed it and threw it away.

And then something happened.

It clicked for the first time that no one else will ever use those cups, and I had just used two when I could have used one.

I realized that there is a somewhat literal pile of trash somewhere that only Ethan Renoe has used, and every time I throw something away I am adding to the pile. (Is *that* what they mean by 'carbon footprint'?) But this realization had to do with more than tree hugging environmentalism. It wasn't just about the small plastic cups, but the attitude behind the action. I realized that as an American, it is of no cost to me to use and dispose of two plastic cups because *someone else* will take care of it. The little cups may be ruining the earth, but *someone else* will be affected, likely a few hundred years from now, or a few thousand miles away in a developing country. And I realized that cups add up. I may have only used one extra cup that day, but how many days of my life have I taken the extra cup? Multiply that by the

503

millions of Americans like me who think nothing of rapid use and quick disposal, and we have a huge pile of unnecessary plastic.

I recently read an article about how every piece of plastic ever created is still in existence. Then I read my friend Benji's response to it about people always making fun of him for his mason jars and wool coats but maybe he's onto something.

I forget where I read it, but Mother Teresa once said that only one thing in the world makes her angry:

Waste.

She said that violence and wars can be traced back to hurt and pain, and to a degree they're understandable, and also much harder to fix.

But waste? Waste is not only easy to fix but it's intentional. It's harmful but it does not come from hurt, it comes from laziness. The problem is that we as Americans are oblivious to the effects of our own waste because it doesn't affect our lives in the least. We are essentially partitioned off from seeing the results of our waste for the sake of our own comfort.

I mean, I don't want to think about how many plastic Starbucks cups I've used because I couldn't be bothered to bring my own cup or bottle and it's more CONVENIENT to just take a new one…

At this point you may be thinking, *Gee, Ethan is starting to sound like one of those turtle-kissing hippies who wears only clothes made of hemp, marches in PETA protests and takes delight in making his friends feel guilty. I only read this blog because of the warm and fuzzy Jesus vibes he usually gives…* and you're right, this is a slight departure for me. But it all ties back to

zooming out.

Because God cares about the environment. He said so when He called it "good," and he reinforced that when he instructed Adam to care for it and maintain it. That initiative remains to this day. We were not given the world to take advantage of it, squeezing every last drop from it for our pleasure. As Christians, we should care the MOST about the world God has given us. Because how we treat the creation reflects how we perceive its Creator.

Yet for some reason this has been largely overlooked in America in favor of tying Christianity to the issues of sexuality, pornography, anger management, and similar scruples. It's easy to walk into an American church building and not see a trace of environmental care. Whether it's the styrofoam coffee cups or the gargantuan power consumption (how many stage lights and fog machines are needed before the Holy Spirit arrives?), Christians have somehow divorced their faith from the environment.

I think that when Jesus says He's going to make all things new, He *does* mean erasing our addictions, shame and sin. But I also think He means trees and oceans and porpoises and marmots. I think that when we talk about joining Christ as He makes all things new, we must also talk about caring for this world we've been given. It means we should be aware of when we use two plastic cups when we could have used one, because that plastic goes SOMEWHERE. We need to

zoom out.

Because when we are so zoomed in on what makes MY life easier, it's easy to generate waste without thinking about it. It's easy to consume

and consume

and consume.

I think solutions can be easy to start out with. Things like taking a mug to the coffee shop with you, or riding your bike. My roommate and I compost everything we can, burn everything that burns, and only throw away what won't burn or compost. Since we moved in together in September, I think we've thrown away about a dozen bags of trash. It's still a lot, but we're trying to get creative in the ways we consume and dispose.

I don't want to reach the end of my life and look behind me to see this imaginary—but very real—mammoth pile of trash in my wake. I want to be able to say I did the best I could with what I had been given. That I did my best to join Jesus as He cultivates the New Heavens and the New Earth.

So join me. Let's be people who are conscious of the waste we produce and who strive to zoom out in order to see the effects it has on the world, not just the ease it contributes to our lives.

WHITE NOISE

I joke about being broke as if my stomach were actually empty.

Elliot and I were asked to watch two dogs this weekend. One is the size of a football player, the other the size of a football.

We walked into the home yesterday and heard the dogs upstairs screaming from their kennels. I ascended the stairs to free them from their cages and they were more than eager to get out. They were ramming their noses into the latch of the cage, pawing the ground because they were so excited to escape. Once the door was unlatched they took off and sprinted throughout the house, glad to be out of their prison.

Last night, I slept in the room where the dogs were kept and noticed something fascinating. Throughout the night, the dogs would return to their cages and lie in them for a few hours at a time, despite the fact the entire house was open to them. The doors of both kennels were wide open, and the pups would go lie comfortably in their crates.

There is a big difference between being locked in a cage and staying in one.

When I lived in Chicago, I volunteered to lead Bible studies in the prison on the South Side, aka, *Chiraq*. Walking into the cells each week, it was rare to see another white face. There were the occasional Hispanics, but the majority of the people in the prison were black.

It was through their eyes I began to see the experience of people who were born into a life of gangs, fatherlessness, violence and drugs. Hip hop was a pathway to salvation for many of them, but this same pathway led many to the same idols worshiped by Chief Keef or Lil' Wayne: Violence, abusive sex, and constant drug use.

They were born in the cage and the door was closed.

The language used in the detention center was barely English: Everything was a code and I realized how very little I knew about this world. Because if you're anything like me, a white person from suburban America, you'll

506

watch *8 Mile* or *Step Up 2* and think you have a comprehensive understanding of American black culture.

White noise.

We're sitting in a cage but the door is open.

Lately I've been streaming more Kendrick Lamar through my headphones and the thing I appreciate about him, for one, is his intelligence. He seems to have a poetic awareness of the story of his people, and he tells it well. There are a lot of false narratives in the world, so it's refreshing to hear an explicit explanation of the situation of millions in our country.

One of my favorite college professors wrote a blog post along the same lines last year, and I gladly borrow his emotion, if not his prosaic prowess.

"Who decides whose lives matter?"

Two dozen black people stand next to one of their burning homes. Arson in the Jim Crow era. Justice isn't a comfortable coffee shop conversation, it's standing near enough to the heat to smell your own hair being singed.

Some people call hip-hop the demon plaguing the inner-city youth,[2] but perhaps it's not quite as it seems. I hear sentiments like this and begin to realize just how much fear they mask. As if the problem could not possibly be systemic, an outcome instituted by our own white ancestors, but rather lies in the art created by the very ones being pushed down.

I used to be scared of swear words too.
We stifle a voice for telling an uncomfortable truth.

We carry in our physical bodies trauma experienced throughout our lives. I wonder how much trauma lies beneath the soil of our feet. How many African bodies lie in American dirt, having taken abuse, neglect, and tears into the grave with them? How many Jewish bodies occupy European soil, still containing the hatred and injustice of their persecutors?

---

[2] A reporter on Fox News once blamed hip-hop music for all of the trouble and hardship befalling black urban youth in America. For some reason, this doesn't seem to be quite accurate…

What are you taking to your grave?

I've come to realize that much of our world is shaped by systems with roots running far deeper than most of us realize, and so few of us make an effort to understand, much less shift these systems. Kids born into fatherless homes on the South Side of Chicago have so few options that their futures are almost pre-arranged.

The kennel door is firmly sealed by the hands of the comfortable.

I was born into a middle-class white family, and there is little I could do to escape this socio-economic position. I joke about being broke as if my stomach were actually empty.

Yet I look in the Scriptures and see Jesus voluntarily kneeling before the feet of His disciples, taking the rag in His hands and touching their disgusting heels. The Master become a slave; the strong become weak. If America is a massive pyramid scheme (something this recent election has made perfectly clear) then the Kingdom of God is an upside-down pyramid. It's a reversal of strengths and a healing of wounds.

It's the glory of a coming system which makes all things right and levels the ground before an all-consuming institution of justice. It's a country where all voices are heard and every soul is intimately known.

What good is a religion that doesn't turn the world on its head?

Once again we are reminded that the first are last, and that true religion, as James tells us, is to attend to the orphan and widow; the prisoner and the poor. The black and the white, the straight and the gay. To swing open our doors to them and usher in a taste of this coming kingdom.

A kingdom led not by the wealthy and aggressive, but by a man who would lay his life down for the very least in the world. Heath McNease raps:

> Where dread and beauty clash, it forces souls to speak
> and knees to bow and tongues to plead the blood that no one bleeds,

the kind that opens gates to welcome home the lowest thieves
the kind that gives us faces so we see what holy means.[3]

What kind of blood pours from a man who has voluntarily joined the ranks of the outcast? What kind of blood is able to open gates to welcome home the lowest thieves?

The blood of a good Father, starving for His children to come home.

The blood of a just Judge, longing for equality among His people.

The blood of the God-man, swapping places with the vile in order that they be made holy.

He has already unlocked the gate of my kennel and invited me out. And He's daily teaching me that I don't need to stay in the prison He's already opened. He has already demolished the power of our sin, shame, and even death.

It is us who often choose to remain in them.
Maranatha. Come soon, Lord Jesus.

READING MARX ON A SNOWY EVENING
the Reformation/Communism primer I wish I'd had years ago.

Tonight I bought two scary books: A novel by Stephen King and *The Communist Manifesto.*

I'm trying to figure out why so may people are so terrified of Marx, but maybe I'll soon figure it out. My uncle tells me I have the ability to write powerful and punchy prose, but my aim is communicate a relatively clear message. What is prose but poetry without line breaks?

Snow is gradually finding its way to the streets in the windless evening. I've got a good chai in me and it's a perfect night for composition. I have had a lot of thoughts lately, perhaps too many to condense into a post.

---

[3] From the song *Till We Have Faces*

Look at it like this: You come across a beach filled with stranded starfish. These poor creatures are utterly unable to move themselves back into the sea, so they simply lie on the sand awaiting their death by drought. There is absolutely no way to rescue every single starfish, so your internal reaction is sadness for such a mass death.

Then you see a man in the distance. He bends over and stands. Bends over and stands. As you get closer, you realize he is picking up starfish, one at a time, and lobbing them back into the water. [Let's pause here and recognize that there are two endings here. First, an emotionally-tugging one, then a realistic one.]

You ask him why he's doing this, because there are far too many to save and it doesn't matter. He bends over and tosses one into the ocean, "It mattered to that one."

And life is beautiful.

Of course, the logical observer will note that the small dent the Good Samaritan makes will still leave thousands of fish dead on the shoreline. His pithy maxim won't save these thousands of other lives, and that is where systems come into play.

A system hires a bulldozer, or a score of bulldozers, and pushes them all into the ocean, saving thousands at a time, though a few may get crushed on the outskirts of the plow.

A system is less warm but more effective at providing care for the masses.

Prior to the Reformation, before Atheism was invented, the Church was the vehicle for this care. It was the machine which took in the sick, the poor and the hungry and provided for them. The Church was the evidence of the coming of the Kingdom of God, witnessed by the world, as God's means of providing care to the world. However, in the wake of Luther's departure from the Catholic church, this machine was splintered. it was stunted and suddenly a space emerged between these two gargantuan forces (the Catholic and Protestant churches) where Western people realized that they could exist outside the world of the Church; outside the realm of God.

In the wake of the Reformation, as these two massive entities pulled away from one another, folks realized they didn't really need God to go on with life.

(Additionally, the splintering brought on by the Reformation effectively rendered the word "God" useless and it's why people like Meryl Streep and Lil' Wayne always seem to thank *It* when they win awards.)

Over time, the system's power shifted from the Church to the government. The State was now the one responsible for bulldozing the stranded and powerless starfish back into the sea. So the State took from the Church the responsibility for healthcare, welfare and soup kitchens, thus rendering, in many people's minds, the Church to be obsolete and useless.

And to be frank, it has left many postmodern Christians confused as to why their giving a PB&J to a homeless man hasn't solved the issue of homelessness in America. Because the issue isn't a single person being hungry; it's millions. And though the sentiment of giving out a sandwich is sweet and we can pat ourselves on the back, it still leaves 999,999 people hungry. And it leaves that same guy hungry tomorrow.

So as Christians, how do we interact with the System, which at this point in time, is the State? How do we join forces in order to feed the hungry and heal the sick in a way that's not ignorant of a bigger system at work? How do we zoom out enough to see the bigger picture?

Marx seeks to connect man to his labor in the absence of a higher power. His aim is 'liberation' from the class system after the divine monarchy dissolved and religion took a back seat to the State.

Think about it: So many kings thought they came to power because God elected them (Romans 13 and all), and the Papacy held enormous power over the empire as well.[4] That alone is enough to create a dichotomy between these people and those people. The more important and the less

---

[4] Pope Leo X even crowned Charlemagne 'Holy Roman Emperor' in 800AD, thus solidifying his control over the empire. I always told my history students that a marriage between the Church and political power will always end badly. Christianity thrives in the counterculture.

important. And the value trickles down from the top through the nobility to the peasants and slaves.

Take away the church's power as well as the existence of God, and in that post-Christian vacuum, you realize that all men are created equal. And no one deserves more than another. And that's where Marx's ideas come into play and sway the crowd.

We are still feeling the effects of his writings whether we know it or not. Whenever someone calls on the name on 'equality' to justify their actions or their cause, they are referring to Marx who upholds both humanism (read: Atheism) and equal rights across the board. (Sound familiar?)

So if this post leaves you, as a Christian, more confused as to how we are to act within the boundaries of our system, then you're not alone. The State is doing (or has potential to do) a lot of good for a lot of people, ever since the catholic (lowercase c) church split into a thousand pieces and left a vacuum for the needy people of the world.

Here is what I'm thinking about now, and invite you to join me:

—How should Christians act in order to shape our respective systems to look more like the Kingdom of God?
—SHOULD Christians fret over socio-political issues within the State, or focus our energies on the Church universal, God's intended vehicle for healing the world?
—Was the Reformation ultimately good or bad for Christianity, as it made many positive theological shifts, but brought about division on a level previously unknown to Christendom.
—What can I do to help?
—Is it worth picking up individual starfish and tossing them into the sea, despite the thousands of others left stranded? Is the parable of the one lost sheep vs. the 99 meant to be literal, or is that a naive reading of it?

SYSTEMS PT. 1: HOW TO UNDERSTAND THE WORLD

the church passes the baton to the state

I've decided to start writing some thoughts on the systems of the world and how they dictate our lives, our thoughts, our pursuit of *eudaimonia*[5] and especially our perceptions of God. These are just thoughts of mine trying to sort everything out in my mind, so they may not be 100% accurate, but they're how the world makes sense to me as I wade through a season of reasoning through and wrestling with them.

I can't remember when exactly my obsession with systems began, but it was sometime in the past year, and is related to many of the lyrics of Kendrick Lamar. I think it began with racism and a slow realization of what it means when people use terms like 'systemic racism' or 'structural oppression.' In short, these terms describe things which are larger than just one person hating another for the color of their skin. I was raised to hate racism and love all people equally, so for the majority of my life, I thought that people of all skin colors were awesome. I thought that, because I am pro-people of all colors, I am doing the best I can to create equality in our culture.

I never understood that historically, there are systems at work which have roots in the beginnings of America and beyond and have yet to be overturned, or at least adjusted. If Charlottesville has shown us anything, it's that racism is alive and well, which was a huge surprise to me, because I thought it was a very, very small percentage of the population which still felt that way. However, I have stumbled across a question which has begun to haunt me and make me ask questions bigger than myself. Questions like, If all racism was suddenly erased from the hearts of all humans, would the black or hispanic population of America still be oppressed and underprivileged? Would places like the South Side of Chicago still be overrun with gangs and underserved by their local government?

This is where questions of systems begin to rise, because it is much deeper and more foundational than simply a white person being nice to a black person. For example, a black boy is born on the South Side of Chicago and

---

[5] a Greek term for how we see the good life, or happiness and fulfillment

(assuming he is the rule and not an exception) his life has a gigantic handicap already. Statistically, he is more likely to have a father who is absent, incarcerated, or dead, and will be raised by his mother or siblings. (I am basing these statistics on my own experience working in the Cook County Juvenile Detention Center.) As a result of a lack of leadership, as well as a responsibility to help provide for his family, he will get involved in gangs, weapons dealing, or drug dealing, ultimately landing him in prison.

The family is the system to end all systems, and barring a few miraculous examples, people born into an unhealthy family system will almost always end up going down a small number of similar paths, none of which are hopeful. Generally speaking, no amount of church activities, after school programs or Good Samaritans will replace a healthy family system.

More shocking is the examination of how these families and neighborhoods go about changing in order to help young boys like our example. Historically, roughly until the time of Marx, help for these communities would have been doled out from the local church, as it was a member of the larger universal church working together to renew our world. Several hundred years ago, though, there was a shift in this responsibility and it was handed over to the State. We Americans live in a culture where there are two sides of the aisle, which can essentially be boiled down to small government versus big government.

While thinking through the divorce of the Church and State and the handling of power between these two, I suddenly realized *why* Republicans (typically the more 'conservative Christian' side of the aisle) generally lean toward a small government while Democrats lean toward a large government. Republicans come from a line of thought which argues that the church, as well as companies with a trickle-down philosophy, should be the entity to look after the poor, the hungry, the sick and the oppressed, and that the state should stick to its world of legislation and implementation of laws as they pertain to governmental responsibilities. Democrats, on the other hand, plea for a larger government to take control of providing for people in trouble, and that the church is unnecessary. This, in my mind, helps me understand why more secular people and liberal-leaning Christians tend to vote Democratic while your typical evangelical, conservative Christian will lean Republican.

However, in the tension of the current world we live in, there is a war over who *actually* steps in to aid our example inner-city boy. Churches try to do their best kingdom work, inviting lower socio-economic communities into their doors or after school programs, while government workers are doing the same thing, just with the religious element removed. Thus, according to one of my professors at Moody Bible Institute, "The humanitarian secular machine will do more to help the poor and needy in the world than you ever will in your lifetime." As we exit the long era of Constantine's Christendom and move into a universally more secular age, the system with the most power, money and resources is undeniably the State (the government). This is why Democrats (big government) call for more welfare, more healthcare, etc. from the State, because they won't count on the Church to provide those things the way it once did prior to the Reformation and/or Enlightenment, depending on how you read history.

One of the most detrimental shifts of the Protestant Reformation is the splintering of the Christian Church, and therefore, the weakening of the aid it is able to give. Each church has its own budget, its own mission, its own creeds, and so on. Rather than being the united mammoth it once was when it was united as one catholic (universal) church, it is hundreds of thousands of smaller denominations which gather and believe, often in relative isolation. This is why it's a joke when a non-denominational church makes a daytrip downtown to hand out peanut butter and jellies to homeless people. Systems are the reason this is ultimately a waste of time. Why would they get excited about a PB&J when they could walk a few blocks and grab a warm meal and maybe a bed for the evening, paid for by the State.

Shifting systems is the way to change people's lives.

Doing the most good for the highest number of people involves understanding systems, not just having a good heart which 'breaks for the poor and oppressed,' but a heart attached to a mind which understands the way things really change in this world. I'm still trying to figure out the role of a Christian in a world which moves slowly like the turning of a cruise ship. It is a slow shift which comes about by people with power, or a large group of people with a loud enough voice, like the slow turning of large gears. I guess the question I catch myself asking is, What can one person with limited resources do to shift the nature of the American system and help it operate in a more kingdom-oriented manner? It's huge, I know.

SYSTEMS PT. 2: I HAVE FAITH IN THE SYSTEM
"scrap the systematic theologies"

"I have faith in the system," said agent Madani.

The fictitious CIA agent in Marvel's *The Punisher* exquisitely encapsulates the modern notion of the government as a suitable replacement for God. In the first season, she and her small team are on the hunt for the truth about a mission gone sour in the Middle East. Rather than assume the corruption of all human nature, she has decided to fully thrust her faith into the system constructed by the American constitution writers. If she can't catch the perpetrators of injustice, the system of government will. Their wrongs will be exposed eventually due to the nature of the way the hierarchy is set up. Of course, in this fictional world, Frank "The Punisher" Castle takes matters into his own hands and sprays bullets everywhere until justice is fully served.

Madani's faith in a human system reflects a much larger epidemic of materialistic (secular) belief we see in our culture. That somehow, sinful, broken and selfish humans can construct a flawless system in which justice will be served and all will be provided for equally. But if the past few years have shown us anything, it's that our system of government, law, and the way those laws are executed is fundamentally flawed. People have placed too much faith in the system of government to dole out equal measures to all people while neglecting the fact that the people pulling the strings are also looking out for their own well-being, usually above that of the masses'.

In the recent election, evangelical Christians put Trump in the most powerful office in the world and I can't help but wonder if their emotions were swayed by a conflated view of the governmental and the ecclesial systems. This leads me to wonder if our systematic theology is in dire need of straightening out, or scrapping entirely.

As a Millennial theologian, it's romantic to push for a razing of systematics in theology with the argument that an infinite God cannot be constrained and described by mere human language. I was in Kansas City for a conference years ago and overheard two guys talking. One was a friend of mine and the other was someone we had just met who was attending a different Bible college. "What do you think when it comes to systematics?" our new acquaintance asked.

"Scrap it," my friend waved his hands in a tree-chopping motion. "Get it out of here. It's useless." Since then, I've seen arguments for both sides of this theological quandary. Is it worthwhile to attempt to construct systems by which God operates? Or by which He is measured and described? After all, doesn't He do as He pleases and our feeble attempts to understand Him are just a chasing after the wind?

What, then, is the work of theology? This question is answered by the fact that we do not worship a God who is silent in His magnitude. He is not distant in His transcendence. We worship a God who is incredibly near and very loud.

We worship a God who reveals Himself to us. He moves toward us.

He knows us and wants to be known by us. This is the difference in worldview between Christianity and every other religion or worldview in the world. Agnostics are people who claim the transcendence and holiness of a god they cannot comprehend, but it doesn't want to be known. It's more akin to the notion of The Force in *Star Wars* than it is a living, active Person who may be described. Buddhism doesn't even refer to itself as a religion, but a philosophy. Roman and Islamic gods leave humans striving just to attain their attention and mercy.

It is *because* Yahweh is a person that we may have any hope at all of knowing and understanding Him. What's more is that this distant, unknowable, inexhaustible God came TO us in the man Jesus of Nazareth and met us in our wickedness. This incarnation of God is the heart of our gospel, for otherwise we would simply be stabbing at the air and constructing humanistic philosophical structures built on little more than conjecture about the nature of the divine. God is knowable and reveals Himself.

With this in mind, let's return to Donald Trump and the Christians who voted him into office. Donald Trump currently sits atop the apex of a human system built by constitution writers, a gigantic military, and an extreme nationalism which rivals that of Ancient Rome and Greek city-states. How did he get there? By working the system, and especially by playing heavily into less educated people's notions of religion and the conflated nature of God and America. One of the reasons I began this series of systems posts is that people often vote with one person in mind: Themselves. By refusing to see the world beyond ourselves, we have crippled the democratic system of voting. When I put myself in the shoes of a rural voter, I can see why they would want to elect someone who promises to make *their* life better in a myriad of ways. He said very nice things to tickle their ears. Then again, so did the false prophets in the Old Testament whom God cursed repeatedly...

Historically, the Western Church was its own freestanding system, operating with a top-down flow of leadership and guidance from the Vatican. It was a much more powerful force because it was not splintered as the churches we see today around the world are, but it could do a lot of good for a lot of people, and had significant political power of its own merit. Not all of these were good things. Look at the crowning of Charlemagne in 800 A.D.. In a disgusting act of symbolic drama, it was the Pope who physically put the crown on the new Holy Roman Emperor, thus indicating that if anyone had control of the empire, it was really the Pope. Power plays like this would ultimately lead to Luther's penning of the 95 theses 500 years ago. The Catholic church got into a lot of trouble getting mixed up in political houses of cards and causing mass violence and destruction because of political vows. This is part of what led to the Reformation, and ironically, Evangelical Christianity, which in turn put Trump in office: A man who heavily used his notion of conservative and 'Christian' ideals (as well as a buttload of cash) to win himself the office.

See how history repeats itself?

When it comes to systematic theology, one of the downfalls is that we think we have worked out a perfectly oiled and functional machine *in which* our little rendition of god can run about and do as he pleases. This is the god I see smeared all over America. With such a small god, it's not surprising that many Americans, while claiming the name of Christ (more as a lifesaver than authentic worship) turned to politics as their source of hope. A man who claimed the same allegiance both to god and country as they do promises them a better life and they're going to jump on board. This also comes with the promises of destroying not only political enemies, but spiritual enemies as well (i.e. the *Islamic State*...Like, could it be more plainly spelled out? *Islamic* = spiritual, *State* = political).

Since I'm friends with a LOT of Christians on Facebook, I saw a lot of similar posts around the time of the election, each containing a similar notion of *I don't care who wins this election because God has put them there*. I couldn't help but think that their statements were a bit trite. While this is true, and it's true that we are citizens of a higher, coming country, this does not call for negligence in our roles in the American governmental system. I can't help but wonder if this notion stems from some kind of union in our minds between the American nationalistic ideal and the kingdom of God. In other words, 'because God loves America the most, He is going to ultimately pick who's in office, and it'll all go swimmingly.' This overlooks a lot of scripture which would demonstrate that yes, God puts every leader into their position of authority, but often these leaders are wicked and evil and are meant to punish the people whom they rule. The sentiment which normally accompanied these types of posts were more optimistic, suggesting that God will take whoever gets elected and use their leadership for good.

We live in a country where the masses have the ability to sway political outcomes (to some degree, anyway), so should we not influence it in favor of doing the *most* good for the *most* people? I struggle to find the balance between trusting that this system can and will do good for her people, but remaining cynical that any manmade system will not ultimately crumble.

This is why we Christians have hope in the coming Theocracy: A governmental system ruled and dictated by a good and just God. A God whom systematics cannot fully define, yet who reveals Himself to us. The kingdom of God is a perfect union of Church and State, you could say. We cannot fully systematize our infinite God, but we can tangibly see how our government works. Perhaps that is why some have settled for a democracy as an adequate substitute for God on earth. Perhaps this is why so many Americans put their faith in the president, because to them, he is the closest their minds can get to God. And for the most part, this isn't their fault, it's the fault of a church system which favors emotion over intellect or political leanings over truth.

My head hurts now from thinking so much about things I know so little about.

I'm hungry so I'll end this here.

SYSTEMS PART 3: YOU CAN'T WIN
sounds pretty simple, right?

James is one of the smartest people I know, and has provided me with much of the framework for thinking through seeing the world and her systems. Today we spent a decent amount of time talking through an issue, only to arrive at a rather hopeless conclusion. We began talking about my resolution, initiated earlier this year, to stop buying new clothes and to patronize only thrift stores. My intentions behind starting the resolution were solid, as I wanted to see an end to my support of companies which profited from the sweat of slave laborers who sourced their goods.

Sounds pretty simple, right?

Buying used clothes sends none of my money to the big corporations which enslave thousands of people and force them into unfair and unsafe working conditions. It hasn't been very hard, but there has been the occasional temptation to snoop around at H&M or Urban Outfitters, but so far I have stayed true to my resolution.

Now, here's why that matters: Because it doesn't.

Because other articles I read while diving into internet research pointed out that some thrift stores are just as detrimental to local economies as the big brand-name stores. Goodwill, for instance, takes crates full of clothes which didn't sell in America and dumps them into third-world countries. Sounds like a win-win, right?

What this actually does is run local clothes-makers out of business, because why is there a need for clothes to be produced when American companies are dumping their goods into your town for free? Not only are they free clothes, they're free *Western* clothes, which for some reason, is how the world wants to look.

To review, my two options are, support gigantic conglomerate companies which employ sweatshops to produce their goods, or support thrift stores which essentially put tailors in developing countries out of business, disrupting local economies. It's a lose-lose situation. James, however, pushed me to follow a logical rabbit trail to its end. He took me back to the history of tribal ethics, which went something like this:

> Imagine you live in a small tribe where your actions are judged according to the tribal systems and if you do something wrong by these, word will spread among your family, your in-laws, the tribal elders, etc. Your morals are self-contained within your tribal system, and your own fear of shame from these people you know intimately will prevent you (for the most part) from breaking this ethical code.

Nowadays, however, the system is universal. you are not judged according to tribal ethical codes, but according to universal codes which are generally abstract and invisible. For instance, you don't want to drop an empty soda can on the sidewalk because of fear that people will see you and hold you accountable to this unwritten universal code of ethics. Not only that, but many people would go so far as to fear dropping it in the trash can as opposed to the recycling, because 'trash is destroying the environment while recycling is saving it.' We modern people hold ourselves, for the most part, to this universal ethic which is heavily cultural, and more and more politically-based.

So when I decide to shop exclusively at thrift stores, I am making a minute change which may or may not make a tangible difference in anyone's life, but I assume it will because of what I have learned about human slavery and production of merchandise. My 'moral good' is more abstract than it is tangible. I will never meet someone who *would have* made that t-shirt I *didn't* buy at Target. Make sense?

In other words, despite my convictions about buying new clothes, it is nearly impossible to trace the effect it is having on the world.

James pushed further.

"Do you drive a car?" he crackled through my headphones.

I do. And this led to the greatest irony. Because, while I've been attempting to save the anonymous Malaysian worker from his laborious job, I've been pumping the atmosphere with exhaust fumes, which help to stir up hurricanes and typhoons which attack Malaysia and destroy his family's home. (Yes, this is heavily hyperbolic and anecdotal, but follow the illustration.) The very person I'm trying to help in one way is the very same person affected by another one of my actions in a different category.

So, does this mean that I sell my car and buy a bike? Will the world be a better place when I do that? No, not really. Because one person, as I've said before, can do very little to change a world run by systems.

Think of the legendary film *Fight Club*, which (spoiler alert!) ends by destroying the American economy in an attempt to reset the world and level the playing ground.

"Revolution will never work," said James. "You cannot simply call to destroy the system because the system is always going to reinstate itself. The same hierarchy is going to surface." Someone will become richer and others will be oppressed. And those at the top of the system will always take advantage of those caught in the gears of it. The poor will always be pushed down.

"If you think revolution is the answer, destroying the system and starting over, all you're doing is creating a new elite." This is why *Fight Club's* proposal is flawed. Because when the credit card companies' skyscrapers fall, Tyler Durden is the new elite. He is the new ruler. And right there, a new system is initiated and he is now atop the hierarchy. Because there will always be jobs people don't want to do and the labor is pushed down the line until someone is poor or weak enough to be forced to do it.

There is a reason for this, and then there is hope. The reason is, ultimately, we live under the jurisdiction of the system of satan. He is the "Prince of the air,"[6] and until he is dethroned once and for all, all of our attempts at righteous systems will be flawed. This is the beauty of the Kingdom of God: A system ruled and governed by God alone. A kingdom where justice is served to all, and where none are oppressed and all are equal. Truly equal.

The hope comes in the form of the very first Christian prayer: *Maranatha; Come soon, Lord Jesus.*

In other words,

Come, Lord Jesus. Disrupt the system. Bring the kingdom of God, where justice and mercy reign and you judge men.

Until that time, I continue to ask myself the question of Francis Schaeffer, which has haunted me for years: *How then shall we live?*

My thinking behind the thrift store resolution was not necessarily to change the world or disrupt the product flow of H&M, but to take responsibility for what *I* am able to change. I cannot control how my neighbor spends his money, but I can control how *I* do. I am not responsible for what is in the pockets of America, but in the pocket of Ethan Renoe. And with *that,* I decide not to fund sweatshop-using conglomerates. I may never see an ounce of change in this, but what I will be able to do is say that "I did the best with what I was given," which is really the best any of us can say. We are not responsible for the world, but we are responsible for what's entrusted to us. Some of us are trusted with more, while others are given less. And from those entrusted with much, much will be expected.

That is a thought which should haunt us.

---

[6] Ephesians 2:2

SYSTEMS PART 4: LORD OF THE SYSTEM

<u>when the kingdom comes, it will not be a handout system of welfare</u>

Many years ago, I got my third tattoo at a shop in Pennsylvania. It was the result of many months of learning about the kingdom of God; it's a passage from the Lord's prayer across my heart: "your kingdom come." Pretty simple, yet profound. In the years since getting it, I have not once regretted putting that phrase over my heart, as I believe it is the sole goal of every Christian: To advance the kingdom of God and pray that it come.

While the tattoo itself has reflected a constant truth I have held close to my heart (pun intended) for almost a decade, my understanding of this concept of the kingdom of God has certainly deepened. Perhaps more so in the past several months, as I have reflected heavily on this notion of systems.

A few days ago, my dad sent me this fantastic yet intense article on capitalism,[7] the kingdom of God and the early church. The author, David Bentley Hart, essentially argues several things over the course of several paragraphs: The teachings of Jesus are extreme. They are not small, anecdotal bits of wisdom meant to gently correct us in our 10-minute daily devotions; they are system-overhauling, paradigm-shifting teachings which are meant to essentially wreck the way the world runs in favor of introducing kingdom concepts. He points out that many English translations modify the original Greek to soften the blow of what the early writers were actually saying. Hart also argues that Capitalism is the most humanistic and secular form of economy, isolating individuals, creating competition, and creating a culture of selfish accumulation. He points out that the early church as described in Acts 4 most accurately looks like a Christian form of communism because everything was held in common and no one was in need. He also argues that wealth itself, not just the love of wealth, is sinful.

Yesterday I brought the article up to a business- and finance-savvy friend of mine while driving him home from the airport to get his take on the anti-biblical nature of Capitalism. By the end of our conversation, I arrived at

---

[7] *Christ's Rabble* by David Bentley Hart

the same conclusion I had before, and to be honest, it is nothing new. In fact, it is the very first prayer ever prayed communally by the Church: *Maranatha, come quickly, Lord Jesus.*

A simple salve for the problem of capitalism would be for Christians to push for communism, because ideally, it solves all our problems. No poor people and no super rich people. Similarly, many Christians have earnestly sought to live in communes where things are held in common, no one is in need, and the elderly are looked after and provided for. There are problems with that model as well, which I won't explore here, save to say that this effectively removes Christians from the rest of society and leaves the rest of the world to rot. It's sort of a hipster way of singing the old gnostic hymn, *I'll fly away, oh glory, I'll fly away. When I die, hallelujah by and by…*

The world is bad and corrupt? Ok, let's just leave it behind and fly away to our own little utopian bubble.

The problem is, no matter where we run in this world, or what systems we try to implement, our world is fallen, broken and corrupt. It is ruled by 'the spirit of the air,' the evil one who wishes for the destruction of humans and their flourishing. It convinces us to desire things which ultimately lead us down twisted paths toward our doom. It makes sin look appealing and allows us to justify our transgressions.

No matter where you look in human history, you see people attempting to create a system which is most effective for the highest number of people. Even the American experiment was founded on the principles of freedom, democracy, and equality, but it has become a popularity contest. The founders who fled European oppression were looking for religious freedom, and some would argue, a theocracy where God would rule over His people. The same idea governed the Holy Roman Empire, the title of which demonstrates the marriage of Church and State (Holy + Roman), which again led to violence, conquest in the name of God, and torture at the hands of inquisitors.

No matter what system is implemented by human hands, people will be neglected, overlooked, hurt, or brainwashed for the very simple reason that humans themselves are flawed and imperfect. No one has complete wisdom to see every possible outcome, or complete vision to *see* every single person and see that their needs are met. No one has the ability to set laws in place which prohibit waste, encourage environmentalism, and maintain a functional and just economy. In essence, no one has the ability to cure the human heart of its twisted and selfish desires and quiet its fears and envies.

For years, I puzzled over the original prayer of the Christians. Why were they so desperate for Jesus to come quickly? *I feel like I'm doing pretty well... Plus, I want to get married, so I sort of hope Jesus takes His time in coming back.*

The more I zoom out from myself, however, and am able to recognize that I am not the only human on earth, and that there is ongoing injustice, persecution, hunger, disease, and pain in the world, the more I am able to honestly pray with the early believers. The more I see that systems are rigged toward the elite and wealthy, the more I lose hope in human systems and in any sort of satisfaction in this life. In fact, I am coming to the conclusion that this world and her systems are *utterly* hopeless and beyond repair by our own hands.

The only solution for a complete system overhaul and healing of the world must come from somewhere else, as we are not going to find it within this world. The only hope is a new system, not conceived and enforced by men, but by a higher power. In light if this realization, it changes the way I read Christ's announcements of the coming of the kingdom. For the longest time, I saw it as a 'bro-ish' motivational message, that I got to be a part of the revolution for the kingdom, like one of the men fighting alongside William Wallace in *Braveheart*. It pumped me up to lift a lot of weight and shamelessly tell people about Jesus (not bad things in and of themselves). Or perhaps it could aid me in looking like a better Christian who was stoked about this idea of the kingdom. In other words, because of my upbringing in a postmodern, consumeristic, individualistic culture, I saw the coming of the kingdom as pretty Ethan-centric. This, of course, is diametrically opposed to the message of what a kingdom *is* by definition. A kingdom is not made up of one person, or even one friend group, nor is a king a ruler over just one person. It is much, much larger than that.

We may read books like *Jesus Calling* and think of Jesus as nothing more than a soft-spoken counselor type who wants to cuddle us to sleep every night and hear all of our complaints. Then we get confused by passages in the Bible where Jesus seems to lose His almighty temper or say harsh things to people which seem unnecessary. It's a "Jesus-for-me" Christianity.

But after looking at the world through the lens of systems, I've realized that Jesus is announcing that *He* is taking the throne. *He* is implementing this new system which will ensure enduring peace, justice, and satisfaction for *all*. He, who can see everyone in every hidden corner of His kingdom, will look after His people with fairness and impartiality. This is why those who are oppressed by human systems have a much better understanding of the implications of the coming of the kingdom than we who are comfortable, self-serving, self-providing Americans.

The way His system works will be perfect. It will bring healing and food. It will not be a hand-out system of welfare, but a kingdom where everyone will do work and be satisfied by what their hands have done. In a semi-Marxist way, His kingdom will reconnect men with the labor of their hands. The more we can think about the hope we have in the coming kingdom (or system), the more excited we will get to hurry the coming of Christ. And it is in *this* way that we may eagerly, not reluctantly, pray *Maranatha, Come, Jesus, and be the Lord of our system.*

When a good, loving and perfect God is the ruler of our system, what could go wrong? I eagerly anticipate this kingdom more and more; not only because I will be healed and made new, but because the entire world and all of her systems will be as well. And that is something worth celebrating.

SYSTEMS PART 5: RIGHTEOUS ANGER
and that's why Jesus went into a fury against an unjust system.

Today I was in the gym (and now I'm in a coffee shop…and now you literally know the entire life of Ethan), and the cardio theater was playing a movie called *Walking Tall*. I had never seen it before, but I had a vague idea that it was a revenge/vigilante story starring Dwayne "The Rock" Johnson which would pump me up to exercise.

I wasn't disappointed.

In summary, the film centers around Johnson's character, who is returning to his small rural hometown after years as a special forces officer. He comes home to find that the town where he grew up has been overrun by corrupt and greedy businessmen who have opened a casino which essentially runs the town. The casino cheats its customers and its employees sell drugs to the local high schoolers, including Johnson's nephew who is hospitalized after a crystal meth overdose.

He goes to the police, only to find that the sheriff is just as corrupt/spineless as the rest of the town, which is when Johnson decides to take matters into his own beefy hands. He trashes the casino, breaks some bones of the employees, and doles out justice to the drug dealers. Without giving the ending away, it is a macho film which revels in the simplicity of vigilante-driven, action-packed justice.

We love to see this satisfying collapse of a corrupt system as we join in the righteous anger of her executor, don't we? Because deep down, humans crave justice. We are wired to hate injustice and oppression, so when we see the fury of a huge islander unleashed on the crooks, we feel satisfied.

This plot is not dissimilar to many we've seen before: *Braveheart's* William Wallace finds his beloved homeland overrun by the English tyrants who are oppressing his people, and we love to see him go primal with that buck antler. The Resistance in *Star Wars* is standing against the enormous Empire whose wicked hands control the galaxy.

Of course, when we look at the world in which we live, it becomes evident that things are rarely this black and white. Systems pull strings and make people look bad from one angle but good from another.

"Everyone is just trying to get by."

The top-down overhauls of systems, as I mentioned in the previous chapter, only results in creating a new elite. Anger rises in my chest the more I think about the absolute hopelessness in every constructed human system. Despite their superficial 'mission statements,' these systems always end up being rigged against the poor and weak and in favor of the wealthy and powerful.

And that's why Jesus went into an angry fury against an unjust system.

This is an oft-brought up, yet frequently misunderstood story found in all four gospels. John 2:14 tells us that He found people selling animals and changing money "in the temple courts."

Now, the location here is the most important piece of understanding why this caused such an intense reaction from the Lord. The temple courts sat outside the heart of the temple, where the Israelites would come and make sacrifices to Yahweh. The courts were reserved for a very specific group of people: The poor, the needy, and the Gentiles (non-Israelites).

The outsiders.

Jesus' rage happened during Passover, which is when thousands of people would have made the pilgrimage to the temple just to worship God and make sacrifices. The holiday was a marvelous time for people to come together and worship God in community, but over time, the religious leaders (much like the modern day Christmas or Easter industry) only saw dollar signs. They saw an opportunity to profit by selling people animals to sacrifice and changing their money into currency which would be acceptable in Jerusalem.

Their greed consumed so much space that it eliminated the opportunity for Gentiles and the poor to come and worship. Much like the casino in *Walking Tall,* the people with the money and power were the ones calling the shots and pushing away those labeled "outsider."

And *this* is why God went nuts.

This is why Jesus turned into Dwayne "The Rock" Johnson and destroyed their marketplace. Because not only was God's house, which was supposed to be a welcoming place for all people to come and connect with God, turning people away, but the religious people were profiting and becoming richer and more powerful because of it.

John notes in verse 17, "His disciples remembered that it is written: 'Zeal for your house will consume me,'" which is a line taken from Psalm 69. And I think that we too are called to this sort of zeal. This righteous anger.

I think each of us is called to lose our minds in the face of injustice, when the rich are oppressing the poor and the religious are profiting off of the outsider. After all, around my wrist is the classic W.W.J.D. bracelet, and in this case, the answer to "What Would Jesus Do?" is, turn over some tables and violently drive some people out of the house of God.

Matthew 11:12, "The kingdom of heaven is taken by violence and the violent seize it."

But what does this look like in tangible terms? In talking about systems, the story of *Walking Tall* is evidently far-fetched, as no man can singlehandedly overturn an entire city's corrupt system. Even Jesus' episode in the temple didn't last long, as there is another recorded event of Him clearing the temple not 3 years later, shortly before He is crucified. The rich and powerful rushed back in and continued what they had been doing before.

Growing up in the church, I've heard the expression dozens of times in messages on anger, especially in relation to this story: *Anger isn't bad, as long as you're angry at the right things.*

For decades I wondered what the "right things" were, but looking again at this story in its context and through the lens of Systems, it starts to make more sense. I begin to understand why we love William Wallace, Luke Skywalker, and obviously, Jesus Christ, because they stand up to corrupt systems of power and oppression and win. I used to feel guilty loving those films because I had an anemic view of Jesus as a weak and soft pacifist. In reality, Jesus stood up to the religious *and* political systems of the time and even announced that a new one was on its way: The kingdom of God.

It's the system where He will rule with justice, mercy and equality. The system where we will no longer have need for a strong hero to rise up and overthrow her wicked leaders, because there will be no injustice or profiting off of outsiders.

Once again I land at the same conclusion I have before: *Maranatha, come swiftly, Lord Jesus.* And in the mean time, may we be people who absolutely lose our cool at the sight of injustice and the oppression of the weak.

SYSTEMS PART 6: RESISTANCE
it's gonna cost us everything.

If you've never listened to Josh Garrels before, what have you been doing with your life? I have had one of his songs spinning on repeat for a week now, partly because Garrels is brilliantly aware of how systems and frameworks shape the lives of everyone in the world. Specifically his song "The Resistance" is phenomenal and actually opens with the line,

> *I was born into a system constructed for failure.*
> *It's a sinking ship being manned by drunken sailors.*

He then proceeds to deconstruct the world from the perspective of one on the outside of it, an objective view of the world we live in:

> *A pyramid scheme with it's cogs and it's pistons.*
> *Mechanization of men, making more and more*
> *Live in a miserable existence*
> *How can so few take so many victims?*

And the last line of the first verse begs the question:

> *How do good men become a part of the regime?*
> *They don't believe in resistance.*

The thing I love about Josh Garrels, possibly more than his jaw-dropping musical ability, is his brilliant understanding of the world and the Word. I had the chance to see him in concert several years ago, and prior to his performance he gave a small lecture. At the time, I was part of a missions organization which was incredibly charismatic, so I just wanted "spiritual pump-up sessions" rather than philosophically rich lectures.

I don't remember the entirety of Josh's message, but I do recall him talking at length about McDonald's and Wal-Mart and how this is so contrary to the way God designed Christians as creatives who should not be industrialized and mass-produced, but should be loud and unique and speak truth in an era of deception and blind obedience.

Looking back on it, it seemed like Garrels was going through a similar season I'm going through now: He was torn about the comfort and injustice he witnessed when he looked around and tried to make sense of it. It seemed like he hadn't prepared for the speech, but had simply stood up and opened up about what he was wrestling with at the time. Don't get me wrong—it was fantastic, and likely the same thing would happen if someone asked me to stand up and speak on something right now without any prep time.

Now I am beginning to understand why he was so passionate about the topic. And since he is exponentially wiser and better-read than I, his solutions come from a much deeper place. "The Resistance" ends with:

Hold fast my people and sing
Through peace and through suffering
All for the joy that it brings, to be free
It's gonna cost us everything
To follow one Lord and King
True love endures everything
To be free

For the past couple months, I have been teaching through the life of Moses in my Sunday School class and the exact magnitude of what Moses and Aaron did has come to life in ways it never has before. Moses literally went up to the head of the human system (Egypt) and demanded that he let 1.2+ million people—their workforce (Hebrews)—leave the country.

Imagine a Jew approaching Hitler and telling him to 'just shut down the whole Nazi thing.'

Or a black slave approaching some southern legislator in the 1800's and telling him to release all the black slaves in America and let them go free.

It simply doesn't happen.

The person would most likely be executed or simply taken as a slave himself. It's fascinating looking at the Moses story through this lens, then, because Moses is no longer just a 'Bible character from Sunday School,' but an actual disruptor of a massive system. The story of God's liberation is so much crazier when you realize that Moses would have had no audience with Pharaoh if he had not been raised by his daughter as an Egyptian noble. He was born pretty darn near the top of the system, yet he was of the people scraping the bottom, the Hebrews.

That, in addition to the wonder-working power of God allowed him to stand up to the wicked regime of the Egyptians (For a refresher, the Egyptians enslaved the Israelites after Joseph had moved his people there and a ruler came to power who forgot what Joseph had done in Egypt. They were unjust rulers to them, and when the Israelites became too numerous for them, the Egyptians began killing their newborns by tossing them in the Nile River).

Put yourself in Moses' shoes for a moment. You, a solitary man, are approaching one of the most powerful men in the world and demanding that he release his entire free labor force. All you have is a stick which sometimes turns into a snake (which isn't that unusual apparently, since the king's magicians can do the same thing by their dark arts) and the promise of YHWH that He has your back.

As mentioned in Part 5, the resistance is often painted as this glorious escapade, as in *Star Wars* or *Braveheart,* but in reality it's rarely that dramatic. Moses was petrified of what he was called to, to the point that his brother Aaron had to do all the speaking for him. All of it, not some of it.

Humans crave this resistance to corrupt human systems, but the work of resisting the powerful systems is not only incredibly hard, it is not appealing or rewarding. Moses pulled his 1.2 million people out of Egypt and then died on the mountaintop before ever entering the Promised Land. Resistance today, as Christians, is wildly unpopular. It means refusing to live in sin and follow the ways of the world. It means recognizing that your body is purposed differently than those of the non-believers and you don't get to use it hedonistically to extract your own pleasure from the bodies of others. When God calls us to be holy as He is holy, this isn't a gentle or minor command. It means looking and acting diametrically opposite to the way *most* people act. And this comes with ridicule.

I can't tell you how many times I've been urged to just get out there and lose my virginity, even by people who have nothing to gain by telling me that! Atheists argue that my faith is outdated and legalistic, and my views on human sexuality is too restrictive. I am pressured from every way to accept and affirm things which are clearly outside the intended will of God as laid out in His Word. Am I a 'resister' like Moses?

Yes and no.

I am far from standing up to an entire nation oppressing my own people and killing their young. But I am also different from them. My most recent tattoo is a small black square next to a large hollow circle. Very simple visually but bottomless in symbolic imagery. One of the meanings I ascribe to it is this notion of 'set-apart-ness' or the holiness demanded of believers from the world. We are divorced from the lures of the flesh and temptations of the world, and there is this forced reconciliation that happens when we live "according to our old ways," as Paul puts it. We are to look—to the world—the way a small black square would to a large white circle. We have nothing in common with them.

And I think this is what resistance looks like today: It may not be a violent revolt or a political upheaval, but I marvel at the strong and quiet power of men and women who take stands simply by living lives to honor God rather than their own flesh. Lives which please Him rather than themselves. Because our culture desperately wants us to be in love with ourselves and ourselves alone, because then they can sell us more goods. Selflessness is the root of resisting this Spirit of the Air and standing against our version of Egypt. Our oppressors are not as blatant as slave driving babykillers, but they are present. We were born into a system, and continue to live in it blindly for the most part. We confess the name of Christ but are swayed by every appealing advertisement on television. Our hearts are pulled between sacrifice and consumerism. And many of us think we can have both.

Be wary if you cannot tell which parts of your life are submitted to Christ.

The way you spend your money, the way you use your body, the way you interact with friends and family, or the thoughts you allow to remain in your head. Have you taken it and made it captive to Christ? Or are you blinded by the human system in which you were raised, unable to discern between the pull of the Holy Spirit and the allure of a model selling expensive clothes for a fashion conglomerate?

James says, Religion that God our Father accepts as pure and faultless is this: to look after orphans and widows in their distress and to keep oneself from being polluted by the world.[8]

Are you polluted or are you willing to resist the system?

Leonard Ravenhill said that something that is 99.9% pure is not pure at all. It is diluted. Purity refers to absolute, 100%, complete perfection and faultlessness.

Grow more aware of the system you are in and how it has shaped and formed you. You many think you are old enough to understand how the world works, yet it took Moses the first 40 years of his life to realize how unjust the Egyptians were to his people, and 40 more to gather up the courage to do something about it. Don't wait till you're 80 to resist the corruption of the system.

We may do our parts to incrementally change our very small portion of the world, but it is not until Jesus returns and institutes the new system, the Kingdom of God, that justice will truly be universal and distributed to all. So, with the very first believers we pray,

Maranatha, come swiftly, Lord Jesus.

Isaiah sings,

> Is this the kind of fast I have chosen,
>> only a day for people to humble themselves?
> Is it only for bowing one's head like a reed
>> and for lying in sackcloth and ashes?
> Is that what you call a fast,
>> a day acceptable to the Lord?
> "Is not this the kind of fasting I have chosen:
> to loose the chains of injustice
>> and untie the cords of the yoke,
> to set the oppressed free
>> and break every yoke?
> Is it not to share your food with the hungry

---

[8] James 1:27

and to provide the poor wanderer with shelter—
when you see the naked, to clothe them,
    and not to turn away from your own flesh and blood?
Then your light will break forth like the dawn,
    and your healing will quickly appear;
then your righteousness will go before you,
    and the glory of the Lord will be your rear guard.
Then you will call, and the Lord will answer;
    you will cry for help, and he will say: Here am I.
"If you do away with the yoke of oppression,
    with the pointing finger and malicious talk,
and if you spend yourselves on behalf of the hungry
    and satisfy the needs of the oppressed,
then your light will rise in the darkness,
    and your night will become like the noonday.
The Lord will guide you always;
    he will satisfy your needs in a sun-scorched land
    and will strengthen your frame.
You will be like a well-watered garden,
    like a spring whose waters never fail.
Your people will rebuild the ancient ruins
    and will raise up the age-old foundations;
you will be called Repairer of Broken Walls,
    Restorer of Streets with Dwellings.[9]

SYSTEMS PT. 7: PASSIVE PARTICIPATION IN THE SYSTEM

his solution to the problem? a public hanging in the town square.

I recently watched the film *Gangs of New York*, and of course, a systems post was born into my mind. The film hyperbolically depicts Bill "The Butcher" Cutting (Daniel Day-Lewis) in his rise to power and prominence

---

[9] Isaiah 58:5-12

as, essentially, the king of New York in the late 1800's. In systems-terms, he is at the top of the system. He is the one who calls the shots which determine how the system runs and who does what within its boundaries. Police serve him out of fear; the fire department works for him because of the prestige it affords him; business owners serve him their goods out of obligation; favors have become countless and all things flow to and from him. The Butcher is the king and center of the system.

The scene that stood out to me was a smaller scene as it does not directly involve any of the main characters, yet it reveals a lot about how systems in general work. At one point in the film, Bill is feeling like he is losing power to rival gangs, and losing respect from the population at large.

His solution to the problem? A public hanging in the town square.

It didn't matter who they were or what they had done, they just needed to find four (exactly four, not three, not five) men and kill them before a crowd to remind people who runs the town.

When the time comes, the four men stand atop the gallows, weeping but filled with pride. It almost seems like they have no idea why they are being killed, they are mere cogs in the wheel of the city. They are small pistons turning so that others more powerful and wealthy than them may be served.

One man, tears streaking his face, stands with his chest high as the rope is tightened around his neck. He looks down on his crying family and makes a short speech about his own willingness to die so that his family may be monetarily compensated for it. Soon the floor of the gallows swings down and the necks of the four men snap.

So, to summarize: One man's sole purpose in the eyes of Bill the Butcher was to die, affording his family a small reward, so that Bill could become more powerful. His role in the system was utterly out of his own control; it was given to him.

In a similar way, I am losing hope in effecting any change I could possibly make in the system I find myself in. Simply by my own incidental traits, I struggle to see how I could escape my God-given role to play in the system, and find that passive submission is possibly my only option. I am a white male, college educated, from a stable middle-class family. There is next to nothing I could do to upend and trainwreck my life, landing me on the streets with empty pockets and no remaining options. I am an American/Westerner, meaning that by merely existing, I was inserted into a point in the world's system where no matter how I live, I am taking advantage of other parts of the world. I have drank coffee harvested by enslaved hands, and I have thrown away more garbage in my life than most people in the world will ever touch. Today alone, I have gone through three plastic 'disposable' water cups, and I will never see them again, nor will I see the effects of my waste.

My given, passive position in the system sets me up to be ignorant to the needs and oppression of the rest of the world, and I have spent 28 years of my life thinking I'm a pretty good person who is not intentionally harming others. And I guess, it's not intentional harm. I harm others because of my passive role in the system—the role I was born into.

Just as the man in *Gangs of New York* was randomly selected to be executed so the powerful may prosper, I was randomly selected to be born and raised in America as a white male, meaning next-to-nothing could ruin my life. The lens through which I see the world is rosy and relatively untainted, as it would take a lot for my life to fall apart. Others, however, born into different places in the system, have to work with everything they have just *not* to end up on the streets. And some still do.

We are all cogs, and the sooner we are able to zoom out and recognize our role in the bigger picture, the sooner we will be able to realize how, exactly, we should live and where the greatest areas of need are. Those of you like me, born into positions of accidentally taking advantage of others in the world, should especially look for ways we participate in the unequal tapestry which is the fabric of the world. Not all threads are created equal. Or perhaps I should say, not all positions in the tapestry are created equal.

I used to think that merely because I was a white guy who loved people of all races and colors, I was doing great. This mindset, however, completely disregards all forms of systemic oppression, racism, injustice and waste. I will only see the effects of these things if I go looking for them.

When you go hiking, the maxim is "Take nothing but pictures; leave nothing but footprints." Yet when it comes to literally every other area of life, we disregard both what we take and what we leave. This varies from person to person depending on their passive participation in the system. When I die, I will have left exponentially more waste than most people in the world. And the alarming part is that not one person has ever called me out for this. Most people I know live the exact same way. We do not think about the trash we produce once it leaves our sight, nor do we think about where everything we consume (clothes, entertainment, food) comes from.

The American Hiker's motto, as it applies to the rest of our lives would be, "Take everything we can afford; leave everything we can pay someone else to discard."

Folks in other parts of the world were born into the position of living in the place our trash goes. They were born in countries used by ours to get products for next to no cost. When I lived in Guatemala for instance, I discovered that when a vehicle can no longer pass emissions tests in the USA, it gets sent down to Central America to pollute their air instead of ours. Black smoke tails nearly every vehicle in those countries.

Become aware of your position and participation in the world system. Refuse to continue passively participating like advertisers and manufacturers want you to.

If you're reading this on a phone or your own computer, chances are you were born into a position which takes advantage of others, at no fault of your own. When you were born, you were handed a position in the system, but you get to choose whether or not you remain there.

While we wait, we pray for the One who will not take advantage of others from the peak of the system. The One who will (and has) serve those below Him rather than exploit them for His own gain. Therefore, as the church visible and invisible, we pray *Maranatha, come swiftly, Lord Jesus.*

SYSTEMS PT. 8: CURSED ARE THE HAPPY

Chris has a nice job, but children are being used as militia soldiers

It turns out that the actor inside the Barney the Dinosaur costume for ten years became a tantric masseuse.

From 1991-2001, David Joyner was inside the big purple dino costume, happily spreading his message of love to children around the world. Conditions inside the costume sometimes reached as high as 120 degrees Fahrenheit, and Joyner said in a recent interview that the only thing that got him through those conditions with a smile on his face was his training in tantric love-giving. Through some odd smearing together of energy, love, light, and spirituality, he explains how his connection to the universe carried him through those crazy conditions and allowed him to continue to put smiles on the faces of thousands of kids.

What a weird introduction to a systems post.

The Barney-the-Tantric-Masseuse story reminded me of something discussed in a theology class in college. As a Christian, growing up within the confines of the Christian bubble in America, I think we can slip into this mindset that everyone who doesn't know Jesus is wildly unhappy and actively searching for something to satiate their soul's hunger. When I was younger, I imagined non-Christians crawling up to me like a starving animal and begging for an introduction to "whatever I had, they must have it…"

Sadly, in all my years of being a proselytizing believer, very few people have come to me and asked me to tell them about Jesus because they simply were not happy. The truth is, many people in the world are quite happy and content without Him (Yes, I would acknowledge that there is a distinct difference between happiness and joy, but generally speaking, many people can become happy outside the sphere of Christ's love).

And that's what my professor at Moody told us: There are plenty of people out there who are happy without Christ. This kind of threw a wrench in my soteriology because I had assumed that everyone was looking for something to fill that massive void inside each of us which only eternity can fill.[10] Yet, as I go on with my life, I find many people who can authentically say that they are generally happy and content as they are. Without knowing God and having active communion with the Holy Spirit and the saints of the Lord.

For years, I was perplexed when I met a non-Christian who seemed to be getting along just fine as they were, not crawling around with a crazed look in their eye, thirsting for the Living Water.

How, then, can I ever tell them the good news of the gospel??

I wondered this endlessly, sure that the only way to announce the news of the coming kingdom was when someone was unhappy and in a dark place.

There are a number of ways to go about this, but today I want to put this line of thought through my "systems filter." What does the worldly system say about a wealthy American's happiness? It's worth noting that Jesus repeatedly instructed His followers to be on their guard against greed, lest it slip in without them noticing as they amassed their wealth.[11]

That aside, there is something worth noting: Jesus' sole mission is not to make people happy and content, in this life, anyway. The fact that someone is happy aside from Him does not mean that Christ is not on the throne and His kingdom is not still on its way. If anything, this simply reflects an ongoing blindness to the plight of the rest of the world on the part of the happy person.

Let's put some hypothetical skin on this: Imagine a man named Chris. Chris is married and has kids and a good job and a good house and a good car and everything in his life is *good*. He would report that he is happy and content and needs to add nothing else to his life. How, then, does one point out Chris' desperate need to know the man Jesus from Nazareth?

Zoom out.

---

[10] Ecclesiastes 3:11

[11] Luke 12:15

Chris is not the only person in the world, nor is he the sole aim of the kingdom of God. For Chris to have such a self-centered understanding of the world (as is common in America) reflects just how blind he is to the sinful and fallen condition of the rest of the world.

Yes, he is happy, but thousands of people will die in third world countries this year because they were starving.

Chris has a nice job, but children are being used as soldiers for cartels around the world.

Chris is in need of nothing, but 27 million humans are currently being trafficked as sex objects.

The point is, anyone who would deny that this world is in desperate need of a savior simply because they themselves are 'happy' are ignorant and self-centered. They are unaware of the system which allows them to continue going on as a wealthy average American, not recognizing that at any second the system could crumble and they could be scavenging for their next meal in the ashes of capitalism. Their happiness is merely predicated on their current conditions, and their hope is in material possessions and their history of self-sufficiency.

In other words, someone who is happy because they have discovered some route to their own happiness—i.e. David Joyner finding satisfaction in his tantric massages—is like saying a gear of a car is happy because it is well-oiled, but the entire car is driving off a cliff.

Just because one's crystals, meditation, energy, bank account, or whatever else they have found to bring them happiness, has satiated them for the time being does not mean they are untouched by sin and live in a world no longer affected by the fall of man. As a whole, our world is in desperate need of a savior and a revolution in the system, but the revolution cannot come from within this world. The happiness, peace and *eudaimonia* we are looking for cannot be found in this world. Those who claim to have found it (and may be genuinely happy) have merely pressed pause on their awareness of their own sin and brokenness, and that of the world.

Many people may turn a blind eye to the fallen state of the world because their own life is going well, but Jesus did not come so that they may be happy. He did not come to comfort the rich of the world, but to heal the entire mechanism. Returning to the car metaphor, He did not come to change a few faulty parts, but to overhaul the entire vehicle and make it brand new into a state that will never decay or breakdown. Ever.

Luke 6 has some scary words for those who live this way:

> But woe to you who are rich,
>> for you have already received your comfort.
> Woe to you who are well fed now,
>> for you will go hungry.
> Woe to you who laugh now,
>> for you will mourn and weep.
> Woe to you when everyone speaks well of you,
>> for that is how their ancestors treated the false prophets.

The thing about temporary satisfaction is just that: It is temporary. Every tantric sex session ends. As does every meditative moment. If fame is what you seek, remember that even if you attain a level of status and acclaim, you will die and the world will spin on and you will be forgotten.

There is *one* source of eternal happiness and satisfaction, and His name is Jesus. However the best part about Him is that He did not come just so that *you* and *your* family may be happy. He did not come to make all Christians more comfortable at the expense of the suffering of non-believers.

He came to heal the entire system.

His message was not "Believe in me and you will be happy if you're not right now;" it was "*Repent*, for the kingdom of heaven is near."

In Ethan's Paraphrase:

> *Change your ways and get on the right side because a systemic overhaul is coming. I don't care if you're happy or not right now, because there are millions of people who are not, and that needs to be fixed. There are millions of people presently suffering injustice and I am going to fix that. Whether you're currently happy and comfortable or not right now, you should get on my team. I'm gonna make things right and you*

can either help me or continue profiting off of an unjust system so that you may be more comfortable.

Hope that makes sense.

To sum it up: Things will be better when Jesus returns, overhauls the system, and creates justice, peace and joy for all. So we pray with the Church universal: *Maranatha, come hastily Lord Jesus.*

SYSTEMS PT. 9: DON'T GIVE TO THE POOR
Jesus didn't give handouts to the poor, but He broke bread with them.

I was in Australia when I first discovered the writing of Shane Claiborne, a Christian writer, activist, and member of a group called the New Monastics. Someone had left a copy of his book *The Irresistible Revolution* on the toilet, so over the course of a couple weeks, I had finished it across daily visits to the throne. If you were to summarize Claiborne's writings, upheld by his own lifestyle, in one word, it would be along the lines of 'radical'.

In short, Claiborne lived and studied under Mother Teresa (Yes, *that* Mother Teresa) and worked in several other impoverished countries around the world after receiving his degrees from Wheaton College and Eastern University. He moved to Philadelphia a number of years ago where he founded The Simple Way, an intentional living community for people living in poverty. Shane is a dude who practices what he preaches.

So if I were to summarize *The Irresistible Revolution* in one sentence, it would be, *Live as Jesus lived and do what He did, literally.*

But that's a lot easier said than done, as highlighted by passages like this from *Revolution:*

> "I asked participants who claimed to be "strong followers of Jesus" whether Jesus spent time with the poor. Nearly 80 percent said yes. Later in the survey, I sneaked in another question, I asked this same group of strong followers whether they spent time with the poor, and less than 2 percent said they did. I learned a powerful lesson: We can

admire and worship Jesus without doing what he did. We can applaud what he preached and stood for without caring about the same things. We can adore his cross without taking up ours. I had come to see that the great tragedy of the church is not that rich Christians do not care about the poor but that rich Christians do not know the poor."

or,

"I'm just not convinced that Jesus is going to say, 'When I was hungry, you gave a check to the United Way and they fed me.'"

I recall one argument built over the course of a few chapters which expounded on Christians who are happy to give to the poor, or give to organizations which are helping the poor, yet none of that is in the same ballpark of what Jesus taught or modeled.

Jesus didn't merely give to the poor, He joined them.

This is what led Claiborne to found The Simple Way: A tension between people maintaining their own comfortable social status while therapeutically giving to the poor, versus the life and teachings of Christ. So Claiborne did just that, he joined the poor. He lived among them. He loved them and was loved by them.

And if I'm honest, this is a really scary thought for me to think: That Christ demands that I give up my social standing in order to follow Him. When I probe the depths of my heart, it becomes clear that things like status, car, home, and friends are idols on a very high pedestal because of my resistance to relinquish them for Christ. My dreams are not His dreams, in other words, and that's a scary thing. Am I longing for the kingdom, or am I longing for my own idea of what a good system is? Am I longing for visible, tangible things like a wife and a comfortable, well-funded life, or do I trust God that He both knows and will give me the desires of my heart in the fullness of His kingdom?

I quoted David Bentley Hart in a previous Systems post, but it's worth repeating. In his article *Christ's Rabble,* Hart builds an argument that all of Jesus' teaching is polarizing and in-or-out language, leaving little room for in-between living.

"Christ condemned not only an unhealthy preoccupation with riches, but the getting and keeping of riches as such. The most obvious citation from all three synoptic Gospels would be the story of the rich young ruler who could not bring himself to part with his fortune for the sake of the Kingdom, and of Christ's astonishing remark about camels passing through needles' eyes more easily than rich men through the Kingdom's gate. As for the question the disciples then put to Christ, it should probably be translated not as "Who then can be saved?" or "Can anyone be saved?" but rather "Then can any [of them, the rich] be saved?" To which the sobering reply is that it is humanly impossible, but that by divine power *even* a rich man might be spared."

Hart proceeds to list several more passages in which God proclaims good news to the poor, but scary woes to the rich. And let me remind you, if you're reading this on a phone or laptop, you are 'the rich'.

I have a friend who is an atheist and has told me in the past that he's a 'pretty good person' because he gives to the homeless whenever he passes them begging on the sidewalk. What I've realized is that the message of Christ asks far more of us than this. It asks us not to hand out spare change to those beneath us on the caste system, thus perpetuating their situation of dependence and ours of Good Samaritans handing out alms, but to join the poor. To do life, not with those of the same social ranking as us, or in the same socio-economic class as us, but with those all across the spectrum.

Jesus didn't just give handouts to the poor, but He broke bread with them. He made friends with them. And even He, Himself did not have a home or a place to lay His head. He didn't just toss medicine to the lepers, or even heal them from a distance; He *touched* the untouchable.

Think about it: What good do handouts do in light of affecting systemic change? Are you helping to overhaul the system of poverty by tossing a five-spot into the cup of a beggar, or are you merely perpetuating the very system you may think you're healing? It's a microcosm of rich nations doing more damage than good by giving handouts to poorer, needy third-world countries who are not then able to themselves.

Now, with all that said, it may be scary to consider abandoning all that you have and all that you cling to for comfort and security. And I myself am still wrestling with where the balance is between preaching a 'poverty gospel'[12] and obeying God. That's why I always refrain from giving specific imperatives and instead let you in on what I'm mulling over in my mind. So for now, I hope this gives you some food for thought.

And now, we continue to pray for the equalizing power of a just King: *Maranatha, come swiftly, Lord Jesus.*

SYSTEMS PART 10: INVISIBLE BODIES
which camp is right and how do we read the Bible?

Every thought you've ever had, every experience you've ever interpreted and every desire you've ever had is, for all intents and purposes, not your own.

I just got off the phone with my friend James, who has influenced many of these Systems posts, and every single conversation with him is like drinking straight from a firehose. There is no 'gentle' switch, and it's great. Today's conversation was sparked by a relatively simple question from me to him via text: "What's the difference between modernism and postmodernism?"

The firemen arrived and busted the cap off the hydrant.

I put my headphones in while James talked and I attempted to type up every single thing we talked about as we went. Now, my burden (as I always feel it is) is to take the philosophical jargon and ideas and present them in a digestible and accessible way to the internet. So, in this post, I'm attempting to answer three (relatively, but not really) simple questions: What is modernism? What is postmodernism? How does this affect our Christian theology and faith?

Modernism
If you're to attach a face to each of these movements, Descartes is the figurehead of modernity. You know his line: *cogito ergo sum.* Or, *I think, therefore I am.* That line in itself is earth shattering, but out of context is

---

[12] A phrase which means you need to be poor in order to be saved

somewhat useless and meaningless. It's not so much where Descartes arrived as much as how he got there. He began asking "How do I know what I know, and how do I know it's accurate?"

Now, when we talk about knowledge, it's much broader than you may imagine. How do you know red is red? How do you know what a doughnut tastes like? How do you know another human?

Descartes wanted empirical, unadulterated truth and accuracy in what he knew, and wanted to know that his experience of the world was true and authentic. All this reasoning led to him realizing that the one reason he knew he existed is because he was capable of conscious thought; therefore, *I think, therefore I am.* By thinking, he empirically proved his own existence. Maybe it doesn't hit you very hard, but this is the nutshell edition.

Descartes wanted a tool with which to do philosophy which he could trust to be accurate. It's as if you had a telescope which was set to 94x magnification, but you thought it was set to 100x. All your measurements would be off because the tool you are using is off. If you can doubt someone's tool or method, you can doubt their knowledge.

Modernists were after solid, universal, concrete truth.

Postmodernism
This line of thinking led to two camps: Rationalists, spearheaded by Descartes; and Empiricists, which was led by Locke or Hume. Rationalists asked the question about knowledge, and Empiricists provided (what we call modern science) the means of experimentation in order to find the answers.

Kant was the first to synthesize the two camps, but the two who sent real shockwaves through modern philosophy were Kierkegaard and Nietzsche. They came along and said 'You guys are fools; it's nice that you want to have sure knowledge, but the fact of the matter is, we're human beings and the ways in which we produce knowledge fundamentally make it so that it's not universal, so it's always couched in human desire and experience. No matter how good your method is, your desires are always informing your methods. All your data stems from presuppositions.'

The whole postmodern school is about reorienting away from a search for universal, unimpeachable knowledge and toward local, varied, diverse expression that's constantly changing and being rewritten.

Put simply: **Modernists** assume and pursue one knowable, universal and concrete truth. **Postmodernists** realize that, because we are human and are shaped by our culture and desire, knowing this truth in its entirety is foolish. Both extremes have consequences, especially in how they relate to Christianity.

Philosophy in Faith

Most conservative, fundamentalist-type Christians (including many Evangelicals) tend to lean toward modernism. After all, don't we believe that there is one universal truth which is absolute and knowable? The problems with resolutely modern thinking is that it can lead to things like the colonialists of the 19th century: Some white missionaries believed that, because there is one, knowable and absolute truth (and *they knew it*), they not only had to tell native Africans about Christ, but also conform them to a degree of 'whiteness.' The truth which they knew exceeded society, culture and religion, meaning that if an African were to become a Christian, it also meant adopting the modern white man's culture as well. That's a synecdoche of the issue with a completely modern approach to theology.

A postmodern approach would mean that the gospel becomes contextualized to every tribe or individual and they can understand it and interpret it as they please. Taken to its extreme, this methodology would say that *nothing* is *wrong*, and humans can live as Christians however they want to read the Scriptures. We could dismiss the instructions of Paul, saying *this* was simply for *that* culture, and doesn't apply to us. Taken to its furthest extreme, postmodern readings of Scripture render it utterly meaningless and its interpretation is left to the whims and desires of the individual.

Don't like Jews? Yank some of Paul's writings out of context and use them to exterminate 6 million of them. Don't like his teaching on homosexuality, premarital sex or gender roles? Just write them off by saying that they were only for *his* culture. This is postmodernity.

Modernists fear that a postmodern claim that there is no knowable, universal truth suggests that people will get carried away, modifying the gospel from society to society until no more truth remains. The fear is real and it is valid, but a balance in the middle must be found. The modern extreme is to construct an idol of truth and knowledge and bow down to it.

However, postmodernity is not all negative. Postmodernity suggests that Christianity can, in fact, be understood as a native African without conforming to colonial 'whiteness.' It can also be understood and applied as a white American, and as an Asian rice farmer. It is read with different eyes by each individual, but is no more or less true based on who is reading it.

So which camp is right and how do we read the Bible?
And of course, how then shall we live?

A professor of James' and mine, Michael McDuffee, says that the best way for the average Christian to read the Bible is literally. Pick it up and read it. Learn and grow as you go, of course, but if there is no literal reading of the text, then it ultimately is meaningless.

James basically summed up the Christian tension thus:

> Modernist theology is difficult because it can easily become arrogant. It's saying that absolute truth exists and we have access to it and can describe it beyond the shadow of a doubt. Unchecked, it's a recipe for exploitation and oppression. However, the ramifications of an unqualified postmodernist theory is equally as dangerous. Because where do you get off the train? How much can we qualify scripture before we're just reading our own desires and interests into what we see in the text?

It's a hard and nearly impossible task, but that doesn't mean we stop trying to grapple with it and understand the Bible we hold in our hands. I think understanding these philosophical backgrounds really help us come to understand how we (how I, Ethan Renoe), read the Bible. How we comprehend our faith and apply it to our lives.

Yet, until our knowledge is completed and our blinders are removed, we ask, *Maranatha! Come hastily, Lord Jesus! Make our knowledge full and our comprehension accurate.*

SYSTEMS PART 11: HUMAN TRAFFICKING IS THE NEW CHURCH

every member is an atheist. come and worship yourself.

In 2013, The Sunday Assembly opened their doors for the first time. in the five years since, they have planted congregations in over 70 cities, with an emphasis on justice, social care, and loving community. They meet on Sundays, go on seasonal retreats, sing songs and listen to messages.

The catch? Every member is an atheist.

The organization's website demonstrates that the movement is spreading like gangrene. What's scarier to me is that is looks virtually no different than most modern church's websites. Smiling, interracial congregants make the community seem welcoming and accepting. There appears to be general warmth and acceptance among the crew, and if you went, you'd hear advice for taking your life in the best direction possible and deepening the intimacy of your relationships.

A couple years ago I joined my first dating app: Coffee Meets Bagel. I immediately noticed that a good number of folks on there had selected the religious option of "Spiritual But Not Religious." I laughed at how ludicrous that option was, because spirituality, by definition, is religious (From the Latin *religare*, 'to bind.' A religious person is one who has bound themselves to their god/s…even if their god looks just like them).

I could go on listing examples of the spiritual climate of our current western culture, but I will stop here and use those two as synecdochical references. The Sunday Assembly shows us several things about humans: We long for community and fellowship with other humans, and when we lack a common ground for gathering (i.e. religion), we create one.

SA also reveals that humans have an innate longing for meaning and purpose. Andy Stanley is the one who pointed out that something's purpose is not to serve itself, but to serve something or someone else. A purpose, by definition, is bigger than the individual. That's why the Sunday Assembly has incorporated things like service projects and social justice movements into their mission.

Meanwhile, the option to be Spiritual But Not Religious on a dating app reveals the inverse. It shows that even when someone may not align with a specific religious denomination, there is some sort of longing for connection with the invisible. Ecclesiastes 3:11 tells us that we are built with eternity in our hearts, and those people on the dating app have inadvertently revealed this truth. Even when we try our hardest to be humanistic and areligious, we are left with a sense that there is more to the world than what we can see and touch.

Secularism is beginning to show her hand and she's bluffing.

Mark Sayers defines secularism as a group of people longing for 'the kingdom without the King.' We want the benefits of the kingdom of God (peace, justice, equality, health, fellowship, acceptance, etc.) without a need for Jesus of Nazareth.

The sad thing is, the more I've learned about secularism taking form in the past several decades, the more I realize that the western church has been happy to follow suit, rather than attempting to lead culture away from so-called 'secular relevance'. The western elite has been preaching a gospel of self-expression and autonomy as the highest good and sadly, the Church has bought this story beginning to end (Have you ever wondered about the origin of the phrase "a personal relationship with Christ"? I can tell you it's not in the Bible).

Despite the individual-centered nature of the American culture, cracks in the dam are beginning to show. When atheists begin to long for community, justice, spirituality and purpose, they betray their confessed beliefs. Kierkegaard pointed out that the (honest) atheist is given two options in life: Hedonism or suicide. An atheist's hedonism must be absolute: they must seek their own pleasure at all costs, even the expense of other people. Thus, sex trafficking is one of the highest expressions of hedonistic atheism; you are using other people for your own pleasure. Have you ever wondered why ancient pagan temples often contained orgies with temple prostitutes? The sex industry (pornography included) is the modern form of the pagan temple.

Come and worship yourself.

The other alternative is equally meaningful: Kill yourself, because without purpose larger than yourself (or larger than the material world), there is no point in forging ahead one more second. Life is meaningless and it's better to end it than go on taking advantage of others.

The problem is that humans are born with at least some iota of conscience. And with this conscience comes an awareness that there are invisible forces, whether we acknowledge them or not. The Sunday Assembly and the option to be Spiritual But Not Religious, rather than disheartening me, give me hope. Changing culture is like turning a cruise ship: it happens slowly, but everyone is on board and aware of it. These things are signs to me that secularism is starting to reveal their hunger for something more.

How long will it take before the SA congregants recognize that there is still some void in their souls? How long before the material world they see stops satisfying their itch for depth, pleasure and purpose?

However, the issue does not simply exist *outside* the walls of the Church. Ask most Christians in America why they should go to church every week, and you'll probably hear everything covered by the Sunday Assembly. Singing, inspirational messages to stroke our egocentric selves, fellowship, service projects. What is it exactly that sets the Christian church apart from the Sunday Assembly?

When I was in Bible college, a sadly large number of my fellow students opted to stay in their rooms on Sunday mornings and listen to sermons online with their buddies. After all, we had community in the dorms, biblical teaching in class, our weekly outreach ministry, and singing songs three days a week in chapel. What were they missing?

Christ.

Sacraments.

You can have a lot of things that look like church and even feel like church, but without the presence of Christ in your midst, you're simply collectively masturbating. If there is no supernatural appearance of Christ (manifest in the bread and the wine, communal prayer and worship, and the indwelling presence of the Holy Spirit), you're just patting each other on the back and going home. To members of the Sunday Assembly, Jesus seems like someone who interrupts the flow. With Him in the picture, you can't go on pleasuring yourself, because He demands that your eyes be lifted off from yourself. To the Christian who has aligned her vision with Christ's, His reign feels like freedom; to the autonomous atheist, His reign looks restrictive.

Only time will tell how long these artificial substitutes will last. Amazingly, The Sunday Assembly is not the first of its kind. Atheistic churches have been launched before and have never lasted longer than one generation. Humans are hungry for eternity. And what is big enough to fill an eternal void? Only the Creator of time and space Himself.

These signs give me hope of revival, and I don't use that word lightly. Running in charismatic circles for several years made me weary of overusing the word, but looking backward through history, I have found that revivals happened in circumstances where the culture seemed most godless and hopeless. In other words, revival happens when it could *only* be the work of God moving in the unfolding of human history. Go figure.

Hopeful, we strive toward that end anyway. The best and simplest way to work for revival is through prayer. Join the Church universal as we pray that God advance His kingdom on earth as it is in heaven. Pray that His presence invade our lives and our churches. And lest we forget, pray the earliest of Christian prayers, *Maranatha, come swiftly Lord Jesus.*

Return our vision to You alone.

SYSTEMS PART 12: FAMILY > SELF
You just skimmed over that, didn't you?

Recently, I heard a sermon which has lingered in my mind for a few weeks. Oddly enough, it was on Matthew 1, which is simply a long list of names. In the Bible, it's called a 'genealogy' and it simply says for many, many paragraphs who is the father of whom, leading all the way from Adam to Jesus. When reading the Bible, most people skim hastily over these sections of Scripture due to how boring they are, but this sermon dove deep into the passage. Just for a sampling, this is the first paragraph:

> This is the genealogy of Jesus the Messiah the son of David, the son of Abraham:
>> Abraham was the father of Isaac,
>> Isaac the father of Jacob,
>> Jacob the father of Judah and his brothers,
>> Judah the father of Perez and Zerah, whose mother was Tamar,
>> Perez the father of Hezron,
>> Hezron the father of Ram,
>> Ram the father of Amminadab,
>> Amminadab the father of Nahshon,
>> Nahshon the father of Salmon,
>> Salmon the father of Boaz, whose mother was Rahab,
>> Boaz the father of Obed, whose mother was Ruth,
>> Obed the father of Jesse,
>> and Jesse the father of King David.

You just skimmed over that, didn't you?

The part of the sermon which stood out to me related closely to what I've been teaching in my history classes this week. We've been doing a unit on Asian countries and cultures and how they are different from Western cultures. For a few classes, we watched Disney's *Mulan* and analyzed how much of that film is drawn from a western mindset, versus how much is authentically Asian. The main thing I tried to highlight in these classes was the Asian mentality of family/tribe over self.

People in Asian countries tend to think about what is best for their families, not necessarily for themselves. This is vastly different from how western people think, which spawns from a capitalistic mindset of "get out of my way, I need to get to the top."

I shared with my students a pattern I observed when I was in Thailand: This is an oversimplification, but this problem is rooted in both western power/lust/strong-arm economy, and that idea of Asian family mindset.

Thailand is notorious for its sex trafficking problem, which is closely aligned (if not identical to) its issue of child brides, or Thai brides who marry wealthy white men. It is extremely common there to see a chubby middle-aged white man holding hands on the sidewalk with a Thai girl half his age (or less). It's disgusting and painful to witness, but the explanation makes sense.

These women see their bodies as mere means to helping out their families. Often, they accompany their new husband back home to Germany, or perhaps just go touring with him around Southeast Asia. In the process, she will get more money than she and her family possibly could have raised on their own, so she sends some back every month to help her family out, despite what it costs her. These women's bodies are mistreated and they marry men they don't love just for the sake of helping their family financially. They see their families as more important than their own bodies. Can you picture a western person thinking like this?

The idea of tribe over self is beautiful, of course, and that example is a toxic twisting of the cultural mindset. What that illustration does do, though, is highlight the degree to which Asians value family over self. This is why certain parts of *Mulan* begin to seem western and contrived, i.e., when she sings to herself in a mirror and talks about being a single, unique grain of rice. I struggle to believe (though correct me if I'm wrong) that most Chinese people at the time of Mulan, would think that way. Theirs is a culture of extreme shame and honor, in which most people would rather die than bring shame to their families.

This brings me back to the sermon on Jesus' genealogy. I had never before heard such an acute description of why genealogies are so key in the Bible, yet it made so much sense when he said it: "That list was Jesus' resume."

Today, when we draft a resume, we list all of the things *we* (the individual) have accomplished in *our* lives. We list the schools we attended and the experience we have gleaned in our dozens of years of life. Think about how small that is, compared with a genealogy/resume that spans centuries and leads up to one man. When discussing Jesus, a first-century person in the Near East would have begun with this genealogical list of people in Jesus' background. If Jesus were to make a resume, it wouldn't describe how many people He raised from the dead, or make bullet points of how many rabbis (teachers of the Scriptures) he stumped. It would have much more to do with His family, and in this case, his ancestors leading all the way back to Adam. This helps to confirm Jesus' words in John 4, when He says "salvation is from the Jews." He could have just said, 'salvation is from me,' but opted for a more culturally powerful statement. What better proves His messiah-ship than an extensive list of all Jesus' important ancestors?

What can we learn from this, and how can this be applied to modern western culture? I think it can help balance out our idea of "Looking out for #1." We tend to fall into a trap of thinking that all of our accomplishments are our own, and no one at all helped us get here but our own sweat and blood. For some people in America, that's true. It's also often married to dumb luck and coincidence, in cases like Eminem and Oprah. For the most part, however, people born into rich families stay rich, and people in poor families stay poor.

To illustrate, think about a hypothetical lawyer (or president...) in New York City. He probably thinks he got there all on his own, as his resume clearly demonstrates that he attended Harvard and got good grades, etc. However, how many people like this got into Harvard because *their* parents could afford to send them there, or had connections, much less to allow them to focus on their studies and not be distracted by paying for their own tuition? And how did those parents earn their substantial wealth? Probably because *their* parents came from money and put them through school, and you can trace it all the way back to some person in the 1800's who actually *did* build the family up from nothing. Therefore, the wealth of the lawyer rests more on the shoulders of his ancestor than it does on his own effort.

However, to whom do you think he attributes his success? His long-dead predecessor, or himself?

It's easy to examine someone like this and cast stones, but if you're reading this on your own phone or laptop, chances are you're in the same boat. Unless you are an orphan who received no assistance whatsoever growing up, you have been given things from your family which should humble you into seeing beyond yourself.

We often lose sight of everything we have been given, and I think that's a big reason gratitude is such a big deal to God. In one case, He killed off

24,000 Israelites just for complaining, which is the opposite of gratitude! These are the two attributes which will begin to shift our perspective and help us learn from more tribal cultures: humility and gratitude. When we see things as a gift, we are less likely to take them for granted, or to boast about working for them. Gratitude keeps us humble, and learning from Asian cultures can be widely beneficial to us all.

May we become known as people of gratitude and humility. They are the hardest things in the world to master, but I think they bring a small slice of the kingdom to earth.

SYSTEMS PT. 13: NO BETTER THAN NAZIS
what if the nearby German farmers took down the Third Reich?

I recently began reading *Man's Search For Meaning* by the annoyingly optimistic Viktor E. Frankl, and if you don't know what that is, it's definitely worth looking into. The book is essentially made up of two parts: The first is simply a detailed account of Frankl's experience inside a Nazi concentration camp for two years, and the second is his explanation of his psychological theory called Logotherapy, or treatment by introducing meaning into someone's life.

Aleksander Solzhenitsyn, renowned commentator on the impact of the Holocaust and Gulag, famously said,

> "If only it were all so simple! If only there were evil people somewhere insidiously committing evil deeds, and it were necessary only to separate them from the rest of us and destroy them. But the line dividing good and evil cuts through the heart of every human being. And who is willing to destroy a piece of his own heart?"

This was related to the Nuremberg Trials, which took place after the end of World War 2, and were of utmost importance because they declared that there are, indeed, actions which are not permissible by humans, regardless of whether or not you were simply ordered to carry out the action by a superior. Interestingly, many of the men ordered to appear in Nuremberg committed suicide before the trails even began, begging the question, did they know in a deep place that they had committed acts which could be universally defined as *evil?*

Of course, by stating that some action is universally evil, you must be prepared to describe why something is evil, and therefore, you must also be able to give an account of something good—the opposite of evil—and acknowledge the existence of the two. Beyond both of these, you must answer the largest question of all: *Why?*

Why is something evil and something else is good? And why should humans be held accountable for what they do? Granted, atheist and agnostic thinkers have struggled to define these boundaries and establish answers to the ethical question of *Why* since the Bronze Age, but no answers have readied themselves within their humanistic boundaries. As a Christian, I find myself (sometimes reluctantly) submitting to the boundaries set by Scripture, and even more than the boundaries, the reasons presented within. Put simply, the reason humans should not be cruel to other humans (or to the environment) is because God made them. Humans especially have a unique spark of the Divine inside us, and to harm another human is to harm God Himself.[13] This is not a place atheists can arrive without acknowledging the fact that there are moral rights and wrongs that they themselves hold to, but can't explain why.

Heck, zoom out far enough, and you'd see that the natural world would be much better off without human beings polluting it and chopping down miles of forest. Therefore, human continuation is not a strong enough argument for an ethical stance unless there *is* something special and worth preserving about us.

Now, when discussing these actions which were so reprehensible that they needed to be punished by a court of the entire world, we need to ask a couple more questions.

1. Were these men unique in their evil, or, as Aleks pointed out, are each of us capable of the heights of evil they reached? Think about what it

---

[13] Genesis 1, Matthew 25

would take for you to perpetrate such vicious acts. Now, acknowledge that the fact that you can imagine doing them means you are, in fact, capable of doing such evil acts. You are not exempt from becoming a Nazi given the right circumstances. [Insert entire Gospel message here]

2. What acts are happening today that future generations may compare to the Holocaust, and criticize us for standing by and doing nothing? After all, in the midst of the Holocaust, there were average citizens going about their business without a qualm while the gas chambers were running just a few miles from them. How terrible to look back and realize that you were one of these farmers who said and did *nothing* while the Nazi regime 'experimented' with human beings just a couple clicks away.

I want to expound on number 2 for a minute. Let's take the recent controversial event of America separating families at the border. I am just using it as an example because most humans on earth would agree that it's wrong to tear apart a family.

Now, if you think this is wrong, who do you blame for the action? Do you blame the man at the top of the command chain, the president? Do you hold accountable the soldiers who were just following orders, but tore children from their parents because they were instructed to? Or do we all hold ourselves accountable because we saw it happen on Facebook shortly before flipping over to Netflix to laugh at some sitcoms? Are we the same as the farmers outside the concentration camps who insisted on voluntary blindness so that we did not have to act against injustice?

As a middle-class American, it's hard for me to not see a direct comparison here, though you could apply it to any modern issue: sex trafficking, systemic racism, modern-day slavery, sweatshops, poverty and hunger, etc. Am I aware of sex trafficking? Yes. Am I doing anything about it? …..no. (The case could be made that many of us actually perpetuate the cycle every time we look at porn…or watch the Super Bowl.)

I'm still torn about what exactly we are called to do here. It's not like the German farmers outside the fences of the camps could have stood up to the Third Reich and taken them down. What do we look back and expect them to have done differently? Maybe if we can answer that question, we can find clarity into what we should do, assuming you are in a similar position to me as an average, middle-class worker who is doing normal work and trying not to hurt anyone.

If these massive systemic problems stress you out as much as they do me, join with me in praying the only real prayer which can solve these problems once and for all: *Maranatha, Lord Jesus. Come swiftly and institute Your kingly system which will be just and fresh and beautiful.*

AN APOLOGY FROM AN ACCIDENTAL RACIST
I do not want to be the type of person who builds walls.

I've reached the point where I need to repent.

A lump wells in my throat as, for the past couple months, I've read article after article on the black experience in America, and become more aware of the suffering taking place at the hands of a very corrupt system.

#BlackLivesMatter was something I once thought was common sense. I've never considered myself a racist and have always extended love and respect to people of every skin color. I thought rooting against slave owners was enough to qualify me as a non-racist.

But in the words of King's Kaleidoscope (fronted by a white singer),

> I'm complicit in the prejudice, it's automatic
> I take advantage being born into my demographic
> But what's a blessing when it generates a struggle of a color
> For the privilege of another?
> In my whitewashed tomb
> I've become immune
> Oh, my God, oh, my God[14]

In the same song, spoken word artist Propaganda notes that "Oh, you tweeted about it? ...Most don't notice the system till it turns against them." That's exactly what I've realized lately. Of course, the system has not turned

---

[14] "Playing With Fire" by King's Kaleidoscope, featuring Propaganda

against me (I'm a white male...come on), but what I have begun to do is seek to understand the system. And I have barely scratched the surface, but what I'm beginning to realize is that I have absolutely taken advantage of my passive participation in a corrupt system.

In this piece, I primarily want to repent and apologize. It's a nuanced tightrope to walk between advocating social justice without falsely accusing all white people of individual sin and inducing unnecessary (and unproductive) white guilt/shame. Here are a few thoughts.

I'm sorry for making racist jokes.
They're harmless, right?

The more I read about people losing brothers, daughters, parents, and other loved ones as a result of gang violence, police violence, or any of the other plethora of sources of violence many black and hispanic people face in America which I will never have to, the harder it is to take it lightly. In fact, I become disgusted at myself for even laughing at or making certain jokes.

I do not think jokes are harmless. We always joke most about the things we are most ashamed of, and I can't help but wonder if there is a collective white shame which is revealed through this sort of joking.

Jokes build walls, not bridges.
I do not want to be the type of person who builds a wall.

I've come to realize that this is a decent way to sum up many of Jesus' social teachings: You can either use everything at your disposal to build fences from others and segregate yourself from those you don't want near you, or you can use your resources to build bridges and span the barriers created by race, economic level, or any other dividing factor.[15]

Christianity is not a gated community.

---

[15] Luke 18:18-25. The Rich Young Ruler had used all of his resources to better himself. Jesus tells him to use all of his wealth to build bridges to others, especially the poor. In the next chapter, Jesus blesses Zacchaeus for giving only *half* of his wealth to the poor rather than all of it. Why? Because he figured out how to use his resources to build bridges rather than walls. The amount was less important than the employed use.

I think racist jokes, though seemingly harmless most of the time, paint mental images of people of different colors as "The Other." *They* are not like *me*, therefore, I construct distance between myself and them, and joking is a way to do that.

One sort of inverse tragedy I've seen in myself and many (white) people I know is a refusal to understand black cultures. I've seen this most exemplified in the character of Kendrick Lamar and many white Christians' response to his work. Most of us do not know that his song "Alright" inadvertently became the anthem for the Black Lives Matter movement, as protesters and activists chanted the peppy, optimistic hook, "N***a we gon' be alright!" (The critically-acclaimed video, which I can't watch without tears rolling down my face, shows Kendrick et al. facing violence of varying types, concluding with Lamar being shot by a white police officer). I can't help but wonder if the reason for this is that we, good moral Christians, shut out Lamar and his ilk because he swears and uses the N-Word.

Have we completely missed the point?

In chasing after 'purity,' and attempting to purge our Spotifys of explicit songs, have we simultaneously become deaf to the cries of the oppressed, standing on a mountaintop with our fingers in our ears? I feel like this is a common pattern in white evangelicalism: We shoot to grow in holiness by eradicating 'dirty' media from our minds (Didn't Jesus say something like "It's not what goes into a man that makes him unclean…"?).[16] This means streaming primarily music made by/for Christians, meaning we unwittingly subject ourselves to a segregated bubble in which we are unaware of what's happening outside of it. We listen to what we want to hear.

We are simply playing intramurals while the rest of the world is happening around us.

No one learned this more explicitly than Christian rapper Lecrae, who recently began speaking out on issues of race and segregation and received ample rejection by his listeners, made up of thousands of white kids who

---

[16] Mark 7:15

wanted him to be who they thought black people were.[17] Once subliminally hailed as the 'cool black rapper for white Christian kids,' Lecrae experienced rejection by them once he began to stand up for movements like BLM and reclaim his black heritage. (He and his clique were not unaware of their cultural tension. Propaganda observed that they could fill a stadium with white kids, raising their 1-1-6 tats, but would make awkward conversation with them in the green room because they hadn't talked to a black person before.)[18]

So again, where does all this lead me? What is the purpose of this piece and what are the next steps?

Of the latter, I am unsure. I don't know what difference I can make today to alleviate the suffering of others, or to shift the American system toward justice and equality. But I think the first steps, as a white man unfamiliar with deep generational suffering, is to apologize and repent.

I believe communal sin is real, so while I can't apologize on behalf of all white people participating in systemic violence and injustice, I can apologize on behalf of Ethan Renoe.

I'm sorry for turning a blind eye to the issues faced by millions in America, and not making much of an effort to educate myself; for assuming I knew what you were going through, or minimizing it.

I'm sorry for making and laughing at racist jokes, as if bolstering the division between cultures is a trivial thing.

I'm sorry for becoming numb to photos of dead bodies in streets and news of yet another South Sider being riddled with bullets.

I'm sorry for playing intramural Christianity instead of seeking to heal the world outside the doors of the Church; for accidentally building fences instead of bridges.

---

[17] Piper, John. "116 Been Real: Lecrae, 'White Evangelicalism,' and Hope." Desiring God, 25 May 2019, www.desiringgod.org/articles/116-been-real.

[18] This is a line from Lecrae's song "Hands Up" feat. Propaganda

And, although I'm still figuring out what exactly this means, I'm sorry for not doing more to mend our divides.

WHITE PEOPLE VS. RACISM

I was a very wealthy and powerful minority.

Dominique Green is one of far too many black men executed in the United States by his own government. Until his final day at the age of 30, he claimed that yes, he committed the robbery, but he did not pull the trigger which killed another man. His final words before his execution by lethal injection were these:

> "There was [sic] a lot of people that got me to this point and I can't thank them all. But thank you for your love and support. They have allowed me to do a lot more than I could have on my own…I am not angry but I am disappointed that I was denied justice. But I am happy that I was afforded you all as family and friends. I love you all. Please just keep the struggle going…I am just sorry and I am not as strong as I thought I was going to be. But I guess it only hurts for a little while. You are all my family. Please keep my memory alive."

Today at the gym, the film *Remember the Titans* was playing on the big screen so I sat and watched it from the stationary bike. I love that film, and I felt a lump welling up inside my throat at points, such as when the white people refuse to shake the black peoples' hands, or when, inversely, the team builds bonds across racial bounds tighter than those outside the team.

On the flight back to the States, I happened to watch the award-winning film *Green Book*, which is set in the same time period as *Titans* and deals with many of the same issues of race in the South. A wealthy, famous and black musician is touring through the southern states, and despite being the guest of honor, is forced to use outhouses rather than white bathrooms, and is only welcomed in certain hotels. The title of the film comes from the book carried by black folks who wanted to travel the US safely during that time period; it described where they would and would not be welcomed.

In both films, pure anger rose up inside me. It was a wild, white-hot anger at the racist characters in the films. Every time I see a scene like those in the films, I boggle my mind to figure out how the victims kept themselves from unleashing hell on the unjust institutions and racist people discriminating against them. *How could they respond with such grace and poise??* If I were in their shoes, my fists would be flying and their jaws would be dangling like a playground swing.

One more anecdote, then I'll begin to tie things together.

I lived in Guatemala for the last ten months; a place where I was very much a minority. Everywhere I went, people stared at the *gringo* walking down the sidewalk or working out. I was surrounded by the beautiful, tan and hardworking Guatemalans, and my experience as a minority there was the polar opposite of most minorities in the States.

As a white minority in Central America, I was not the underdog or the poor outcast; I was the wealthy and powerful minority. People stared at me not because I was a pariah the way they would stare at a freed slave after the Civil War; they stared at me knowing I could travel anywhere on the globe, had obscene amounts of education and wads of money in my bank account.

I was a *powerful* minority.
I experienced no prejudice or discrimination based on my race or status.

Now, compare that to the experience of basically any minority in the States for the majority of her history. The minorities are the ones who are enslaved, taken advantage of, or victimized by a system which has no problem executing them just to get them out of the way. They tend to be a powerless minority in a country set up to function against them.

Did you see that?

When I—a wealthy white American—am a minority, I still expect to maintain privilege, comfort and power. I think that's why, when I watch those scenes in *Remember the Titans* and *Green Book*, anger wells up within me. I *expect* there to be resolution for injustice. I *expect* people to treat me with dignity, the same way they treat their friends and family. I *expect* that when a white idiot dehumanizes a black person, the black person deserves to level them.

I've never had to learn how to respond to bigotry or stigma because I've never been oppressed by them. That's why my mind boggles when people of different races can respond with silence or love when some white fool insults spits in their face (literally or metaphorically). As a white, 'powerful' person, my gut reaction is anger and rage.

The scenes from *Titans* fueled the rest of my workout, as I funneled my rage at the very notion of racism into my reps. It ran through my mind and I found myself asking, then, *what is the solution?* Here are a few thoughts:

It made me respect Martin Luther King Jr. and all the people working in the Civil Rights Act era all the more as they called for *peaceful* protest against absolute bastards who were literally killing their friends and family. Black people, Jews, and countless other oppressed minorities have learned how to respond to violence with peace and grace—something we powerful majorities can learn from.

If the roles were reversed, I don't see many white people calling for non-violent protest against their oppressors. How strong does one have to be to turn the other cheek to the person killing you and your family members, or spraying you with a firehose?[19]

Secondly, it made me ask the question (again), what can I as a white person do to combat these issues? Granted, the US has made steps in the right direction since the 60's, but we have a way to go. Without giving concrete instructions, **I believe it is the obligation of those in power to use their power to aid and stand up for those with less power.** Guatemala gave me a better first-hand witness to people oppressed by a system taking advantage of them from which they can't escape.

Powerful people are essentially given two choices for how to use their power in relation to the less-powerful: Enslave/take advantage of them, or fight for them and stand up for them. This is one reason Jesus was so hard

---

[19] For a gut-wrenchingly beautiful reversal of this image, please watch Leon Bridges' music video for his song "River." The same hose which once tortured the southern black people now baptizes them. You will sob.

on the teachers of the Law in the Bible: they were the powerful men of the time, but were using their power to get wealthy by taking advantage of the poor. How utterly opposite to the message of the entirety of Scripture! Genesis to the eschaton, the message of YHWH could not be more clear. Aid the powerless minorities living among you.

How do white people go about undoing the wrongs done by our ancestors? I hope to find a balance between violently lashing out at the oppressors while still *fighting* racism and injustice. May we identify the issues on which we can affect change. May we ask God to scour our hearts of any racism, conscious or subconscious, dwelling in our guts. May we worship God together, with bonds much deeper than the things which may divide us.

HOW HOLLYWOOD HIJACKED YOUR MIND
once you understand Soft Power, you understand everything.

Today I was introduced to the idea of Soft Power and the term alone caused so many things to instantly click in my head. Soft Power is a clear paradox to Hard Power, and once you grasp the simple concept, so much will make sense. It's the reason you always feel like you're offending someone, or that if you disagree with someone, you're anathema to the cultural tide.

For example, take the two Koreas as embodiments of the two notions. North Korea has nuclear weaponry aimed at the soil of the world, hovering her finger above the launch button if someone pries too closely. Hard Power. It's the bully with the bigger muscles and the baseball bat.

By contrast, South Korea is a rising star in the music scene with numerous breakout boy bands which my students are obsessed with. K-Pop is infecting radio waves alongside the behemoth of entertainment which is the United States. Soft power is far more subliminal, but perhaps even more powerful than her counterpart. South Korea, with its intellectual Soft Power, is growing the ability to influence fans however they want. Of course, this is slow and takes time compared to the blatant force of North Korea's nukes.

The reason this is so important is because we in the West are far more likely to give in to Soft Power than Hard.

For instance, look no further than the third chapter of Genesis. Does the serpent come to Eve with a crossbow and tell her to eat the fruit "or else…"? No, of course not! He slips subtle lies into her mind. He makes her question things she was once so sure of. Before long, she has given in and doomed the progeny of the world to death and toil.

I would wager that most of us are not threatened with AK-47's or barbed wire clubs on the daily, but we face a far more insidious power. We face another foe: Intellectual Colonialism.

What is Colonialism? It's the invasion of Western culture into indigenous lands. It was the white man coming in and saying that they're doing things wrong and they should be done like THIS (to put it lightly).

Without realizing it, Christians living in the West have become slaves to the machine of Intellectual Colonialism. We have been told that the way we have been thinking is wrong and we need to do it like THEM. We need to be sexually liberated (as long as it's safe and consensual), and we need to be tolerant of every belief, simply because someone *feels* that it's true.

Problem is, feelings turn out to not be great dictators of truth.

Just today, someone commented on a YouTube video of mine saying that I shouldn't be so hard on Christians who may believe something contrary to the Bible. "If they believe it strongly, then it can be true for them."

That phrase, in addition to being one of the most ridiculous and ignorant things a human can say, was disproven in the 300's B.C. Something cannot be simultaneously true and false depending on who feels what way about it. No matter how hard I *feel* that winter should be sunny and 75, reality is going to keep dumping snow on me.

But now I'm off track.

In the Bible, let's take another look at Hard Power and how we bend the knee to the same entities who now use Soft Power instead. Nebuchadnezzar strong armed the Israelites into exile where he made them kneel to his gigantic statue under pain of death.[20] Guards were on watch to see anyone who would not bow the knee to his image. If you've been in Sunday School at any point in the past century, you're familiar with the three boys who did not bow to the statue: Shadrach, Meshach and Abednego. They faced a very real and physical power ordering them to follow its decrees.

Today, we are simply peer pressured into accepting every sexy wind of heresy and affirming every possible sexual orientation our sideways imaginations can conjure up. More often than not though, this peer pressure takes the form of appealing sitcoms and catchy lyrics. It's taken time, but media has so influenced our culture that to frown upon such media or behavior doesn't make you pious, it makes you a prude.

We have moved into a new era where pursuing righteousness isn't just foreign to people, it's downright offensive. In the past, when I told people I was a virgin, they would applaud my restraint. Now, however, I may be told that I am actually repressing my good desires for sex and am therefore doing something bad. It's insane.

It seems that these strong and invisible pressures have worked their magic on more than a few Western Christians. They are SO subliminal, and following the way of Christ will always be less popular and more difficult.

Take for instance the recent release of the film *Boy Erased*. The observant Christian will note that the thesis boils down to this: Either your sexual urges are set in stone or your religion is. If one won't bend, the other should. I'll let you imagine which one the movie suggests should be more malleable (Apparently God is not 'progressive' enough to keep up with our advanced culture).

In order to end with a glimmer of hope, let's remind ourselves who Jesus is. The classic verse John 14:6 states simply that He is truth. He does not simply say the occasional truism, but He is the embodiment of all that is right, straight, aligned and worth believing. He is the definition of reality.

One thing He constantly tells us to watch out for is, essentially, Soft Power. When He tells us how to fight the devil, Jesus does not give some mystical

---

[20] See Daniel 2

sort of instruction for putting on an exorcism. He simply tells us to listen to Him because He speaks the truth and to watch out for the devil, because "when he lies, he speaks his native tongue."[21]

Later, in Ephesians 6, Paul draws up a pretty explicit dichotomy between the Hard and Soft Powers: "For our struggle is not against flesh and blood (Hard Power), but against the rulers, against the authorities, against the powers of this dark world and against the spiritual forces of evil in the heavenly realms (Soft Power)."

I think the Bible spends a lot more time warning us against Soft Power because it's harder to spot. It's easy to point to wars, child slavery, and spousal abuse as the only evil in the world. It's harder to identify greed, wandering sexual mores, and self worship in our own hearts.

As Tim Keller often says in his sermons, "You always know when you're committing adultery. You're never having sex and stop and say, 'Wait a minute! You're not my wife!' It's harder to be aware of things like greed and pride because they are invisible and insidious."

Beware of America's Soft Power. Don't passively absorb media of any form with your brain turned off. Just because every show on Netflix makes casual sex not only permissible but necessary, doesn't mean that God has changed His mind on adultery.

Keep your brain turned on because it's far easier to flick it off and slip into the appealing ebb of the cultural current.

Identify the ubiquitous use of Soft Power.

May we be those who cling to truth and think with wisdom. Moreover, may we cling to Truth Himself as we grow closer to the person of Jesus Christ, although it will NEVER be the easy or popular route. May we never lose hope that He will come again to expose every lie and make plain all that is true and real.

---

[21] John 8:44

FILM REVIEW: A GHOST STORY

A film succeeds inasmuch as it makes you feel something.

I wanted to throw in this film review because of the way it illuminates so many of the themes of this book. The film and this review tie together a lot of loose ends and leave us with a glimmer of gravity, meaning and hope.

When a director sets out to create a film, he or she has a massive number of tools at their disposal, and we typically think of these tools along the lines of dialogue, color, cinematography, characterization, casting, etc, but perhaps the most overlooked is *time*.

Time can pull a viewer into a film in a way few other cinematic elements can. And David Lowery, writer and director of the ethereal *A Ghost Story* succeeds in using this tool to full and long-suffering effect.

Part of the use of time in this film reflects the overall theme of the film: That time, and everything that happens within its span, is utterly pointless. It's the book of Ecclesiastes rendered into a gripping visual display.

The plot is simple enough: A young couple, madly in love (though not without their flaws), moves into a home and odd things begin unraveling. This is not a horror film, but they see random flecks of light dart or hover in the corner of their room, and eerie sounds resound from the house. We are not given access to much of their personalities, nor are we welcomed into the precise dynamics of their relationship, though these things are not necessary for the point of the film to ultimately be made.

The important thing to note in the early stages of the film, however, is that the shots are LONG. They do not relent. You are forced to watch Casey Affleck and Rooney Mara kiss gently in bed for at least three full minutes. You must watch her drag a piece of trash all the way from the house down the long driveway to the curb, then pause, then walk all the way back…then watch the house sit there for another minute.

In other words, time passes naturally in the first half of the film. It is not chopped up into the lightning-fast edits we are accustomed to.

Not long into the plot, the husband is killed in a car accident and we are only given the aftermath. We see his body resting lazily against the steering wheel. And then we watch it a bit longer.

Then we see his corpse in the hospital lying beneath a white sheet. We watch as Mara comes in, looks at her late lover, and walks out. With prolonged expectation, his form lies on the table without a moving pixel in the frame for another solid minute until it bursts upward in fitful life.

And the ghost is born.

It paces around the hospital, and at one point eternity seems to open up before him, but closes before he has a chance to enter. This causes him to walk back to his small home and remain indefinitely. He watches his wife consume an entire pie in grief over another 5-minute shot, and the viewer senses an odd mix of curiosity and sympathy emanating from the draped form.

It is not long, however, before the ghost begins to become more and more removed from the time he once inhabited. The shots of the film become much faster, symbolizing his removal from time as experienced by the living, and we see episodic events occur before him. His wife soon moves out of the home with a new lover and a young family moves in. They slip from summer to Christmas in the blink of an eye, and then they are gone and new tenants occupy the small home.

The most haunting exchange is when Casey Affleck's ghost—still a man draped in a simple white sheet with two black eye holes—looks out the window and sees another ghost in the window of the house next door. Through subtitles, the viewer is given their exchange:

> "Hello," says the neighbor.
> "Hi," replies Casey's ghost.
> "I'm waiting for someone."
> "Who?"
> "I don't remember."

I got chills as that silent scene played out.

Within the functional world of the film, each ghost is only allowed to 'rest in peace' when their purpose has been fulfilled. For the neighbor, her purpose turns out to be realizing that the person she is waiting for will never arrive (more chills).

For Casey's ghost, the relief is more hard-earned. The last thing his wife does before leaving the house is write something on a tiny slip of paper, fold it up and slide it into a crack in the wall. For the rest of the film, Casey's ghost is seen periodically hunched before the crack and scratching to get the piece of paper. All the future tenants are haunted by the terribly subtle sound of a ghost scratching at a wall.

As the film picks up, the long shots die away more and time itself speeds up. The house is demolished and an office building is built. We see the ghost pace its halls as it is built, then cut directly to its finished state with businessmen pacing its halls in such a hurry.

The next scene is the end of all time, as a dystopian future is painted and the entire world is populated by flashing lights and high rises. Casey jumps from one of their ledges, only to land on the same patch of land at the beginning of all time. Settlers are preparing to build a home there and as they do, a little girl from the covered wagon writes something on a slip of paper and slides it under a rock. Before Casey's ghost can read it though, they are slaughtered by native Americans. In the next shot, their arrow-riddled corpses have rotted away and been overgrown by grass.

Time spins madly on once more until his wife once again slips the note into the wall and he can finally scrape at it enough to pull it free.

He uncrumples the note.

His sheet hollows and collapses to the ground and he is at rest.

His purpose in the cyclical spin of time has been realized and he is required to haunt the earth no more.

When the credits appeared at the end of this mostly silent film, I felt a mix of depression and existential angst. Not only did it take your emotions (and your expectations) and play hackie-sack with them, but it painted a universe in which any straggling sense of purpose a human could scrape together will blow away with the infuriating march of time and the hopelessness of realizing one's meaning.

On the one hand, if all this world is is a confused array of atoms which burped themselves into existence out of nothing, then yes, our mad march of history and time will utterly be worthless in the end. Every loving embrace and created art form will have been for naught, and will be lost to the annals of trivium.

On the other hand, however, if we were crafted with a longing for purpose, inheriting an image of the Creator Himself, and instructed to go forth and multiply our humanness, our creativity, our love and the work of our hands, then every movement we make has meaning. Every stroke of a pen has the potential to take the created order of things and rearrange them for better or for worse.

Jesus breathes meaning into matter.

History reveals her Creator just as much as a delicious meal or a breathtaking sunset does.

A Ghost Story hearkens back to *Garden State,* which also portrays characters longing for significance and uniqueness. Recall the scene where Natalie Portman squeaks out a weird sound and contorts her body in an abnormal fashion, then explains to Zach Braff that no one else will ever be able to say they did that exact thing in that exact spot.

We are longing not only to be meaningful, but unique. Set apart. And in the utterly depressing and apathetic world painted by *A Ghost Story,* none of those things are possible. The dead forget the living and vice-versa.

The neighbor ghost remembers not whom they are waiting for. And they never come.

I began the film expecting it to be a mourning of Casey's character over the life he had and the woman he loved.

Instead, it was far more horrifying.

It was a removal of connection and of meaning. It was existence without purpose. It was a painful ripping of a human being from his humanity. The outlook of the film is bleak, and the greatest form of sentiment one can muster in this universe is, if you can merely discover a few words left for you by someone you used to know, you will be fulfilled.

Yet this is not the mindset of the Christian. We have hope that yes, there is life after death, but it is not a departure from meaning. It is not a removal from the world of creativity, love and significance. Rather, because of the resurrection of Jesus Christ (in a tangible body, not an ethereal, invisible sheet), all lives have meaning and all humans have hope.

We are not left lonely to wander the earth, forgetting who we are waiting for. No, we specifically pray along with the church universal, *Marantha, come swiftly, Lord Jesus.*

OUTRODUCTION
you made it this far...may as well keep going

Time kills all things, but it also heals all things.

I am usually tempted to agree with Conor Oberst, who sang, "There is nothing the road cannot heal." And I've lived like that. It may be impressive to list the places I've been, but if that wandering was in search of healing, I have traveled in vain. There are some wounds the road cannot heal.

Healing and dying are the only way the world can work. Think of a rollercoaster: The first hill is the highest, the second is a little shorter, and the drops keep getting shorter until the ride concludes. This is how healing works as we make our way toward death—the recoveries grow smaller and smaller the closer we draw to the end of the ride as it loses momentum.

I'm 28 and my body is already less resilient than it used to be.

With each rise and fall of my coaster, I learn that I'm not as immortal as I once thought I was. With this realization comes both joy and gravity. Joy that, as my ride hurdles toward its end, I anticipate an even greater one. But gravity because there is so much work to do. So much healing to complete —in myself, in those I love, and in the world at large.

If nothing else, this book has been me wadding up my thoughts and tossing them across the room to you, hoping they make your world a little better.

May we remember that time will eventually kill us all; numbering our days.

May we date better, and have better sex.

May we make better music and art and films, reflecting our creative God.

May we never stop learning how the world works.

May we be people who take it upon ourselves to heal the world, joining God as He makes all things new.

e

ALL THINGS

time kills all things